Montmartre &
Northern Paris
p123

Champs Élysées &
Grands Boulevards
p65

Louvre &
Les Halles p87

Eiffel Tower &
Western Paris
p47

The Islands
p177

Le Marais &
Bastille p145

St-Germain,
Les Invalides &
Montparnasse
p219

Latin Quarter
p197

The Islands p177

Paris' landmark cathedral
dominates the larger Île
de la Cité, while little Île
St-Louis is graced with
elegant buildings.

Don't Miss Notre Dame

Latin Quarter p197

The hub of academic
life, filled with lively
student haunts and
institutions, and featuring
Paris' beautiful botanic
gardens.

St-Germain,
Les Invalides &
Montparnasse p219

Literature lovers and
fashionistas flock to this
mythological Left Bank
neighbourhood.

Don't Miss Musée d'Orsay,
Jardin du Luxembourg

Contents

lonely planet

Discover
Paris

Experience the best
of Paris

This edition written and researched by

Catherine Le Nevez,

Discover Paris

Eiffel Tower & Western Paris p47

Home to the city's signature spire and La Défense's forest of skyscrapers.

Don't Miss Eiffel Tower

Champs-Élysées & Grands Boulevards p65

Paris' grandest avenue, department stores and the palatial opera house.

Don't Miss Arc de Triomphe

Louvre & Les Halles p87

The world's mightiest museum, market streets and the capital's cutting-edge cultural centre showcasing modern and contemporary art.

Don't Miss The Louvre, Centre Pompidou

Montmartre & Northern Paris p123

The Paris of myth and films, Montmartre's hilly streets adjoin the red-light district Pigalle, home to the Moulin Rouge.

Don't Miss Sacré-Cœur

Le Marais & Bastille p145

Hip boutiques, bars and restaurants, mansion-housed museums and a celebrity-filled cemetery.

Don't Miss Cimetière du Père Lachaise

This Is Paris

Paris has a timeless familiarity for first-time and frequent visitors, with instantly recognisable architectural icons. But against its iconic backdrop, Paris' real magic lies in the unexpected: hidden parks, small museums and tucked-away boutiques, bistros and neighbourhood cafes where you can watch Parisian life unfold.

Famous landmarks abound throughout the French capital.
The spire of the Eiffel Tower piercing the clouds, the Arc de Triomphe guarding Paris' most glamorous avenue, the Champs-Élysées, the gargoyled Notre Dame cathedral and lamplit bridges spanning the Seine are etched in the minds of anyone who's visited the city – and the imaginations of anyone who hasn't (yet). But despite initial appearances, Paris' cityscape isn't static: there are some stunning modern icons too, from the inside-out Centre Pompidou to the *mur végétal* (vertical garden) gracing the striking Musée du Quai Branly.

Paris' cuisine is renowned.
From cosy neighbourhood bistros to triple-Michelin-starred temples of gastronomy, you'll find every establishment prides itself on exquisite preparation and presentation of quality produce. Enticing *patisseries* (cake shops), *boulangeries* (bakeries), *fromageries* (cheese shops) and colourful street markets are perfect for packing a picnic to take to the city's parks and gardens.

Fashion shopping is this city's forte.
Paris remains at the forefront of international fashion trends, and browsing designer boutiques and *haute couture* (high fashion) houses is a quintessential part of any visit. You'll also find uberhip concept stores and art nouveau department stores, along with a trove of flea markets, bookshops, adorable children's wear, art and antique dealers, and, of course, gourmet food and wine shops galore.

Paris is one of the great art repositories of the world.
In addition to big hitting museums, including the world's largest, the Louvre, there are scores of smaller museums housing collections of every imaginable genre – tangible reminders of the city's illustrious artistic legacy, which endures to this day.

> 66
> Paris'
> real magic
> lies in the
> unexpected
> 99

Eiffel Tower (p52)

25
Top Highlights

25 Paris' Top Highlights

Eiffel Tower (p52)

No one could imagine Paris today without its signature spire. But Gustave Eiffel only constructed this graceful tower – then the world's tallest, at 320m – as a temporary exhibit for the 1889 Exposition Universelle. Luckily, its acceptance and ultimate popularity (and its usefulness as a perfect platform for the transmitting antennae needed for the new science of radiotelegraphy) assured its survival beyond the World Fair, and its elegant art nouveau webbed-metal design has become the defining fixture of the city's skyline.

Sacré-Cœur (p128)

Sacré-Cœur is a place of pilgrimage in more ways than one. Staircased, ivy-clad streets wind up the hill of the fabled artists' neighbourhood of Montmartre to the dove-white domes of Basilique du Sacré-Cœur. The chapel-lined basilica crowns the 130m-high Butte de Montmartre (Montmartre Hill). Its lofty position provides dizzying vistas across Paris from the basilica's front steps and, above all, from up inside its main dome.

Arc de Triomphe (p70)

If anything rivals the Eiffel Tower as the symbol of Paris, it's this magnificent monument to Napoleon's 1805 victory at Austerlitz. Commissioned in 1806, the intricately sculpted triumphal arch stands sentinel in the centre of the Étoile (star) roundabout – be sure to use the underground pedestrian tunnels to reach it! Some of the best vistas in Paris radiate from the top, including sweeping views along Paris' most glamorous avenue, the Champs-Élysées.

The Best...
Views

EIFFEL TOWER
Not only the city's most iconic building but also its highest. (p52)

NOTRE DAME
Scale the cathedral's spiralling steps for a view you'll never forget. (p182)

ARC DE TRIOMPHE
Little known fact: you can climb to the top of the arch. (p70)

TOUR MONTPARNASSE
The saving grace of this otherwise-hideous high-rise is its panoramic observation deck. (p232)

CENTRE POMPIDOU
Captivating views extend from this distinctive cultural centre's rooftop. (p98)

NAZLIE ABU SEMAN/GETTY IMAGES ©

The Best...
Places of Worship

SACRÉ-CŒUR
Paris' landmark basilica lords it over the city. (p128)

ÉGLISE ST-SULPICE
Featured in *The Da Vinci Code*, it has frescoes by Eugène Delacroix. (p228)

NOTRE DAME
The city's mighty cathedral is without equal. (p182)

SAINTE-CHAPELLE
Sunlight streams through exquisite stained glass in this hidden Gothic gem. (p187)

MOSQUÉE DE PARIS
This 1920s art deco–Moorish tiled mosque has a wonderful tearoom and *hammam* (steam baths). (p207)

4 The Louvre (p92)

The *Mona Lisa* and the *Venus de Milo* are just two of the priceless treasures resplendently housed inside this former royal palace, now France's first national museum. Stretching along the Seine, the world's biggest museum can seem overwhelming, but there are plenty of ways to experience it, even if you don't have nine months to glance at every artwork and artefact here. One of the best is the thematic trails – from the 'Art of Eating' to 'Love in the Louvre'.

5 Centre Pompidou (p98)

This primary-coloured, inside-out building houses France's national modern and contemporary art museum, the Musée National d'Art Moderne, containing works from 1905 through to the present. The centre's cutting-edge cultural offerings include exhibition spaces, a public library, cinemas and entertainment venues. Topping it off is a spectacular rooftop panorama.

Musée National du Moyen Âge (p203)

Medieval weapons, suits of armour, gold and ivory aren't the only reasons to visit France's National Museum of the Middle Ages. You can also see the sublime series of late-15th-century tapestries, *The Lady with the Unicorn*; the flowering gardens planted with flowers, and France's finest civil medieval building, the Hôtel de Cluny. Medieval tapestry

Musée d'Orsay (p224)

Magnificent renovations at the Musée d'Orsay display the celebrated canvases by impressionist and postimpressionist masters (including Renoir, Gauguin, Cézanne, Manet, Monet, Degas and Toulouse-Lautrec) as if they're hung in an intimate home. The grand former railway station housing the museum is still an exemplar of art nouveau architecture, of course, but France's treasured national collection of masterpieces from 1848 to 1914 are now – more than ever – the stars of the show.

Musée Rodin (p234)

The lovely Musée Rodin is the most romantic of Paris' museums. Auguste Rodin's former workshop, the 1730-built Hôtel Biron, is filled with masterpieces like the marble monument to love, *The Kiss*, as well as works by his muse and protégé, sculptor Camille Claudel, and by other artists including Van Gogh and Renoir. The real treat, though, is the mansion's rambling sculpture garden, which provides an entrancing setting for contemplating works like *The Thinker*. Rodin's *The Thinker*

The Best...
Smaller Museums

MUSÉE DE L'ORANGERIE
Monet conceived a stunning cycle of his *Waterlilies* series especially for this one-time greenhouse. (p107)

MUSÉE MARMOTTAN MONET
More Monet – in fact the world's largest collection – inside an intimate hunting lodge. (p60)

MUSÉE PICASSO
An incomparable overview of Picasso's work and life. (p156)

MAISON DE VICTOR HUGO
A must for literary buffs, the writer's former apartment overlooks picturesque place des Vosges. (p152)

Parisian Cafes (p245)

Paris' cafes are the city's 'communal lounge rooms': places to eat, drink, read, write, flirt and fall in – and out – of love. Many, such as Les Deux Magots, are gilded, dark-wood-panelled belle époque treasures, where past patrons like Picasso and Sartre still haunt the air. It's the quintessential Parisian experience: settle inside a cosy cafe and press pause, or perch at an outdoor cafe table and watch the parade of Parisians go about their daily lives...all for the price of a *café au lait*. Marché aux Enfants Rouges (p158)

The Best...
Cafes

LES DEUX MAGOTS
A must-visit address in literary St-German des Prés. (p245)

LE PURE CAFÉ
Still as quintessentially Parisian as Ethan Hawke's character found it in *Before Sunset*. (p165)

CHEZ PRUNE
The original *bobo* (bourgeois bohemian) hangout on the banks of Canal St-Martin. (p141)

CAFÉ LA FUSÉE
A relaxed escape from the bustle of Centre Pompidou. (p169)

Cimetière du Père Lachaise (p150)

10

Paris is a collection of villages, and these sprawling hectares of cobbled lanes and elaborate tombs, with a population (as it were) of over one million, qualify as one in their own right. The world's most visited cemetery was founded in 1804, and initially attracted few funerals because of its distance from the city centre. The authorities responded by exhuming famous remains and resettling them here. Their marketing ploy worked and Cimetière du Père Lachaise has been Paris' most fashionable final address ever since.

Jardin des Tuileries (p107)

11

Filled with fountains, ponds and sculptures, the Jardin des Tuileries is a verdant oasis that offers a chance to enjoy Paris at its symmetrical best. These 28-hectare formal gardens, where Parisians paraded in all their finery in the 17th century, are now a Unesco World Heritage Site and form part of the *axe historique* (historic axis), Paris' line of monuments running from the Louvre's glass pyramid in the east to La Défense's modern, box-like Grande Arche in the west.

BRIGITTE SMITH/GETTY IMAGES ©

12

Versailles (p254)

No wonder revolutionaries massacred the palace guard and ultimately dragged King Louis XVI and Marie Antoinette back to Paris: this monumental, 700-room palace and sprawling estate – with its fountains, gardens, ponds and canals – could not have been in starker contrast to the average Parisian's living conditions at the time. A Unesco World Heritage–listed wonder, Versailles is easily reached from central Paris; try to time your visit to catch musical fountain displays and equestrian shows.

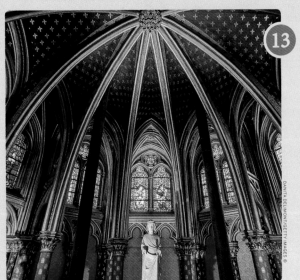

13

Sainte-Chapelle (p187)

Richly coloured biblical tales are exquisitely told with a stained-glass grace and beauty at Sainte-Chapelle, the Gothic 'Holy Chapel' near Notre Dame on the Île de la Cité. A masterpiece of delicacy, with a curtain of glazing across the 1st floor of deeply coloured stained glass (marvel at that incredible deep blue), Sainte-Chapelle is at its most dazzling when the sun is shining and the glass flickers in a glorious rainbow of colours.

Street Markets (p174)

Stalls of cheeses, raspberries, baguettes, sun-ripened tomatoes, pigs' trotters, horsemeat sausages, spit-roasted chickens, bottles of olives and olive oils, quail and duck eggs, boxes of chanterelle mushrooms and knobbly truffles, long-clawed langoustines and prickly sea urchins on beds of crushed ice – along with belts, boots, wallets, cheap socks, chic hats, colourful scarves, striped T-shirts, wicker baskets, wind-up toys, buckets of flowers... Paris' street markets, such as the wonderful Marché Bastille, are a feast for the senses. Marché Mouffetard on Rue Mouffetard (p210)

The Best...
Markets

MARCHÉ BASTILLE
One of the city's largest, liveliest street markets. (p174)

RUE MOUFFETARD
An old Roman road is now a sensory feast of street stalls. (p210)

MARCHÉ AUX ENFANTS ROUGES
Paris' oldest covered market, with communal tables where you can eat lunch. (p158)

MARCHÉ AUX FLEURS REINE ELIZABETH II
Fragrant flower market. (p193)

MARCHÉ AUX PUCES DE ST-OUEN
Europe's largest flea market. (p143)

The Best...
Nights Out

PALAIS GARNIER
Paris' palatial opera house.
(p83)

MOULIN ROUGE
The cancan creator is
touristy but spectacular all
the same. (p142)

SUNSET & SUNSIDE
Respected double venue
on a street famed for its
jazz clubs. (p117)

POINT ÉPHÉMÈRE
Edgy cultural centre, club
and performance venue
booking emerging and
established DJs, artists
and bands. (p142)

REX CLUB
Paris' first dedicated
techno club is still cutting
edge. Phenomenal sound
system. (p116)

15

Canal St-Martin (p134)

Bordered by shaded tow-paths and traversed by iron footbridges, the charming, 4.5km-long Canal St-Martin was slated to be concreted over when barge transportation declined, until local residents rallied to save it. The quaint setting lured artists, designers and students, who set up artists' collectives, vintage and offbeat boutiques and a bevy of neo-retro cafes and bars. Enduring maritime legacies include old swing-bridges that still pivot 90 degrees when boats pass through the canal's double-locks; a canal cruise is the best way to experience Paris' lesser-known waterway.

BELOW: CULTURA TRAVEL/PHILIP LEE HARVEY/GETTY IMAGES © LEFT: CULTURA TRAVEL/PHILIP LEE HARVEY/GETTY IMAGES ©

Parisian Dining (p59)

There's a reason that boxes of leftovers aren't done in Paris, and it has nothing to do with portion sizes. Whether you're at an unchanged-in-decades bistro, an art nouveau brasserie, a switched-on neobistro or a gastronomic extravaganza, the food and the dining experience are considered inseparable. France pioneered what is still the most influential style of cooking in the Western world and Paris is its showcase. Do as Parisians do and savour every moment.

BRUNO DE HOGUES/GETTY IMAGES ©

MING TANG-EVANS/LONELY PLANET ©

Stylish Shopping (p84)

Paris, like any major city, has its international chains. But what really sets Parisian shopping apart is the incredible array of specialist shops. Candles from the world's oldest candle maker, pigments from the art supply shop that developed 'Klein blue' with the artist, soft leather handbags made in the hip Haut Marais and green-metal *bouquiniste* (secondhand bookshop) stalls lining the banks of the Seine are just some of the goodies in store.

Notre Dame (p182)

A vision of stained glass rose windows, flying buttresses and frightening gargoyles, Paris' glorious cathedral on the larger of the two inner-city islands is the city's geographic and spiritual heart. This Gothic wonder took nearly 200 years to build, but it would have been demolished following damage during the French Revolution had it not been for the popularity of Victor Hugo's timely novel, *The Hunchback of Notre Dame,* which sparked a petition to save the building. Climb its 400-odd spiralling steps for magical rooftop views.

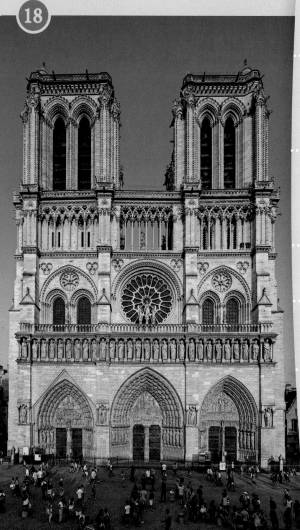

The Best...
Street Snacks

ROAST CHESTNUTS
In the chilly winter months, warm up with *marrons chauds* (roast chestnuts) from street vendors citywide.

CRÊPES
Unlike at sit-down Breton crêperies, crêpes cooked at Parisian street stalls are rolled up and eaten on the move.

BREAD & BAKERY TREATS
Boulangeries (bakeries) are omnipresent.

ICE CREAM
Berthillon's ice cream and sorbets can't be beaten. (p188)

FELAFELS
Join the queue for scrumptious sandwiches from L'As du Fallafel. (p158)

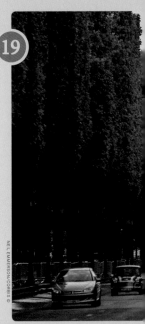

Champs-Élysées (p72)

19

Baron Haussmann famously reshaped the Parisian cityscape around the Arc de Triomphe, from which 12 avenues radiate like the spokes of a wheel. The most celebrated (and the scene of many major celebrations, including the final stretch of the Tour de France) is the av des Champs-Élysées, which is named for the Elysian Fields (heaven in Greek mythology). No trip to Paris is complete without strolling this broad, tree-shaded avenue lined with luxury shops, car showrooms and restaurant terraces.

NEIL EMMERSON/CORBIS ©

The Best...
Shopping

GALERIES LAFAYETTE
France's most famous department store, crowned by a magnificent art nouveau cupola, with free fashion shows. (p84)

E DEHILLERIN
Paris' professional chefs stock up at this c 1820 cookware shop. (p119)

SHAKESPEARE & COMPANY
A 'wonderland of books', as Henry Miller described it. (p216)

ADAM MONTPARNASSE
Historic art supply shop with paints, canvases and paraphernalia galore. (p248)

DIDIER LUDOT
Couture creations of yesteryear including the timeless little black dress. (p118)

RUNE JOHANSEN/GETTY IMAGES ©

20 Les Catacombes (p243)

Down below the streets of Paris, you can take a spine-tingling wander through Les Catacombes. These one-time quarries were packed with exhumed bodies relocated here due to overflowing cemeteries, and later served as the head-quarters of the Resistance during WWII. Today, the skull- and bone-lined tunnels are at once horrid yet intriguing, and offer a macabre way to experience the city's history in a way that is both figuratively and literally chilling (dress warmly), but above all unique.

Jardin du Luxembourg (p226)

The Jardin du Luxembourg offers a snapshot of Parisian life. Couples stroll through the chestnut groves. Children chase sailboats around the pond. Old men play rapid-fire chess at weathered tables. Students pore over books between lectures. Office workers snatch some sunshine, lounging in sage-green metal chairs. Joggers loop past stately statues. And friends meet and make plans to meet again.

Cruising on the Seine (p299)

Paris' most beautiful 'boulevard' of all is the Seine, which runs through the heart of the city. A river cruise with an operator such as the Bateaux Mouches is an idyllic way to watch the city's landmarks float past. Alternatively you can board the Batobus, which allows you to hop on and off at its eight stops: the Eiffel Tower, Musée d'Orsay, St-Germain des Prés, Notre Dame cathedral, Paris' botanic gardens the Jardin des Plantes, the Hôtel de Ville (town hall), the Louvre and the Champs-Élysées.

Gourmet Food Shops (p249)

Instead of stocking up at a supermarket, Parisians will buy their bread at a *boulangerie* (bakery), cheese at a *fromagerie* (cheese shop), meat at a *charcuterie* (specialist butcher), fruit and vegetables at street-market stalls and other delectable items from small shops specialising in everything from honey to mustard, truffles and foie gras, as well as at glorious food emporiums like La Grande Épicerie de Paris. The goods are fresher and better, and the social interaction forms part of the city's village atmosphere. Boutique Maille (p81)

The Best...
Tours

FAT TIRE BIKE TOURS
Friendly cycling tours around the city as well as further afield. (p299)

LEFT BANK SCOOTERS
Zoom around the capital in Parisian style aboard a scooter. (p299)

L'OPEN TOUR
Hop-on, hop-off open-topped bus tours. (p299)

PARISIEN D'UN JOUR – PARIS GREETERS
See Paris through local eyes with free walking tours led by resident volunteers. (p299)

THATLOU
Treasure hunts in high-profile museums and neighbourhoods. (p300)

Cooking & Wine-Tasting Courses (p251)

If dining in the city's sublime restaurants whets your appetite for cooking, there are stacks of cookery schools, from famous institutions like École Le Cordon Bleu to private Parisian homes, most of which include shopping and market visits. Where there's food in France, wine is never more than an arm's length away, and plenty of places offer wine tastings and instruction. Courses cater to all abilities, schedules and budgets. Many are run in English; confirm language requirements when you book.

The Best...
For Free

CITY MUSEUMS
Free entry to permanent exhibits (temporary exhibitions command an additional fee).

NATIONAL MUSEUMS
Free on the first Sunday of the month (temporary exhibitions cost extra).

NATIONAL MONUMENTS
Some national monuments (eg Arc de Triomphe and Notre Dame towers) are free on the first Sunday of the month from November to March.

CEMETERIES
Celebrity-filled cemeteries including Père Lachaise are free to wander.

25

Maison et Jardins de Claude Monet (p261)

The prized drawcard of tiny Giverny is the home and flower-filled garden of the seminal impressionist painter and his family from 1883 to 1926. Here Monet painted some of his most famous series, including *Décorations des Nymphéas* (Waterlilies). The house and garden are open from April to October. From early to late spring, daffodils, tulips, wisteria and irises appear, followed by poppies and lilies. By June, nasturtiums, roses and sweet peas are in blossom. Around September, there are dahlias, sunflowers and hollyhocks.

Top Days in
Paris

Central Right Bank

The central Right Bank is the ideal place to kick off your Parisian trip. As well as the ancient art and artefacts in the world's largest museum, the Louvre, you'll also see ground-breaking modern and contemporary art inside the striking Centre Pompidou.

DAY 1

① Jardin des Tuileries (p107)

Start your day with a stroll through the elegant Jardin des Tuileries, stopping to view Monet's *Waterlilies* at the Musée de l'Orangerie and/or photography exhibits at the Jeu de Paume.

JARDIN DES TUILERIES ➲ MUSÉE DU LOUVRE
🏃 Stroll through the gardens to the Louvre.

② Musée du Louvre (p92)

Visiting the world's largest museum could easily consume a full day, but bear in mind that tickets are valid all day, so you can come and go as you please. Various tours help you maximise your time.

MUSÉE DU LOUVRE ➲ RACINES 2
🏃 Racines 2 is just northeast of the Louvre's Cour Carée.

③ Lunch at Racines 2 (p113)

Nip out for contemporary food at Racines 2.

MUSÉE DU LOUVRE ➲ JARDIN DU PALAIS ROYAL
🏃 Walk north through place du Palais Royal.

Exterior of the Centre Pompidou (p98), designed by Renzo Piano and Richard Rogers
NEIL FARRIN/GETTY IMAGES ©

④ Jardin du Palais Royal (p101)

Browse the colonnaded arcades of the exquisite Jardin du Palais Royal.

JARDIN DU PALAIS ROYAL ➲ ÉGLISE ST-EUSTACHE
🏃 Exit the gardens on rue St-Honoré, turn left into rue du Louvre and right on rue Coquillière.

⑤ Église St-Eustache (p103)

One of Paris' most beautiful churches, Église St-Eustache has a magnificent organ – catch a classical concert here if you can.

ÉGLISE ST-EUSTACHE ➲ CENTRE POMPIDOU
🏃 Continue east on to place Georges Pompidou.

⑥ Centre Pompidou (p98)

Head to the late-opening Centre Pompidou for amazing modern and contemporary art. For dinner, try Georges, the Centre's swish-est dining option, with a spectacular view.

CENTRE POMPIDOU ➲ LE PICK-CLOPS
🏃 Follow rue Rambuteau, turning right into rue Vieille du Temple.

⑦ Le Pick-Clops (p168)

The Marais really comes into its own at night, with a cornucopia of hip clubs and bars like Le Pick-Clops.

Western & Southern Paris

*It's a day of Parisian icons today – from the triumphal span of the Arc de
Triomphe to the world-famous avenue, the Champs-Élysées, and, of course,
the city's stunning art nouveau Eiffel Tower, with some surprises too, such as
floating nightclubs.*

① Arc de Triomphe (p70)

Climb the mighty Arc de Triomphe for a pinch-yourself Parisian panorama. Back down on ground level, take the time to check out the intricate sculptures and historic bronze plaques, and pay your respects to the Tomb of the Unknown Soldier.

ARC DE TRIOMPHE ➲ CHAMPS-ÉLYSÉES
🏃 Walk down the Champs-Élysées.

② Champs-Élysées (p72)

Promenade along Paris' most glamorous avenue, the Champs-Élysées, and perhaps give your credit card a workout in the adjacent Triangle d'Or (Golden Triangle), home to flagship *haute couture* fashion houses.

CHAMPS-ÉLYSÉES ➲ MUSÉE DU QUAI BRANLY
Ⓜ Franklin D Roosevelt to Alma Marceau.

③ Musée du Quai Branly (p59)

From Alma Marceau metro station, cross the Pont d'Alma and turn right along quai Branly to check out indigenous art as well as the awesome architecture of the Musée du Quai Branly.

MUSÉE DU QUAI BRANLY ➲ CAFÉ BRANLY
🏃 Head to the museum's Café Branly.

④ Lunch at Café Branly (p63)

Casual yet classy, Café Branly has ringside Tower views.

CAFÉ BRANLY ➲ PALAIS DE TOKYO
🏃 Cross the Passerelle Debilly and walk up rue de la Manutention, turning right on av du Président Wilson.

⑤ Palais de Tokyo (p54)

This stunning building takes on major temporary cutting-edge exhibits – the rooftop, for example, has been the setting for projects like the transient Hotel Everland and the see-through restaurant Nomiya.

PALAIS DE TOKYO ➲ EIFFEL TOWER
Ⓜ Iéna to Trocadéro.

⑥ Eiffel Tower (p52)

Exiting the Trocadéro metro station, walk east through the Jardins du Trocadéro for the ultimate Eiffel Tower snapshot, and cross Pont d'Iéna to the tower itself (600m total). Sunset is the best time to ascend the Eiffel Tower, to experience both the dazzling views during daylight and then the twinkling *la ville lumière* (the City of Light) by night. (Prepurchase your tickets to minimise queuing!)

EIFFEL TOWER ➲ LE CASSE NOIX
🏃 Head southwest along Quai Branly to rue de la Fédération.

⑦ Dinner at Le Casse Noix (p61)

Dining inside the Eiffel Tower itself is unforgettable. Alternatively, book ahead for cracking bistro fare at Le Casse Noir.

LE CASSE NOIX ➲ LE BATOFAR
Ⓜ Bir-Hakeim to Quai de la Gare.

⑧ Le Batofar (p247)

Shadow the Seine by metro to party aboard several floating nightclubs permanently moored here, including Le Batofar. Other nightlife options in this area include the Docks en Seine (aka Cité de la Mode et du Design), home to the French fashion institute, and ultrahip bars, clubs and restaurants and huge riverside terraces.

Arc de Triomphe (p70)
PAWEL LIBERA/GETTY IMAGES ©

The Islands & Left Bank

Begin the day in the heart of Paris at the city's colossal cathedral then venture across to Paris' elegant Left Bank to see impressionist masterpieces in the Musée d'Orsay, and visit the city's oldest church and its loveliest gardens.

DAY
3

1 Notre Dame (p182)

Starting your day at the Notre Dame gives you the best chance of beating the crowds. As well as the stained-glass interior, allow an hour to climb up to the top to check out the gargoyles, and another to explore the crypt.

NOTRE DAME ➲ SAINTE-CHAPELLE

🏃 Walk south along rue de la Cité, turning right on quai du Marché-Neuf, then right on bd du Palais.

2 Sainte-Chapelle (p187)

For even more beautiful stained-glasswork, don't miss the chapel Sainte-Chapelle. Consecrated in 1248, its stained glass forms a curtain of glazing on the 1st floor.

SAINTE-CHAPELLE ➲ CUISINE DE BAR

Ⓜ Cité to St-Sulpice, then walk west on rue du Vieux Colombier and left on rue du Cherche-Midi.

3 Lunch at Cuisine de Bar (p233)

This stylish lunch spot serves gourmet *tartines* (open sandwiches) on sourdough made by famous bakery Poilâne next door. Nip into Poilâne afterwards to pick up some *punitions* (crispy butter biscuits).

CUISINE DE BAR ➲ MUSÉE D'ORSAY

Ⓜ Sèvres-Babylone to Solférino, then northwest on bd St-Germain and right up rue de Bellechasse.

4 Musée d'Orsay (p224)

Visit the magnificent Musée d'Orsay, filled with impressionist masterpieces including works by Renoir, Monet, Van Gogh, Degas and dozens more.

MUSÉE D'ORSAY ➲ ST-GERMAIN DES PRÉS

Ⓜ Solférino to Sèvres-Babylone, then change lines for Mabillon.

5 Église St-Germain des Prés (p228)

Paris' oldest church, the Église St-Germain des Prés, sits in the heart of the buzzing St-Germain des Prés district, with chic boutiques and historic literary cafes including Les Deux Magots, just opposite the church.

ÉGLISE ST-GERMAIN DES PRÉS ➲ JARDIN DE LUXEMBOURG

🏃 Head south on rue Bonaparte to place St-Sulpice and continue on to rue Vaugirard.

6 Jardin du Luxembourg (p226)

Enter the lovely Jardin du Luxembourg from rue Vaugirard and stroll among its chestnut groves, paths and statues.

JARDIN DU LUXEMBOURG ➲ BOUILLON RACINE

🏃 From rue Vaugirard, turn left on rue Monsieur-le-Prince and right on rue Racine.

7 Dinner at Bouillon Racine (p235)

Feast on French classics at the art nouveau jewel Bouillon Racine.

BOUILLON RACINE ➲ SHAKESPEARE & COMPANY

🏃 Head east on rue Racine, turning left at bd St-Michel then right at rue de la Huchette and cross rue St-Jacques to reach tiny rue de la Bûcherie.

8 Shakespeare & Company (p216)

Scour the shelves of late-night bookshops like the fabled Shakespeare & Company.

Sainte-Chapelle (p187)
DANITA DELIMONT/GETTY IMAGES ©

Northern & Eastern Paris

Montmartre's sinuous streets and steep staircases lined with crooked ivy-clad buildings are especially enchanting to meander in the early morning when tourists are few. Afterwards, explore charming Canal St-Martin and futuristic Parc de la Villette before drinking, dining and dancing in lively Bastille.

1 Musée de Montmartre (p130)

Brush up on the area's fabled history at the local museum, the Musée de Montmartre. Not only was Montmartre home to seminal artists, but Renoir and Utrillo are among those who lived in this very building.

MUSÉE DE MONTMARTRE ➲ SACRÉ-CŒUR

🚶 Walk east along rue Cortot and right on rue du Mont Cenis then left on rue Azais.

2 Sacré-Cœur (p128)

Head to the hilltop Sacré-Cœur basilica and, for an even more extraordinary panorama over Paris, up into the basilica's main dome. Regular metro tickets are valid on the funicular that shuttles up and down the steep Butte de Montmartre (Montmartre Hill).

SACRÉ-CŒUR ➲ LE MIROIR

🚶 At the bottom of the hill, walk west along rue Tardieu and rue Yvonne le Tace, turning left on rue des Martyrs.

3 Lunch at Le Miroir (p137)

Dining-wise Montmartre has more than its fair share of tourist traps, but locals' favourite Le Miroir offers lunch *menu* specials that offer superb quality and value, as do its wines from its own shop across the street. You'll also find wonderful food shops along the street, including award-winning *boulangerie* (bakery) Arnaud Delmontel.

LE MIROIR ➲ CANAL ST-MARTIN

Ⓜ Abbesses to Marcadet-Poissonniers, then change lines for Gare de l'Est.

4 Canal St-Martin (p134)

A postcard-perfect vision of iron footbridges, swing bridges and shaded tow paths,

Canal St-Martin's banks are lined with funky cafes and boutiques. Also here are the historic Hôtel Du Nord (the setting for stories that formed the basis for the eponymous film and now a restaurant/bar) and the ubercool cultural centre Point Éphémère.

CANAL ST-MARTIN ➲ PARC DE LA VILLETTE

Ⓜ Jacques Bonsergent to Porte de Pantin.

5 Parc de la Villette (p135)

In addition to its striking geometric gardens, innovative Parc de la Villette has a slew of attractions including the kid-friendly Cité des Sciences museum. Sailing schedules permitting, you can take a two-and-a-half-hour cruise to Bastille with canal cruise operator Canauxrama. Alternatively, head for the metro.

PARC DE LA VILLETTE ➲ SEPTIME

Ⓜ Porte de Pantin to Oberkampf, then change lines for Charonne.

6 Dinner at Septime (p164)

After a pre-dinner *apéro* (aperitif) at the classic, cherry-red corner cafe Le Pure Café, head around the corner to enjoy Modern French culinary magic at Septime.

SEPTIME ➲ RUE DE LAPPE

🚶 Head west on rue de Charonne for 450m to rue de Lappe.

7 Rue de Lappe

The Bastille neighbourhood and its surrounds spill over with nightlife venues. A good place to start the evening off is heading little rue de Lappe, not far from place de la Bastille, where you can salsa your socks off at the 1936 dance hall Le Balajo or simply hop between the street's buzzing bars.

Sacré-Cœur (p128)

Month by Month

January

 Who's Next Prêt-à-porter

Who's Next Prêt-à-porter (www.whosnext.com), a ready-to-wear fashion salon held twice a year (in late January and early July), is a must for fashion buffs. Held at Parc des Expositions at Porte de Versailles, 15e.

February

 Salon International de l'Agriculture

At this nine-day fair (www.salon-agriculture.com), produce and animals from all over France are turned into gourmet fare at the Parc des Expositions, from late February to early March.

March

 Banlieues Bleues

Big-name acts perform during the 'Suburban Blues' jazz, blues and R&B festival (www.banlieues bleues.org) from mid-March to mid-April in Paris' northern suburbs.

April

 Foire du Trône

Dating back some 1000 years (!), this huge funfair (www.foiredutrone.com) is held on the pelouse de Reuilly of the Bois de Vincennes from around early April to early June.

 Marathon International de Paris

On your marks... The Paris International Marathon (www.parismarathon.com), usually held on the second Sunday of April, starts on the av des Champs-Élysées, 8e, and finishes on av Foch, 16e, attracting more than 40,000 runners from over 100 countries.

May

 La Nuit des Musées Européenne

Key museums across Paris stay open late for the European Museums Night (www.nuitdesmusees.culture.fr), on one Saturday/Sunday in mid-May.

 French Open

The glitzy Internationaux de France de Tennis Grand Slam hits up from late May to early June at Stade Roland Garros (www.rolandgarros.com) at the Bois de Boulogne, 16e.

June

 Fête de la Musique

This national music festival (http://fetedelamusique.culture.fr) welcomes in summer on the solstice (21 June) with staged and impromptu live performances of jazz, reggae, classical and more all over the city.

(left) Paris Plages on the banks of the Seine
PAWEL LIBERA/GETTY IMAGES ©

◉ Gay Pride March

Late June's colourful Saturday-afternoon Marche des Fiertés (www.gaypride.fr) through the Marais to Bastille celebrates Gay Pride Day with floats and costumes.

✪ Paris Jazz Festival

Free jazz concerts swing every Saturday and Sunday afternoon in June and July in the Parc Floral de Paris (www.parisjazzfestival.paris.fr); park entry fee applies (adult/under 25 €5.50/2.75).

July

✪ Paris Cinéma

Rare and restored films screen in selected cinemas citywide during this 12-day festival (www.pariscinema.org) in the first half of July.

◉ Bastille Day (14 July)

The capital celebrates France's national day with a morning military parade along av des Champs-Élysées accompanied by a fly-past of fighter aircraft and helicopters, and *feux d'artifice* (fireworks) lighting up the sky above the Champ de Mars by night.

✪ Paris Plages

Sand and pebble 'beaches'– complete with sun beds, umbrellas and palm trees – line the banks of the Seine from mid-July to mid-August.

✪ Tour de France

The last of 21 stages of this legendary, 3500km-long cycling event (www.letour.fr) finishes with a dash up av des Champs-Élysées on the third or fourth Sunday of July.

August

✪ Rock en Seine

Headlining acts rock the Domaine National de St-Cloud on the city's southwestern edge at this popular three-day, late-August music festival. (www.rockenseine.com)

September

✪ Festival d'Automne

Painting, music, dance and theatre take place at venues throughout the city from mid-September to late December as part of the long-running Autumn Festival of arts (www.festival-automne.com).

◉ Journées Européenes du Patrimoine

The third weekend in September sees Paris opening the doors of otherwise-off-limits buildings – embassies, ministries and so forth – during European Heritage Days (www.journees dupatrimoine.culture.fr).

October

✪ Nuit Blanche

From sundown until sunrise on the first Saturday and Sunday of October, museums and recreational facilities like swimming pools stay open, along with bars and clubs, for one 'White Night' (ie 'All Nighter').

✪ Fête des Vendanges de Montmartre

The grape harvest from the Clos Montmartre in early October is followed by five days of festivities including a parade (www.fetedesvendangesde montmartre.com).

November

✪ Africolor

From mid-November to late December, this six-week African music festival (www.africolor.com) is primarily held in surrounding suburbs, such as St-Denis, St-Ouen and Montreuil.

December

✪ New Year's Eve

Bd St-Michel (5e), place de la Bastille (11e), the Eiffel Tower (7e) and, above all, av des Champs-Élysées (8e) are the places to be to welcome in the New Year.

What's New

For this new edition of Discover Paris, our authors hunted down the fresh, the transformed, the hot and the happening. Here are a few of our favourites. For up-to-the-minute recommendations, see lonelyplanet.com/paris.

1 LEGENDARY HOTELS

Landmark hotel openings include illustrious addresses like Les Bains, formerly thermal baths and later a steamy nightclub, and the art deco swimming pool now housing the Hôtel Molitor (p290). And reopenings see the 2015 return of the Hôtel de Crillon (www.crillon.com), with two suites designed by Karl Lagerfeld, as well as belle époque beauty the Ritz (www.ritzparis.com), following head-to-toe renovations of its rooms, bars, restaurants, gardens and Ritz Escoffier cooking school.

2 EIFFEL TOWER REFIT

On the 1st floor of Paris' emblematic tower, two glitzy new glass pavilions house interactive history exhibits; outside them, peer d-o-w-n through glass flooring to the ground below. (p52)

3 RIVERSIDE RENAISSANCE

A breath of fresh air, the former expressway Les Berges de Seine has fitness areas, floating gardens and a string of bars, restaurants and clubs, and also hosts year-round activities and events. (p229)

4 ISLAMIC CULTURAL INSTITUTE

Art exhibitions and a hammam top the billing at the new Institut des Cultures d'Islam cultural institute in northern Paris' Goutte d'Or neighbourhood. (p131)

5 COFFEE REVOLUTION

Bitter Parisian coffee is becoming a thing of the past thanks to local roasteries like Belleville Brûlerie and Coutume, with a wave of cafes citywide now producing world-class brews. (p169)

6 HIP HOSTELS

For years, Paris' crash pads were as good as its coffee was(n't), but that's changing too with the opening of state-of-the-art flash pads such as St Christopher's. (p290)

7 MOVEABLE FEASTS

Street food is taking the city by storm as food trucks specialising in everything from French favourites like *tartiflette* to gourmet burgers and wildly flavoured ice creams roll out across Paris. (p62)

8 VISIONARY ARCHITECTURE

Frank Gehry's Fondation Louis Vuitton building topped by 3600 glass panels forming 12 giant 'sails' competes for attention with the artistic creations inside. (p61)

9 STIRRING SYMPHONIES

For a classical concert to remember, visit the 2400-seat, Jean Nouvel–designed Philharmonie de Paris when it opens in the Parc de la Villette in 2015. (p135)

10 TREASURE HUNTS

Tours with a twist organised by THATLou challenge participants to undertake themed treasure hunts in high-profile museums and neighbourhoods. (p300)

11 FORUM OVERHAUL

On the site of Paris' old wholesale markets, a rainforest-inspired giant glass canopy and meadow-like gardens atop the rejuvenated subterranean mall Forum des Halles will reach final completion in 2016. (p102)

Get Inspired

Books

○ **The Flâneur: A Stroll Through the Paradoxes of Paris** (Edmund White) White muses about his beloved adopted city.

○ **Les Misérables** (Victor Hugo) Epic novel tracing convict Jean Valjean through the battles of early-19th-century Paris.

○ **Life: A User's Manual** (Georges Perec) Intricate tale of Parisian life told through characters inhabiting an apartment block between 1833 and 1975.

○ **Down and Out in Paris and London** (George Orwell) Follows Eric Blair's (aka Orwell's) days as a downtrodden hotel dishwasher.

Films

○ **Le Fabuleux Destin d'Amélie Poulain** (Amélie) Feel-good fable about Montmartre cafe waitress Amélie Poulain.

○ **La Môme** (La Vie en Rose) Acclaimed biopic of Édith Piaf, uncannily portrayed by Marion Cotillard.

○ **Last Tango in Paris** Marlon Brando steams up the screen.

♫ Music

○ **She: the Best of Charles Aznavour** (Charles Aznavour) Hits from 'France's Frank Sinatra' including 'La Bohème' and 'The Old Fashioned Way'.

○ **Anthologie** (Serge Gainsbourg) Famous tracks include 'Le Poinçonneur des Lilas' and 'Je t'aime...Moi Non Plus', a duet with Brigitte Bardot.

○ **Le Voyage dans la Lune** (AIR) The seventh album from innovative electronica duo AIR (which stands for '*Amour*, *Imagination*, *Rêve*' meaning 'Love, Imagination, Dream').

○ **La Nouvelle Chanson Française** (Various Artists) Everything from traditional and cabaret to folk-electronic and Paris club sound.

Websites

○ **Paris By Mouth** (http://parisbymouth.com) Foodie heaven.

○ **My Little Paris** (www.mylittleparis.com) Little-known local treasures.

○ **Secrets of Paris** (www.secretsofparis.com) Loads of resources and reviews.

Short on time?

This list will give you an instant insight into the city.

Read Hemingway's classic *A Moveable Feast* recounts his early Parisian career, with priceless vignettes of fellow writers including F Scott Fitzgerald.

Watch Paris' timeless magic is palpable in Woody Allen's *Midnight in Paris*.

Listen *Live at the Paris Olympia* features Édith Piaf's classics, including 'Milord', 'Padam... Padam' and, of course, 'Non, Je Ne Regrette Rien'.

Log on Paris Convention & Visitors Bureau (www.parisinfo.com).

Montmartre grocer seen in the film *Amélie*
KRISTIN PILJAY/GETTY IMAGES ©

Need to Know

Currency
Euro (€)

Language
French

Visas
Generally no restrictions for EU citizens. Usually not required for most other nationalities for stays of up to 90 days.

Money
ATMs widely available. Visa and MasterCard accepted in most hotels, shops and restaurants; fewer establishments accept American Express.

Mobile Phones
Check with your provider before you leave about roaming costs or ensure your phone is unlocked to use a French SIM card.

Time
Central European Time (GMT plus one hour).

Wi-Fi
Paris has hundreds of free wi-fi hotspots; locations are mapped at www.paris.fr/wifi.

Tipping
Tips are included under French law, though for good service you might tip an extra 10% in restaurants. Round taxi fares up to the nearest euro.

For more information, see Survival Guide (p300).

When to Go

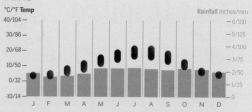

Spring and autumn are ideal times to visit. Summer is the main tourist season, but some businesses close during August. Sights are quieter and prices lower during winter.

Advance Planning

As early as possible Book accommodation.

Two months before Book a cooking or wine-tasting course, organise opera, ballet or cabaret tickets and make reservations for high-end and/or popular restaurants for a Parisian feast.

Two weeks before Sign up for a free, local-led tour and start narrowing down your choice of museums, pre-purchasing tickets online where possible to avoid lengthy ticket queues on the ground in Paris.

Two days before Pack your comfiest pair of shoes for all that walking you'll be doing.

Daily Costs

Budget less than €100
○ Dorm beds €25–50
○ Self-catering supermarkets and markets
○ Inexpensive public transport; stand-by theatre tickets

Midrange €100–250
○ Double room €130–250
○ Two-course meals €20–40
○ Affordable museums

Top End over €250
○ Historic luxury hotels
○ Gastronomic restaurants
○ Designer boutiques

Arriving in Paris

Charles de Gaulle Airport Trains (RER), buses, night buses to the city centre €5.70–€17.50; taxi around €50–€65.

Orly Airport Trains (Orlyval then RER), buses, night buses to the city centre €7.50–€12.50; taxi around €40–€65.

Beauvais Airport Buses (€17) to Porte Maillot then metro (€1.70); taxi from at least €100 (probably more than the cost of your flight!).

Gare du Nord Train Station Within central Paris; served by metro (€1.70).

Getting Around

Walking is a pleasure in Paris, but the city also has one of the most efficient and inexpensive public transport systems in the world, making getting around a breeze.

○ **Metro & RER** The fastest way to get around. Runs from about 5.20am to 1.15am (around 2.15am on Friday and Saturday nights), depending on the line.

○ **Bicycle** Virtually free pick-up, drop-off Vélib' bikes operate across 1800 stations citywide.

○ **Bus** Good for parents with prams/strollers and people with limited mobility.

○ **Boat** The Batobus is a handy hop-on, hop-off service stopping at eight key destinations along the Seine.

Sleeping

Paris has a wealth of accommodation options, but they're often *complet* (full) well in advance. Reservations are recommended any time of year, and are essential during the warmer months (April to October) and all public and school holidays. Accommodation outside central Paris is marginally cheaper, but it's almost always a false economy, as travelling into the city consumes time and money. Try to choose somewhere within Paris' 20 *arrondissements* (city districts), where you can experience Parisian life the moment you step out the door.

Useful Websites

○ **Paris Hotel** (www.hotels-paris.fr) Well-organised site with lots of user reviews.

○ **Paris Hotel Service** (www.parishotelservice.com) Specialises in boutique gems.

○ **Paris Hotels** (www.parishotels.com) Loads of options and locations.

○ **Lonely Planet** (www.lonelyplanet.com/hotels) Reviews and bookings.

What to Bring

○ **Phrase book** The more French you attempt, the more rewarding your visit will be.

○ **Corkscrew** For picnics complete with French wines.

○ **Adaptor** Especially to charge your phone/camera to snap Parisian panoramas.

○ **Bike helmet** Not supplied with Vélib' bikes, so you may want to bring your own.

○ **Your appetite** France's reputation for fine food precedes it.

Be Forewarned

○ **Museums** Most close Monday or Tuesday. All museums and monuments shut their doors 30 minutes to one hour before listed closing times.

○ **Summer closures** Many restaurants and shops close for summer holidays, generally during August.

○ **Restaurants** *Menus* (fixed-price meals) offer infinitely better value than ordering à la carte. Meals are often considerably cheaper at lunch than dinner.

○ **Bars & cafes** A drink costs more sitting at a table than standing, on the terrace rather than indoors, and on a fancy square rather than a back street. Come 10pm many cafes apply a pricier *tarif de nuit* (night rate).

○ **Shopping** Paris' twice-yearly *soldes* (sales) usually last around six weeks, starting in mid-January and again in mid-June.

○ **Metro stations** Worth avoiding late at night: Châtelet-Les Halles and its seemingly endless corridors, Château Rouge (Montmartre), Gare du Nord, Strasbourg St-Denis, Réaumur Sébastopol and Montparnasse Bienvenüe.

○ **Pickpockets** Pickpockets prey on busy places; *always* stay alert to the possibility of someone surreptitiously reaching for your pockets or bags.

Eiffel Tower & Western Paris

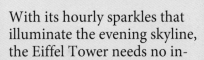

With its hourly sparkles that illuminate the evening skyline, the Eiffel Tower needs no introduction. Heading up to its viewing platforms offers you a panorama over the whole of Paris, with the prestigious neighbourhood of Passy (the 16e *arrondissement*) stretching out along the far banks of the Seine to the west.

In the 18th and 19th centuries, Passy was home to luminaries such as Benjamin Franklin and Balzac. Defined by its sober, elegant buildings from the Haussmann era, it was only annexed to the city in 1860.

Passy boasts some fabulous museums, both big-hitters and a host of smaller collections devoted to everything from Balzac to fashion, crystal, wine and sub-Saharan art. At the city's western edge is the leafy refuge of the Bois de Boulogne. Beyond this lies the high-rise business district of La Défense, home to some great urban art.

Eiffel Tower (p52)

Eiffel Tower & Western Paris Highlights

Eiffel Tower (p52)

Almost any time is a good time to visit the tower (except in inclement weather when views are diminished or high winds force it to shut). But the best time to ascend this famous landmark – more Parisian than Paris itself – is at dusk for day- and night-time views of the glittering city. Celebrate making it to the top at the tower's sparkling champagne bar.

HISHAM IBRAHIM/GETTY IMAGES ©

Musée du Quai Branly (p59)

Like in all good Paris museums, the collection of indigenous artwork at the Musée du Quai Branly – the brainchild of former French President Jacques Chirac – is as controversial as it is innovative. Check out its 'vertical living garden', which scales the exterior of the structure, before heading inside to contemplate anthropological artefacts from every continent except Europe.

MUSÉE DU QUAI BRANLY, VUE EXTÉRIEURE DU BÂTIMENT MUSÉE ET DES BOÎTES SCÉNOGRAPHIQUES/ MUSÉE DU QUAI BRANLY / LOIS LAMMERHUBER / ARCHITECT JEAN NOUVEL ©

VÉRONIQUE DELAUX PHOTOGRAPHY & CREATING/GETTY IMAGES©

Bois de Boulogne (p61)

The leafy Bois de Boulogne is where city-dwellers head to escape the concrete, whether on bikes, skates or by *footing* (jogging). Other activities and attractions include paddling row boats around the lake, the delightful Jardin d'Acclimatation amusement park for littlies, the Stade Roland Garros and its adjacent tennis museum, and the stunning new Frank Gehry–designed fine-arts centre Fondation Louis Vuitton pour la Création. Bagatelle park, Bois de Boulogne

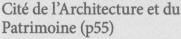

Cité de l'Architecture et du Patrimoine (p55)

Wander past cathedral portals, gargoyles and intricate scale models at the Cité de l'Architecture et du Patrimoine. This colossal 23,000-sq-metre space overlooking the Jardins du Trocadéro houses a comprehensive collection of elements of French architecture and heritage. It's an education and a delight, and the views of the Eiffel Tower from the windows are equally monumental.

Musée Marmottan Monet (p60)

Take a trip out to the Musée Marmottan Monet, on the edge of the Bois de Boulogne, to see the world's largest collection of Monet canvases. Some of the masterpieces to look out for include *La Barque* (1887), *Cathédrale de Rouen* (1892), *Londres, le Parlement* (1901) and the various *Nymphéas* (Waterlilies; many of these canvases were smaller studies for the works in the Musée de l'Orangerie).

Eiffel Tower & Western Paris Walk

The ultimate symbol of Paris, the Eiffel Tower, is never far from view on this walk, but you'll also explore a little-known artificial island in the middle of the Seine, and see one of the city's innovative vertical gardens at the Musée du Quai Branly.

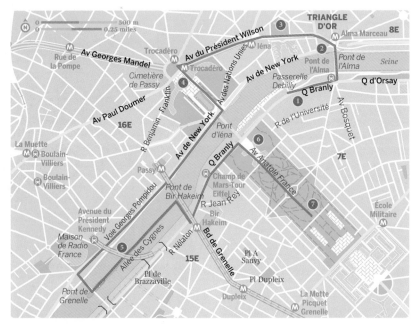

WALK FACTS

- **Start** Musée du Quai Branly
- **Finish** Parc du Champ de Mars
- **Distance** 5km
- **Duration** 2½ hours

① Musée du Quai Branly

Facing the Seine at the **Musée du Quai Branly** (p59) is a *mur végétal* (vegetation wall; ie a vertical garden) designed by Patrick Blanc, with some 15,000 low-light foliage plants on a surface of 800 sq metres. They're held in place by a frame of metal, PVC and non-biodegradable felt, but no soil. The museum itself, showcasing indigenous art from Oceania, Asia, Africa and the Americas, is in a striking building designed by Jean Nouvel.

② Flame of Liberty Memorial

Walk east along quai Branly and cross the Pont de l'Alma to place de l'Alma. Near the end of bridge, the bronze **Flame of Liberty Memorial** (p55) is a replica of the Statue of Liberty's flame. You'll see floral tributes for Diana, Princess of Wales, who died in a car accident here in 1997.

③ Musée Galliera de la Mode de la Ville de Paris

Walk west along av du Président Wilson. On your left you'll pass the modern art museum the **Musée d'Art Moderne de la Ville de Paris** (p55), then the **Palais de Tokyo** (p54), built for the 1937 Exposition Universelle and now hosting contemporary art installations. On your right, set back behind lavish gardens in the 19th-century Palais Galliera, is Paris' fashion museum, the **Musée Galliera de la Mode de la Ville de Paris**.

Palais de Chaillot

Continue to place du Trocadéro et du 11 Novembre to the **Palais de Chaillot**. The two curved, colonnaded wings of this palace and the terrace in between them afford an exceptional panorama of the Eiffel Tower. The eastern wing houses the excellent architectural museum the **Cité de l'Architecture et du Patrimoine** (p55).

5 Île aux Cygnes

From the Palais de Chaillot's terrace, descend the steps and walk through the Jardins du Trocadéro; on your left you'll see the kid-pleasing **Cinéaqua aquarium** (p55) and cinemas. Continue to the river and turn right to cross the Pont de Grenelle's eastern side. Descend to the artificially created island **Île aux Cygnes** (Isle of Swans), formed in 1827 to protect the river port, and measuring just 850m long by 11m wide. On the western side of the bridge is a 11.5m-high replica of the Statue of Liberty, inaugurated in 1889. Walk east along the **Allée des Cygnes** – the tree-lined walkway that runs the length of the island.

6 Eiffel Tower

Ascend the steps on Pont de Bir Hakeim and turn right to cross to the Left Bank. West of the Musée du Quai Branly, the **Eiffel Tower** (p52) is at its most monumental as you stand beneath it.

7 Parc du Champ de Mars

From the tower, stroll the lawns of the **Parc du Champ de Mars** (p54), perhaps stopping for an ultrascenic picnic.

★★★ The Best…

PLACES TO EAT

Hugo Desnoyer Feast for meat lovers courtesy of Paris' most famous butcher. (p61)

Tokyo Eat The funkiest dining option in the otherwise sedate west. (p62)

Choux d'Enfer Gourmet takeaway pastry puffs for Eiffel Tower picnicking. (p60)

58 Tour Eiffel Affordable dining inside the Eiffel Tower under the direction of Alain Ducasse. (p62)

MUSEUMS

Musée du Quai Branly Indigenous art, artefacts, music and more from every continent bar Europe. (p59)

Cité de l'Architecture et du Patrimoine Huge space with exhibits covering Paris' architectural history and its future. (p55)

Musée Marmottan Monet The world's largest collection of Monet's works. (p60)

Musée Guimet des Arts Asiatiques France's foremost repository of Asian art. (p55)

SPORTS & ACTIVITIES

Bois de Boulogne Bike rides, row boats and more. (p61)

Stade Roland Garros France's premier tennis stadium, with an extravagant tennis museum. (p61)

Stade Roland Garros (p61)
PASCAL LE SEGRETAIN/GETTY IMAGES ©

Don't Miss
Eiffel Tower

There are many ways to experience the Eiffel Tower, from an evening ascent amid the lights to a meal in one of its two restaurants, and even though some 6.7 million people come annually, few would dispute the fact that each visit is unique. Like many Parisian icons, it has gone from being roundly criticised by city residents to much loved.

Map p56

☎ 08 92 70 12 39

www.tour-eiffel.fr

Champ de Mars, 5 av Anatole France, 7e

lift to top adult/ child €15/10.50, lift to 2nd fl €9/4.50, stairs to 2nd fl €5/3, lift 2nd fl to top €6

⊙ lifts & stairs 9am-midnight mid-Jun–Aug, lifts 9.30am-11pm, stairs 9.30am-6.30pm Sep–mid-Jun

Ⓜ Bir Hakeim or RER Champ de Mars-Tour Eiffel

1st Floor

Of the tower's three floors, the 1st (57m) has the most space (hence its appealing museum-like layout) but the least impressive views. Two glass pavilions, Pavillon Ferrié and Salle Gustave Eiffel – open since summer 2014 – showcase interactive history exhibits, an immersion film and other features designed to help visitors learn more about the tower's ingenious design. Outside the pavilions, glass floors proffer a dizzying view of the ant-like people walking on the ground far, far below.

This level also hosts the affordable 58 Tour Eiffel restaurant.

Not all lifts stop at the 1st floor (check before ascending), but it's an easy walk down from the 2nd should you accidentally end up one floor too high.

2nd Floor

Views from the 2nd floor (115m) are generally considered to be the best, as they are impressively high but still close enough to see the details of the city below. Telescopes and panoramic maps placed around the tower pinpoint locations in Paris and beyond. Other sights to look out for include the story windows, which give a nuts-and-bolts overview of the lifts' mechanics, and the vision well, which allows you to gaze down (and down, and d-o-w-n) through glass panels to the ground. Also up here is the Michelin-starred restaurant Le Jules Verne, now run by Alain Ducasse.

Top Floor

Views from the wind-buffeted top floor (276m) can stretch up to 60km on a clear day, though at this height the panoramas are more sweeping than detailed. Celebrate your ascent with a glass of bubbly from the champagne bar while you try to pick out the monuments below, or check out Gustave Eiffel's restored top-level office, where life-like wax models of Eiffel and his daughter Claire greet Thomas Edison.

To access the top floor, you will need to take a separate lift on the 2nd level. Note that it will close in the event of heavy winds.

Ticket Purchases & Queueing Strategies

Ascend as far as the 2nd floor (either on foot or by lift), from where it is lift-only to the top floor. Pushchairs must be folded in lifts and you are not allowed to take bags or backpacks larger than aeroplane-cabin size.

Buying tickets in advance online usually means you avoid the monumental queues at the ticket offices. Print your ticket or show it on a smart-phone screen. If you can't reserve your tickets ahead of time expect waits of well over an hour in high season.

Stair tickets can't be reserved online. They are sold at the south pillar, where the staircase can also be accessed: the climb consists of 360 steps to the 1st level and another 360 steps to the 2nd pillar.

If you have reservations for either restaurant, you are granted direct access to the lifts.

Nightly Sparkles

Every hour on the hour, the entire tower sparkles for five minutes with 20,000 gold-toned lights. First installed for Paris' millennium celebration in 2000, it took 25 mountain climbers five months to install the bulbs and 40km of electrical cords. For the best view of the light show, head across the Seine to the Jardins du Trocadéro.

Eiffel Tower & Western Paris

◀▶ Getting There & Away

○ **Metro** Line 6 runs south from Charles de Gaulle–Étoile past the Eiffel Tower (views are superb from the elevated section); line 9 runs southwest from the Champs-Élysées.

○ **RER** RER A runs west to La Défense; RER C runs east–west along the Left Bank, with a stop at the Eiffel Tower.

○ **Bus** Scenic bus 69 runs from the Champ du Mars (Eiffel Tower) along the Left Bank, crosses the Seine at the Louvre, and then continues east to Père Lachaise.

○ **Bicycle** Handy Vélib' stations include 2 av Octave Creard (for the Eiffel Tower) and 3 av Bosquet (for Musée du Quai Branly).

○ **Boat** Eiffel Tower

◉ Sights

Eiffel Tower & 16e

Parc du Champ de Mars　　Park

Map p56 (Champ de Mars, 7e; M Champ de Mars–Tour Eiffel or École Militaire) Running southeast from the Eiffel Tower, the grassy Champ de Mars – an ideal summer picnic spot – was originally used as a parade ground for the cadets of the 18th-century **École Militaire**, the vast French-classical building at the southeastern end of the park which counts Napoléon Bonaparte among its graduates. The steel-and-etched glass **Wall for Peace memorial** (2000) is by Clara Halter.

Musée Dapper　　Art Museum

Map p56 (www.dapper.com.fr; 35 rue Paul Valéry, 16e; adult/child €6/free; ⏱11am–7pm Wed & Fri-Mon; M Victor Hugo) Focused on African and Caribbean art, this museum is an invitation to leave Paris behind for an hour or two. Exhibits rotate throughout the year, but the permanent collection is superb: ritual and festival masks and costumes accompanied by several video presentations. The auditorium hosts film screenings, concerts, storytelling and other cultural events.

Palais de Tokyo　　Art Museum

Map p56 (www.palaisdetokyo.com; 13 av du Président Wilson, 16e; adult/child €10/free; ⏱noon-midnight Wed-Mon; M Iéna) The Tokyo Palace, created for the 1937 Exposition Universelle, has no permanent collection. Rather its shell-like interior of concrete and steel is a stark backdrop to interactive contemporary art installations. Its bookshop is fabulous for art and design magazines, and its eating/drinking options are magic.

Flame of Liberty Memorial
YVES TALENSAC/GETTY IMAGES ©

Cité de l'Architecture et du Patrimoine
Museum

Map p56 (www.citechaillot.fr; 1 place du Trocadéro et du 11 Novembre, 16e; adult/child €8/free; ◎11am-7pm Wed & Fri-Mon, to 9pm Thu; Ⓜ Trocadéro) This mammoth 23,000-sq-metre space is an ode on three floors to French architecture. The highlight is the light-filled ground floor with a beautiful collection of plaster and wood *moulages* (casts) of cathedral portals, columns and gargoyles, and replicas of murals and stained glass originally created for the 1878 Exposition Universelle. Views of the Eiffel Tower are equally monumental.

Musée de la Marine
Naval Museum

Map p56 (Maritime Museum; www.musee-marine.fr; 17 place du Trocadéro et du 11 Novembre, 16e; adult/child €8.50/free; ◎11am-6pm Wed-Mon, to 7pm Sat & Sun; Ⓜ Trocadéro) Located in the western wing of Palais de Chaillot, the Maritime Museum examines France's naval adventures from the 17th century until today and boasts one of the world's finest collections of model ships, as well as ancient figureheads, compasses, sextants, telescopes and paintings. Temporary exhibitions command an additional admission fee.

Musée d'Art Moderne de la Ville de Paris
Museum

Map p56 (www.mam.paris.fr; 11 av du Président Wilson, 16e; ◎10am-6pm Tue, Wed, Fri-Sun, 10am-10pm Thu; Ⓜ Iéna) FREE The permanent collection at Paris' modern-art museum displays works representative of just about every major artistic movement of the 20th and (nascent) 21st centuries, with works by Modigliani, Matisse, Braque and Soutine. The real jewel though is the room hung with canvases by Dufy and Bonnard. Look out for cutting-edge temporary exhibitions (not free).

Musée de la Mode de la Ville de Paris
Museum

Map p56 (www.galliera.paris.fr; 10 av Pierre 1er de Serbie, 16e; adult/child €8/free; ◎10am-6pm Tue, Wed, Fri-Sun, 10am-9pm Thu; Ⓜ Iéna) Paris' Fashion Museum, housed in 19th-century Palais Galliera, warehouses some 100,000 outfits and accessories – from canes and umbrellas to fans and gloves – from the 18th century to the present day. The sumptuous Italianate palace and gardens dating from the mid-19th century are worth a visit in themselves, as are the excellent temporary exhibitions the museum hosts.

Aquarium de Paris Cinéaqua
Aquarium

Map p56 (www.cineaqua.com; av des Nations Unies, 16e; adult/child €20.50/16; ◎10am-7pm; Ⓜ Trocadéro) Paris' aquarium, on the eastern side of the Jardins du Trocadéro, has a shark tank and 500-odd fish species to entertain families on rainy days. Three cinemas screen ocean-related and other films (dubbed in French, with subtitles). Budget tip: show your ticket from the nearby Musée de la Marine to get reduced aquarium admission (adult/child €16.40/10.40).

Flame of Liberty Memorial
Monument

Map p56 (place de l'Alma, 8e; Ⓜ Alma Marceau) This bronze sculpture, a replica of the one topping the Statue of Liberty, was placed here in 1987 as a symbol of friendship between France and the USA. More famous is its location, above the place d'Alma tunnel where, on 31 August 1997, Diana, Princess of Wales, was killed in a car accident. Graffiti remembering the princess covers the entire wall next to the sculpture.

Musée Guimet des Arts Asiatiques
Art Museum

Map p56 (www.museeguimet.fr; 6 place d'Iéna, 16e; adult/child €7.50/free; ◎10am-6pm Wed-Mon; Ⓜ Iéna) France's foremost Asian art museum has a superb collection. Observe the gradual transmission of both Buddhism and artistic styles along the Silk Road in pieces ranging from 1st-century Gandhara Buddhas from Afghanistan and Pakistan, to later Central Asian, Chinese and Japanese Buddhist sculptures and art. Part of the collection is housed in the nearby Galeries du **Panthéon Bouddhique** Map p56 (19 av d'Iéna, 16e; ◎10am-5.45pm Wed-Mon, garden to 5pm) FREE with a **Japanese garden**.

Eiffel Tower & 16e

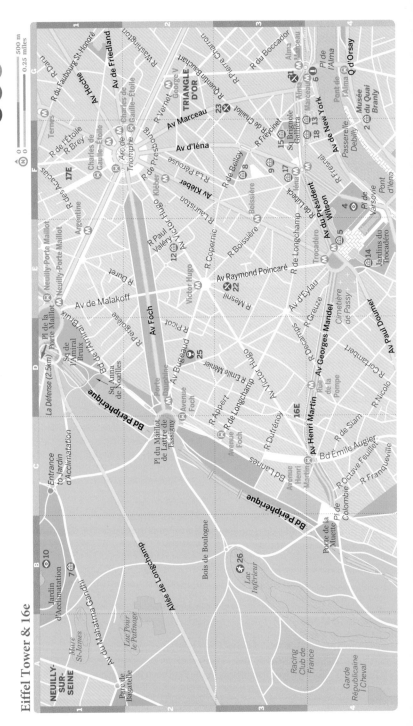

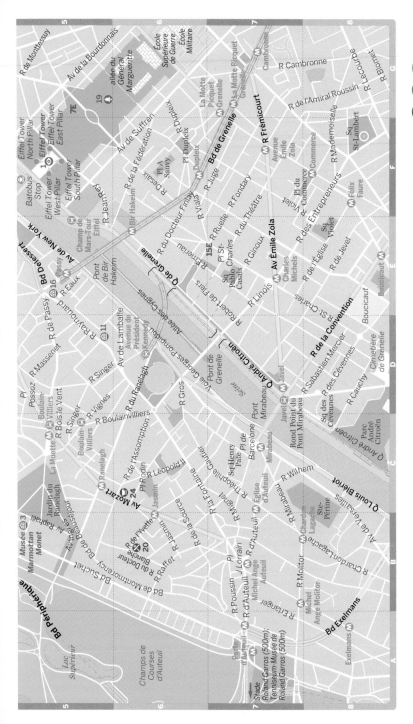

Galerie-Musée Baccarat   Museum

Map p56 (www.baccarat.com; 11 place des États-Unis, 16e; adult/child €7/free; ⊙10am-6pm Mon & Wed-Sat; Ⓜ Boissière or Kléber) Showcasing 1000 stunning pieces of crystal, many of them custom-made for princes and dictators of former colonies, this flashy museum is at home in its striking new rococo-style premises designed by Philippe Starck in the ritzy 16e. It is also home to an upmarket restaurant called – what else? – **Le Cristal Room**.

Musée du Vin   Museum

Map p56 (🖉 01 45 25 63 26; www.museeduvinparis.com; 5 sq Charles Dickens, 16e; adult/child €10/free; ⊙10am-6pm Tue-Sun; Ⓜ Passy) The Wine Museum, headquarters of the prestigious International Federation of Wine Brotherhoods, introduces visitors to the fine art of viticulture with mock-ups and tool displays. End museum visits with a glass of AOP wine (€5) or a two-hour wine-tasting workshop (€63). If you lunch in the attached restaurant (noon to 3pm Tuesday to Saturday) museum admission is free.

Maison de Balzac   Museum

Map p56 (www.balzac.paris.fr; 47 rue Raynouard, 16e; ⊙10am-6pm Tue-Sun; Ⓜ Passy or Avenue du Président Kennedy) FREE This pretty, three-storey spa house is where realist novelist Honoré de Balzac (1799–1850) lived and worked from 1840 to 1847, editing the entire *La Comédie Humaine* here. There's lots of memorabilia, letters, prints and portraits – perfect for die-hard Balzac fans.

La Défense

Paris' high-rise business district La Défense, is an engaging, open-air art gallery. Calder, Miró, Agam, César and Torricini are among the international artists behind the colourful and often surprising sculptures and murals that pepper the central 1km-long promenade. Pick up a map and excellent booklets in English outlining walks to discover its art and surprising green spaces at the **Info Défense** (🖉 01 47 74 84 24; www.ladefense.fr; place de la Défense; ⊙9am-6pm Mon-Fri, 10am-5pm Sat & Sun; Ⓜ La Défense) kiosk, to the side of the moon-shaped CNIT building on the main drag.

Grande Arche de la Défense   Landmark

(1 Parvis de la Défense; Ⓜ La Défense) La Défense's landmark edifice is the white marble Grande Arche, a cube-like arch built in the 1980s to home government and business offices. The arch marks

EIFFEL TOWER & WESTERN PARIS SIGHTS

ATELIERS JEAN NOUVEL/PHILIPPE RUAULT ©

 Don't Miss
Musée du Quai Branly

No other museum in Paris so inspires travellers, armchair anthropologists and those who simply appreciate the beauty of traditional craftsmanship. A tribute to the diversity of human culture, Musée du Quai Branly presents an overview of indigenous and folk art. Its four main sections focus on Oceania, Asia, Africa and the Americas.

An impressive array of masks, carvings, weapons, jewellery and more make up the body of the rich collection, displayed in a refreshingly unique interior without rooms or high walls. Be sure to check out the temporary exhibits and performances, both of which are generally excellent.

NEED TO KNOW
Map p56 www.quaibranly.fr; 37 quai Branly, 7e; adult/child €8.50/free; ⏱11am-7pm Tue, Wed & Sun, 11am-9pm Thu-Sat; Ⓜ Alma Marceau or RER Pont de l'Alma

the western end of the *axe historique* (historic axis), though Danish architect Johann Otto von Spreckelsen deliberately placed the Grande Arche fractionally out of alignment. It's not possible to visit inside or access the roof.

Musée de la Défense   Museum
(www.ladefense.fr; 15 place de la Défense; Ⓜ La Défense) FREE Set to reopen after renovations in early 2015, this museum evokes the area's development and architecture

through drawings, architectural plans and scale models.

 # Eating

This neighbourhood is best known for its monuments and museums and, conveniently, there are a number of good restaurants located in the sights themselves, including the Eiffel Tower.

HEMIS/ALAMY ©

★ Don't Miss
Musée Marmottan Monet

This museum showcases the world's largest collection of works by impressionist painter Claude Monet (1840-1926) – about 100 – as well as paintings by Gauguin, Sisley, Pissarro, Renoir, Degas, Manet and Berthe Morisot. It also contains an important collection of French, English, Italian and Flemish miniatures from the 13th to the 16th centuries.

NEED TO KNOW

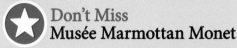

Map p56 📞01 44 96 50 33; www.marmottan.com; 2 rue Louis Boilly, 16e; adult/child €10/5; 🕙10am-6pm Tue-Sun, to 8pm Thu; Ⓜ La Muette

Choux d'Enfer   Patisserie €
(📞01 47 83 26 67; cnr rue Jean Rey & quai Branly, 15e; bag sweet/savoury choux €5/7, with cream filling €6-17; 🕙10am-8pm; Ⓜ Bir Hakeim or RER Champ de Mars-Tour Eiffel) This kiosk gives street food a whole new spin. The creation of top French chefs Alain Ducasse and Christophe Michalak, it cooks up *choux* (pastry puffs). Grab a brown paper bag of nine *choux salées* (savoury cheese puffs) spiced with pepper, curry or cumin; or go sweet with almond, cocoa, coffee, lemon and vanilla *chouquettes,* with or without cream filling.

La Mascotte   Brasserie €
Map p56 (📞01 40 36 03 86; 4 av du Président Wilson, 16e; mains €14-19; 🕙7.30am-midnight; Ⓜ Alma Marceau) In an area with few budget eating options, this buzzing neighbourhood brasserie with terrace in the lunchtime sun is a hot spot. Its kitchen prepares meal-size salads, steak tartare and other typical brasserie fare. Come dusk, afterwork drinks kick in. Inside, a mezzanine with cushioned seating and shelves of books provides a peaceful sanctuary.

Hugo Desnoyer

Butcher €€

Map p56 (☏01 46 47 83 00; www.hugodesnoyer.
fr; 28 rue du Docteur Blanche, 16e; menu €50,
mains €16-32; ⏰7am-8pm Tue-Fri, 7am-7.30pm
Sat; Ⓜ Jasmin) Hugo Desnoyer is Paris' most
famous butcher and the trip to his shop in
the 16e is well worth it. Arrive by noon or
reserve to snag a table and settle down to
a *table d'hôte* feast of homemade terrines,
quiches, foie gras and cold cuts followed
by the finest meat in Paris – cooked to
perfection *naturellement*. Watch out for
another Desnoyer opening in 2015.

Le Casse Noix

Modern French €€

(☏01 45 66 09 01; www.le-cassenoix.fr; 56 rue
de la Fédération, 15e; 2-/3-course lunch menus
€21/26, 3-course dinner menu €33; ⏰noon-
2.30pm & 7-10.30pm Mon-Fri; Ⓜ Bir Hakeim)
Proving that a location footsteps from the
Eiffel Tower doesn't mean compromising
on quality, quantity or authenticity, 'the
nutcracker' is a neighbourhood gem with
a cosy retro interior, affordable prices
and exceptional cuisine that changes by
season and by the inspiration of owner/
chef Pierre Olivier Lenormand, who has
honed his skills in some of Paris' most
fêted kitchens. Book ahead.

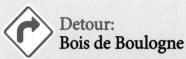

Detour:
Bois de Boulogne

On the western edge of Paris just beyond the 16e, the 845-hectare **Bois de
Boulogne** (bd Maillot; Ⓜ Porte Maillot) owes its informal layout to Baron Haussmann,
who was inspired by Hyde Park in London. Be warned that the Bois de Boulogne
becomes a distinctly adult playground after dark, especially along the allée de
Longchamp, where male, female and transvestite prostitutes cruise for clients.

The southern part of the wood has two horse-racing tracks, the Hippodrome
de Longchamp for flat races and the Hippodrome d'Auteuil for steeplechases.

Families adore the green and flowery **Jardin d'Acclimatation** (Map p56; www.
jardindacclimatation.fr; av du Mahatma Gandhi; admission €3, attraction single/carnet of 10
€2.90/15; ⏰10am-7pm Apr-Sep, to 6pm Oct-Mar; Ⓜ Les Sablons) on the northern fringe of
wooded Bois de Boulogne. There are swings, roundabouts and playgrounds for
all ages galore (included in the admission fee), as well as dozens of attractions
such as puppet shows, boat rides, fun-fair rides, a small water park, pony rides
and so on which you pay extra for.

The **Stade Roland Garros** (www.fft.fr; 2 av Gordon Bennett, 16e; adult/child €10.50/8.50,
with stadium visit €15.50/10.50; ⏰10am-6pm Wed, Fri-Sun; Ⓜ Porte d'Auteuil), home of the
French Open tennis tournament, also shelters the world's most extravagant
tennis museum which traces the sport's 500-year history through paintings,
sculptures and posters. Guided stadium tours in English depart at 11am and
3pm; reservations required.

The stunning **Fondation Louis Vuitton** (Map p56; www.fondationlouisvuitton.fr; av
du Mahatma Gandhi, 16e; Ⓜ Les Sablons) contemporary art centre, designed by Frank
Gehry in the Bois de Boulogne, opened its doors in late 2014. As impressive
as the world-class works of art destined to be displayed here is the 'iceberg'
architecture – imagine 12 curvaceous giant 'sails' crafted from 3600 glass panels.

Rent an old-fashioned rowing boat through **Le Chalet des Îles** (Map p56; ☏01 42
88 04 69; Carrefour du Bout des Lacs; 30/60/90/120 minutes €6/10/15.50/19, plus €50 deposit;
⏰noon-5pm Mon-Fri, 10am-6pm Sat & Sun mid-Feb-Oct; Ⓜ Av Henri Martin) to explore Lac
Inférieur, the largest of Bois de Boulogne's lakes – romance guaranteed.

Tokyo Eat

Fusion €€

Map p56 (☎01 47 20 00 29; www.palaisdetokyo.com; Palais de Tokyo, 13 av du Président Wilson, 16e; mains €15-28; ☷noon-2am Wed-Tue; Ⓜléna) This artsy canteen attached to contemporary-art museum Palais de Tokyo is industrially chic, with colourful flying saucers hovering above the tables and changing art exhibits on the walls. Cuisine is unpredictable and fun – anything from chicken curry served on a banana leaf to caramelised chicory. DJs hit the decks some evenings.

Food Trucks

Hour-long queues? Organic ingredients? TV spots? Welcome to the hip new world of Parisian food trucks. Find the day's location online or follow them on Twitter or Facebook.

Camion Qui Fume (www.lecamionquifume.com; burger & fries €10.50) The smoking food truck that started it all, with gourmet burgers grilled by SoCal chef (and now local food celeb) Kristin Frederick. Follow @lecamionquifume

Cantine California (www.cantinecalifornia.com; burger & fries €11) Organic burgers, tacos and homemade desserts from San Fran transplant Jordan Feilders. Follow @CantineCali

Mes Bocaux (Map p56; www.mesbocaux.fr; 37 rue Marceau, 8e; 2-/3-course menu €11/13.50; Ⓜ Alma Marceau) Savoyard chef Marc Veyrat upped the takeaway stakes when he put his small fleet of smart black food trucks on the road. Order gastronomic-to-go sandwiches and main dishes online before noon, then collect from the truck; the nearest stop to the Eiffel Tower is in front of the Anglo-American pharmacy at 37 rue Marceau, on the corner of rue de Chaillot.

Le Petit Rétro

Bistro €€

Map p56 (☎01 44 05 06 05; www.petitretro.fr; 5 rue Mesnil, 16e; mains €17-26, 2-/3-course menus €25/29; ☷noon-2.30pm & 7-10.30pm Mon-Wed, to 11pm Thu-Sat; Ⓜ Victor Hugo) From the gorgeous 'Petit Rétro' emblazoned on the zinc bar to the ceramic, art nouveau folk tiles on the wall, this is a handsome old-style bistro. Its fare is French classic: for example, blood sausage, *blanquette de veau* (veal in a butter and cream sauce) and *oreilles de cochon* (pig's ears). Delicious.

58 Tour Eiffel

Brasserie €€

Map p56 (☎01 45 55 20 04; www.restaurants-toureiffel.com; 1st level, Eiffel Tower, Champ de Mars, 7e; 2-/3-course lunch menu €21/26, dinner menu €66/75; ☷11.30am-4.30pm & 6.30-11pm; Ⓜ Bir Hakeim or RER Champ de Mars–Tour Eiffel) If you're intrigued by the idea of a meal in the Tower, reserve a table at 58 Tour Eiffel. It may not be the caviar and black truffles of the tower's Michelin-starred address one floor up, but Alain Ducasse did sign off on the menu, ensuring it's far more than a tourist cafeteria.

Monsieur Bleu

Modern French €€

Map p56 (☎01 47 20 90 47; www.monsieurbleu.com; Palais de Tokyo, 20 av de New York, 16e; mains €15-20; ☷noon-2am; Ⓜléna) An 'in' address with the uber-cool fashion set since opening in 2013, this darling of a restaurant has bags going for it – superb interior design by Joseph Dirand, excellent seasonal cuisine and a summer terrace with a monumental Eiffel Tower view. Find it inside Palais de Tokyo; reserve in advance.

Le Jules Verne

Gastronomic €€€

Map p56 (☎01 45 55 61 44; www.lejulesverne-paris.com; 2nd fl, Eiffel Tower, Champ de Mars, 7e; lunch/dinner menus €98/185-230; ☷noon-1.30pm & 7.30-9.30pm; Ⓜ Champ de Mars–Tour Eiffel or Bir Hakeim) Book way ahead (online only) to feast on Michelin-starred cuisine and the most beautiful view of Paris at this magical address, on the Eiffel Tower's 2nd level. Cuisine is contemporary, with a five- or six-course 'experience' menu allowing you to taste the best of chef

Camion Qui Fume food truck

GAUTIER STEPHANE/SAGAPHOTO.COM/ALAMY ©

Pascal Féraud's stunning gastronomic repertoire.

Les Ombres
Modern French €€€

Map p56 (01 47 53 68 00; www.lesombres-restaurant.com; 27 quai Branly, 7e; 2-/3-course lunch menu €32/42, dinner menu €68, mains €32-44; noon-2.15pm & 7-10.20pm; M Iéna or RER Pont de l'Alma) This glass-enclosed rooftop restaurant on the 5th floor of the Musée du Quai Branly is named the 'Shadows' after the patterns cast by the Eiffel Tower's webbed ironwork. Dramatic Eiffel views are complemented by kitchen creations such as *gambas* (prawns) with black rice and fennel, or pan-seared Burgundy snails in watercress sauce. Reserve.

🍷 Drinking & Nightlife

St James Paris
Bar

Map p56 (01 44 05 81 81; www.saint-james-paris.com; 43 rue Bugeaud, 16e; drinks €15-25, Sun brunch €65; 7-11pm; M Porte Dauphine) It might be a hotel bar, but a drink at St James might well be one of your most memorable in Paris. Tucked behind

a stone wall, this historic mansion opens its bar each evening to non-guests – and the setting redefines extraordinary. Winter drinks are in the library, in summer they're in the impossibly romantic garden.

Café Branly
Cafe

Map p56 (27 quai Branly, 7e; 9.30am-6pm Tue, Wed & Sun, to 8pm Thu, Fri & Sat; M Pont de l'Alma or Iéna) This casual spot at the Musée du Quai Branly has ringside views of the Eiffel Tower and quality cafe fare (foie gras salad, XL *croque monsieur*) to tuck into over a drink or three. The setting, within the museum's modernist garden, is peaceful and fantastic.

Bô Zinc Café
Cafe, Bar

Map p56 (01 42 24 69 05; 59 rue Mozart, 16e; 8am-midnight or 2am; M Ranelagh) With its soft sage-green façade and buzzing pavement terrace, Bô Zinc is one of those great hybrid addresses – perfect for hanging with locals over coffee, tea or after-work cocktails. Seating is a mix of wooden bistro chairs and 'flop-in' armchairs, while potted palm trees – inside and out – add a touch of chic. Top-notch nosh too, served until 11pm.

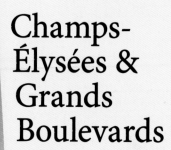

Champs-Élysées & Grands Boulevards

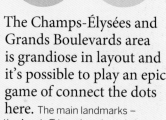

The Champs-Élysées and Grands Boulevards area is grandiose in layout and it's possible to play an epic game of connect the dots here. The main landmarks – the Arc de Triomphe, place de la Concorde, place de la Madeleine and the Opéra – are all joined by majestic boulevards, each lined with harmonious rows of Haussmann-era buildings.

Fans of *haute couture* à la Dior, Chanel, Louis Vuitton et al will be pulled into the Triangle d'Or (Golden Triangle), which neighbours the Champs-Élysées. Further east along the Grands Boulevards are the historic and more affordable *grands magasins* (department stores) like Le Printemps and Galeries Lafayette.

The vestiges of the 1900 World's Fair – the Grand Palais and Petit Palais – play host to a variety of excellent exhibits. Entertainment, too, has a strong tradition, most notably at the famed 19th-century opera house, the Palais Garnier.

Arc de Triomphe (p70)

Champs-Élysées & Grands Boulevards Highlights

Arc de Triomphe (p70)

Climb to the top of Paris' signature arch and gasp at the breathtaking, bird's-eye view of the *axe historique* (historic axis), extending from the Louvre's Grande Pyramide through the Jardin des Tuileries and along the av des Champs-Élysées to the Arc de Triomphe, then west all the way to the modern Grande Arche in the skyscraper district of La Défense.

Grand Palais (p73)

It's worth reserving ahead to catch exhibitions at the stunning art nouveau Grand Palais, erected for the 1900 Exposition Universelle (World's Fair), especially for big-name shows in the Galeries Nationales. Advance reservations are also highly recommended for one of Paris' most exciting restaurants, the Grand Palais' architecturally and culinarily stunning Mini Palais.

TOYOHIRO YAMADA/GETTY IMAGES ©

Palais Garnier (p83)

3

By day, take a tour – guided or DIY – of this classic example of opulent, Second-Empire architecture, the 19th-century Palais Garnier. By night the original home of Parisian opera focuses on ballet, theatre and dance. Book tickets in advance and pack your finery for an unforgettable performance by the Opéra National de Paris' affiliated orchestra and ballet companies.

PHOTOGRAPHY BY BERT/DESIGNPICS/GETTY IMAGES ©

4

5

Champs-Élysées (p72)

Over-the-top, grandiose and even kind of kitsch, you can't leave Paris without strolling the av des Champs-Élysées. A wide, overwhelming and bustling commercial artery full of enormous big-name shops and clogged traffic, it's anchored by the Arc de Triomphe at one end and place de la Concorde – the enormous square where Louis XVI and thousands more were guillotined – at the other. Obelisk on the place de la Concorde

Galeries Lafayette (p84)

Get the inside edge on Parisian fashion while shopping beneath the stained-glass dome of the capital's best-known and most resplendent department store. The free Friday-afternoon fashion shows (advance bookings required) and the panoramic views from the rooftop terrace will sweep you off your feet, as will the contemporary art gallery and a cocktail or stylish bite at one of the on-site eateries.

Champs-Élysées & Grands Boulevards Walk

This glamorous walk takes you from the Arc de Triomphe along the famed av des Champs-Élysées, ending at the opulent Palais Garnier opera house.

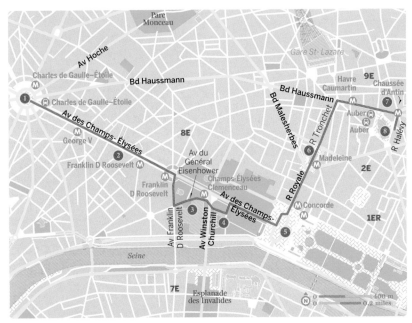

WALK FACTS

- **Start** Arc de Triomphe
- **Finish** Palais Garnier
- **Distance** 3.5km
- **Duration** Two hours

1 Arc de Triomphe

The city's sense of grandeur peeks beneath the soaring **Arc de Triomphe** (p70), the mighty arch commissioned by Napoleon in 1806 in Roman triumphal style. Just don't try to cross the traffic-choked Étoile ('star') roundabout above ground – use the subterranean pedestrian tunnels. For great views from the arch, climb to the top.

2 Champs-Élysées

A dozen avenues radiate out from the Étoile but none is more famous than the **av des Champs-Élysées** (p72). Take your time strolling this broad, tree-shaded avenue past car showrooms and luxury shops such as **Louis Vuitton's flagship store** (p84), which has a free contemporary art gallery, the **Louis Vuitton Espace Culturel**, at the top.

3 Grand Palais

Parkland unfolds in front of you at the Ront Point Champs-Élysées Marcel Dassault roundabout; turn right (south) here on av Franklin D Roosevelt then left on av du Général Eisenhower to find the vast glass-roofed **Grand Palais** (p73). In addition to major gallery spaces, it houses the children's science museum the **Palais de la Découverte**, with excellent temporary exhibits (such as moving lifelike dinosaurs) as well as a hands-on, interactive permanent collection focusing on astronomy, biology, physics and the like.

4 Petit Palais

Heading south across av Winston Churchill, the smaller but equally striking art nouveau **Petit Palais** (p73) was also built for the 1900 World Fair. Today it houses the **Musée des Beaux-Arts de la Ville de Paris**, the city's fine arts museum.

5 Place de la Concorde

Beyond the Petit Palais, turn right to rejoin the Champs-Élysées and continue east to **place de la Concorde** (p72), the vast square between the Champs-Élysées and the Jardin des Tuileries. Paris spreads out around you, with views taking in the Eiffel Tower and Seine. In the centre, the pink granite obelisk stands on the site of a French Revolution guillotine.

6 Place de la Madeleine

Head left on rue Royal to **place de la Madeleine** (p81). The Greek-temple-style **Église de la Madeleine** dominates the centre, while the place itself is home to some of the city's finest gourmet shops, as well as the **Marché aux Fleurs Madeleine**, a colourful flower market trading since 1832.

7 Galeries Lafayette

Continue north along rue Tronchet and right onto bd Haussmann. On your left you'll see the grands magasins (department stores) **Le Printemps** (p85), followed by **Galeries Lafayette** (p84), topped by a stained-glass dome – be sure to head inside and up to Galeries Lafayette's rooftop for a fabulous, free panorama over Paris.

8 Palais Garnier

Turn right on rue Halévy to reach the entrance to Paris' resplendent **Palais Garnier** opera house (p83).

 The Best…

PLACES TO EAT

Le Hide Smart, affordable French cuisine including decadent desserts. (p77)

Makoto Aoki The name suggests otherwise, but this is traditional French *haute cuisine*. (p79)

Le Boudoir Beguiling decor and bistro cuisine. (p77)

Le J'Go Spirited Southwest French cuisine and wines. (p81)

ENTERTAINMENT

Palais Garnier Paris' palatial 19th-century opera house is where the fabled Phantom of the Opera lurked. (p83)

Au Limonaire Perfect little Parisian wine bar with traditional French *chansons*. (p83)

Salle Pleyel Classical concerts and recitals in art deco surrounds. (p84)

PLACES TO SHOP

Galeries Lafayette This quintessential department store has fabulous fashions beneath a dramatic cupola. (p84)

Le Printemps Grand Parisian department store. (p85)

Triangle d'Or Go on a *haute couture* treasure hunt in Paris' 'Golden Triangle'. (p84)

Place de la Madeleine Garlanded by gourmet food shops. (p81)

Interior of Galeries Lafayette (p84)
MARK THOMAS/DESIGN PICS/GETTY IMAGES ©

Don't Miss
Arc de Triomphe

Napoléon's armies never did march through the Arc de Triomphe showered in honour, but the monument has nonetheless come to stand as the very symbol of French patriotism. The Tomb of the Unknown Soldier and the names of the numerous generals engraved onto the arch's inner walls pay homage to those who have fought and died for France. It's not for nationalistic sentiments, however, that so many visitors huff up the narrow, spiralling staircase every day. Rather it's the sublime panoramas from the top, which extend out over the Paris skyline.

Map p74

www.monuments-nationaux.fr

place Charles de Gaulle, 8e

adult/child €9.50/free

⏱10am-11pm Apr-Sep, to 10.30pm Oct-Mar

Ⓜ Charles de Gaulle–Étoile

Napoléon's Arch

The arch was first commissioned in 1806, following Napoléon's victory at Austerlitz the year before. At the time, the victory seemed like a watershed moment that confirmed the tactical supremacy of the French army, but a mere decade later, Napoléon had already fallen from power and his empire had crumbled. The Arc de Triomphe, however, was never fully abandoned and in 1836, after a series of starts and stops under the restored monarchy, the project was finally completed. In 1840 Napoléon's remains were returned to France and passed under the arch before being interred at Invalides.

Today, the military parade commemorating France's national Bastille Day (14 July) kicks off from the arch (adorned by a billowing tricolour).

Beneath the Arch

Beneath the arch at ground level lies the Tomb of the Unknown Soldier. Honouring the 1.3 million French soldiers who lost their lives in WWI, the Unknown Soldier was laid to rest in 1921, beneath an eternal flame that is rekindled daily at 6.30pm.

Also here are a number of bronze plaques laid into the ground. Take the time to try to decipher some: these mark significant moments in modern French history, such as the proclamation of the Third French Republic (4 September 1870) or the return of Alsace and Lorraine to French rule (11 November 1918). The most notable plaque is the text from Charles de Gaulle's famous London broadcast on 18 June 1940, which sparked the French Resistance to life.

The Sculptures

The arch is adorned with four main sculptures, six panels in relief, and a frieze running beneath the top. Each was designed by a different artist; the most famous sculpture is the one to the right as you approach from the Champs-Élysées: *La Marseillaise* (Departure of the Volunteers of 1792). Sculpted by François Rude, it depicts soldiers of all ages gathering beneath the wings of victory, en route to drive back the invading armies of Prussia and Austria. The higher panels depict a series of important victories for the Revolutionary and imperial French armies, from Egypt to Austerlitz, while the detailed frieze is divided into two sections: the *Departure of the Armies* and the *Return of the Armies*. Don't miss the multimedia section beneath the viewing platform, which provides more detail and historical background for each of the sculptures.

Viewing Platform

Climb the 284 steps up to the viewing platform at the top of the 50m-high arch and you'll be suitably rewarded with magnificent panoramas over western Paris. From here, a dozen broad avenues – many of them named after Napoléonic victories and illustrious generals – radiate out towards every compass point. The Arc de Triomphe is the highest point in the line of monuments known as the *axe historique* (historic axis; also called the grand axis); it offers views that swoop east down the Champs-Élysées to the gold-tipped obelisk at place de la Concorde (and beyond to the Louvre's glass pyramid), and west to the skyscraper district of La Défense, where the colossal Grande Arche marks the *axe*'s western terminus.

Tunnels

Don't cross the traffic-choked roundabout above ground if you value your life! Stairs lead from the northern side of the Champs-Élysées to pedestrian tunnels (not linked to metro tunnels) that bring you out safely beneath the arch. Tickets to the viewing platform are sold in the tunnel.

71

Champs-Élysées & Grands Boulevards

⟷ Getting There & Away

- **Metro** Line 1, which follows the Champs-Élysées below ground, is the most useful, followed by lines 8 and 9, which serve the Grands Boulevards.

- **RER** RER A stops at Auber (Opéra) and Charles de Gaulle–Étoile.

- **Bicycle** You'll find Vélib' stations in side streets off the Champs-Élysées.

- **Boat** Champs-Élysées

◎ Sights

Champs-Élysées

Avenue des Champs-Élysées — Street

Map p74 (8e; Ⓜ Charles de Gaulle–Étoile, George V, Franklin D Roosevelt or Champs-Élysées-Clemenceau) No trip to Paris is complete without strolling this broad, tree-shaded avenue lined with luxury shops. Named for the Elysian Fields ('heaven' in Greek mythology), the Champs-Élysées was laid out in the 17th century and is part of the *axe historique,* linking place de la Concorde with the Arc de Triomphe. It's where presidents and soldiers strut their stuff on Bastille Day, where the Tour de France holds its final sprint, and where Paris turns out for organised and impromptu celebrations.

Louis Vuitton Espace Culturel — Gallery

Map p74 (☎ 01 53 57 52 03; www.louisvuitton-espaceculturel.com; 60 rue de Bassano, 8e; ⏲ noon-7pm Mon-Sat, 11am-7pm Sun; Ⓜ George V) **FREE** At the top of Louis Vuitton's flagship store is this contemporary art gallery with changing exhibits throughout the year. The entrance is via the mammoth store, which, of course, is something of a sight in itself.

Place de la Concorde — Square

Map p74 (8e; Ⓜ Concorde) Paris spreads around you, with views of the Eiffel Tower, the Seine and along the Champs-Élysées, when you stand in the city's largest square. Its 3300-year-old pink granite obelisk was a gift from Egypt in 1831. The square was first laid out in 1755 and originally named after King Louis XV, but its royal associations

Egyptian obelisk, Place de la Concorde
PAWEL LIBERA/GETTY IMAGES ©

meant that it took centre stage during the Revolution – Louis XVI was the first to be guillotined here in 1793.

Grand Palais — Art Museum
Map p74 (www.grandpalais.fr; 3 av du Général Eisenhower, 8e; adult/child €13/9; ⏰10am-10pm Tue-Sat, to 8pm Sun & Mon; Ⓜ Champs-Élysées–Clemenceau) Erected for the 1900 Exposition Universelle (World's Fair), the Grand Palais today houses several exhibition spaces beneath its huge 8.5-ton art nouveau glass roof. Some of Paris' biggest shows (Renoir, Chagall, Turner) are held in the Galeries Nationales, lasting three to four months. Hours, prices and exhibition dates vary significantly for all galleries. Those listed here generally apply to the Galeries Nationales, but always check the website for exact details. Reserving a ticket online for any show is strongly advised.

Petit Palais — Art Museum
Map p74 (www.petitpalais.paris.fr; av Winston Churchill, 8e; permanent collections free; ⏰10am-6pm Tue-Sun; Ⓜ Champs-Élysées–Clemenceau) FREE Like the Grand Palais

opposite, this architectural stunner was also built for the 1900 Exposition Universelle, and is home to the Paris municipality's Museum of Fine Arts, the Musée des Beaux-Arts de la Ville de Paris. It specialises in medieval and Renaissance objets d'art such as porcelain and clocks, tapestries, drawings and 19th-century French painting and sculpture; and also has paintings by such artists as Rembrandt, Colbert, Cézanne, Monet, Gaugin and Delacroix.

Jardin de la Nouvelle France — Park
Map p74 (cnr av Franklin D Roosevelt & cours la Reine, 8e; ⏰24hr; Ⓜ Franklin D Roosevelt) Descending rustic, uneven staircases (by the white-marble Alfred de Musset sculpture on av Franklin D Roosevelt, or the upper garden off cours la Reine) brings you to the tiny, 0.7 hectare Jardin de la Nouvelle France, an unexpected wonderland of lilacs, lemon, orange, maple and weeping beech trees, with a wildlife-filled pond, waterfall, wooden footbridge and benches to soak up the serenity.

Champs-Élysées

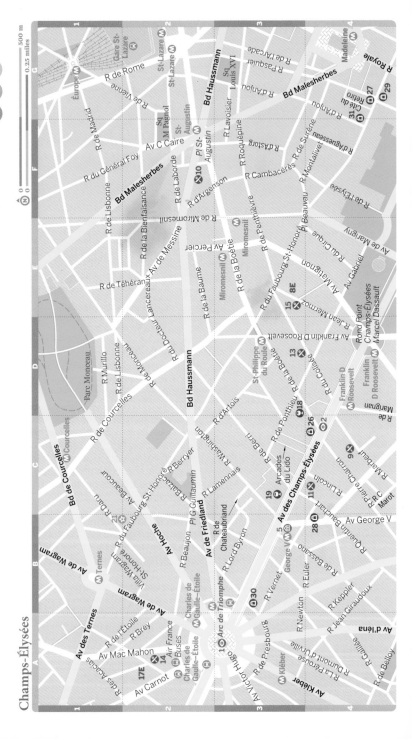

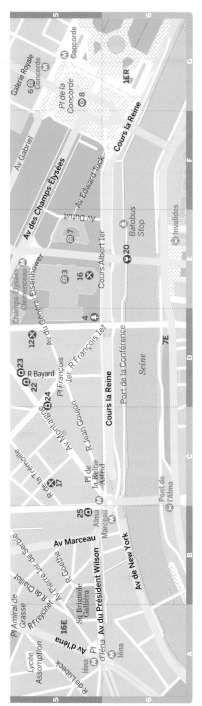

Musée Maxim's   Museum

Map p74 (☏ 01 42 65 30 47; www.maxims-musee-artnouveau.com; 3 rue Royale, 8e; admission €15; ⊙ tours 2pm, 3.15pm & 4pm Wed-Sun; Ⓜ Concorde) During *la belle époque,* Maxim's bistro was the most glamorous place to be in the capital. The restaurant has lost much of its cachet (though the food is actually excellent), but for art nouveau buffs, the real treasure is the upstairs museum. Opened by Maxim's owner, fashion designer Pierre Cardin, it's filled with some 550 pieces of art nouveau artworks, objets d'art and furniture detailed during 40-minute guided tours (available in English).

Grands Boulevards

Église de la Madeleine   Church

Map p78 (Church of St Mary Magdalene; www.eglise-lamadeleine.com; place de la Madeleine, 8e; ⊙ 9.30am-7pm; Ⓜ Madeleine) Place de la Madeleine is named after the 19th-century neoclassical church at its centre, the Église de la Madeleine. Constructed in the style of a massive Greek temple, 'La Madeleine' was consecrated in 1842 after almost a century of design changes and construction delays.

The church is a popular venue for classical-music concerts (some free); check the posters outside or the website for dates.

On the south side, the monumental staircase affords one of the city's most quintessential Parisian panoramas. From here, you can see down rue Royale to place de la Concorde and its obelisk and across the Seine to the Assemblée Nationale. Les Invalides' gold dome appears in the background.

La Pinacothèque   Art Museum

Map p78 (www.pinacotheque.com; 28 place de la Madeleine, 8e; adult/child from €12.30/10.80; ⊙ 10.30am-6pm Sat-Tue & Thu, to 9pm Wed & Fri; Ⓜ Madeleine) The top private museum in Paris, La Pinacothèque organises three to four major exhibits per year. Its nonlinear approach to art history, with exhibits that range from Mayan masks to retrospectives covering the work of artists such as Edvard Munch, has shaken

Champs-Élysées

up the otherwise rigid Paris art world and won over residents used to more formal presentations.

Musée du Parfum   Museum

Map p78 (www.fragonard.com; 9 rue Scribe, 9e; ◷9am-6pm Mon-Sat, to 5pm Sun; Ⓜ Opéra) **FREE** If the art of perfume-making entices, stop by this collection of copper distillery vats and antique flacons and test your nose on a few basic scents. Run by the parfumerie Fragonard, it's located in a beautiful old *hôtel particulier* (private mansion); free guided visits are available in multiple languages. A short distance south, a separate wing in a 20th-century theatre, the **Théâtre-Musée des Capucines** Map p78 (39 blvd des Capucines, 2e; ◷9am-6pm Mon-Sat; Ⓜ Opéra), concentrates largely on the bottling and packaging side of perfume production.

Eating

The area around the Champs-Élysées is known for its big-name chefs (Alain Ducasse, Pierre Gagnaire) and culinary icons (Taillevent), but there are a few under-the-radar restaurants here too, where the Parisians who live and work in

the area actually dine on a regular basis. For a more diverse selection, head east to the Grands Boulevards, where you'll find everything from hole-in-the-wall wine bars to organic cafes.

Champs-Élysées

Ladurée   Patisserie €

Map p74 (www.laduree.com; 75 av des Champs-Élysées, 8e; pastries from €1.50; ◷7.30am-11.30pm Mon-Fri, 8.30am-12.30am Sat, 8.30am-11.30pm Sun; Ⓜ George V) One of the oldest patisseries (cake shops) in Paris, Ladurée has been around since 1862 and was the original creator of the lighter-than-air macaron. Its tearoom is the classiest spot to indulge on the Champs. Alternatively, pick up some pastries to go – from croissants to its trademark macarons, it's all quite heavenly.

Aubrac Corner   Burgers €

Map p74 (www.maison-aubrac.com/aubrac-corner; 37 rue Marbeuf, 8e; sandwiches from €5, burgers €9-11; ◷7.45am-6.30pm Mon-Fri, 11am-6pm Sat; Ⓜ Franklin D Roosevelt) At this gourmet deli of famous steakhouse Maison Aubrac, burgers come with bowls of fries or *aligot* (mashed potatoes with melted cheese); take them downstairs into the hidden wine cellar, a refuge from the nonstop commotion outside. Afterwards, browse the deli for Laguiole (the special *aligot* cheese).

Le Hide
French €€

Map p74 (📞 01 45 74 15 81; www.lehide.fr; 10 rue du Général Lanrezac, 17e; 2-/3-course menus €25/34; 🕙noon-2pm Mon-Fri & 7-10pm Mon-Sat; Ⓜ Charles de Gaulle–Étoile) A perpetual favourite, Le Hide is a tiny neighbourhood bistro serving scrumptious traditional French fare: snails, baked shoulder of lamb with pumpkin purée or monkfish in lemon butter. Unsurprisingly, this place fills up faster than you can scamper down the steps of the nearby Arc de Triomphe. Reserve well in advance.

Mini Palais
Modern French €€

Map p74 (📞 01 42 56 42 42; www.minipalais. com; av Winston Churchill, 8e; lunch menu €28, mains €22-45; 🕙10am-2am, kitchen to midnight; Ⓜ Champs-Élysées-Clemenceau or Invalides) Set inside the fabulous Grand Palais, the Mini Palais resembles an artist's studio on a colossal scale, with unvarnished hardwood floors, industrial lights suspended from ceiling beams and a handful of plaster casts on display. Its sizzling success means that the crowd is anything but bohemian; dress to impress for a taste of the lauded modern cuisine.

Philippe & Jean-Pierre
Traditional French €€

Map p74 (📞 01 47 23 57 80; www.philippeetjean-pierre.fr; 7 rue de Boccador, 8e; 4-/5-course menu €40/50, mains €24-26; 🕙noon-2.15pm & 7.15-10.45pm Mon-Sat; Ⓜ Alma Marceau) Philippe graciously oversees the elegant, parquet-floored, white tableclothed dining room, while co-owner Jean-Pierre helms the kitchen. Seasonal menus incorporate dishes like cauliflower cream soup with mushrooms and truffles, sautéed scallops with leek and Granny Smith sauce and melt-in-the-middle *moelleux au chocolat* cake. Given the service, quality and gilt-edged Triangle d'Or location, prices are a veritable bargain.

Le Boudoir
French €€

Map p74 (📞 01 43 59 25 29; www.boudoir-paris.fr; 25 rue du Colisée, 8e; 2-/3-course lunch menus €30/33 mains €26-30; 🕙12.30-3.30pm Mon-Fri, 7.30-11.30pm Mon-Sat; Ⓜ St-Philippe du Roule or Franklin D Roosevelt) Spread across two floors, the quirky salons – Marie Antoinette, Palme d'Or, le Fumoir – are individual works of art with a style befitting the name. Expect classy bistro fare (quail stuffed with dried fruit and foie gras, chateaubriand steak with chestnut purée) prepared by chef Arnaud Nicolas, a recipient of France's top culinary honour, Meilleur Ouvrier de France.

The Unsung Museums of Paris

Marc Restellini, director of the excellent **La Pinacothèque** (p75), filled us in on his favourite art museums in Paris.

Musée d'Art Moderne de la Ville de Paris (p55) An intelligent museum with high-quality, original exhibits, it carries out its mission as a modern-art museum with courage.

Musée Dapper (p54) The greatest collection of African art in the world, imbued with a magical setting. It's a small museum, but when you leave it's as if returning from an incredible journey.

Musée Jacquemart-André (p138) The second major private museum in Paris along with La Pinacothèque, it stages real art-history exhibits that are both original and daring.

Grands Boulevards

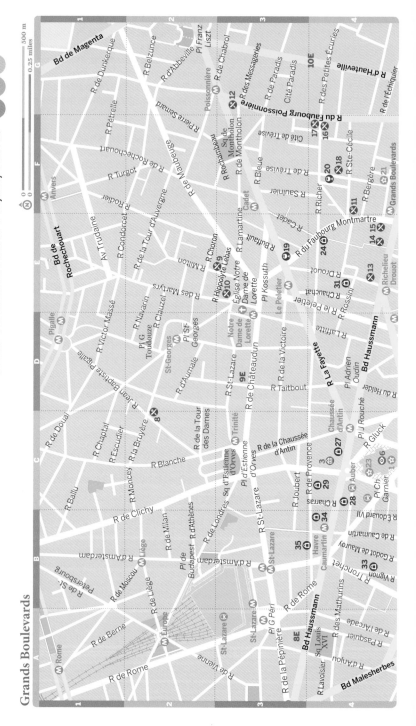

Makoto Aoki Traditional French €€
Map p74 (☏01 43 59 29 24; 19 rue Jean Mermoz, 8e; lunch menu €22, mains €34-38; ◷noon-2pm Mon-Fri, 7.30-9.30pm Tue-Sat; ⓂFranklin D Roosevelt) In an *arrondissement* (city district) known for grandiose interiors and superstar chefs who are often elsewhere, this intimate neighbourhood restaurant is a real find. The Japanese chef is a French-trained *haute cuisine* perfectionist; lunch might include an extravagant bacon-morel brioche; dinner a divine risotto with John Dory or truffles.

Lasserre Gastronomic €€€
Map p74 (☏01 43 59 02 13; www.restaurant-lasserre.com; 17 av Franklin Roosevelt, 8e; lunch menus €90-120, degustation menu €220, mains €82-125; ◷noon-2pm Thu-Fri, 7-10pm Tue-Sat; ⓂFranklin D Roosevelt) Since 1942 this exceedingly elegant restaurant in the Triangle d'Or has hosted style icons like Audrey Hepburn and is still a superlative choice for a twin-Michelin-starred meal to remember. A bellhop-attended lift/elevator, white-and-gold chandeliered decor, extraordinary retractable roof and flawless service set the stage for head chef Christophe Moret's and pastry chef Claire Heitzer's inspired creations. Dress code required.

Grands Boulevards

Le Valentin Tearoom €
Map p78 (www.le-valentin.fr; 30-32 passage Jouffroy, 9e; dishes €4-14; ◷8.30am-7.30pm Mon-Sat, 10am-7pm Sun; ⓂGrands Boulevards) Inside beautiful covered arcade passage Jouffroy, this enchanting, two-storeyed *salon de thé* slash patisserie slash *chocolaterie* is an equally lovely spot for breakfast, light lunches like quiches, salads, *feuilletés* (savoury-filled puff pastries) and *brochettes* (skewers), and dozens of varieties of tea, accompanied by exquisite *tartelettes* and delectable cakes.

Chez Plume Rotisserie €
Map p78 (www.chezplume.fr; 6 rue des Martyrs, 9e; dishes €3.50-8.50; ◷10.15am-2.45pm Mon-Fri, 5-8pm Tue-Fri, 9.30am-8.30pm Sat, 9.30am-3pm Sun; ⓂNotre Dame de Lorette) This rotisserie specialises in free-range

Grands Boulevards

chicken from southwest France, prepared in a variety of fashions: simply roasted, as a crumble, or even in a quiche or sandwich. It's wonderfully casual: add a side or two (potatoes, polenta, seasonal veggies) and pull up a counter seat.

Le Zinc des Cavistes   Wine Bar €

Map p78 (☎01 47 70 88 64; 5 rue du Faubourg Montmartre, 9e; lunch menu €15.50, mains €13.50-18; ⊗kitchen noon-11pm; ⋈Grands Boulevards) Don't tell the masses standing dutifully in the queue at the iconic, old-fashioned restaurant Chartier that there's a much better restaurant right next door. Local secret Le Zinc des Cavistes is as good for a full-blown meal (duck confit with mash, chicken fricassée with crushed potatoes) as it is for sampling new vintages.

SuperNature   Organic €

Map p78 (☎01 47 70 21 03; www.super-nature. fr; 12 rue de Trévise, 9e; 2-/3-course lunch menu €17/20; ⊗noon-2.30pm Mon-Fri, 11.30am-3.30pm Sun; ⋈Cadet or Grands Boulevards) 🍃 Clever veggie creations at this funky organic cafe include curried split-pea soup and cantaloupe, pumpkin seed and

feta salad but, being France, it's not all legumes – you can still order a healthy cheeseburger with sprouts. A takeaway branch two doors down (at 8 rue de Trévise, 9e) serves sandwiches, salads and thick slices of sweet potato and gorgonzola quiche.

Richer   Neobistro €€

Map p78 (2 rue Richer, 9e; mains €16-25; ⊗kitchen noon-2.30pm & 7.30-10.30pm; ⋈Poissonnière or Bonne Nouvelle) Run by the same team as across-the-street neighbour **L'Office** (p81), Richer's pared-back, exposed-brick decor is a smart setting for genius creations like trout tartare with cauliflower and tomato and citrus mousse, and quince and lime cheesecake for dessert. It doesn't take reservations, but if it's full, Richer posts a list of recommended local addresses outside. Fantastic value.

Floquifil   Traditional French €€

Map p78 (☎01 84 19 42 12; www.floquifil.fr; 17 rue de Montyon, 9e; mains €14-25; ⊗11am-midnight Mon-Fri, from 6.30pm Sat; ⋈Grands Boulevards) If you were to envision the ultimate backstreet Parisian wine bar, it would probably look a lot like Floquifil:

table-strewn terrace, dark timber furniture, aquamarine-painted walls and bottles galore. But while the by-the-glass wines are superb, you're missing out if you don't dine here (on rosemary-roasted lamb with ratatouille or at the very least a charcuterie platter).

Bistrot La Bruyère   Bistro €€
Map p78 (☎ 09 81 22 20 56; 31 rue la Bruyère, 9e; 2-/3-course lunch menus €18/21, dinner menus €28/35; ⏰ noon-2.30pm & 7.30-10.30pm Mon-Sat; Ⓜ St-Georges) Young-gun chef Loïc Buisson is the wunderkind behind winning dishes like tomato gazpacho, pigs trotter pancakes with apple chips, tuna with fried leeks, and beef from celebrated butcher Hugo Desnoyer at this unassuming but brilliant little bistro. One to watch.

Le Grenier à Pain   Boulangerie €
Map p78 (91 rue Faubourg Poissonnière, 9e; ⏰ 7.30am-8pm Thu-Tue, to 1.30pm Sun; Ⓜ Poissonnière) Michel Galloyer founded this string of artisan bakeries, which also includes an award-winning **branch** Map p132 (38 rue des Abbesses, 18e; ⏰ 7.30am-8pm Thu-Mon; Ⓜ Abbesses) in Montmartre.

Le J'Go   Regional Cuisine €€
Map p78 (☎ 01 40 22 09 09; www.lejgo.com; 4 rue Drouot, 9e; 2-/3-course menus €16/22, mains €13.50; ⏰ noon-3pm & 6-11.30pm Tue-Sat; Ⓜ Richelieu Drouot) With sunflower-coloured

walls decorated with bull-fighting posters, this contemporary bistro magics you away to southwestern France (perfect on a grey Parisian day). Flavourful regional cooking is based around the rotisserie and other Gascogne standards like *cassoulet* and foie gras.

The roasting takes a minimum 20 minutes, giving you the opportunity to sample a choice selection of sunny southern wines.

Caillebotte   Modern French €€
Map p78 (☎ 01 53 20 88 70; 8 rue Hippolyte Lebas, 9e; 2-course lunch menu €19, 3-/5-course dinner menus €35/49; ⏰ noon-2.30pm & 7.30-10.30pm Mon-Fri; Ⓜ Notre Dame de Lorette) Although named for impressionist painter Gustave Caillebotte, the clattering interior – slate tiles, blond wood and tightly packed marble-topped tables – means this isn't the place for a romantic meal. But it is the place for amazing flavour combinations like scallops with creamy fennel and coffee purée and sea urchin foam, by the same team as **Le Pantruche** (p137).

L'Office   Modern French €€
Map p78 (☎ 01 47 70 67 31; 3 rue Richer, 9e; 2-/3-course lunch menus €22/27, dinner menus €28/34; ⏰ noon-2.30pm & 7.30-10.30pm Mon-Fri; Ⓜ Poissonnière or Bonne Nouvelle) Don't judge this one by the simple chalkboard

Place de la Madeleine Gourmet Food Shops

Ultragourmet food shops garland **place de la Madeleine** (Map p78; place de la Madeleine, 8e; Ⓜ Madeleine); many have in-house dining options, too. Notable names include truffle dealers **La Maison de la Truffe** (Map p78; ☎ 01 42 65 53 22; www.maison-de-la-truffe.com; 19 place de la Madeleine, 8e; ⏰ 10am-10pm Mon-Sat; Ⓜ Madeleine); luxury food shop **Hédiard** (Map p78; www.hediard.fr; 21 place de la Madeleine, 8e; ⏰ 9am-8pm Mon-Sat; Ⓜ Madeleine); mustard specialist **Boutique Maille** (Map p78; ☎ 01 40 15 06 00; www.maille.com; 6 place de la Madeleine, 8e; ⏰ 10am-7pm Mon-Sat; Ⓜ Madeleine); and Paris' most famous caterer, **Fauchon** (Map p78; ☎ 01 70 39 38 00; www.fauchon.fr; 26 & 30 place de la Madeleine, 8e; ⏰ 8.30am-8.30pm Mon-Sat; Ⓜ Madeleine), selling incredibly mouthwatering delicacies, from foie gras to jams, chocolates and pastries. Nearby is 'honey house' **La Maison du Miel** (Map p78; ☎ 01 47 42 26 70; www.maisondumiel.com; 24 rue Vignon, 9e; ⏰ 9.30am-7pm Mon-Sat; Ⓜ Madeleine).

descriptions ('beef/polenta'), which belie the rich and complex flavours emerging from the kitchen. The market-inspired menu is mercifully short – as in there are only two choices for lunch – but outstanding. Alternatively, cross the street to its newer, sleeker sibling, **Richer** (p80).

Bistrot du Sommelier   Bistro €€€

Map p74 (01 42 65 24 85; www.bistrotdusom-melier.com; 97 bd Haussmann; lunch menus €34-55, dinner menus €70-118; noon-2.30pm & 7-10.30pm Mon-Fri; St-Augustin) If you like *haute cuisine* with your wine (rather than the other way around), this freshly refurbished brain child of star sommelier Philippe Faure-Brac offers superb degustation menus with pre-paired wines. Fridays are an institution, offering a three-course tasting lunch with wine for €55 and five-course dinner with wine for €75 (reservations essential).

 Drinking & Nightlife

Champs-Élysées

Autour d'un Verre   Wine Bar

Map p78 (01 48 24 43 74; 21 rue de Trévise, 9e; 10.30am-10.30pm Tue-Sat; Cadet or Grands Boulevards) You'd be forgiven for thinking that Autour d'un Verre is one of those pop-up places: the interior doesn't appear to have been renovated since the 1950s. But that's all part of its undercover appeal – and after a few glasses of Clos

---

du Tue-Boeuf, who cares about decoration anyway? The selection of natural wines is superb (as is the food).

Charlie Birdy   Pub

Map p74 (www.charliebirdy.com; 124 rue de la Boétie, 8e; noon-5am; ; Franklin D Roosevelt) This kick-back brick-walled place just off the Champs Élysées is easily the most inviting pub in the neighbourhood. The usual array of bar food (burgers, hot dogs, more burgers...) is available; DJs hit the decks on weekend nights.

Queen   Club

Map p74 (01 53 89 08 90; www.queen.fr; 102 av des Champs-Élysées, 8e; 11.30pm-6.30am; George V) These days this doyen of a club is as popular with a straight crowd as it is with its namesake clientele but Monday's disco nights are still prime dancing queen territory. While right on the Champs-Élysées, it's not nearly as inaccessible as the other nearby clubs.

ShowCase   Club

Map p74 (www.showcase.fr; Port des Champs-Élysées, 8e; 11.30pm-6am Thu-Sat; Invalides or Champs-Élysées-Clemenceau) This gigantic electro club has solved the neighbour-versus-noise problem that haunts so many Parisian nightlife spots: it's secreted beneath the Pont Alexandre III bridge alongside the Seine. Unlike other exclusive Champs backstreet clubs, the Showcase can pack 'em in (up to 1500 clubbers) and is less stringent about its door policy, though you'll still want to dress like a star.

Grands Boulevards

Au Général La Fayette   Brasserie

Map p78 (52 rue la Fayette, 9e; 10am-3am Mon-Sat, to 2am Sun; Le Peletier) With its archetypal belle époque decor (brass fittings, polished wood, large murals) and excellent wines by the glass, this old-style brasserie is an atmospheric spot for an afternoon coffee or evening drink.

Discount Tickets

Head to **Kiosque Théâtre Madeleine** (Map p78; opp 15 place de la Madeleine, 8e; 12.30-8pm Tue-Sat, to 4pm Sun; Madeleine) to pick up half-price tickets for same-day performances of ballet, opera and music at this freestanding kiosk.

CHICUREL ARNAUD/HEMIS.FR/GETTY IMAGES ©

Don't Miss
Palais Garnier

The fabled 'phantom of the opera' lurked in this opulent opera house designed in 1860 by Charles Garnier (then an unknown 35-year-old architect). You can reserve a spot on an English-language guided tour or take an unguided tour of the attached museum, with posters, costumes, backdrops, original scores and other memorabilia, which includes a behind-the scenes peek (except during matinees and rehearsals). Highlights include the Grand Staircase and horseshoe-shaped, gilded auditorium with red velvet seats, a massive chandelier and Chagall's gorgeous ceiling mural.

Interestingly, a prop man at the opera set up beehives on the roof some 20 years ago – the honey is now sold at the gift shop when available.

NEED TO KNOW

Map p78 ☎08 25 05 44 05; www.operadeparis.fr; cnr rues Scribe & Auber, 9e; unguided tour adult/child €10/6, guided tour adult/child €14/12.50; ☺unguided tour 10am-5pm, to 1pm on matinee performance days, guided tour by reservation; Ⓜ Opéra

⭐ Entertainment

Palais Garnier — Opera
Map p78 (☎08 92 89 90 90; www.operadeparis.fr; place de l'Opéra, 9e; Ⓜ Opéra) The city's original opera house is smaller than its Bastille counterpart, but has perfect acoustics. Due to its odd shape, some seats have limited or no visibility – book carefully. Ticket prices and conditions (including last-minute discounts) are available from the **box office** Map p78 (cnr rues Scribe & Auber; ☺11am-6.30pm Mon-Sat).

Au Limonaire — Live Music
Map p78 (☎01 45 23 33 33; http://limonaire.free.fr; 18 cité Bergère, 9e; ☺6pm-2am Tue-Sat, from 7pm Sun & Mon; Ⓜ Grands Boulevards) This perfect little wine bar is one of the

Historic Haute Couture

A stroll around the legendary **Triangle d'Or** (bordered by avs Georges V, Champs-Élysées and Montaigne, 8e) constitutes the walk of fame of top French fashion. Rubbing shoulders with the world's top international designers are Paris' most influential French fashion houses:

Chanel (Map p74; www.chanel.com; 42 av Montaigne, 8e; 🕙10am-7pm Mon-Sat; Ⓜ George V) Box jackets and little black dresses, chic ever since their first appearance in the 1920s.

Christian Dior (Map p74; www.dior.com; 30 av Montaigne, 8e; 🕙10am-7pm Mon-Sat; Ⓜ George V) Post-WWII, Dior's creations dictated style, re-establishing Paris as the world fashion capital.

Givenchy (Map p74; www.givenchy.com; 3 av George V, 8e; 🕙10am-7pm Mon-Sat; Ⓜ George V) The first to present a luxurious collection of women's prêt-à-porter.

Hermès Map p74 (www.hermes.com; 24 rue du Faubourg St-Honoré, 8e; 🕙10.30am-6.30pm Mon-Sat; Ⓜ Concorde) Founded in 1837 by a saddle-maker, Hermès' famous scarves are *the* fashion accessory.

Jean-Paul Gaultier (Map p74; www.jeanpaulgaultier.com; 44 av George V, 8e; 🕙10.30am-7pm Mon-Sat; Ⓜ George V) A shy kid from the Paris suburbs, JPG morphed into the *enfant terrible* of the fashion world with his granny's corsets, men dressed in skirts and Madonna's conical bra.

Lanvin (Map p74; www.lanvin.com; 22 rue du Faubourg St Honoré, 8e; 🕙10.30am-7pm Mon-Sat; Ⓜ Concorde) One of Paris' oldest fashion houses, established in 1909.

Louis Vuitton (Map p74; www.louisvuitton.com; 101 av des Champs-Élysées, 8e; 🕙10am-8pm Mon-Sat, 11am-7pm Sun; Ⓜ George V) Take home a Real McCoy canvas bag with the 'LV' monogram.

Yves Saint Laurent (Map p74; www.ysl.com; 38 rue du Faubourg St-Honoré, 8e; 🕙11am-7pm Mon, 10.30am-7pm Tue-Sat; Ⓜ Concorde) One of the top Parisian designers from the 1960s on, YSL was the first to incorporate non-European styles into his work.

best places to listen to traditional French *chansons* and local singer-songwriters. Performances begin at 10pm Tuesday to Saturday and 7pm on Sunday. Entry is free; reservations are recommended if you plan on dining.

Salle Pleyel — Classical
Map p74 (📞01 42 56 13 13; www.sallepleyel.fr; 252 rue du Faubourg St-Honoré, 8e; 🕙box office noon-7pm Mon-Sat, to 8pm on day of performance, 11am to 2hrs prior to performance Sun; Ⓜ Ternes) Dating from the 1920s, this highly regarded hall hosts many of Paris' finest classical-music recitals and concerts.

🔒 Shopping

Galeries Lafayette — Department Store
Map p78 (http://haussmann.galerieslafayette. com; 40 bd Haussmann, 9e; 🕙9.30am-8pm Mon-Sat, to 9pm Thu; Ⓜ Auber or Chaussée d'Antin) *Grande dame* department store Galeries Lafayette is spread across the main store (whose magnificent stained-glass dome is over a century old), **men's store** Map p78 and **home design** Map p78 store, and includes a gourmet emporium.

Catch modern art in the **gallery** (www. galeriedesgaleries.com; 1st fl; 🕙11am-7pm Tue-Sat) FREE, or take in a **fashion show** (📞bookings 01 42 82 30 25; 🕙3pm Fri Mar-Jul

& Sep-Dec by reservation); a free, windswept rooftop panorama; or a break at one of its 19 restaurants and cafes.

Publicis Drugstore   Concept Store
Map p74 (www.publicisdrugstore.com; 133 av des Champs-Élysées, 8e; ◷8am-2am Mon-Fri, 10am-2am Sat & Sun; Ⓜ Charles de Gaulle–Étoile) An institution since 1958, Publicis incorporates cinemas and late-opening shops including an *épicerie* (specialist grocer), pharmacy, beauty counter, international newsagent, a wine *cave* (cellar) and cigar bar. At street level there's a glassed-in brasserie and steakhouse, but its newest and chicest dining space is downstairs at the glossy black and red Étoile branch of **L'Atelier de Joël Robuchon**.

Le Printemps   Department Store
Map p78 (www.printemps.com; 64 bd Haussmann, 9e; ◷9.35am-8pm Mon-Wed & Fri & Sat, to 10pm Thu; 🛜; Ⓜ Havre Caumartin) Famous department store Le Printemps encompasses Le Printemps de la Mode (women's fashion), **Le Printemps de l'Homme** Map p78 (men's fashion), both with established and up-and-coming designer wear, and Le Printemps de la Beauté et Maison (beauty and homewares), offering a staggering display of perfume, cosmetics and accessories. There's a free panoramic rooftop terrace and luxury eateries including Ladurée.

À la Mère de Famille   Food, Drink
Map p78 (www.lameredefamille.com; 35 rue du Faubourg Montmartre, 9e; ◷9.30am-8pm Mon-Sat, 10am-1pm Sun; Ⓜ Le Peletier) Founded in 1761, this is the original location of Paris' oldest chocolatier. Its beautiful belle époque façade is as enchanting as the rainbow of sweets, caramels and chocolates inside.

Guerlain   Perfume
Map p74 (🎝 spa 01 45 62 11 21; www.guerlain.com; 68 av des Champs-Élysées, 8e; ◷10.30am-8pm Mon-Sat, noon-7pm Sun; Ⓜ Franklin D Roosevelt) Guerlain is Paris' most famous parfumerie, and its shop (dating from 1912) is one of the most beautiful in the city. With its shimmering mirror and marble art-deco interior, it's a reminder of the former glory of the Champs-Élysées. For total indulgence, make an appointment at its decadent spa.

Chloé   Fashion
Map p74 (www.chloe.com; 44 av Montaigne, 8e; ◷10.30am-7pm Mon-Sat; Ⓜ Franklin D Roosevelt) Bold prints, bohemian layers and uneven hemlines have given street cred to this 1950s-established Parisian label.

Hôtel Drouot   Art, Antiques
Map p78 (www.drouot.com; 7-9 rue Drouot, 9e; ◷11am-6pm most days; Ⓜ Richelieu Drouot) Selling everything from antiques and jewellery to rare books and art, Paris' most established auction house has been in business for more than a century. Viewings are from 11am to 6pm the day before and from 11am to noon the morning of the auction. Pick up the catalogue *Gazette de l'Hôtel Drouot,* published Fridays, in-house or at newsstands.

Louvre & Les Halles

Carving its way through the city, Paris' *axe historique* (historic axis) passes through the Jardin des Tuileries and the Arc de Triomphe du Carrousel before reaching IM Pei's glass pyramid at the city's mightiest museum, the Louvre. Many smaller museums and galleries also cluster around this art lovers' Holy Grail.

Shoppers crowd along rue de Rivoli, which has beautiful cloisters along its western end, and congregate within the Forum des Halles – the underground mall that supplanted the city's ancient marketplace and is undergoing a major renaissance. The original markets' spirit lives on in Les Halles' lively backstreets, such as rue Montorgueil.

The bright blue and red Centre Pompidou attracts art aficionados with its amazing hoard of modern art. Outside, place Georges Pompidou is a hub for buskers, while place Igor Stravinsky's mechanical fountains are a riot of outlandish creations.

View of the Louvre from the *Jardins des Tuileries* (p107)

Louvre & Les Halles Highlights

The Louvre (p92)

The Musée du Louvre, the mother of all museums, houses Western art from the Middle Ages to about 1848, as well as the works of ancient civilisations that formed the starting point for Western art – all under one seemingly endless roof. Successive French governments have amassed works from all over Europe, including collections of Assyrian, Etruscan, Greek, Coptic and Islamic art and antiquities.

OLIVER STREWE/GETTY IMAGES ©

Centre Pompidou (p98)

The Centre Pompidou, a kind of Louvre for the 21st century, offers a day of culture and amusement for the whole family. From the modern and contemporary masterpieces at its fabulous National Museum of Modern Art to the whimsical mechanical fountains and the buskers performing in the adjacent square, this is where art and fun fuse together seamlessly.

CENTRE POMPIDOU DESIGNED BY RENZO PIANO, RICHARD ROGERS; GARDEL BERTRAND/GETTY IMAGES ©

Jardin des Tuileries (p107)

The Jardin des Tuileries' verdant oasis is a great place to recharge your batteries and enjoy Paris at its symmetrical best. While wandering, you can admire its exquisite sculptures, including Rodin's *The Kiss* and Louise Bourgeois' delicate *Welcoming Hands*. Within the gardens, the Musée de l'Orangerie is an exquisite space in which to enjoy Monet's *Decorations des Nymphéas* (Waterlilies). *L'Ombre* sculpture by Auguste Rodin

Église St-Eustache (p103)

One of the least-known (and most beautiful) churches in Paris, the Église St-Eustache is also one of the best examples of early Renaissance style on the Right Bank, with a magnificent mix of Flamboyant Gothic and neoclassical architectural features. Don't miss the colossal organ inside, which you can catch in action during recitals.

Jardin du Palais Royal (p101)

With pristine lawns, designer fashion shops, galleries, sculptures and history (the French Revolution effectively started at a cafe here), the gardens of this former royal palace are a perfect hang-out spot for a warm day. Don't miss the sculpture at the southern end of the garden: legend says if you can toss a coin onto one of the columns, your wish will come true.

Louvre & Les Halles Walk

Exploring the immense Musée du Louvre takes as many hours as you have free after finishing this walk at the museum's cobbled square courtyard, the Cour Carrée. But there's much more to see in this neighbourhood, including-glorious gardens, churches and centuries-old towers.

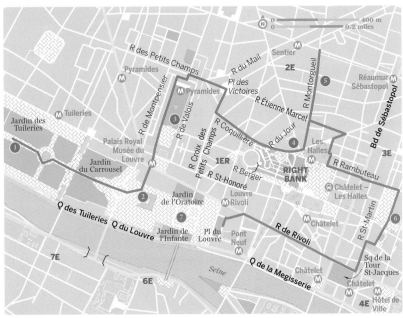

1 Jardin des Tuileries

With the Parisian panorama of the **place de la Concorde** behind you, step into the Unesco World Heritage–listed **Jardin des Tuileries** (p107). On your left is the **Jeu de Paume** photography gallery, while on your right, a 19th-century greenhouse now contains the **Musée de l'Orangerie**, showcasing Monet's enormous *Waterlilies*.

2 Louvre Grande Pyramide

Promenade through the Tuileries past the Arc de Triomphe du Carrousel to the **Grande Pyramide** (p95). Egypt's original pyramid builders couldn't have imagined this 21m-high glass wonder, which has been the Musée du Louvre's main entrance since 1989.

3 Jardin du Palais Royal

Turn left at the pyramid and cross rue de Rivoli, past the **Palais Royal-Musée du Louvre metro entrance**, featuring two crown-shaped cupolas (one representing the day, the other night) consisting of 800 pieces of red, blue, amber and violet glass. Enter the exquisite **Jardin du Palais Royal** (p101), and browse its colonnaded arcades.

④ Église St-Eustache

Exit next to the historic restaurant **Le Grand Véfour** (p115) onto rue de Beaujolais, turn left into Passage du Perron and right onto rue des Petits Champs. Continue to place des Victoires, with its equestrian **Louis XIV Memorial**. Turn right on rue Croix des Petits Champs and left into rue Coquillière. On your right is the subterranean shopping mall the **Forum des Halles** (p102), currently undergoing a massive, much-needed makeover, while up ahead **Église St-Eustache** (p103) is one of the city's most beautiful churches.

⑤ Rue Montorgueil

A splinter of the former *halles* (markets), **rue Montorgueil** (p112) was previously the oyster market. Grocery and speciality street stalls set up daily, except Monday. Look out for patisserie **Stohrer** at No 51, which opened in 1730, with pastel murals added in 1864 by Paul Baudry (who also decorated the Palais Garnier's Grand Foyer); and, at the northern end (rue des Petite Carreaux), horse-meat butcher **J Davin** at No 9.

⑥ Centre Pompidou

From rue Montorgueil, head down rue Étienne Marcel, passing the Gothic **Tour Jean sans Peur** (p106), turning right on rue Pierre Lescot then left again on rue Rambuteau to find the extraordinary **Centre Pompidou** (p98). The inside-out-designed building is such a sight in its own right that it's easy to forget that it houses France's foremost contemporary and modern art museum, the **Musée National d'Art Moderne** (p99).

⑦ Cour Carrée

Cross the fountain-filled **place Igor Stravinsky** and head south to rue de Rivoli and turn right – on your left you'll see the Flamboyant Gothic **Tour St-Jacques** (p102). Take rue Parrault to the place du Louvre. At the **Église Saint-Germain-l'Auxerrois**, cross the place du Louvre and enter the grand Louvre courtyard, the **Cour Carrée**.

 The Best...

PLACES TO EAT

Frenchie Hidden alleyway bistro serving sensational menus. (p114)

Verjus A hidden but hyped contemporary restaurant you need to know about to find. (p115)

Spring One of the Right Bank's 'talk-of-the-town' addresses, with an American in the kitchen and stunning food. (p115)

PLACES TO DRINK

Experimental Cocktail Club Parisian style blends with New York street cred. (p116)

Jefrey's Sink into a leather Chesterfield to sip swish cocktails and whiskies. (p116)

Kong Seine views stretch from this Philippe Starck–designed stunner. (p117)

ENTERTAINMENT

Le Grand Rex A landmark art deco cinema with behind-the-scenes tours and an epic techno nightclub. (p118)

Comédie Française The world's longest-established national theatre, founded in 1680. (p118)

Le Baiser Salé Jazz club combining big names and unknown artists. (p117)

Le Grand Rex cinema (p118)
GUIZIOU FRANCK/GETTY IMAGES ©

Don't Miss
The Louvre

Few art galleries are as prized or as daunting as the Musée du Louvre, Paris' pièce de résistance. Showcasing 5000 works of art, it would take nine months to glance at every piece, making advance planning essential.

Map p104

☎ 01 40 20 53 17

www.louvre.fr

rue de Rivoli & quai des Tuileries, 1er

adult/child €12/free

🕐 9am-6pm Mon, Thu, Sat & Sun, to 9.45pm Wed & Fri

Ⓜ Palais Royal–Musée du Louvre

Palais du Louvre

The Louvre today rambles over four floors and through three wings: the **Sully Wing** creates the four sides of the Cour Carrée (literally 'square courtyard') at the eastern end of the complex; the **Denon Wing** stretches 800m along the Seine to the south; and the northern **Richelieu Wing** skirts rue de Rivoli. The building started life as a fortress built by Philippe-Auguste in the 12th century – medieval remnants are still visible on the Lower Ground Floor (Sully). In the 16th century it became a royal residence and after the Revolution, in 1793, it was turned into a national museum. Its booty was no more than 2500 paintings and objets d'art.

Over the centuries French governments amassed the paintings, sculptures and artefacts displayed today. The 'Grand Louvre' project inaugurated by the late President Mitterrand in 1989 doubled the museum's exhibition space, and both new and renovated galleries have since opened, including the state-of-the-art **Islamic art galleries** (Lower Ground Floor, Denon) in the stunningly restored Cour Visconti.

Mona Lisa

Easily the Louvre's most admired work (and world's most famous painting) is Leonardo da Vinci's *La Joconde* (in French; *La Gioconda* in Italian), the lady with that enigmatic smile known as *Mona Lisa* (Room 6, 1st floor, Denon). For centuries admirers speculated on everything from the possibility that the subject was mourning the death of a loved one to the possibility that she might have been in love or in bed with her portraitist.

Mona (*monna* in Italian) is a contraction of madonna, and Gioconda is the feminine form of the surname Giocondo. Canadian scientists used infrared technology to peer through paint layers and confirm *Mona Lisa*'s identity as Lisa Gherardini (1479–1542), wife of Florentine merchant Francesco de Giocondo. Scientists also discovered her dress was covered in a transparent gauze

Local Knowledge

Don't Miss List

BY ELISE MAILLARD, HEAD OF PROMOTIONAL DEVELOPMENT, MUSÉE DU LOUVRE

I've been working at the Louvre for 5 years, so I'm quite new in this old house! It's an everyday pleasure to work here, enjoying the palace, the gardens and, of course artworks.

1 DEPARTMENT OF ISLAMIC ART

The design and installation of these new galleries is the museum's single largest expansion project since IM Pei created the Pyramid 20 years ago. The new department is home to one of the most exceptional collections of Islamic art in the world, owing to its geographic diversity (from Spain to India), the historical periods covered (from the 8th to the 19th century), and the wide variety of materials and techniques represented.

2 PORTRAIT OF THE MARQUISE DE POMPADOUR BY MAURICE-QUENTIN DELATOUR (DEPARTMENT OF THE 18TH CENTURY)

What impresses me the most in this portrait is the technique: using only pastel pencils heightened with gouache, Delatour successfully reinvents the style of official portraits. The sumptuousness of her clothing is also a delight, and a perfect representation of a French-style dress of the 18th century.

3 EBIH-IL, THE SUPERINTENDENT OF MARI (DEPARTMENT OF MESOPOTAMIA)

I love this statuette, made of translucent alabaster. The bust is sculpted in a subtle way and the eyes! Made of lapis lazuli, they look at you in a very gentle and calm way. It inspires serenity and wisdom in me, and it's the favorite artwork of my little son.

4 JEUNE FILLE EN BUSTE BY PIERRE-NARCISSE GUÉRIN (DEPARTMENT OF PAINTING)

I love the modernity and the freshness of this young lady, with her short hair, hiding her breasts. The light on her pearly skin is very smooth. This painting is seated in a calm part of the museum, so you can stay for a while in front of this very beautiful portrait.

93

veil typically worn in early-16th-century Italy by pregnant or new mothers; it's surmised that the work was painted to commemorate the birth of her second son around 1503, when she was aged about 24.

Antiquity to Renaissance

One of the most famous works from antiquity is the cross-legged *Squatted Scribe* (Room 22, 1st floor, Sully), a painted limestone statue with rock-crystal inlaid eyes dating from c 2620–2500 BC. Measuring 53.7cm tall, the unknown figure is depicted holding a papyrus scroll in his left hand; he's thought to have been holding a brush in his right hand that has since disappeared. Equally compelling is the *Code of Hammurabi* (Room 3, ground floor, Richelieu), and the armless duo of the **Venus de Milo** (Room 16, ground floor, Sully) and the **Winged Victory of Samothrace** (top of Daru staircase, 1st floor, Denon).

The eastern side of the Sully Wing's ground and 1st floors house the Louvre's astonishing cache of Pharaonic Egyptian treasures. Don't miss the mummy of a man from the Ptolemaic period (Room 15, ground floor, Sully) and the funerary figurine of pharaoh Ramesses IV (Room 13, ground floor, Sully). From the Renaissance, Michelangelo's marble masterpiece *The Dying Slave* (Room 4, ground floor, Denon) and works by Raphael, Botticelli and Titian (1st floor, Denon) draw big crowds.

Northern European & French Painting

The 2nd floor of the Richelieu Wing allows for a quieter meander through the Louvre's inspirational collection of Flemish and Dutch paintings spearheaded by works by Peter Paul Rubens and Pieter Bruegel the Elder.

Trails & Tours

Self-guided thematic trails range from Louvre masterpieces and the art of eating to family-friendly topics. Download

trail brochures in advance from the website. Another good option is to rent a **Nintendo 3DS multimedia guide** (adult/child €5/3; ID required). More formal, English-language **guided tours** (📞01 40 20 51 77; 🕙11am & 2pm except 1st Sun of month) depart from the Hall Napoléon. Reserve a spot up to 14 days in advance or sign up on arrival at the museum.

The Pyramid: Inside & Out

Almost as dazzling as the masterpieces inside is the 21m-high glass pyramid designed by Chinese-born American architect IM Pei that bedecks the main entrance to the Louvre in a dazzling crown of shimmering sunbeams and glass. Beneath Pei's **Grande Pyramide Map p104 (place du Louvre)** is the **Hall Napoléon**, a split-level public area comprising a temporary exhibition hall, bookshop, souvenir store, cafe and auditoriums for lectures and films. To revel in another Pei pyramid of equally dramatic dimensions, head towards the **Carrousel du Louvre** (p121), a busy shopping mall that loops underground from the Grande Pyramide to the **Arc de Triomphe du Carrousel** (p101) – its centrepiece is Pei's **Pyramide Inversée** (inverted glass pyramid).

Queue-Dodging

You need to queue twice to get in: once for security and then again to buy tickets. The longest queues are outside the Grande Pyramide; use the Carrousel du Louvre entrance (99 rue de Rivoli or direct from the metro) or the Porte de Lions entrance (closed Wednesday and Friday) instead. A Museum Pass gives you priority; buying tickets in advance will also help expedite the process.

The Louvre

A HALF-DAY TOUR

Successfully visiting the Louvre is a fine art. Its complex labyrinth of galleries and staircases spiralling three wings and four floors renders discovery a snakes-and-ladders experience. Initiate yourself with this three-hour itinerary – a playful mix of Mona Lisa obvious and up-to-the-minute unexpected.

Arriving by the stunning main entrance, pick up colour-coded floor plans at the lower-ground-floor **information desk ①** beneath IM Pei's glass pyramid, ride the escalator up to the Sully Wing and swap passport for multimedia guide (there are limited descriptions in the galleries) at the wing entrance.

The Louvre is as much about spectacular architecture as masterly art. To appreciate this zip up and down Sully's Escalier Henri II to admire **Venus de Milo ②**, then up parallel Escalier Henri IV to the palatial displays in **Cour Khorsabad ③**. Cross room 1 to find the escalator up to the 1st floor and staircase-as-art **L'Esprit d'Escalier ④**. Next traverse 25 consecutive galleries (thank you, floor plan!) to flip conventional contemplation on its head with Cy Twombly's **The Ceiling ⑤**, and the hypnotic **Winged Victory of Samothrace sculpture ⑥** – just two rooms away – which brazenly insists on being admired from all angles. End with the impossibly famous **The Raft of Medusa ⑦**, **Mona Lisa ⑧** and **Virgin & Child ⑨**.

TOP TIPS

➡ **Floor Plans** Don't even consider entering the Louvre's maze of galleries without a Plan/Information Louvre brochure, free from the information desk in the Hall Napoléon

➡ **Crowd dodgers** The Denon Wing is always packed; visit on late nights Wednesday or Friday or trade Denon in for the notably quieter Richelieu Wing

➡ **2nd floor** Not for first-timers: save its more specialist works for subsequent visits

MISSION MONA LISA

If you just want to venerate the Louvre's most famous lady, use the Porte des Lions entrance (closed Tuesday and Friday), from where it's a five-minute walk. Go up one flight of stairs and through rooms 26, 14 and 13 to the Grande Galerie and adjoining room 6.

L'Esprit d'Escalier
Escalier Lefuel, Richelieu
Discover the 'Spirit of the Staircase' through François Morellet's contemporary stained glass, which casts new light on old stone. DETOUR» Napoleon III's gorgeous gilt apartments.

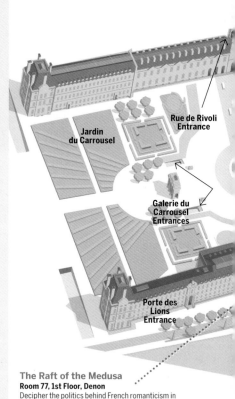

Rue de Rivoli Entrance

Jardin du Carrousel

Galerie du Carrousel Entrances

Porte des Lions Entrance

The Raft of the Medusa
Room 77, 1st Floor, Denon
Decipher the politics behind French romanticism in Théodore Géricault's *Raft of the Medusa*.

Cour Khorsabad
Ground Floor, Richelieu
Time travel with a pair of winged human-headed bulls to view some of the world's oldest Mesopotamian art. DETOUR» Night-lit statues in Cour Puget.

Venus de Milo
Room 16, Ground Floor, Sully
No one knows who sculpted this seductively realistic goddess from Greek antiquity. Naked to the hips, she is a Hellenistic masterpiece.

The Ceiling
Room 32, 1st Floor, Sully
Admire the blue shock of Cy Twombly's 400-sq-metre contemporary ceiling fresco – the Louvre's latest, daring commission. DETOUR» *The Braque Ceiling*, room 33.

Cour Khorsabad

③

④
Cour Marly

Cour Puget

SULLY WING

Cour Carrée

⑤

RICHELIEU WING

Cour Napoléon

①

Pyramid Main Entrance

②

Inverted Pyramid

⑥

⑦ ⑧
Cour Visconti

⑨

DENON WING

Pont des Arts

Pont du Carrousel

Virgin & Child
Room 5, Grande Galerie, 1st Floor, Denon
In the spirit of artistic devotion save the Louvre's most famous gallery for last: a feast of Virgin-and-child paintings by Raphael, Domenico Ghirlandaio, Giovanni Bellini and Francesco Botticini.

Mona Lisa
Room 6, 1st Floor, Denon
No smile is as enigmatic or bewitching as hers. Da Vinci's diminutive *La Joconde* hangs opposite the largest painting in the Louvre – sumptuous, fellow Italian Renaissance artwork *The Wedding at Cana*.

Winged Victory of Samothrace
Escalier Daru, 1st Floor, Sully
Draw breath at the aggressive dynamism of this headless, handless Hellenistic goddess. DETOUR» The razzle-dazzle of the Apollo Gallery's crown jewels.

Don't Miss
Centre Pompidou

The Pompidou Centre has amazed and delighted visitors ever since it opened in 1977, not just for its outstanding collection of modern art but also for its radical architectural statement. The dynamic and vibrant arts centre delights and enthralls with its irresistible cocktail of galleries and exhibitions, hands-on workshops, dance performances, bookshop, design boutique, cinemas and other entertainment venues.

Map p108

☎ 01 44 78 12 33

www.centrepompidou.fr

place Georges Pompidou, 4e

museum, exhibitions & panorama adult/child €13/free

⏱ 11am-9pm Wed-Mon

Ⓜ Rambuteau

Musée National d'Art Moderne

Europe's largest collection of modern art fills the bright and airy, well-lit galleries of the National Museum of Modern Art, covering two complete floors of the Pompidou. For art lovers, this is one of the jewels of Paris. On a par with the permanent collection are the two temporary exhibition halls (on the ground floor/basement and the top floor), which showcase some memorable blockbuster exhibits. Also of note is the fabulous children's gallery on the 1st floor.

The permanent collection changes every two years, but the basic layout generally stays the same. The 5th floor showcases artists active between 1905 and 1970 (give or take a decade); the 4th floor focuses on more contemporary creations, roughly from the 1980s onward.

The most recent 5th-floor layout was a refreshing change from the old Eurocentric model. The dynamic presentation mixed up works by Picasso, Matisse, Chagall and Kandinsky with lesser-known contemporaries from as far afield as Brazil and China, as well as more famous cross-Atlantic names such as Rivera, Kahlo, Warhol, Pollock and Rothko.

One floor down on the 4th, you'll find monumental paintings, installation pieces, sculpture and video take centre stage. The focus of the latest exhibition here is on art, architecture and design from the 1980s onward. The 4th floor also has an Espace des Collections Nouveaux Médias et Film, where visitors can discover 40 years of image and sound experimentation.

Architecture & Views

Former French President Georges Pompidou wanted an ultracontemporary artistic hub and he got it: competition-winning architects Renzo Piano and Richard Rogers designed the building inside out, with utilitarian features like plumbing, pipes, air vents and electrical cables forming part of the external façade. The building was completed in 1977.

Viewed from a distance (such as from Sacré-Cœur), the Centre Pompidou's primary-coloured, box-like form amid a sea of muted grey Parisian rooftops makes it look like a child's Meccano set abandoned on someone's elegant living-room rug. Although the Centre Pompidou is just six storeys high, the city's low-rise cityscape means stupendous views extend from its roof (reached by external escalators enclosed in tubes). Rooftop admission is included in museum and exhibition admission – or buy a **panorama ticket** (admission €3; ⏱11am-10pm Wed-Mon) just for the roof.

Tours & Guides

Guided tours are only in French (the information desk in the central hall on the ground floor has details), but the gap is easily filled by the excellent **multimedia guide** (adult/under 13yr €5/3), which explains 62 works of art in the Musée National d'Art Moderne in detail on a 1½-hour trail. There is also a guide for each temporary exhibit; another covering the unique architecture of the Centre Pompidou; and one created with kids (ages eight to 12) in mind.

Outdoor Entertainment

The full Pompidou experience is as much about hanging out in the busy squares around it, packed with souvenir shops and people, as absorbing the centre's contents. Fun-packed place Georges Pompidou and its nearby pedestrian streets attract bags of buskers and musicians. Don't miss place Igor Stravinsky with its mechanical fountains of skeletons, hearts, treble clefs and a big pair of ruby-red lips.

Dining Options

Georges' outdoor terrace on the 6th floor is a fabulous spot for a drink with a view, though it's not so great for dining. The inexpensive mezzanine cafe on the 1st floor is also unmemorable: walk instead to **Dame Tartine** (p110) for an affordable lunch or well-deserved postmuseum aperitif.

Louvre & Les Halles

 Getting There & Away

o **Metro & RER** The Louvre has two metro stations: Palais Royal–Musée du Louvre (lines 1 and 7) and Louvre–Rivoli (line 1). Many metro and RER lines converge at Paris' main hub, Châtelet–Les Halles.

o **Bus** Major bus lines include the 27 from rue de Rivoli (for bd St-Michel and place d'Italie) and the 69 near the Louvre–Rivoli metro (for Invalides and Eiffel Tower).

o **Bicycle** Vélib' stations at 1 place Ste-Marguerite de Navarre and 2 rue de Turbigo are best placed for the Châtelet–Les Halles metro/RER hub; for the Louvre pedal to/from 165 rue St-Honoré or 2 rue d'Alger next to the Tuileries metro station.

o **Boat** Louvre.

◎ Sights

History and culture meet head on along the banks of the Seine. It was in this same neighbourhood that Louis VI created *halles* (markets) in 1137 for merchants who converged on the city centre to sell their wares and for over 800 years they were, in the words of Émile Zola, the 'belly of Paris'. The wholesalers were moved lox, stock and cabbage out to the suburbs in 1971.

Les Arts Décoratifs   Art Museum
Map p104 (www.lesartsdecoratifs.fr; 107 rue de Rivoli, 1er; adult/child €11/free; ⊙11am-6pm Tue-Sun, to 9pm Thu; MPalais Royal–Musée du Louvre) A trio of privately administered collections – Applied Arts, Advertising, and Fashion & Textiles – sit in the Rohan Wing of the vast Palais du Louvre. They are collectively known as the Decorative Arts; admission includes entry to all three. For an extra €2, you can scoop up a combo ticket that also includes the **Musée Nissim de Camondo** (www. lesartsdecoratifs.fr; 63 rue de Monceau, 8e; adult/18-25yr/under 18yr €9/6.50/ free; ⊙11am-6pm Tue, Wed & Fri-Sun, to 9pm Thu; MMonceau or Villiers) in the 8e.

The **Arts Décoratifs** (Applied Arts) section takes up the majority of the space and displays furniture, jewellery and such objets d'art as ceramics and glassware from the Middle Ages and the Renaissance through the art-nouveau and art-deco periods to modern times. Its collections span from Europe to East Asia.

On the other side of the building is the smaller **Musée de la Publicité** (Advertising Museum), which has some 100,000 posters in its collection dating as far back as the 13th century and innumerable

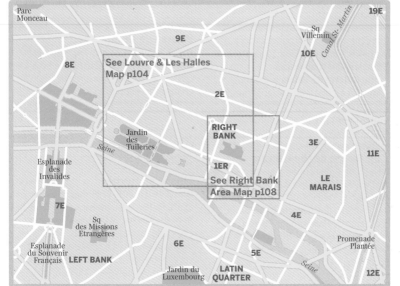

promotional materials. Most of the space is given over to special exhibitions.

Haute couture (high fashion) creations by the likes of Chanel and Jean-Paul Gaultier can be ogled in the **Musée de la Mode et du Textile** (Museum of Fashion & Textiles), home to some 16,000 costumes from the 16th century to the present day. Items are only on display during regularly scheduled themed exhibitions.

Arc de Triomphe du Carrousel — Monument

Map p104 (place du Carrousel, 1er; M Palais Royal–Musée du Louvre) This triumphal arch, erected by Napoléon to celebrate his battlefield successes of 1805, sits with aplomb in the **Jardin du Carrousel**, the gardens immediately next to the Louvre. The eastern counterpoint to the other Arc de Triomphe (the more famous one), it is one of several monuments that comprise the *axe historique* (historical axis), which terminates with the statue of Louis XIV next to the Pyramide du Louvre.

Place Vendôme — Square

Map p104 (M Tuileries or Opéra) Octagonal place Vendôme and the arcaded and colonnaded buildings around it were constructed between 1687 and 1721. In March 1796 Napoléon married Joséphine, Viscountess Beauharnais, in the building at No 3. Today, the buildings surrounding the square house the posh Hôtel Ritz Paris and some of the city's most fashionable boutiques.

Jardin du Palais Royal — Gardens

Map p104 (2 place Colette, 1er; ⏱7am-10.15pm Apr & May, to 11pm Jun-Aug, shorter hours rest of year; M Palais Royal–Musée du Louvre) FREE The Jardin du Palais Royal is a perfect spot to sit, contemplate, and picnic between boxed hedges or shop in the trio of arcades that frame the garden so beautifully: the Galerie de Valois (east), Galerie de Montpensier (west) and Galerie Beaujolais. However, it's the southern end of the complex, polka-dotted with sculptor Daniel Buren's 260 black-and-white striped columns, that has become the garden's signature feature.

This elegant urban space is fronted by the neoclassical **Palais Royal** (closed to the public), constructed in 1633 by Cardinal Richelieu but mostly dating to the late 18th century. Louis XIV hung out here in the 1640s; today it is home to the **Conseil d'État** Map p104 (State Council).

The **Galerie de Valois** is the most upmarket arcade with designer boutiques like Stella McCartney, Pierre Hardy, **Didier Ludot** (p118) and coat-of-arms engraver Guillaumot, at work at Nos 151 to 154 since 1785. Across the garden, in the **Galerie de Montpensier**, the Revolution broke out on a warm mid-July day just three years after the galleries opened in the Café du Foy. The third arcade, tiny **Galerie Beaujolais**, is crossed by **Passage du Perron**, a passageway above which the writer Colette (1873–1954) lived out the last dozen years of her life.

Forum des Halles   Shopping Mall

Map p108 (www.forumdeshalles.com; 1 rue Pierre Lescot, 1er; ⏰shops 10am-8pm Mon-Sat; MChâtelet–Les Halles) Paris' main wholesale food market stood here for nearly 800 years before being replaced by this underground shopping mall in 1971. Four floors of stores extend down to the city's busiest metro hub, while a massive renovation project – with an enormous golden-hued translucent canopy as centrepiece – is under way, with a target completion date of 2016.

Spilling out from the curvilinear, leaf-like rooftop will be new gardens designed by landscaper David Mangin, with pétanque and chess tables, a central patio and pedestrian walkways. The project will also open up the shopping centre, allowing for more natural light.

Renovation is being undertaken in stages; hence business should continue more or less as usual, with minimal disruption. Follow the project at www.parisleshalles.fr or pop into the information centre on place Joachim du Bellay, a pretty square pierced by the Fontaine des Innocents (1549). The multi-tiered Renaissance fountain is named after the Cimetière des Innocents, a cemetery formerly on this site from which

two million skeletons were disinterred after the Revolution and transferred to the Catacombes.

Bourse de Commerce   Monument

Map p108 (2 rue de Viarmes, 1er; ⏰9am-6pm Mon-Fri; MLes Halles) FREE At one time the city's grain market, the circular Trade Exchange was capped with a copper dome in 1811. The murals running along internal walls below the galleries were painted by five different artists in 1889 and restored in 1998. They represent French trade and industry through the ages.

Musée en Herbe   Art Museum

Map p104 (☎01 40 67 97 66; www.musee-en-herbe.com; 21 rue Hérold, 1er; admission €6; ⏰10am-7pm Fri-Wed, to 9pm Thu; MLes Halles) One of the city's great backstreet secrets, this children's museum is a surprise gem for art lovers of every age, not just kids. Its permanent exhibition changes every March and focuses on the work of one artist or theme through a series of interactive displays.

Captions are in English as well as French, children get a *jeu de piste* (activity sheet) to guide and entertain, and additional workshops and guided visits for kids and adults – think hands-on art workshops, afternoon tea, early-evening aperitifs and so on (€6 to €10, reserve in advance) – add to the playful experience.

Tour St-Jacques   Tower

Map p108 (39 rue de Rivoli, 4e; adult €6; MChâtelet) Just north of place du Châtelet, the Flamboyant Gothic, 54m-high St James Tower is all that remains of the Église St-Jacques la Boucherie, built by the powerful butchers guild in 1523 as a starting point for pilgrims setting out for the shrine of St James at Santiago de Compostela in Spain. Recently restored, it should open to the public in the near future, allowing visitors to climb 300 stairs up to an expansive panorama.

59 Rivoli   Gallery

Map p108 (http://59rivoli-eng.org; 59 rue de Rivoli, 1er; ⏰1pm-8pm daily; MLouvre-Rivoli) FREE In such a classical part of Paris crammed with elegant historic architecture, 59 Rivoli is

GARDEL BERTRAND/GETTY IMAGES ©

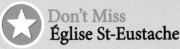

Don't Miss
Église St-Eustache

Just north of the gardens snuggling up to the city's old marketplace, now the bustling Forum des Halles, is one of the most beautiful churches in Paris. Majestic, architecturally magnificent and musically outstanding, St-Eustache has made spirits soar for centuries.

Constructed between 1532 and 1637, St-Eustache is primarily Gothic, though a neoclassical façade was added on the western side in the mid-18th century. Highlights include a work by Rubens and the colourful bas-relief of Parisian market porters (1969) by British sculptor Raymond Mason in the side chapels. Outside the church is a gigantic sculpture of a head and hand entitled *L'Écoute* (Listen; 1986) by Henri de Miller.

France's largest organ, above the church's western entrance, has 101 stops and 8000 pipes dating from 1854. Organ recitals at 5.30pm on Sunday are a must for music lovers.

NEED TO KNOW
Map p108 www.st-eustache.org; 2 impasse St-Eustache, 1er; ⊙9.30am-7pm Mon-Fri, 9am-7pm Sat & Sun; Ⓜ Les Halles

quite the bohemian breath of fresh air. Take time out to watch artists at work in the 30 *ateliers* (studios) strung on six floors of the long-abandoned bank building, now a legalised squat where some of Paris' most creative talent works (but doesn't live).

The ground-floor gallery hosts a new exhibition every fortnight and free gigs, concerts and shows pack the place out most weekends. Look for the sculpted façade festooned with catchy drapes, banners and unconventional recycled piping above the shop fronts.

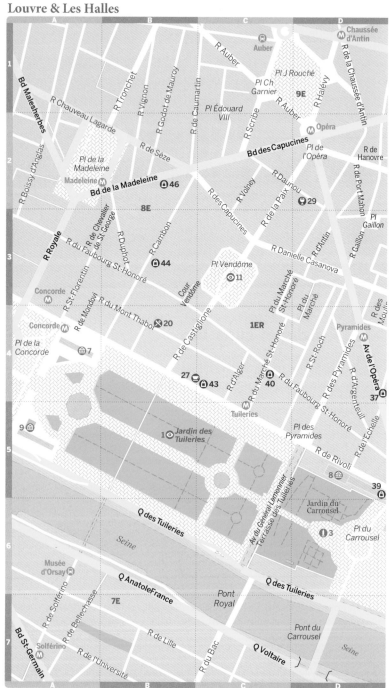

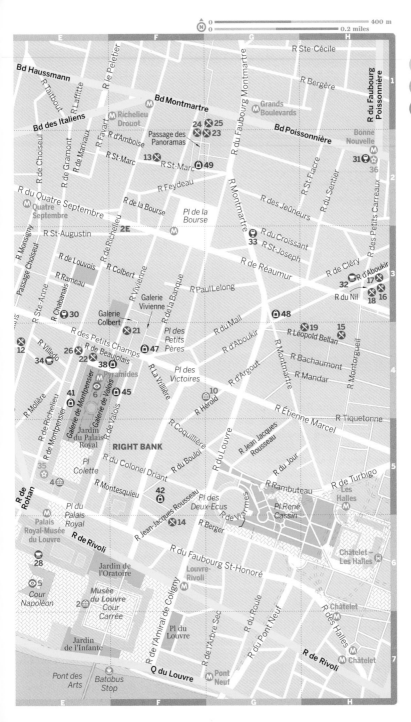

Bd Haussmann

R le Peletier

R Laffitte

R Tattbout

Bd Montmartre

R Favart

R d'Amboise

Richelieu
Drouot

Passage des
Panoramas

24 ✕ 25
✕ 23

Bd des Italiens

R de Choiseul

R de Gramont

R de Marivaux

R St-Marc

13 ✕

R St-Marc

49

R Ste-Cécile

R Bergère

R du Faubourg Montmartre

Grands
Boulevards

Bd Poissonnière

R du Faubourg Poissonnière

Bonne
Nouvelle

31

36

R du Quatre Septembre

R de la Bourse

R Feydeau

R Montmartre

R des Jeûneurs

R St-Fiacre

R du Sentier

R des Petits Carreaux

Quatre
Septembre

R St-Augustin

R de Richelieu

2E

Pl de la
Bourse

33

R du Croissant
R St-Joseph

R Monsigny

R de Louvois

R Colbert

R de Réaumur

R de Cléry

R d'Aboukir

R Rameau

R Ste-Anne

R Chabanais

30

Galerie
Colbert

Galerie
Vivienne

R Vivienne

R de la Banque

R Paul Lelong

32

17

R du Nil

18 16

48

✕ 21

Pl des
Petits
Pères

R du Mail

R d'Aboukir

15
✕

✕
12

R Villedo

26 ✕

R de Beaujolais

22 ✕

38

R des Petits Champs

47

R La Villière

Pl des
Victoires

R d'Aboukir

R d'Argout

19

R Léopold Bellan

R Bachaumont

R Mandar

R Montmartre

R Montorgueil

34

41

Galerie de Montpensier

6

Galerie de Valois

45

R Molière

R de Richelieu

R de Montpensier

Jardin
du Palais
Royal

RIGHT BANK

R Hérold

10

R Coquillière

R du Bouloi

R du Louvre

R Jean Jacques Rousseau

R du Jour

R Étienne Marcel

R Tiquetonne

R de Turbigo

Les
Halles

35

4

Pl
Colette

R Montesquieu

42

Pl des
Deux-Ecus

R Rambuteau

Pl René
Cassin

Châtelet –
Les Halles

R de
Rohan

Pl du
Palais
Royal

Palais
Royal-Musée
du Louvre

R de Rivoli

R Jean-Jacques Rousseau

14

R Berger

R de Viarmes

Pl des
Deux-Ecus

28

Jardin de
l'Oratoire

R du Faubourg St-Honoré

Louvre-
Rivoli

Châtelet

R des Halles

5

Cour
Napoléon

2

Musée
du Louvre
Cour
Carrée

Pl du
Louvre

R du Roule

R du Pont Neuf

R de Rivoli

Châtelet

Jardin
de l'Infante

R de l'Amiral de Coligny

R de l'Arbre Sec

Pont des
Arts

Batobus
Stop

Q du Louvre

Pont
Neuf

Louvre & Les Halles

Tour Jean sans Peur — Tower

Map p108 (Tower of John the Fearless; www.
tourjeansanspeur.com; 20 rue Étienne Marcel,
2e; adult/7-18yr €5/3; ⏱1.30-6pm Wed-Sun
Apr-early Nov, 1.30-6pm Wed, Sat & Sun early Nov-
Mar; MÉtienne Marcel) This 29m-high Gothic
tower was built during the Hundred Years'
War by the Duke of Bourgogne so that he
could take refuge from his enemies –
such as the supporters of the Duke of
Orléans, whom he had assassinated. Part
of a splendid mansion in the early 15th
century, it is one of the few examples of
feudal military architecture extant in Paris.
Climb 140 steps up the spiral staircase to
the top turret (no views).

Atelier Brancusi — Museum

Map p108 (55 rue Rambuteau, 4e; ⏱2-6pm Wed-
Mon; MRambuteau) FREE West of the Centre
Pompidou main building, this reconstruc-
tion of the studio of Romanian-born
sculptor Constantin Brancusi (1876–1957)

designed by Renzo Piano contains some
160 examples of the sculptor's work.

Eating

Blend — Burgers €

Map p108 (www.blendhamburger.com; 44 rue
d'Argout, 2e; burger & fries €14; ⏱noon-11pm
daily; MSentier) A burger cannot simply be
a burger in gourmet Paris, where burger
buffs dissolve into raptures of ecstacy
over gourmet creations at Blend. Think
homemade brioche buns and ketchup,
hand-cut meat and the most inventive
of toppings that transforms the humble
burger into something rather special.

Crêpe Dentelle — Crêperie €

Map p104 (☎01 40 41 04 23; 10 rue Léopold Bellan, 2e; crêpes €4.90-14.60, lunch menu €11.20;
⏱noon-3pm & 7.30-11pm Mon-Fri; 🍴; MSentier) Named after a style of crêpe that's as

JEAN-PIERRE LESCOURRET/GETTY IMAGES ©

⭐ Don't Miss
Jardin des Tuileries

Filled with fountains, ponds and sculptures, the formal, 28-hectare Tuileries Garden, which begins just west of the Jardin du Carrousel, was laid out in its present form, more or less, in 1664 by André Le Nôtre, who also created the gardens at Vaux-le-Vicomte and Versailles. The Tuileries soon became the most fashionable spot in Paris for parading about in one's finery. It now forms part of the Banks of the Seine World Heritage Site listed by Unesco in 1991.

The *axe historique* (historic axis), the western continuation of the Tuileries' east–west axis, follows the av des Champs-Élysées to the Arc de Triomphe and, ultimately, to the Grande Arche in the skyscraper district of La Défense.

Located in the southwestern corner of the Jardin des Tuileries, the **Musée de l'Orangerie** (www.musee-orangerie.fr; Jardin des Tuileries, 1e; adult/child €9/6.50; ⏰9am-6pm Wed-Mon; Ⓜ Concorde), with the Jeu de Paume, is all that remains of the former Palais des Tuileries, which was razed during the Paris Commune in 1871. It exhibits important impressionist works, including a series of Monet's Decorations des Nymphéas (Water Lilies) in two huge oval rooms purpose-built in 1927 on the artist's instructions, as well as works by Cézanne, Matisse, Picasso, Renoir, Sisley, Soutine and Utrillo. An audioguide costs €5.

The **Galerie du Jeu de Paume** (📞01 47 03 12 50; www.jeudepaume.org; 1 place de la Concorde, 8e; adult/child €8.50/free; ⏰11am-9pm Tue, to 7pm Wed-Sun; Ⓜ Concorde), which stages innovative photography exhibitions, is housed in an erstwhile *jeu de paume* (royal tennis court) in the northwestern corner of the Jardin des Tuileries.

NEED TO KNOW
Map p104 ⏰7am-11pm Jun-Aug, shorter hours rest of year; Ⓜ Tuileries or Concorde

107

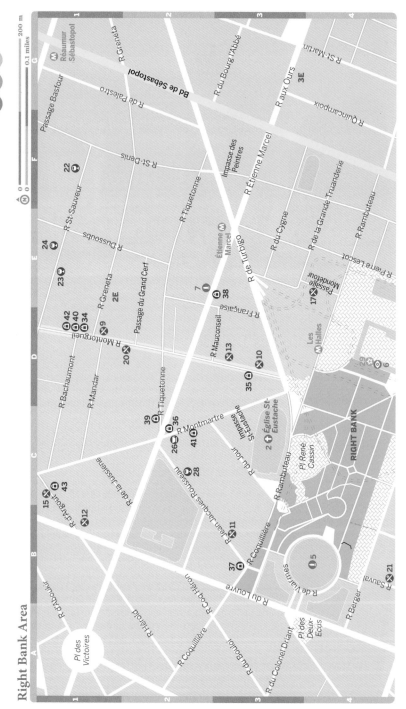

Right Bank Area

LOUVRE & LES HALLES

200 m
0.1 miles

Pl des Victoires

R d'Aboukir

R Hérold

R Coquillière

R du Coq Héron

R du Bouloi

R du Colonel Driant

Pl des Deux-Écus

R de Viarmes

R du Louvre

R de la Jussienne

R Jean-Jacques Rousseau

R Bachaumont

R Mandar

R Montorgueil

R Tiquetonne

R du Jour

R Montmartre

R Coquillière

R Étienne

R Rambuteau

Pl René Cassin

RIGHT BANK

R Berger

R Sauval

R de la Grande Truanderie

R Pierre Lescot

Passage Mondétour

R Rambuteau

R de Turbigo

R Française

R Mauconseil

R du Cygne

R Étienne Marcel

Impasse des Peintres

R de Palestro

Bd de Sébastopol

R St-Denis

R Greneta

R Tiquetonne

R St-Sauveur

R Dussoubs

R Greneta

Passage du Grand Cerf

Passage Basfour

R du Bourg l'Abbé

R aux Ours

R Quincampoix

R St-Martin

Impasse St-Eustache

M Réaumur Sébastopol

M Étienne Marcel

M Les Halles

2E

3E

2E

15
43
12
39
36
41
26
28
11
37
5
21
42
40
34
20
9
23
24
22
7
38
13
10
35
17
2
6
29

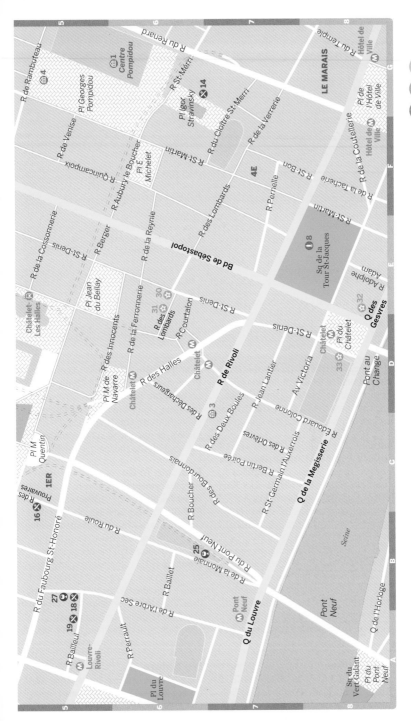

LOUVRE & LES HALLES

109

Right Bank Area

delicate as fine lace (*dentelle*), this is an excellent choice for a light and inexpensive lunch, and is certainly the best bet for crêpes near the Louvre. Arrive by 12.15pm or you may not get a seat.

Claus
Breakfast €

Map p104 (01 42 33 55 10; www.clausparis.com; 14 rue Jean-Jacques Rousseau, 1er; breakfasts €13-18, plat du jour €13; 8am-5pm Mon-Fri, 9.30am-5pm Sat & Sun; Étienne Marcel) Dubbed the '*haute-couture* breakfast specialist' in Parisian foodie circles, this inspired *épicerie du petit-dej* (breakfast grocery shop) has everything for the ultimate gourmet breakfast and brunch – organic cereals, fresh juices, jams, honey and so on.

Breakfast or brunch on site, shop at Claus to create your own or ask for a luxury breakfast hamper to be delivered to your door. Its lunchtime salads, soups and tarts are equally tasty.

Dame Tartine
Cafe €

Map p108 (2 rue Brisemiche, 4e; tartines €8.90-11.20; 9am-11.30pm; Hôtel de Ville) One of the few reasonable dining options near the Centre Pompidou, Dame Tartine makes the most of its lively location across from the whimsical Stravinsky Fountain. Don't expect miracles on the culinary front, but its speciality – the tartine, or open-face sandwich – will hit the spot after a morning in the museum.

Frenchie To Go
Fast Food €

Map p104 (www.frenchietogo.com; 9 rue du Nil, 2e; sandwiches €8-14; 8.30am-4.30pm Mon-Fri, 9.30am-5.30pm Sat & Sun; Sentier) Despite the drawbacks – limited seating, eye-poppingly expensive donuts – the fast-food outpost of the burgeoning **Frenchie** (p114) empire is a wildly popular destination. Bilingual staff transform choice ingredients (eg cuts of meat from the Ginger Pig in Yorkshire) into American classics like pulled-pork and pastrami sandwiches, accompanied by cornets of fries, coleslaw and pickled veggies.

Fée Nature
Organic €

Map p108 (67 rue d'Argout, 2e; plat du jour €8.50; noon-4pm Mon-Sat; Sentier) Fée Nature thinks green with its inventive, wholly 'bio et sain' (organic & healthy) menu – there are even a few gluten-free options. Orange blossom tapioca anyone?

Cojean
Sandwiches, Salads €

(www.cojean.fr; 3 place du Louvre, 1er; sandwiches €5.30-6.80; ⏱10am-4pm Mon-Fri, 11am-6pm Sat; 📶; Ⓜ Palais Royal–Musée du Louvre) Across the street from the Louvre, this stylish sandwich and salad bar promises a quick lunch for less than €10 beneath the splendour of an elegant moulded period ceiling.

Ace Gourmet Bento
Japanese €

Map p104 (18 rue Thérèse, 1er; ⏱noon-10.30pm Mon-Sat; Ⓜ Pyramides) It's as cheap as chips, a mug of sweet lemon tea gets you change from €2, and punters can eat in or take away. In the heart of Paris' Japantown, Ace Gourmet Bento is a bijou Japanese-Korean canteen-bistro with bright white walls, flowery pop-art deco, and an unbeatable-value €9 lunch deal.

Pick your meat or fish main with rice or noodles, choose five veggie salads and side dishes, and plop yourself and fuchsia-pink tray down at a table.

Pirouette
Neobistro €€

Map p108 (📞01 40 26 47 81; 5 rue Mondétour, 1er; lunch menu €18, 3-/6-course dinner menu €40/60; ⏱noon-2.30pm & 7.30-10.30pm Mon-Sat; Ⓜ Les Halles) In one of the best restaurants in the vicinity of the old 'belly of Paris', chef Tomy Gousset's kitchen crew is working wonders at this cool loft-like space, serving up tantalising creations that range from seared duck, asparagus and Buddha's hand fruit to rum baba with chantilly and lime. Some unique ingredients and a new spin for French cuisine.

La Tour de Montlhéry – Chez Denise
Traditional French €€

Map p108 (📞01 42 36 21 82; 5 rue des Prouvaires, 1er; mains €23-28; ⏱noon-2.30pm & 7.30pm-5am Mon-Fri; Ⓜ Châtelet) The most traditional eatery near the former Les Halles marketplace, this boisterous old bistro with red-chequered tablecloths has been run by the same team for 30-some years. If you've just arrived and are ready to feast on all the French classics – snails in garlic sauce, veal liver, steak tartare, braised beef cheeks and housemade pâtés – reservations are in order. Open till dawn.

Racines (p113)

Rue Montorgueil

A splinter of the historic Les Halles, rue Montorgueil was once the oyster market and the final stop for seafood merchants hailing from the coast. Immortalised by Balzac in *La Comédie Humaine,* this compelling strip still draws Parisians to eat and shop – it's lined with *fromageries* (cheese shops), cafes, and street stalls selling fruit, veg and other foodstuffs.

Aux Tonneaux des Halles (Map p108; 28 rue Montorgueil, 1er; ⏰noon-11pm Mon-Sat; Ⓜ Les Halles) Originally a hotel, Aux Tonneaux only became a cafe in the 1920s – a relatively recent addition compared to some of the other addresses here. It boasts great wines and a fine outdoor terrace, as well as classic bistro fare such as *steak-frites.*

Charles Chocolatier (Map p108; 15 rue Montorgueil, 1er; ⏰10am-7.45pm Tue-Sat; Ⓜ Les Halles) Delectable artisan chocolates made with 100% cocoa butter (no milk, butter or cream). If the weather is chilly, pop in for a rich cup of hot chocolate to go.

Caldo Freddo (Map p108; 34 rue Montorgueil, 1er; pizza slices €4.90; ⏰noon-11pm daily; ♿; Ⓜ Les Halles) Pizzas by the pie and the slice (with a truffle topping!) along with *arancini* (fried rice balls), antipasti and panini.

Stohrer (Map p108; www.stohrer.fr; 51 rue Montorgueil, 2e; ⏰7.30am-8.30pm daily; Ⓜ Les Halles) This bakery was opened in 1730 by the Polish pastry chef of queen consort Marie Leczinska (wife of Louis XV). Specialities include its very own *baba au rhum* (sponge cake soaked in rum-flavoured syrup) and *puits d'amour* (puff pasty with vanilla cream and caramel).

Au Rocher de Cancale (Map p108; ☎01 42 33 50 29; www.aurocherdecancale.fr; 78 rue Montorgueil, 2e; mains €10.50-22; ⏰8am-2am daily; Ⓜ Sentier or Les Halles) This 19th-century timber-lined restaurant (first opened in 1804 at No 59) is the last remaining legacy of the old oyster market. You can feast on oysters and seafood from Cancale (in Brittany) as well as other *plats du jour.*

À La Mère de Famille (Map p108; www.lameredefamille.com; 82 rue Montorgueil, 2e; ⏰10am-8pm Mon-Sat, to 1pm Sun; Ⓜ Sentier or Les Halles) The oldest confectionery house in Paris, with over 250 years of experience creating chocolates, *bonbons* and other sweet temptations.

La Fermette (Map p108 ; www.lafermettemontorgueil.com; 86 rue Montorgueil, 2e; ⏰4-8pm Mon, 7.30am-8.30pm Tue-Sat, 7.30am-2pm Sun; Ⓜ Sentier or Les Halles) Not the most stylish *fromagerie* in town, but it always has great deals out front, where you can pick up a preselected assortment of cheese for under €10.

Nysa (Map p108; www.nysa.fr; 94 rue de Montorgueil, 2e; ⏰10.30-2pm & 4-9pm Wed-Mon, 4-9pm Tue; Ⓜ Sentier) This unpretentious wine store supports independent vineyards and has an interesting selection of bottles for under €15.

L'Ardoise Bistro €€

Map p104 (☎01 42 96 28 18; www.lardoise-paris.com; 28 rue du Mont Thabor, 1er; menu €38; ⏰noon-2.30pm Mon-Sat, 7.30-10.30pm Mon-Sun; Ⓜ Concorde or Tuileries) This is a lovely little bistro with no menu as such (*ardoise* means 'blackboard', which is all there is), but who cares? The food – *fricassée* of corn-fed chicken with morels, pork cheeks in ginger, hare in black pepper, prepared dexterously by chef Pierre Jay (ex-Tour d'Argent) – is superb.

La Mauvaise Réputation
Modern French €€

Map p104 (📞01 42 36 92 44; www.lamauvaisereputation.fr; 28 rue Léopold-Bellan, 2e; 2-/3-course menu lunch €18/22, dinner €28/35; 🕐noon-2.30pm Mon-Fri, 7.30-10.30pm Tue-Sat; Ⓜ Sentier) The name alone – Bad Reputation (yep, also a Georges Brassens album) – immediately makes you want to poke your nose in and see what's happening behind that bright-orange canopy and oyster-grey façade just footsteps from busy rue Montorgueil. Great bistro cooking and warm, engaging service in a catchy designer space with coloured spots on the wall and fresh flowers on each table is the answer.

Racines
Wine Bar €€

Map p104 (📞01 40 13 06 41; 8 Passage des Panoramas, 2e; mains €23-30; 🕐noon-2.30pm & 7.30-10.30pm Mon-Fri; Ⓜ Grands Boulevards or Richelieu-Drouot) Snug inside a former 19th-century *marchand de vin* (wine merchant's; look up to admire the lovely old gold lettering above the door), Racines (meaning 'Roots') is an address that shouts Paris at every turn. Shelves of wine bottles curtain the windows, the old

patterned floor smacks of feasting and merriment, and the menu chalked on the blackboard is straightforward.

Racines 2
Modern French €€

Map p108 (📞01 42 60 77 34; 39 rue de l'Arbre Sec, 1er; 2-course lunch menu €18.50, mains €28-31; 🕐noon-2.30pm & 7.30-10.30pm Mon-Fri; Ⓜ Louvre–Rivoli) R2 is a cousin of Racines in Passage des Panoramas, but that is about the extent of the family resemblance. No 2 is a thoroughly modern, urban bistro with a contemporary, Philippe Starck interior and an open stainless-steel kitchen where you can watch the hip, young, black-dressed chefs, tattoos and all, at work.

What's cooking – just two or three choices for each course – is chalked on the board, and the Louvre, handily so, is just around the corner.

Le Grand Colbert
Traditional French €€

Map p104 (📞01 42 86 87 88; www.legrandcolbert.fr; 2-4 rue Vivienne, 2e; 2-/3-course menu lunch €29/36, dinner €46/54; 🕐noon-1am; 🛜; Ⓜ Pyramides) This former workers' *cafétéria* transformed into a *fin de siècle* (end of the century) showcase is more relaxed

Sweet treats for sale at Stohrer

STEVE HAMBLIN/ALAMY ©

than many similarly restored restaurants and is a convenient spot for lunch after visiting the neighbouring covered shopping arcades – the daily *formule ardoise* (blackboard fixed menu; €17) is good value – or cruising the streets at night (last orders: midnight).

Aux Lyonnais
Lyonnais €€

Map p104 (☎ 01 58 00 22 06; www.auxlyonnais. com; 32 rue St-Marc, 2e; lunch menu €32, mains €26-33; ⏰ noon-2.30pm Tue-Fri, 7.30-10.30pm Tue-Sat; Ⓜ Richelieu-Drouot) This is where top French chef Alain Ducasse and his followers 'slum' it. The venue is an art-nouveau masterpiece that feels more real than a movie set; the food is perfectly restructured Lyonnais classics, such as quenelles (creamed fish or meat shaped like a dumpling) and blood sausage.

Beef Club
Steak €€

Map p108 (☎ 09 54 37 13 65; www.eccbeefclub. com; 58 rue Jean-Jacques Rousseau, 1er; mains €25-38; ⏰ dinner daily; Ⓜ Les Halles) No steakhouse is more chic or hipper than this. Packed out ever since it threw its

first T-bone on the grill in spring 2012, this beefy address is all about steak, dry aged and prepared to tender perfection. The vibe is hip New York and the downstairs cellar bar, the Ballroom, shakes a mean cocktail courtesy of the cool guys from the **Experimental Cocktail Club** (p116).

Fish Club
Peruvian €€

Map p108 (☎ 01 40 26 68 75; 58 rue Jean-Jacques Rousseau, 1er; tapas €7-22; ⏰ noon-3pm & 8-10.15pm Tue-Fri, 8-10.15pm Sat; Ⓜ Les Halles) In contrast to the North American-influenced Beef Club, the impeccably chic Fish Club hails from south of the equator, with a distinctly Peruvian influence in its *ceviches* (marinated raw fish), *tiraditos* (thinly sliced raw fish) and pisco sours.

Frenchie
Bistro €€€

Map p104 (☎ 01 40 39 96 19; www.frenchie-restaurant.com; 5-6 rue du Nil, 2e; prix fixe menu €48; ⏰ 7-11pm Mon-Fri; Ⓜ Sentier) Tucked down an alley you wouldn't venture down otherwise, this bijou bistro with wooden tables and old stone walls is iconic. Frenchie is always packed and for good reason: excellent-value dishes are modern, market-driven (the menu changes daily with a choice of two dishes) and prepared with just the right dose of unpretentious creative flair by French chef Gregory Marchand.

The only hiccup is snagging a table: reserve for one of two sittings (7pm or 9.30pm) two months in advance, arrive at 7pm and pray for a cancellation (it does happen) or – failing that – share tapas-style small plates with friends across the street at **Frenchie Bar à Vins** Map p104 (dishes €10-20; ⏰ 7-11pm Mon-Fri). No reservations at the latter – write your name on the sheet of paper strung outside, loiter in the alley and wait for your name to be called.

Pot-au-feu at Spring

MING TANG-EVANS/LONELY PLANET ©

Verjus   Modern American €€€

Map p104 (☎01 42 97 54 40; www.verjusparis.
com; 52 rue de Richelieu, 1er; prixe-fixe menu
€60; ⏱7-10pm Mon-Fri; Ⓜ Bourse or Palais
Royal–Musée du Louvre) Opened by American
duo Braden Perkins and Laura Adrian,
Verjus was born out of a wildly successful clandestine supper club known as the
Hidden Kitchen. The restaurant builds on
that tradition, offering a chance to sample
some excellent, creative cuisine (gnocchi
with shiitake relish and parmesan, wild-
boar confit with cherry compote) in a
casual space. The tasting menu is a series
of small plates, using ingredients sourced
straight from producers.

Reservations are advised, but walk-ins
sometimes end up with a table, especially
if you don't mind eating late. If you're just
after an apéritif or a prelude to dinner,
the **Verjus Bar à Vins** Map p104 (47 rue de
Montpensier, 1er; small plates €8-14, sandwiches
€10; ⏱12.30-2pm Tue-Fri, 6-11pm Mon-Fri;
Ⓜ Bourse or Palais Royal–Musée du Louvre)
cooks up what foodies rightfully claim
to be the best buttermilk-fried chicken
(€10) in the city, among other small
plates. No reservations – arrive early to
snag one of 10 bar stools. It also serves
gourmet sandwiches at lunch.

Spring   Modern French €€€

Map p108 (☎01 45 96 05 72; www.springparis.
fr; 6 rue Bailleul, 1er; prix-fixe menu €84; ⏱dinner
Tue-Sat; Ⓜ Palais Royal–Musée du Louvre) One
of the Right Bank's talk-of-the-town addresses, with Chicago-born Daniel Rose in
the open kitchen and stunning food. It has
no printed menu, meaning hungry gourmets put their appetites in the hands of the
chefs and allow multilingual waiting staff
to reveal what's cooking as each course is
served. Reserve one month in advance.

Yam'Tcha   Fusion €€€

Map p108 (☎01 40 26 08 07; www.yamtcha.
com; 4 rue Sauval, 1er; prix-fixe menu €100;
⏱noon-2.30pm Wed-Sat, 7.30-10.30pm Tue-
Sat; Ⓜ Louvre-Rivoli) Adeline Grattard's
ingeniously fused French and Cantonese
flavours (fried squid with sweet-potato
noodles) has earned the female chef no
shortage of critical praise. Pair dishes on

Gluten-free Dining

Gluten-free kitchens are hard to find
in France, but that's only one of the
reasons that **Noglu** (Map p104; ☎01
40 26 41 24; www.noglu.fr; 16 Passage des
Panoramas, 2e; mains €16-20, menu €24;
⏱noon-2.30pm Mon-Sat, 7.30-10.30pm
Tue-Sat; ✎; Ⓜ Richelieu-Drouot or Grands
Boulevards) is such a jewel – this chic
address builds on French tradition
(*boeuf bourguignon*) while simultaneously drawing on newer culinary
trends from across the Atlantic to
create some devilishly good pastries,
vegetarian plates and superb pizzas
and salads. Don't skip the chocolate-
passion tart. Reserve.

the frequently changing menu with wine
or tea, or sample the special lunch menu
(€60) offered Wednesday through Friday.
Reserve up to two months in advance.

Passage 53   Modern French €€€

Map p104 (☎01 42 33 04 35; www.passage53.
com; 53 Passage des Panoramas, 2e; lunch/
dinner menu €60/130; ⏱noon-2.30pm &
7.30-10.30pm Tue-Sat; Ⓜ Grands Boulevards or
Bourse) No address inside Passage des
Panoramas contrasts more dramatically
with the outside hustle and bustle than
this elegant restaurant at No 53. An oasis
of calm and tranquillity (with window
blinds pulled firmly down when closed),
this gastronomic address is an ode to the
best French produce – worked to perfection in a series of tasting courses by
Japanese chef Shinichi Sato. Reserve.

Le Grand
Véfour   Traditional French €€€

Map p104 (☎01 42 96 56 27; www.grand-vefour.
com; 17 rue de Beaujolais, 1er; lunch/dinner menu
€98/298; ⏱noon-2.30pm & 7.30-10.30pm Mon-
Fri; Ⓜ Pyramides) This 18th-century jewel
on the northern edge of the Jardin du
Palais Royal has been a dining favourite
of the Parisian elite since 1784; just look

at who gets their names ascribed to each table – from Napoléon and Victor Hugo to Colette (who lived next door). The food is tip-top; expect a voyage of discovery in one of the most beautiful restaurants in the world.

🍷 Drinking & Nightlife

Experimental Cocktail Club
Cocktail Bar

Map p108 (www.experimentalcocktailclub. com; 37 rue St-Saveur, 2e; ⊙7pm-2am daily; ⓂRéaumur Sébastopol) Called ECC by trendies, this fabulous speakeasy with grey façade and old-beamed ceiling is effortlessly hip. Oozing spirit and soul, the cocktail bar – with retro-chic decor by American interior designer Cuoco Black and sister bars in London and New York – is a sophisticated flashback to those *années folles* (crazy years) of Prohibition New York.

The City's Most Famous Hot Chocolate

Clink china with lunching ladies, their posturing poodles and half the students from Tokyo University at **Angelina** (Map p104; 226 rue de Rivoli, 1er; ⊙8am-7pm Mon-Fri, 9am-7pm Sat & Sun; ⓂTuileries), a grand dame of a tearoom dating to 1903. Decadent pastries are served here, against a fresco backdrop of belle époque Nice, but it is the superthick, decadently sickening 'African' hot chocolate (€8.20), which comes with a pot of whipped cream and a carafe of water, that prompts the constant queue for a table at Angelina.

Harry's New York Bar
Cocktail Bar

Map p104 (www.harrysbar.fr; 5 rue Daunou, 2e; ⊙noon-2am; ⓂOpéra) One of the most popular American-style bars in the pre-war years, Harry's once welcomed writers like F Scott Fitzgerald and Ernest Hemingway, who no doubt sampled the bar's unique cocktail and creation: the Bloody Mary. The Cuban mahogany interior dates from the mid-19th century and was brought over from a Manhattan bar in 1911.

Ô Chateau
Wine Bar

Map p108 (www.o-chateau.com; 68 rue Jean-Jacques Rousseau, 1er; ⊙4pm-midnight Mon-Sat; 🛜; ⓂLes Halles or Étienne Marcel) Wine aficionados can thank this young, fun, cosmopolitan *bar à vins* for bringing affordable tasting to Paris. Sit at the long bar and savour your pick of 40-odd *grands vins* served by the glass (500-odd by the bottle!). Or sign up in advance for an intro to French wine (€30) or a guided cellar tasting in English over lunch (€75) or dinner (€100).

Le Rex Club
Club

Map p104 (www.rexclub.com; 5 bd Poissonnière, 2e; ⊙midnight-7am Thu-Sat; ⓂBonne Nouvelle) Attached to the art-deco Grand Rex cinema, this is Paris' premier house and techno venue where some of the world's hottest DJs strut their stuff on a 70-speaker, multidiffusion sound system.

Le Conchon à l'Oreille
Cafe

Map p108 (☎01 42 36 07 56; 15 rue Montmartre, 1er; ⊙10am-2am Tue-Sat; ⓂLes Halles) A Parisian jewel, the heritage-listed hole-in-the-wall Le Conchon à l'Oreille retains 1890-laid tiles depicting vibrant market scenes of the old halles. Hours can vary.

Jefrey's
Cocktail Bar

Map p108 (www.jefreys.fr; 14 rue St-Saveur, 2e; ⊙Tue-Sat 7pm-2am; ⓂRéaumur Sébastopol) Oh how dandy this trendy drawing room with wooden façade, leather Chesterfields and old-fashioned gramophone is! It's a gentlemen's club in soul, yes, but creative cocktails are shaken for both him and her, and never more so during happy hour

(7pm to 10.30pm Tuesday and Thursday) when cocktails dip in price.

Kong   Bar
Map p108 (www.kong.fr; 1 rue du Pont Neuf, 1er; ⏱12.15-11.30pm daily; Ⓜ Pont Neuf) Evenings at this Philippe Starck–designed riot of iridescent champagne-coloured vinyl booths, Japanese cartoon cut-outs and garden-gnome stools see Paris' glam young set guzzling Dom Pérignon, nibbling at tapas-style platters (mains €20 to €40) and shaking their designer-clad booty on the tables.

Telescope   Cafe
Map p104 (www.telescopecafe.com; 5 rue Villedo, 1er; ⏱8.30am-5pm Mon-Fri, 9.30am-6.30pm Sat; Ⓜ Pyramides) The barista delivers at this minimalist coffee shop, which brews frothy cappuccinos and serves sweet pastries to boot.

Le Garde Robe   Wine Bar
Map p108 (41 rue de l'Arbre Sec, 1er; ⏱12.30-2.30pm & 7.30-11pm Mon-Fri; Ⓜ Louvre-Rivoli) The Garde Robe is possibly the only bar in the world to serve alcohol alongside a 'Detox' menu. While you probably shouldn't come here for the full-on cleansing experience, you can definitely expect excellent, affordable natural wines, a casual atmosphere and a good selection of eats, ranging from the standard cheese and charcuterie plates to more adventurous veg-friendly options.

Social Club   Club
Map p104 (www.parissocialclub.com; 142 rue Montmartre, 2e; ⏱11pm-6am Tue-Sat; Ⓜ Grands Boulevards) These subterranean rooms showcasing electro, hip hop, funk and live acts are a magnet for clubbers who take their music seriously. Across the street at No 146 is the cafe where French socialist Jean Jaurès was assassinated in 1914.

Depur   Bar
Map p108 (4bis rue St-Saveur, 2e; ⏱9am-11pm daily; Ⓜ Étienne Marcel or Sentier) It's glitzy and chic, a definite after-dark dress-up. But what really gives this hybrid bar-restaurant wow-factor is its courtyard

Jazz Duo

Rue des Lombards, 2e, is the street to swing by for live jazz.

Le Baiser Salé (Map p108; www.lebaisersale.com; 58 rue des Lombards, 1er; ⏱daily; Ⓜ Châtelet) Known for its Afro and Latin jazz, and jazz fusion concerts, the Salty Kiss combines big names and unknown artists. The place has a relaxed vibe, with sets usually starting at 7.30pm or 9.30pm.

Sunset & Sunside (Map p108; www.sunset-sunside.com; 60 rue des Lombards, 1er; ⏱daily; Ⓜ Châtelet) Two venues in one at this trendy, well-respected club: electric jazz, fusion and the odd salsa session downstairs; acoustics and concerts upstairs.

terrace – covered in winter, open and star-topped in summer. Cocktails are shaken from 5pm.

Lockwood   Cafe
Map p104 (73 rue d'Aboukir, 2e; ⏱8am-2am Mon-Sat; Ⓜ Sentier) A handy address for hip coffee lovers. Savour beans from the Belleville Brûlerie during the day and well-mixed cocktails in the subterranean candle-lit cave (wine cellar) at night.

La Champmeslé   Bar
Map p104 (www.lachampmesle.com; 4 rue Chabanais, 2e; ⏱4pm-dawn Mon-Sat; Ⓜ Pyramides) The grande dame of Parisian dyke bars, around since 1979, is a cosy, relaxed spot that attracts an older crowd (about 75% are lesbians, the rest mostly gay men). Cabaret nights, tarot-card reading and fortune-telling sessions, and art exhibitions.

Café Marly   Cafe
Map p104 (📞01 46 26 06 60; 93 rue de Rivoli, 1er; ⏱8am-2am; Ⓜ Palais Royal–Musée du Louvre) This chic venue facing the Louvre's inner courtyard is an unparalled spot for a drink with some serious wow factor. Food

117

Backstage at the Flicks

A trip to 1932 art-deco cinematic icon **Le Grand Rex** (Map p104; www.legrandrex.com; 1 bd Poissonnière, 2e; tour adult/child €11/9; ⊘tours 10am-7pm Wed-Sun; MBonne Nouvelle) is like no other trip to the flicks. Screenings aside, the cinema runs 50-minute behind-the-scene tours (English soundtracks available) during which visitors – tracked by a sensor slung around their neck – are whisked right up (via a lift) behind the giant screen, tour a soundstage and get to have fun in a recording studio. Whizz-bang special effects along the way will stun adults and kids alike.

is also served throughout the day, though it's painfully expensive for what you get – unless you consider the view of the glass pyramid, which is, of course, priceless.

Entertainment

Comédie Française   Theatre
Map p104 (www.comedie-francaise.fr; place Colette, 1er; MPalais Royal–Musée du Louvre) Founded in 1680 under Louis XIV, this state-run theatre bases its repertoire around the works of classic French playwrights. The theatre has its roots in an earlier company directed by Molière at the Palais Royal – the French playwright and actor was seized by a convulsion on stage during the fourth performance of the *Imaginary Invalid* in 1673 and died later at his home on nearby rue de Richelieu.

Forum des Images   Cinema
Map p108 (www.forumdesimages.fr; 1 Grande Galerie, Porte St-Eustache, Forum des Halles, 1er; ⊘1-10pm Tue-Fri, from 2pm Sat & Sun; MLes Halles) Cinemas showing films set in Paris are the centrepiece of the city's film archive, the Forum des Images. Created in 1988 to establish 'an audiovisual

memory bank of Paris', and renovated in dramatic shades of pink, grey and black, the five-screen centre has a new library and research centre with newsreels, documentaries and advertising. Check its program online for thematic series and frequent festivals and events.

Louvre Auditorium   Music
Map p104 (☎01 40 20 55 00; www.louvre.fr/musiques; Hall Napoléon, Louvre, 1er; MPalais Royal–Musée du Louvre) Excellent classical-music concerts are staged several times a week at the Louvre Auditorium (off the main entrance hall). Don't miss the Thursday lunchtime concerts, which cost a mere €6 to €12. The season runs from September to April or May, depending on the concert series.

Théâtre de la Ville   Dance
Map p108 (www.theatredelaville-paris.com; 2 place du Châtelet, 4e; MChâtelet) It hosts theatre and music too, but this theatre is best known for its contemporary dance productions.

Théâtre du Châtelet   Classical
Map p108 (www.chatelet-theatre.com; 1 place du Châtelet, 1er; MChâtelet) This venue hosts concerts as well as operas, musical performances, theatre, ballet and popular Sunday-morning concerts.

🔒 Shopping

Didier Ludot   Fashion
Map p104 (www.didierludot.fr; 19-20 & 23-24 Galerie de Montpensier, 1er; ⊘10.30am-7pm Mon-Sat; MPalais Royal–Musée du Louvre) In the rag trade since 1975, collector Didier Ludot sells the city's finest couture creations of yesteryear in his exclusive twinset of boutiques, hosts exhibitions, and has published a book portraying the evolution of the little black dress, brilliantly brought to life in his shop that sells just that, **La Petite Robe Noire** Map p104 (125 Galerie de Valois, 1er; ⊘11am-7pm Mon-Sat; MPalais Royal–Musée du Louvre).

E Dehillerin
Homewares

Map p108 (www.dehillerin.com; 18-20 rue Coquillière, 1er; ⊙9am-12.30pm & 2-6pm Mon, 9am-6pm Tue-Sat; M Les Halles) Founded in 1820, this extraordinary two-level store carries an incredible selection of professional-quality *matériel de cuisine* (kitchenware). Poultry scissors, turbot poacher, professional copper cookware or Eiffel Tower–shaped cake tin – it's all here.

Colette
Concept Store

Map p104 (www.colette.fr; 213 rue St-Honoré, 1er; ⊙11am-7pm Mon-Sat; M Tuileries) Uber-hip is an understatement. Ogle designer fashion on the 1st floor, and streetwear, limited-edition sneakers, art books, music, gadgets and other high-tech, inventive and/or plain unusual items on the ground floor. End with a drink in the basement 'water bar' and pick up free design magazines and flyers for some of the city's hippest happenings by the door upon leaving.

Room Service
Fashion

Map p108 (www.roomservice.fr; 52 rue d'Argout, 2e; ⊙11am-7.30pm Mon-Sat; M Les Halles) *'Atelier Vintage'* (vintage workshop) is the thrust of this chic boutique that reinvents vintage pieces as new. Scarves, headpieces, sequins, bangles and beads casually strung up to be admired...the place oozes the femininity and refinement of an old-fashioned Parisian boudoir.

Galignani
Books

Map p104 (http://galignani.com; 224 rue de Rivoli, 1er; ⊙10am-7pm Mon-Sat; M Concorde) Proudly claiming to be the 'first English bookshop established on the continent', this ode to literature stocks French and English books and is the best spot in Paris for picking up just-published titles.

Antoine
Fashion

Map p104 (10 av de l'Opéra, 1er; ⊙10.30am-1pm & 2-6.30pm Mon-Sat; M Pyramides or Palais Royal–Musée du Louvre) Antoine has been the Parisian master of bespoke canes, umbrellas, fans and gloves since 1745.

Jamin Puech
Fashion

Map p104 (www.jamin-puech.com; 26 rue Cambon, 1er; ⊙noon-7pm Tue, 11am-7pm Wed-Sat; M Concorde) Among Paris' most creative handbag designers, Jamin Puech is known for its bold mix of colours, fabrics, leathers and textures – lots of beads,

Didier Ludot

pompoms, shells, feathers and so on. Its Cocotte handbag starred in *Sex in the City 2*.

Comptoir de la Gastronomie
Food, Drink

Map p108 (www.comptoirdelagastronomie.com; 34 rue Montmartre, 1er; ⊙6am-8pm Tue-Sat, 9am-8pm Mon; Ⓜ Les Halles) This elegant *épicerie fine* (specialist grocer) stocks a scrumptious array of gourmet goods to take away (particularly in the foie-gras department); it adjoins a striking art-nouveau dining room dating to 1894.

Librairie Gourmande
Books

Map p104 (www.librairie-gourmande.fr; 92 rue Montmartre, 1er; ⊙11am-7pm Mon-Sat; Ⓜ Sentier) The city's leading bookshop dedicated to things culinary and gourmet.

Lavinia
Food, Drink

Map p104 (www.lavinia.com; 3 bd de la Madeleine, 1er; ⊙10am-8pm Mon-Sat; Ⓜ Madeleine) Among the largest and most exclusive drinks shops is this bastion of booze with a top collection of *eaux-de-vie* (fruit brandies).

Legrand Filles & Fils
Food, Drink

Map p104 (www.caves-legrand.com; 1 rue de la Banque, 2e; ⊙noon-7.30pm Mon-Sat; Ⓜ Pyramides) Tucked inside Galerie Vivienne since 1880, Legrand sells fine wine and all the accoutrements: corkscrews, tasting glasses, decanters etc. It also has a fancy wine bar, *école du vin* (wine school) and *éspace dégustation* (tasting room) with several tastings a month; check its website for details.

Boîtes à Musique Anna Joliet
Gifts, Souvenirs

Map p104 (Passage du Perron, 1er; ⊙noon-7pm Tue-Sat; Ⓜ Pyramides) This wonderful shop at the northern end of the Jardin du Palais Royal specialises in music boxes, new and old, from Switzerland.

MORA
Homewares

Map p108 (13 rue Montmartre, 1er; ⊙9am-6.15pm Mon-Fri, 10am-1pm & 1.45-6.30pm Sat; Ⓜ Les Halles) Both amateur and professional pastry chefs will want to stop by MORA to pick up all manner of specialist culinary items, from unique cake and pastry moulds to macaron mats, pasta makers, piping bags and cream chargers (in case you're considering some fresh-baked éclairs back home).

Kiliwatch
Fashion

Map p108 (http://espacekiliwatch.fr; 64 rue Tiquetonne, 2e; ⊙10.30am-7pm Mon, to 7.30pm Tue-Sat; Ⓜ Étienne Marcel) A Parisian institution, Kiliwatch gets jampacked with hip guys and gals rummaging through racks of new and used streetwear. Startling vintage range of hats and boots plus art/photography books, eyewear and the latest sneakers.

Galerie Véro Dodat
HEMIS/ALAMY ©

Flâneurie

Parisian writer Charles Baudelaire (1821–67) came up with the whimsical term *flâneur* to describe a 'gentleman stroller of city streets' or a 'detached pedestrian observer of a metropolis'.

Paris' ornate arcades were closely tied to the concept of *flâneurie* in philosopher Walter Benjamin's Arcades Project (written between 1927 and 1940, and published posthumously). Known as *passages couverts* (covered passages), these marble-floored, iron-and-glass-roofed shopping arcades, streaming with natural light, were the elegant forerunners to department stores and malls.

The term *flâneurie* is now widely used, especially in the context of architecture and town planning. But Paris – with its village-like backstreets, its riverbank paths, parks and gardens, and its passages – remains the ultimate place for a *flâneur* to meander without any particular destination in mind.

Two of the finest *passages couverts*:

Passage des Panoramas (Map p104; 10 rue St-Marc, 2e; ⊙6am-midnight daily; Ⓜ Bourse) Built in 1800, this is the oldest covered arcade in Paris and the first to be lit by gas (1817). It's a bit faded around the edges now but retains a real 19th-century charm with several outstanding eateries, a theatre from where spectators would come out to shop during the interval, and autograph dealer Arnaud Magistry (at No 60).

Galerie Véro Dodat (Map p104; btwn rue Jean-Jacques Rousseau & 2 rue du Bouloi; ⊙vary; Ⓜ Louvre-Rivoli) For a quick taste of 19th-century Paris, it's hard to beat this shopping arcade, which opened in 1826 and retains its original skylights, ceiling murals, Corinthian columns and gas globe lamps (now electric). Bijou art galleries, jewellers, a music shop and furniture restorer fill its quaint shop fronts.

Kabuki Femme   Fashion
Map p108 (www.barbarabui.com; 25 rue Étienne Marcel, 2e; ⊙11am-7pm Mon-Sat; Ⓜ Étienne Marcel) Opened some 20 years ago, this is the shop that brought Barbara Bui to world attention. Her own eponymous store is next door and you'll find Kabuki for men two doors down. Judicious selections from other brands, too, including Prada, Balenciaga, Stella McCartney, Yves Saint Laurent and Dior.

Carrousel du Louvre   Shopping Mall
Map p104 (www.carrouselddulouvre.com; 99 rue de Rivoli; ⊙8am-11pm, shops 10am-8pm; 🛜; Ⓜ Palais Royal–Musée du Louvre) The Carrousel du Louvre is a shopping centre containing more than 30 shops (Apple, L'Occitane, Pylones) and a food court with more than a dozen restaurants. It runs underground from the Grande Pyramide to the Arc de Triomphe du Carrousel, the centrepiece is the Pyramide Inversée (inverted glass pyramid).

Montmartre & Northern Paris

A wellspring of Parisian myth, Montmartre has always stood apart. From its days as a simple village on the hill to its place at the centre of the bohemian lifestyle immortalised by Toulouse-Lautrec and other artists in the late 19th and early 20th centuries, the area has repeatedly woven itself into the city's collective imagination.

Today, of course, the area thrives on busloads of tourists, who come to climb the cascading steps up to Sacré-Cœur and wander through the alluring narrow hillside lanes. But even with the all the souvenir kitsch and milling crowds, it's hard not to appreciate the views looking out over Paris, or to find some romance relaxing in a backstreet cafe.

Back down at the foot of the hill is the rough-and-ready charm of the city's red-light district, a mix of erotica shops, striptease parlours, trendy nightspots and cabarets. If you take the time to wander, you'll find some unusual, less-touristy areas.

The Moulin Rouge (p142)

Montmartre &
Northern Paris Highlights

Sacré-Cœur (p128)

Once you've climbed the Butte de Montmartre (Montmartre Hill) and then the terraced steps of this very Parisian icon, climb a further 234 spiralling steps up inside the main dome – on a clear day, the view from the top is spectacular. Inside the basilica, the glittering mosaics and chapel-lined crypt illuminated by flickering candles also merit a look.

SENG CHYE TEO/GETTY IMAGES ©

Parc de la Vilette (p135)

Catch a performance at the Parc de la Villette, the city's largest cultural playground. Events span world, rock and classical music concerts, art exhibits, outdoor cinema, circuses and modern dance, while venues include the wonderful old Grande Halle (formerly a slaughterhouse – the Parisian cattle market was located here from 1867 to 1974) and giant yurt-like Cabaret Sauvage.

ADRIEN FAINSILBER/CHICUREL ARNAUD/HEMIS.FR/GETTY IMAGES ©

Musée Jacquemart-André (p138)

MASSIMO LISTRI/CORBIS ©

3

Step back into 19th-century opulence at this elegant residence-turned-museum. In addition to the exquisite furnishings and artworks, don't miss the Jardin d'Hiver (Winter Garden), with its marble statuary, tropical plants and double-helix staircase; the delightful *fumoir* (the erstwhile smoking room) filled with exotic objects; and the *salon de thé* (tearoom) – one of the most beautiful in the city.

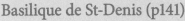

4

5

Basilique de St-Denis (p141)

For 1200 years the hallowed burial place of French royalty, St-Denis today is a vibrant multicultural suburb situated just a short metro ride north of Paris' 18e *arrondissement*. The ornate royal tombs, adorned with some truly remarkable sculptures, and the magnificent Basilique de St-Denis, whose construction dates from around 1136, are well worth the trip.

Cité des Sciences (p135)

If you only have time to visit one museum *en famille* (as a family), make it the Cité des Sciences. Here, kids from ages two and up can explore a variety of interactive exhibits including the brilliant Cité des Enfants' construction site, a TV studio, robots, and water-based physics experiments, all designed for children. Book sessions in advance to avoid grappling with gravely disappointed kids.

Montmartre & Northern Paris Walk

For centuries Montmartre was a country village filled with moulins (mills) that supplied Paris with flour. After it was incorporated into the capital in 1860, its picturesque charm and low rents attracted painters and writers, especially during its late 19th- and early 20th-century heyday.

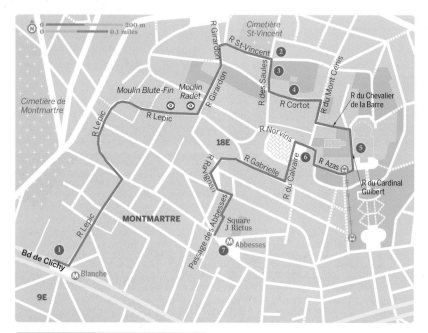

WALK FACTS

- **Start** Moulin Rouge
- **End** Metro Abbesses
- **Distance** 2.5km
- **Duration** Two hours

1 Moulin Rouge

Just west of rue Lepic you'll see the legendary **Moulin Rouge** (p142) cabaret beneath its trademark red windmill – it first opened as a dance hall in 1889. Uphill at 15 rue Lepic is **Café des Deux Moulins**, where Amélie worked in the eponymous film. Theo Van Gogh owned the house at **54 rue Lepic**; his brother, the artist Vincent, stayed

here for two years from 1886. Further north, two original windmills remain, the **Moulin Blute-Fin** and, about 100m east, the **Moulin Radet**. The Debray family, who owned both, turned them into a popular open-air dance hall Le Moulin de la Galette in the 19th century, which Renoir immortalised in his 1876 tableau *Le Bal du Moulin de la Galette* (displayed at the Musée d'Orsay).

2 Au Lapin Agile

Continue north into rue Girardon; descending the stairs you'll see **Cimetière St-Vincent**, the final resting place of artist Maurice Utrillo. Just over rue des Saules is the celebrated cabaret **Au Lapin Agile** (p142), whose name comes from *Le Lapin* *à Gill*, caricaturist André Gill's mural of a rabbit jumping out of a cooking pot on the western exterior wall.

③ Clos Montmartre

Opposite Au Lapin Agile is the **Clos Montmartre** vineyard, planted in 1933 to thwart real-estate development. Across rue des Saules is **La Maison Rose**, the famous subject of an Utrillo painting.

④ Musée de Montmartre

Turn left on rue Cortot; the **Musée de Montmartre** (p130) occupies Montmartre's oldest building, a 17th-century manor once home to painters Renoir, Utrillo and Raoul Dufy.

⑤ Sacré-Cœur

At the end of rue Cortot turn right (south) onto rue du Mont Cenis, left onto (tiny) rue de Chevalier de la Barre then right onto rue du Cardinal Guibert: the entrance to Paris' landmark basilica **Sacré-Cœur** (p128) is just south.

⑥ Place du Tertre

From the basilica follow rue Azaïs west, then turn north to the **Église St-Pierre de Montmartre**, built on the site of a Roman temple. Across from the church is the **place du Tertre** (p130). Cossack soldiers allegedly first introduced the term *bistro* (Russian for 'quickly') into French at No 6 (La Mère Catherine) in 1814. On Christmas Eve, 1898, Louis Renault's first car was driven up the Butte to Place du Tertre, marking the start of the French auto industry. Just off the southwestern side of the square is rue Poulbot, leading to the **Dalí Espace Montmartre** (p130).

⑦ Abbesses metro entrance

From place du Calvaire take the steps into rue Gabrielle, turning right (west) to reach place Émile Goudeau. Take the steps down and follow rue des Abbesses south into place des Abbesses. The glass-canopied **Abbesses metro entrance** is the finest remaining example designed by Hector Guimard.

 The Best…

PLACES TO EAT

Vivant Where else will you get to dine in a century-old exotic bird shop? (p139)

Cul de Poule Countryside produce meets city savvy at this neobistro. (p137)

Le Verre Volé Idyllic wine bar dining. (p139)

Le Miroir Stylish, creative bistro fare. (p137)

PLACES TO DRINK

La Fourmi This Pigalle stalwart has a dynamic energy both day and night. (p140)

Chez Prune Canal St-Martin's original and still coolest cafe. (p141)

ENTERTAINMENT

Parc de la Villette A host of venues, both indoors and out. (p135)

Point Éphémère Ubercool cultural centre, club and performance venue. (p142)

Chez Prune (p141)
PARIS CAFE/ALAMY ©

Don't Miss
Sacré-Cœur

Although some may poke fun at Sacré-Cœur's unsubtle design, the view from its parvis is one of those perfect Paris postcards. More than just a basilica, Sacré-Cœur is a veritable experience, from the musicians performing on the steps to the groups of friends picnicking on the hillside park. Touristy, yes. But beneath it all, Sacré-Cœur's heart still shines gold.

Map p132

www.sacre-coeur-montmartre.com

place du Parvis du Sacré-Cœur

dome adult/child €6/4, cash only

⊙6am-10.30pm, dome 9am-7pm Apr-Sep, to 5.30pm Oct-Mar

Ⓜ Anvers

The Basilica

It may appear to be a place of peaceful-ness and worship today, but in truth Sacré-Cœur's foundations were laid amid bloodshed and controversy. Its construction began in 1876, in the wake of France's humiliating defeat to Prussia and the chaotic Paris Commune, when workers overthrew the reactionary government and took over the city. The resulting battle for control was essentially a civil war, ending with mass executions, exiles and rampant destruction.

In this context, the construction of an enormous basilica to expiate the city's sins seemed like a gesture of peace and forgiveness – indeed, the seven million French francs needed to construct the church came solely from the contributions of local Catholics. Unfortunately, the Montmartre location was no coincidence: the conservative old guard desperately wanted to assert their power in what was then a hotbed of revolution. The battle between the two camps – Catholic versus secular, royalists versus republican – raged on, and it wasn't until 1919 that Sacré-Cœur was finally consecrated, even then standing in utter contrast to the bohemian lifestyle that surrounded it.

While criticism of its design and white travertine stone has continued throughout the decades (one poet called it a giant baby's bottle for angels), the interior is enlivened by the glittering apse mosaic *Christ in Majesty*, designed by Luc-Olivier Merson in 1922 and one of the largest in the world.

The Dome

Outside, some 234 spiralling steps lead you to the basilica's dome, which affords one of Paris' most spectacular panoramas; they say you can see for 30km on a clear day. Weighing in at 19 tonnes, the bell called La Savoyarde in the tower above is the largest in France. The chapel-lined crypt, visited in conjunction with the dome, is huge but not very interesting.

You can avoid some of the climb up to the basilica by taking the short but useful **funicular railway** (1 metro ticket; ⏰6am-midnight) or the **tourist train** (per person €6; ⏰10am-midnight Apr-Sep, to 6pm Oct-Mar), which leaves from place Blanche.

A Place of Pilgrimage

In a sense, atonement here has never stopped: a prayer 'cycle' that began in 1835 before the basilica's completion still continues around the clock, with perpetual adoration of the Blessed Sacrament continually on display above the high altar. The basilica's travertine stone exudes calcite, ensuring it remains white despite weathering and pollution.

WWII

In 1944, 13 Allied bombs were dropped on Montmartre, falling just next to Sacré-Cœur. Although the stained glass windows all shattered from the force of the explosions, miraculously no one died and the basilica sustained no other damage.

Montmartre & Northern Paris

↔ **Getting There & Away**

○ **Metro** Lines 2 and 12 serve Montmartre; lines 5 and 7 serve northeastern Paris (Canal St-Martin and La Villette). Further west, the museums in Clichy are accessed via line 2.

○ **RER** RER B links Gare du Nord with central Paris.

○ **Bicycle** There are quite a few Vélib' stations along the Canal St-Martin, including place République and 8 place Jacques Bonsergent.

Cimetière de Montmartre
BRUNO DE HOGUES/GETTY IMAGES ©

◉ **Sights**

Montmartre & Pigalle

Place du Tertre   Square
Map p132 (M Abbesses) It would be hard to miss the place du Tertre, one of the most touristy spots in all of Paris. Although today it's filled with visitors, buskers and portrait artists, it was originally the main square of the village of Montmartre before it was incorporated into the city proper.

Musée de Montmartre   Museum
Map p132 (www.museedemontmartre.fr; 12 rue Cortot, 18e; adult/child €9/5; ◷10am-6pm; M Lamarck–Caulaincourt) The Montmartre Museum displays paintings, lithographs and documents mostly relating to the area's rebellious and bohemian past. It's located in one of the oldest houses in Montmartre, a 17th-century manor home where over a dozen artists, including Renoir and Utrillo, once lived. Suzanne Valadon's restored studio was set to open here at the time of writing.

Dalí Espace Montmartre   Museum
Map p132 (www.daliparis.com; 11 rue Poulbot, 18e; adult/8-25yr €11.50/6.50; ◷10am-6pm, to 8pm Jul & Aug; M Abbesses) More than 300 works by Salvador Dalí (1904–89), the flamboyant Catalan surrealist printmaker, painter, sculptor and self-promoter, are on display at this surrealist-style basement museum located just west of place du Tertre. The collection includes Dalí's strange sculptures (most in reproduction), lithographs, and many of his illustrations and furniture, including the famous Mae West lips sofa.

Musée de l'Érotisme   Art Museum

Map p132 (www.musee-erotisme.com; 72 bd de Clichy, 18e; admission €10; ☺10am-2am; Ⓜ Blanche) The Museum of Erotic Art attempts to raise around 2000 titillating statuary, stimulating sexual aids and fetishist items to a loftier plane, with antique and modern erotic art from four continents spread out across several floors. Some of the exhibits are, well, breathtaking, to say the least.

Cimetière de Montmartre   Cemetery

Map p132 (☺8am-5.30pm Mon-Fri, from 8.30am Sat, from 9am Sun; Ⓜ Place de Clichy) Established in 1798, this 11-hectare cemetery is perhaps the most celebrated necropolis in Paris after Père Lachaise. It contains the graves of writers Émile Zola (whose ashes are now in the Panthéon), Alexandre Dumas (fils) and Stendhal, composers Jacques Offenbach and Hector Berlioz, artist Edgar Degas, film director François Truffaut and dancer Vaslav Nijinsky, among others.

Musée de la Vie Romantique   Museum

Map p132 (www.vie-romantique.paris.fr; 16 rue Chaptal, 9e; ☺10am-6pm Tue-Sun; Ⓜ Blanche or St-Georges) FREE This small museum is dedicated to two artists active during the Romantic era: the writer George Sand and the painter Ary Scheffer. Located at the end of a film-worthy cobbled lane, the villa housing the museum originally belonged to Scheffer and was the setting for popular salons of the day, attended by such notable figures as Delacroix, Liszt and Chopin (Sand's lover).

Institut des Cultures d'Islam   Cultural Centre

Map p132 (www.institut-cultures-islam.org; 19 rue Léon, 18e; ☺10am-8pm Tue-Sat; Ⓜ Château Rouge) FREE The Islam Cultural Institute, located in the heart of the Goutte d'Or neighbourhood, hosts concerts, poetry readings, film screenings and temporary art exhibits, generally related to North Africa or the Middle East. There's also a pleasant cafe on site. A nearby branch (56 rue Stephenson, 18e; ☺10am-9pm Tue-Sat, from 4pm Fri, noon-7pm

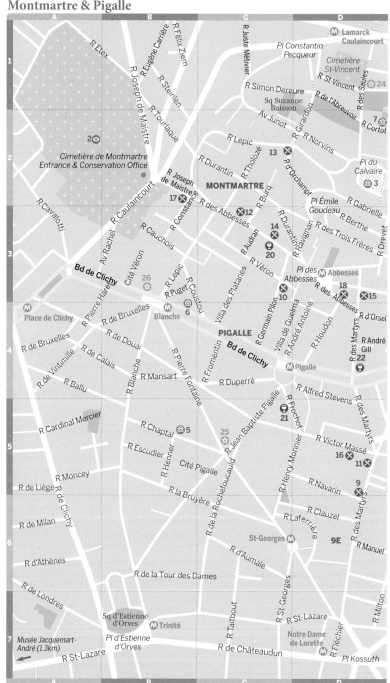

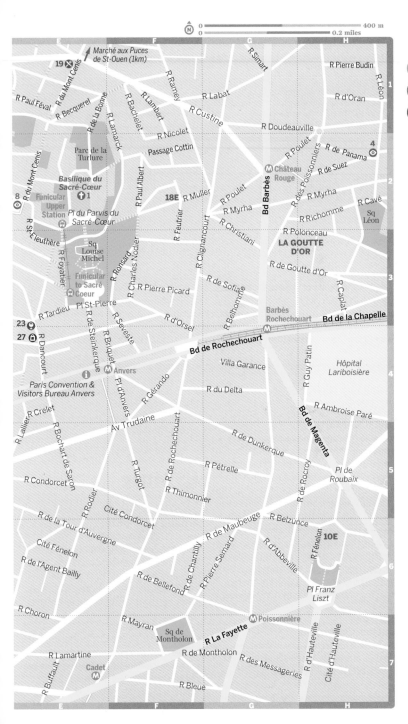

0   400 m
0   0.2 miles

Marché aux Puces
de St-Ouen (1km)

19

R Pierre Budin
R Léon
R d'Oran
R Simart
R Ramey
R Labat
R Custine
R Paul Féval
R du Mont Cenis
R Becquerel
R de la Bonne
R Bachelet
R Lambert
R Nicolet
R Doudeauville
R de Panama   4
R Poulet   R de Suez
Passage Cottin
Parc de la
Turlure
R du Mont Cenis
Château
Rouge
Bd Barbès
R des Poissonniers
Basilique du
Sacré-Cœur   1
18E   R Muller
R Paul Albert
R Poulet
R Myrha
R Cavé
Funicular
Upper
Station
Pl du Parvis du
Sacré-Cœur
R Feutrier
R Christiani
R Richomme   Sq
Léon
R St-Eleuthère
R Foyatier
R Ronsard
R Charles Nodier
R Clignancourt
R Polonceau
LA GOUTTE
D'OR
Sq
Louise
Michel
R de Sofia
R de Goutte d'Or
Funicular
to Sacré
Cœur
R Pierre Picard
R Caplat
R Tardieu
Pl St-Pierre
R de Steinkerque
R Séveste
R de Sofia
R d'Orsel
R Belhomme
Barbès
Rochechouart
Bd de la Chapelle
23
27
R Dancourt
R Briquet
Anvers
Pl d'Anvers
M
Bd de Rochechouart
Villa Garance
R Guy Patin
Hôpital
Lariboisière
Paris Convention &
Visitors Bureau Anvers
R Gérando
R du Delta
R Lallier
R Crelet
Av Trudaine
R Ambroise Paré
Bd de Magenta
R Bochart de Saron
R de Rochechouart
R de Dunkerque
R Condorcet
R Turgot
R Pétrelle
Pl de
Roubaix
R Rodier
R Thimonnier
R de Rocroy
R de la Tour d'Auvergne
Cité Condorcet
Cité Fénelon
R de Maubeuge
R Belzunce
10E
R de l'Agent Bailly
R de Chantilly
R Pierre Semard
R d'Abbeville
R Fénelon
R Choron
R de Bellefond
Pl Franz
Liszt
R Mayran
Poissonnière
M
R Lamartine
Sq de
Montholon
R La Fayette
R d'Hauteville
Cité d'Hauteville
R Buffault
Cadet
M
R de Montholon
R des Messageries
R Bleue

Montmartre & Pigalle

Sun; Ⓜ Marx Dormoy or Château Rouge) FREE, opened in 2013, holds more temporary exhibition space as well as a **hammam** (☏ 01 42 58 02 02; www.azharspa.fr; 56 rue Stéphenson, 18e; ⏱ women 10am-9pm Tue-Thu & Sat, men 4-9pm Fri & noon-7pm Sun; Ⓜ Marx Dormoy or Château Rouge).

Gare du Nord & Canal St-Martin

Canal St-Martin   Park
Map p136 (Ⓜ République, Jaurès or Jacques Bonsergent) The tranquil, 4.5km-long Canal St-Martin was inaugurated in 1825 to provide a shipping link between the Seine and the northeastern Parisian suburbs. Emerging from below ground near place République, its shaded towpaths take you past locks, metal bridges and ordinary Parisian neighbourhoods. It's a great place for a romantic stroll or cycle.

Note that some of the neighbourhood bistros here are closed or have limited opening hours on Sunday and Monday.

Parc des Buttes-Chaumont   Park
(rue Manin & rue Botzaris, 19e; ⏱ 7am-10pm May-Sep, to 8pm Oct-Apr; Ⓜ Buttes Chaumont or Botzaris) This quirky park is one of the city's largest green spaces; its landscaped slopes hide grottoes, waterfalls, a lake and

even an island topped with a temple to Sybil. Once a gypsum quarry and rubbish dump, it was given its present form by Baron Haussmann in time for the opening of the 1867 Exposition Universelle.

It's a favourite with Parisians, who come here to practise tai chi, take the kids to a puppet show or simply to relax with a bottle of wine and a picnic dinner. The tracks of an abandoned 19th-century railway line (La Petite Ceinture, which once circled Paris) also run through the park.

✗ Eating

Montmartre & Pigalle

Arnaud Delmontel   Boulangerie €
Map p132 (39 rue des Martyrs, 9e; ⏱ 7am-8.30pm Wed-Mon; Ⓜ Pigalle) One of several Montmartre bakeries to win Paris' 'best baguette' prize in the past decade, Delmontel specialises in gorgeous pastries, cakes and a variety of artisanal breads.

Le Relais Gascon   Gascon €
Map p132 (☏ 01 42 58 58 22; www.lerelaisgascon. fr; 6 rue des Abbesses, 18e; mains €11.50-16.50, lunch/dinner menus €17.50/27.50; ⏱ 10am-2am; Ⓜ Abbesses) Situated just a short stroll from the place des Abbesses, the Relais Gascon has a relaxed atmosphere and

CARLOS SANCHEZ PEREYRA/JAI/CORBIS ©

⭐ Don't Miss
Parc de la Villette

The largest park in Paris, Parc de la Villette is a cultural centre, kids' playground and landscaped urban space at the intersection of two canals, the L'Ourcq and the St-Denis. Its futuristic layout includes the colossal mirror-like sphere of the Géode cinema and the bright-red cubical pavilions known as folies. Among its themed gardens are the Jardin du Dragon (Dragon Garden), with a giant dragon's tongue slide for kids, the Jardin des Dunes (Dunes Garden) and Jardin des Miroirs (Mirror Garden).

Cité des Sciences (📞 01 56 43 20 20; www.cite-sciences.fr; Parc de la Villette, 19e; adult/under 26yr €9/6; 🕐 10am-6pm Tue-Sat, to 7pm Sun; Ⓜ Porte de la Villette) is the city's top museum for kids, with three floors of hands-on exhibits for children aged two and up, plus two special-effects cinemas, a planetarium and a retired submarine. The only drawback is that each exhibit has a separate admission fee (though some combined tickets do exist), so you'll have to do some pretrip research in order to figure out what's most appropriate.

The **Cité de la Musique** (www.cite-musique.fr; 221 av Jean Jaurès, 19e; 🕐 noon-6pm Tue-Sat, 10am-6pm Sun; Ⓜ Porte de Pantin), on the southern edge of Parc de la Villette, is a striking, triangular-shaped concert hall whose mission is to introduce music from around the world to Parisians. The **Musée de la Musique** (Music Museum; adult/child €7/free; Ⓜ Porte de Pantin) inside displays some 900 rare musical instruments; you can hear many of them being played on the audioguide.

The **Philharmonie de Paris** (www.philharmoniedeparis.com; Parc de la Villette, 19e; Ⓜ Porte de Pantin) is the ambitious new home of the Orchestre de Paris, in the Parc de la Villette. It has an auditorium of 2400 'terrace' seats surrounding the orchestra. It's due to be completed in 2015.

NEED TO KNOW
www.villette.com; Ⓜ Porte de la Villette or Porte de Pantin

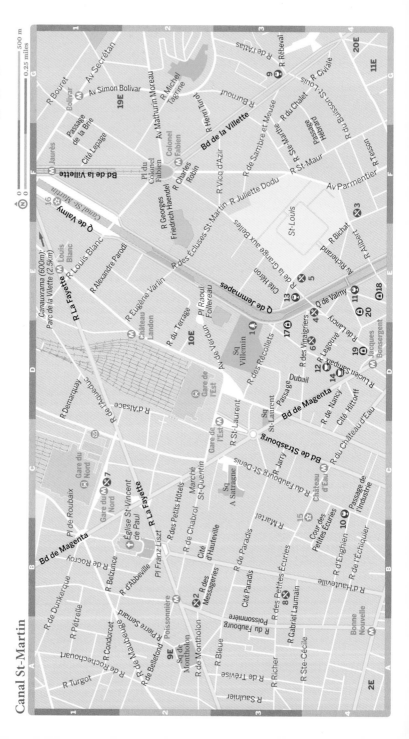

Canal St-Martin

authentic regional cuisine at very reasonable prices. The salads and *confit de canard* will satisfy big eaters, while the traditional *cassoulet* and *tartiflette* are equally delicious.

Another **branch** Map p132 (📞 01 42 52 11 11; 13 rue Joseph de Maistre; Ⓜ Abbesses) is just down the street. No credit cards at the main restaurant.

Soul Kitchen   Vegetarian €

Map p132 (33 rue Lamarck, 18e; menu €13.50; 🕐 8.30am-6.30pm Tue-Fri, 10am-7pm Sat & Sun; 📶 📶; Ⓜ Lamarck-Caulaincourt) For a more typically residential Montmartre neighbourhood, head to the backside of the hill. There's plenty to discover here, such as this inviting vegetarian eatery housed in an old cafe, where you can pick up market-driven dishes that change daily, including scrumptious soups, quiches and lasagna.

Le Miroir   Bistro €€

Map p132 (📞 01 46 06 50 73; http://restaurantmiroir.com; 94 rue des Martyrs, 18e; lunch menu €19.50, dinner menus €27-34; 🕐 noon-2.30pm & 7.30-11pm Tue-Sat; Ⓜ Abbesses) This modern bistro is smack in the middle of the Montmartre tourist trail, yet it remains a local favourite. There are lots of delightful pâtés and rillettes to start off with – guinea hen with dates, duck with mushrooms, haddock and lemon – followed by well-prepared standards like stuffed veal shoulder.

Le Pantruche   Bistro €€

Map p132 (📞 01 48 78 55 60; www.lepantruche.com; 3 rue Victor Massé, 9e; lunch/dinner menus €19/35; 🕐 12.30-2.30pm & 7.30-10.30pm Mon-Fri; Ⓜ Pigalle) Named after a nearby 19th-century theatre, classy Pantruche has been making waves in the already crowded dining hot spot of South Pigalle. No surprise, then, that it hits all the right notes: seasonal bistro fare, reasonable prices and an intimate setting. The menu runs from classics (steak with béarnaise sauce) to more daring creations (scallops served in a parmesan broth with cauliflower mousseline).

Chez Toinette   Traditional French €€

Map p132 (📞 01 42 54 44 36; 20 rue Germain Pilon, 18e; mains €19-24; 🕐 7-11.30pm Mon-Sat; Ⓜ Abbesses) The atmosphere of this convivial restaurant is rivalled only by its fine cuisine (seared duck with honey, venison with foie gras). In the heart of one of the capital's most touristy neighbourhoods, Chez Toinette has kept alive the tradition of old Montmartre with its simplicity and culinary expertise. An excellent choice for a traditional French meal.

Cul de Poule   Modern French €€

Map p132 (📞 01 53 16 13 07; 53 rue des Martyrs, 9e; 2-/3-course menus lunch €16/19, dinner €24/29; 🕐 noon-2.30pm & 8-11pm Mon-Sat; Ⓜ Pigalle) With plastic, orange cafeteria seats outside, you probably wouldn't wander into the Cul de Poule by accident. But the light-hearted spirit (yes, there is a mounted chicken's derrière on the wall) is deceiving; this is one of the most affordable quality kitchens in the Pigalle neighbourhood, with neobistro fare that emphasises quality ingredients from the French countryside.

GLENN HARPER/ALAMY ©

⭐ Don't Miss
Musée Jacquemart-André

If you belonged to the cream of Parisian society in the late 19th century, chances are you would have been invited to one of the dazzling soirées held at this mansion. The home of art collectors Nélie Jacquemart and Édouard André, this opulent residence was designed in the then-fashionable eclectic style, which combined elements from different eras – seen here in the presence of Greek and Roman antiquities, Egyptian artefacts, period furnishings and portraits by Dutch masters.

A wander through the 16 rooms offers an absorbing glimpse of the lifestyle and tastes of Parisian high society: from the library, hung with canvases by Rembrandt and Van Dyck, to the marvelous Jardin d'Hiver – a glass-paned garden room backed by a magnificent double-helix staircase. Upstairs is more art – an impressive collection of Italian Renaissance works by Botticelli, Donatello and Titian, among others.

After the tour, stop in at the **salon de thé** (11.45am to 5.30pm), which serves pastries as extravagant as the decor.

NEED TO KNOW

www.musee-jacquemart-andre.com; 158 bd Haussmann, 8e; adult/child €11/9.50; ⊘10am-6pm, to 9.30pm Mon & Sat during temporary exhibits; Ⓜ Miromesnil

---

La Mascotte Seafood, Cafe €€€
Map p132 (🕾 01 46 06 28 15; www.la-mascotte-montmartre.com; 52 rue des Abbesses, 18e; lunch/dinner menus €29/45, mains €23-39; ⊘8am-11.30pm; Ⓜ Abbesses) Founded in 1889, this bar is as authentic as it gets in Montmartre. It serves quality seafood and regional dishes (Auvergne sausage), but you can also pull up a seat at the bar for a glass of wine and a plate of charcuterie.

Le Coq Rico
Poultry €€€

Map p132 (01 42 59 82 89; www.lecoqrico.com; 98 rue Lepic, 18e; mains €22-39, whole roast chicken €95; noon-2pm & 7-11pm daily; M Abbesses) The first *haute cuisine* restaurant to open in Montmartre in years, Le Coq Rico specialises in poultry – and not just any poultry, but red-ribbon birds that have been raised in luxurious five-star chicken coops.

Gare du Nord & Canal St-Martin

Pink Flamingo
Pizzeria €

Map p136 (01 42 02 31 70; www.pinkflamingopizza.com; 67 rue Bichat, 10e; pizzas €11.50-17; 7-11.30pm Mon-Thu, noon-3pm & 7-11.30pm Fri-Sun; M Jacques Bonsergent) Not another pizza place? *Mais non, chérie!* Once the weather warms up, the Flamingo unveils its secret weapon – pink helium balloons that the delivery guy uses to locate you and your perfect canal-side picnic spot (GPS not needed).

Sunken Chip
Fast Food €

Map p136 (www.thesunkenchip.com; 39 rue des Vinaigriers, 10e; fish & chips €12-14; noon-2.30pm & 7-10.30pm Wed-Sun; M Jacques Bonsergent) Although it's hard to believe anyone would come to Paris in search of fish 'n' chips, it's hard to argue with the battered, fried goodness at this ideally located takeaway. Nothing frozen here: it's all line-caught fish fresh from Brittany (three varieties per day), accompanied with thick-cut chips (peeled and chopped *sur place*), malt vinegar and mushy peas.

Helmut Newcake
Cafe €

Map p136 (www.helmutnewcake.com; 36 rue Bichat, 10e; mains €7.80-9.80; noon-7.30pm Tue-Sat, to 6pm Sun; M Goncourt) Combining the French genius for pastries with a 100% gluten-free kitchen, Helmut Newcake is one of those Parisian addresses that some will simply have to hang on to. Eclairs, fondants, cheesecake and tarts are some of the dessert options, while you can count on lunch (salads, quiches, soups, pizzas) to be scrumptious and market driven.

Le Verre Volé
Bistro €€

Map p136 (01 48 03 17 34; 67 rue de Lancry, 10e; mains lunch €15-17, dinner €15-26; noon-2.30pm & 7-10.30pm; M Jacques Bonsergent) The tiny 'Stolen Glass' – a wine shop with a few tables – is just about the most perfect wine bar–restaurant in Paris, with excellent wines and expert advice. Unpretentious and hearty *plats du jour* (dishes of the day) are superb. Reserve well in advance for meals, or stop by to pick up a bottle.

Albion
Neobistro €€

Map p136 (01 42 46 02 44; 80 rue du Faubourg Poissonnière, 10e; mains €21-28; noon-2pm & 7-10.30pm Tue-Sat; M Poissonnière) Albion is the ancient Greek name for England and it's no coincidence that it's a mere five-minute jaunt from the Gare du Nord, and, what's more, run by two affable English speakers. But don't read into the name too much: this sleek new place is still very Paris, with bottles of wine lining one wall, waiting to be paired with the modern cuisine.

Terminus Nord
Brasserie €€

Map p136 (01 42 85 05 15; 23 rue de Dunkerque, 10e; mains €18.50-35.50, menus €28 & €34.50; 7.30am-midnight; M Gare du Nord) Directly across from the Gare du Nord, this landmark brasserie has a copper bar, wait staff in white uniforms, brass fixtures and mirrored walls that look as they did when it opened in 1925. Breakfast is available from 7.30am to 10.30am.

Vivant
Modern French €€€

Map p136 (01 42 46 43 55; http://vivantparis.com; 43 rue des Petites Écuries, 10e; mains €23-29; noon-2.30 & 7-10.30pm Mon-Fri; M Bonne Nouvelle) Pierre Jancou, the mind behind natural-wine bars like **Racines** (p113) and La Crèmerie, has moved on to his latest adventure set in a century-old exotic-bird shop, where simple but elegant dishes – creamy burrata, crispy duck leg with mashed potatoes, foie gras and roasted onion, an Italian cheese plate – are created to showcase the carefully sourced ingredients.

🍷 Drinking & Nightlife

Montmartre & Pigalle

La Fourmi   Bar
Map p132 (74 rue des Martyrs, 18e; ⌚8am-1am Mon-Thu, to 3am Fri & Sat, 10am-1am Sun; Ⓜ Pigalle) A Pigalle institution, La Fourmi hits the mark with its high ceilings, long zinc bar and unpretentious vibe. Get up to speed on live music and club nights or sit down for a reasonably priced meal and drinks.

Cave des Abbesses   Wine Bar
Map p132 (43 rue des Abbesses, 18e; cheese & charcuterie €7-13; ⌚5-9.30pm Tue-Sun; Ⓜ Abbesses) Pass through the door at the back of the Cave des Abbesses wine shop and you'll discover, no, not a storage room or a portal to another dimension, but instead a quirky little bar. It feels like one of those places only regulars know about, but don't be intimidated; sit down, order a plate of cheese and a glass of Corbières, and you'll blend right in.

La Machine du Moulin Rouge   Club
Map p132 (90 bd de Clichy, 18e; ⌚hours vary; Ⓜ Blanche) Part of the original Moulin Rouge (well, the boiler room, anyway), this club packs 'em in on weekends with a dance floor, concert hall, Champagne bar and outdoor terrace.

Glass   Bar
Map p132 (7 rue Frochot, 9e; ⌚7pm-2am; Ⓜ Pigalle) Pop into this old girly bar, tinted windows and all, for Brooklyn Brewery and Demury beers on tap, beef hot dogs, and punk rock on the stereo. With €4 half pints it's certainly no dive bar, however much it may look the part.

Le Progrès   Bar
Map p132 (7 rue des Trois Frères, 18e; ⌚9am-2am; Ⓜ Abbesses) A real live *café du quartier* perched in the heart of Abbesses, the 'Progress' occupies a corner site with huge windows and simple seating and attracts a relaxed mix of local artists, shop staff, writers and hangers-on. It's great for convivial evenings, but it's also a good place to come for inexpensive meals and cups of coffee.

Bread and Wine by the Gare du Nord

Yes, restaurant owners and chefs go out to eat, too. Charles Compagnon, owner of **L'Office** (p81), filled us in on his staff's top dining picks in Paris' burgeoning culinary hotspot, the 10e *arrondissement*.

○ **Le Grenier à Pain** They bake the bread we serve at L'Office. We really like *le pain de trois,* which is a kind of country bread that's made with three different types of flour. We also recommend their *gâteau basque* (a small round pastry filled with sweet almond paste).

○ **Vivant** This is a great restaurant. The quality of the products is simply outstanding and the atmosphere is really *charmant*. It's located in an old *oisellerie* (a place where exotic birds were raised and sold); the original faience tiling is still on the walls.

○ **Albion** We really like this restaurant because of the quality of the cooking and the diverse wine selection.

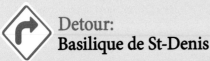

Detour:
Basilique de St-Denis

Once one of the most sacred sites in the country, the **Basilique de St-Denis** (www.monuments-nationaux.fr; 1 rue de la Légion d'Honneur; tombs adult/senior & 18-25yr €7.50/4.50, basilica free; ⊙10am-6.15pm Mon-Sat, from noon Sun Apr-Sep, to 5pm Oct-Mar; Ⓜ Basilique de St-Denis) was built atop the tomb of St Denis, the 3rd-century martyr and alleged 1st bishop of Paris who was beheaded by Roman priests. A popular pilgrimage site, by the 6th century it had become the royal necropolis: all but a handful of France's kings and queens from Dagobert I (r 629–39) to Louis XVIII (r 1814–24) were buried here (today it holds the remains of 42 kings and 32 queens).

The single-towered basilica, begun around 1136, was the first major structure in France to be built in the Gothic style, serving as a model for other 12th-century French cathedrals, including the one at Chartres. Features illustrating the transition from Romanesque to Gothic can be seen in the choir and double ambulatory, which are adorned with a number of 12th-century stained-glass windows.

The tombs in the crypt – Europe's largest collection of funerary art – are the real reason to make the trip out here, however. Adorned with gisants (recumbent figures), those made after 1285 were carved from death masks and are thus fairly life-like; earlier sculptures are depictions of how former rulers might have looked.

Gare du Nord & Canal St-Martin

Holybelly
Cafe

Map p136 (http://holybel.ly; 19 Rue Lucien Sampaix, 10e; ⊙9am-6pm Thu-Mon, from 10am Sat & Sun; Ⓜ Jacques Bonsergent) The largest and liveliest of Paris' new wave of barista-run coffee shops, this soulful hangout features distressed decor and a serious kitchen serving up breakfast and lunch, with a list of seasonal fruits and veggies scrawled on the blackboard in the brick-walled back room. Bonus: pinball machine.

Chez Prune
Bar

Map p136 (71 quai de Valmy, 10e; ⊙8am-2am Mon-Sat, 10am-2am Sun; Ⓜ République) This Soho-boho cafe put Canal St-Martin on the map a decade ago and its good vibes and rough-around-the-edges look show no sign of fading in the near future.

Café Chéri(e)
Bar

Map p136 (44 bd de la Villette, 19e; ⊙noon-1am; Ⓜ Belleville) An imaginative, colourful bar with its signature red lighting, infamous mojitos and caipirinhas and commitment to quality tunes, Chéri(e) is everyone's darling in this part of town. Gritty art-chic crowd and electro DJs Thursday to Saturday.

Le Petit Château d'Eau
Cafe

(34 rue du Château d'Eau, 10e; ⊙8am-2am Mon-Fri, 9am-5pm Sat; Ⓜ Jacques Bonsergent or Château d'Eau) Don't miss this unchanged-in-decades neighbourhood cafe (with cracked lemon-and-lime tiles, oversized mirrors, time-worn maroon-leather booths), where locals chat with staff over the zinc bar.

Hôtel du Nord
Bar

Map p136 (www.hoteldunord.org; 102 quai de Jemmapes, 10e; ⊙9am-1.30am; 🛜; Ⓜ Jacques Bonsergent) The setting for the eponymous 1938 film starring Louis Jouvet and Arletty, the interior of this vintage cafe feels as if it was stuck in a time warp with its zinc counter, red velvet curtains and old piano. Skip the food.

Chez Jeanette   Bar

Map p136 (www.chezjeannette.com; 47 rue du Faubourg St-Denis, 10e; ⏰8am-2am; Ⓜ Château d'Eau) Cracked tile floors and original 1950s decor have turned Chez Jeanette into one of the 10e's most popular hot spots. Local hangout by day, pints by night and reasonably priced meals around the clock.

Tuck Shop   Cafe

Map p136 (13 rue Lucien Sampaix, 10e; ⏰10am-5pm Tue-Fri, 11am-6pm Sat & Sun; Ⓜ Jacques Bonsergent) Superb coffee at this Aussie-run vegetarian hangout. Food is as affordable as it gets in Paris (€10 or under for a meal), though the space is small – getting a seat may require patience.

Entertainment

Montmartre & Pigalle

Moulin Rouge   Cabaret

Map p132 (📞01 53 09 82 82; www.moulinrouge.fr; 82 bd de Clichy, 18e; Ⓜ Blanche) Immortalised in the posters of Toulouse-Lautrec and later on screen by Baz Luhrmann, the Moulin Rouge twinkles beneath a 1925 replica of its original red windmill. Yes, it's rife with bus-tour crowds. But from the opening bars of music to the last high kick it's a whirl of fantastical costumes, sets, choreography and Champagne. Booking advised.

Au Lapin Agile   Cabaret

Map p132 (📞01 46 06 85 87; www.au-lapin-agile.com; 22 rue des Saules, 18e; adult €28, student except Sat €20; ⏰9pm-1am Tue-Sun; Ⓜ Lamarck-Caulaincourt) This rustic cabaret venue was favoured by artists and intellectuals in the early 20th century and traditional *chansons* (songs) are still performed here. The four-hour show starts at 9.30pm and includes singing and poetry. Some love it, others feel it's a bit of a trap.

Bus Palladium   Live Music

Map p132 (www.lebuspalladium.com; 6 rue Pierre Fontaine, 9e; ⏰hours vary; Ⓜ Blanche) Once the place to be back in the 1960s, the Bus is now back in business 50 years later, with funky DJs and a mixed bag of performances by indie and pop groups.

Gare du Nord & Canal St-Martin

Point Éphémère   Live Music

Map p136 (www.pointephemere.org; 200 quai de Valmy, 10e; ⏰12.30pm-2am Mon-Sat, 12.30-11pm Sun; 📶; Ⓜ Louis Blanc) This arts and music venue by the Canal St-Martin attracts an underground crowd from noon till past midnight, for drinks, meals, concerts, dance nights and even art exhibitions. At the time of writing there were three different food trucks setting up shop here three days a week after 7pm.

Rosa Bonheur   Dance Hall

(www.rosabonheur.fr; Parc des Buttes Chaumont, 19e; ⏰noon-midnight Wed-Sun; Ⓜ Botzaris) This self-styled *guinguette* (old-fashioned dance hall) morphs from outdoor cafe by day into a jam-packed dance floor by night. Its setting inside the Parc des Buttes Chaumont is surely the most bucolic getaway in the city, and even if the tapas aren't to die for, good vibes are virtually guaranteed. If the park is closed, you'll need to enter at 7 rue Botzaris.

New Morning   Jazz, Blues

Map p136 (www.newmorning.com; 7-9 rue des Petites Écuries, 10e; ⏰hours vary; Ⓜ Château d'Eau) New Morning is a highly regarded auditorium with excellent acoustics that hosts big-name jazz concerts (Ravi Coltrane, Lake Street Dive) as well as a variety of blues, rock, funk, salsa, Afro-Cuban and Brazilian music.

🔒 Shopping

Montmartre & Pigalle

La Citadelle Fashion, Accessories

Map p132 (1 rue des Trois Frères, 18e; ⏱10am-7pm; Ⓜ Abbesses) This designer discount shop hidden away in Montmartre has some real finds from new French, Italian and Japanese designers. Look out for such labels as Les Chemins Blancs and Yoshi Kondo.

Gare du Nord & Canal St-Martin

Liza Korn Fashion

(19 rue Beaurepaire, 10e; ⏱11.30am-7.30pm Mon-Sat; Ⓜ Jacques Bonsergent) From rock 'n' roll fashion to a new children's line, this designer's tiny boutique is a portal into a rich and playful imagination.

La Crèmerie Cheese

Map p136 (41 rue de Lancry, 10e; ⏱9.30am-1pm Mon, 9.30am-1.30pm & 4-8pm Tue-Sat; Ⓜ Jacques Bonsergeant) If you're in need of supplies for a picnic on the canal quays, pop into local deli La Crèmerie for heavenly cheeses (brie with truffles, soft goat cheese rolled in raisins), cured ham, saucisson, and housemade jams.

Maje Fashion, Accessories

Map p136 (6 rue de Marseille, 10e; ⏱11am-8pm Mon-Sat, 1.30-7.30pm Sun; Ⓜ Jacques Bonsergent) A Parisian prêt-à-porter brand featured regularly on the pages of *Elle, Glamour* and *Marie Claire,* Maje doesn't come cheaply – that is, unless you know about this outlet store, which sells most items at a 30% discount.

Antoine et Lili Fashion, Homewares

Map p136 (95 quai de Valmy, 10e; ⏱11am-8pm Tue-Fri, to 7pm Sun & Mon; Ⓜ Jacques Bonsergent or Gare de l'Est) All the colours of the rainbow and all the patterns in the world congregate in this wonderful Parisian institution with designer clothing for

Detour:
Marché aux Puces de St-Ouen

The vast **Marché aux Puces de St-Ouen** (www.marcheauxpuces-saintouen.com; rue des Rosiers, av Michelet, rue Voltaire, rue Paul Bert & rue Jean-Henri Fabre; ⏱9am-6pm Sat, 10am-6pm Sun, 11am-5pm Mon; Ⓜ Porte de Clignancourt) flea market, founded in the late 19th century and said to be Europe's largest, has more than 2500 stalls grouped into a dozen *marchés* (market areas), each with its own speciality (eg Paul Bert for 17th-century furniture, Malik for clothing, Biron for Asian art). There are miles upon miles of 'freelance' stalls; come prepared to spend some time.

women (pink store) and children (green store), and hip home decorations (yellow store).

Idéco Homewares

(19 rue Beaurepaire, 10e; ⏱11.30am-7.30pm Mon-Sat, 2-7pm Sun; Ⓜ République or Jacques Bonsergent) Pick up quirky knick-knacks and fun souvenirs at this idea-filled decor store. French recipe books, Eiffel Tower paper weights, Japanese trays, jewellery made from *bonbons* and all sorts of other weird and wonderful creations.

Frivoli Boutique

Map p136 (26 rue Beaurepaire, 10e; ⏱11am-7pm Mon-Fri, 2-7pm Sat & Sun; Ⓜ Jacques Bonsergent) Flip through colour-coded racks of cast-offs at this vintage boutique.

Le Marais & Bastille

Hip bars, boutiques, restaurants and the city's thriving gay and Jewish communities all squeeze cheek-by-jowl into this vibrant patch.

Paris' *marais* (marsh) was cleared in the 12th century, with grand aristocratic mansions built here from the 16th century onwards. Haussmann's reformations largely bypassed the area, leaving its tangle of medieval laneways intact. After falling from grace, the Marais underwent a revitalisation in the 1960s that hasn't stopped since, and it remains a see-and-be seen spot for a *soirée* (evening out) on the town.

The adjoining Bastille was a flashpoint for the French Revolution and is still the focal point of Paris' not-infrequent political protests. This longtime grassroots district now continues to boom alongside its intertwined neighbour as a pumping party hub. Above the Bastille, the raised Promenade Plantée walkway provides a peaceful retreat from the urban action.

Le Marais

Le Marais & Bastille Highlights

Musée Carnavalet (p157)

Take an elegant walk through the history of Paris, from prehistory to modern times, at the city's atmospheric Musée Carnavalet. It is secreted inside a twinset of richly furnished 16th- and 17th-century *hôtels particuliers* (private mansions): the mid-16th-century Renaissance-style Hôtel Carnavalet, home to the letter-writer Madame de Sévigné from 1677 to 1696, and the Hôtel Le Peletier de St-Fargeau, which dates from the late 17th century.

SONEP, SYLVAIN/HEMIS/CORBIS ©

Opéra Bastille (p158)

Although not as visually spectacular or palatial as the Palais Garnier, this opera house is the main opera venue in the capital. It features a 2700-seat auditorium with perfect acoustics and hosts some of the most ambitious opera productions in the city. Designed by the Uruguayan architect Carlos Ott, it was inaugurated on 14 July 1989, the 200th anniversary of the storming of the Bastille.

Place des Vosges (p152)

No square thrills Paris-hungry souls more than Place des Vosges, a triumph of symmetry and understated *bon goût* (good taste). Inaugurated in 1612 as place Royale and thus the oldest square in Paris, place des Vosges is a strikingly elegant ensemble of 36 symmetrical houses with ground-floor arcades, steep slate roofs and large dormer windows arranged around a large and leafy square.

3

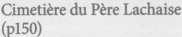

4

Cimetière du Père Lachaise (p150)

Pay your respects to the rich, famous and infamous at Cimetière du Père Lachaise. Gravestones in the world's most opulent cemetery read like a Who's Who of French history and the arts: some 800,000 deceased call this enormous necropolis home, including urchin sparrow Édith Piaf, rock legend Jim Morrison, writer Oscar Wilde and painter Eugene Delacroix.

5

Hôtel de Ville (p152)

Enjoy Paris for free with an art exhibition incorporating a Parisian theme inside the city's magnificent neo-Renaissance Hôtel de Ville. Paris' town hall rises from one of the city's busiest and best shopping thoroughfares, the rue de Rivoli. During winter, you can twirl on the ice at the open-air skating rink that sets up outside; summer often sees concerts and other events take place here. *Hall of Feasts*

Le Marais & Bastille Walk

Although the Marais district might be best known today for its hip shopping, dining and nightlife, this walk also takes you past many of the hôtels particuliers (private mansions) so characteristic of this neighbourhood, which are among the most beautiful Renaissance structures in the city.

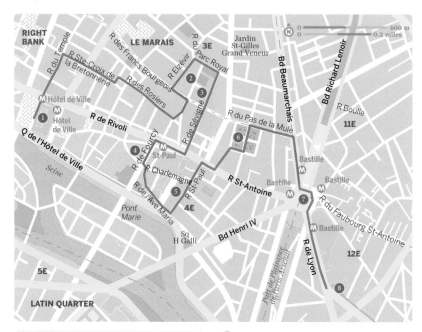

1 Hôtel de Ville

If Paris' statue-adorned, neo-Renaissance **Hôtel de Ville** (p152) looks familiar, it may be because photographer Robert Doisneau snapped his world-famous black-and-white portrait *Le baiser de l'hôtel de ville* (The Kiss at the Hôtel de Ville) here in 1950.

2 Musée Cognacq-Jay

Cross rue de Rivoli and walk up rue du Temple. Turn right at rue Ste-Croix de la Bretonnerie into the heart of the medieval Marais. Take a left on rue Vielle du Temple and right onto rue des Roisiers, in the **Pletzl**, and join the queue at **L'As du Fallafel** (p158). Continue left on rue Pavée, left on rue des Francs Bourgeois and right on rue Elzévier to reach the **Musée Cognacq-Jay** (p153) an exquisite collection of 18th-century art.

3 Musée Carnavalet

Turn right on rue du Parc Royal (**Hôtel de Vigny** at No 10 and **Hôtel Duret de Chevry** at No 8 date from around 1620). Past square Léopold Achille, turn right again on rue de

Sévigné where Paris' impressive, history museum the **Musée Carnavalet** (p157) is set back behind manicured gardens.

Maison Européenne de la Photographie

Continue south until turning right rue de Rivoli and left on rue de Fourcy. Despite the striking contemporary entrance to the European photography centre, the **Maison Européenne de la Photographie** (p153), the building dates from the early 18th century.

⑤ Village St-Paul

Turn left on rue Charlemagne, right into rue du Figuier and continue on to rue St-Paul. Past the quaint magic museum, the **Musée de la Magie** (p156), is the entrance to **Village St-Paul** (p174): five cobbled courtyards dotted with tiny boutiques.

⑥ Place des Vosges

The stone cloisters of this 1612-built ensemble of mansions (one of which houses the **Maison de Victor Hugo** (p152)) resonate with busking violinists and cellists, who provide an atmospheric soundtrack for browsing the arcaded galleries. In the centre of **place des Vosges** (p152) you'll see au pairs playing with their charges in the little gated park.

⑦ Place de la Bastille

Take rue du Pas de la Mule, passing the astonishing displays in the window of **Chocolaterie Joséphine Vannier** (p174) (such as chocolate shoes that look good enough to wear and far too good to eat), then turn right on bd Beaumarchais down to the historic site turned skirmishly busy roundabout at **place de la Bastille** (p158).

⑧ Promenade Plantée

Cross to rue de Lyon (the monolithic opera house **Opéra Bastille** (p158) is on your left) and follow it to the stairs leading to the **Promenade Plantée** (p158)– a disused 19th-century railway viaduct now planted with a fragrant profusion of cherry trees, maples, rose bushes and lavender, which stretches above the **Viaduc des Arts** (p173).

⭐ The Best...

PLACES TO EAT

Septime A beacon of modern cuisine. (p164)

Au Passage Creative bistro fare and back-alley simplicity combine for a devastating one-two punch. (p159)

Derrière Cheeky apartment-style venue for a sophisticated home-cookin' feel. Ping-pong table included. (p159)

Le Chateaubriand Some of Paris' most inventive cuisine is cooked up at this quintessential neobistro. (p164)

Le Petit Marché Traditional French fare with a fusion twist. (p161)

PLACES TO DRINK

Le Baron Rouge Wonderfully convivial barrel-filled wine bar. (p165)

Le Pure Café Still as quintessentially Parisian as Ethan Hawke's character found it in *Before Sunset*. (p165)

La Fée Verte Old-fashioned neighbourhood cafe specialising in absinthe. (p168)

La Chaise au Plafond An oasis from the frenzy of the Marais. (p169)

Le Barav Hipster wine bar in the Haut Marais. (p169)

Andy Wahloo Cool, multicoloured cocktail lounge. (p168)

Le Baron Rouge (p165)
HEMIS/ALAMY ©

Don't Miss
Cimetière du Père Lachaise

The world's most visited cemetery opened in 1804. Its 44 hectares hold more than 70,000 ornate tombs – a stroll here is akin to exploring a verdant sculpture garden. Père Lachaise was intended for Parisians, a response to local neighbourhood graveyards being full. It was groundbreaking for Parisians to be buried outside the quartier in which they'd lived.

Map p160

☎ 01 43 70 70 33

www.pere-lachaise.com

16 rue du Repos & bd de Ménilmontant, 20e

🕙 8am-6pm Mon-Fri, 8.30am-6pm Sat, 9am-6pm Sun

Ⓜ Père Lachaise or Gambetta

Jesuits Roots

Cimitière du Père Lachaise is named after Louis XIV's confessor, a Jesuit father known as Le Père La Chaise, who was resident on the estate where the cemetery is now located. The Jesuits bought the land in the 17th century but sold it a century later and in 1803 the land fell into city hands. Père Lachaise was built at the same time as cemeteries in Montmartre and Montparnasse, but Parisians, wary of entombing their dead so far from home, proved reluctant to purchase grave space here. It was only in 1817, after the remains of immortal 12th-century lovers Abélard and Héloïse were disinterred and reburied here beneath a neo-Gothic tombstone, that the cemetery really took off.

Famous Occupants

The only criteria to become a permanent resident of Cimitière du Père Lachaise was Paris residency; nationality did not matter, hence the cosmopolitan population of the city's most extravagant cemetery.

Among the 800,000 or so buried here include: the composer Chopin; the playwright Molière; the poet Apollinaire; writers Balzac, Proust, Gertrude Stein and Colette; the actors Simone Signoret, Sarah Bernhardt and Yves Montand; the painters Pissarro, Seurat, Modigliani and Delacroix; the *chanteuse* (songstress) Édith Piaf alongside her two-year-old daughter; and the dancer Isadora Duncan.

Oscar Wilde

One of the most visited graves is that of Oscar Wilde (1854–1900), interred in division 89 in 1900. The flamboyant Irish playwright and humorist proclaimed on his deathbed in what is now **L'Hôtel** (p292): 'My wallpaper and I are fighting a duel to the death – one of us has *got* to go.'

Jim Morrison

The cemetery's other big hitter is 1960s rock star Jim Morrison (1943–71), who died in a flat in the Marais at **17-19 rue Beautreillis** Map p154, 4e, in 1971 and is now buried in division 6. His tomb is something of a concern for the cemetery these days, however: a security guard had to be posted near the grave of the rock singer not long ago after fans began taking drugs and having sex on his tomb.

Mur des Fédérés

On 27 May 1871, the last of the Communard insurgents, cornered by government forces, fought a hopeless, all-night battle among the tombstones. In the morning, the 147 survivors were lined up against the **Mur des Fédérés** (Wall of the Federalists), shot and buried where they fell in a mass grave.

A Perfect City Stroll

For those visiting in Paris for its exceptional art and architecture, this vast cemetery – the city's largest – is not a bad starting point. It's one of central Paris' biggest green spaces, laced with 5300 trees and a treasure trove of magnificent 19th-century sculptures by artists such as David d'Angers, Hector Guimard, Visconti and Chapu. Many graves are crumbling, overgrown and in need of a good scrub and polish, but such is the nature of the cemetery's exquisite faded-grandeur charm. Consider the walking tour detailed in the photographic book *Meet Me At Père Lachaise* by Anna Eriksson and Mason Bendewald, or simply start with architect Étienne-Hippolyte Godde's neoclassical chapel and portal at the main entrance and get beautifully lost.

The cemetery has five entrances, two of which are on bd de Ménilmontant. Maps indicating the location of noteworthy graves are available for free from the **Conservation Office** in the southwestern corner of the cemetery.

Le Marais & Bastille

Getting There & Away

○ **Metro** Stops for the lower Marais include St-Paul (line 1), Rambuteau (line 11); for the Haut Marais, Temple (line 3) or Filles du Calvaire and St-Sébastien-Froissart (line 8); for Ménilmontant, Belleville (lines 2 and 11), Ménilmontant (line 2) or Oberkampf (line 5). Bastille metro station is a central hub.

○ **Bus** Bus 29 runs from rue des Francs Bourgeois to Bastille and Gare de Lyon; and bus 76 from rue de Rivoli to the 20e and Porte de Bagnolet.

○ **Bicycle** Handy Vélib' stations: 7 place de l'Hôtel de Ville; in Ménilmontant 81bis rue Jean-Pierre Timbaud or 137 bd Ménilmontant.

○ **Boat** Hôtel de Ville.

Houses around Place des Vosges
VISIONS OF OUR LAND/GETTY IMAGES ©

◉ Sights

Place des Vosges　　　Square
Map p154 (place des Vosges, 4e; Ⓜ St-Paul or Bastille) Inaugurated in 1612 as place Royale and thus Paris' oldest square, place des Vosges is a strikingly elegant ensemble of 36 symmetrical houses with ground-floor arcades, steep slate roofs and large dormer windows arranged around a leafy square with four symmetrical fountains and an 1829 copy of a mounted statue of Louis XIII. The square received its present name in 1800 to honour the Vosges *département* (administrative division) for being the first in France to pay its taxes.

Maison de Victor Hugo　　House Museum
Map p154 (www.musee-hugo.paris.fr; 6 place des Vosges, 4e; ⊙10am-6pm Tue-Sun; Ⓜ St-Paul or Bastille) FREE Between 1832 and 1848 writer Victor Hugo lived in an apartment on the 3rd floor of Hôtel de Rohan-Guéménée, overlooking one of Paris' most elegant squares. He moved here a year after the publication of *Notre Dame de Paris* (The Hunchback of Notre Dame), completing *Ruy Blas* while living here. His house is now a small museum devoted to the life and times of the celebrated novelist and poet, with an impressive collection of his personal drawings and portraits.

Hôtel de Ville　　　City Hall
Map p154 (www.paris.fr; place de l'Hôtel de Ville, 4e; Ⓜ Hôtel de Ville) FREE Paris' beautiful town hall was gutted during the Paris Commune of 1871 and rebuilt in luxurious neo-Renaissance style between 1874 and 1882. The ornate façade is decorated with

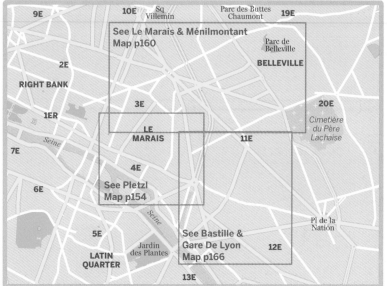

108 statues of illustrious Parisians, and the outstanding temporary exhibitions (admission free) held inside its **Salle St-Jean** almost always have a Parisian theme.

From December to early March, an ice-skating rink sets up outside this beautiful building, creating a real picture-book experience.

Musée Cognacq-Jay   Art Museum

Map p154 (www.cognacq-jay.paris.fr; 8 rue Elzévir, 3e; ⏰10am-6pm Tue-Sun; Ⓜ St-Paul or Chemin Vert) **FREE** This museum inside Hôtel de Donon displays oil paintings, pastels, sculpture, *objets d'art,* jewellery, porcelain and furniture from the 18th century assembled by Ernest Cognacq (1839–1928), founder of La Samaritaine department store, and his wife Louise Jay.

Although Cognacq appreciated little of his collection, boasting that he had never visited the Louvre and was only acquiring collections for the status, the artwork and *objets d'art* give a good idea of upper-class tastes during the Age of Enlightenment.

Musée des Arts et Métiers   Museum

Map p160 (www.arts-et-metiers.net; 60 rue de Réaumur, 3e; adult/child €6.50/free; ⏰10am-6pm Tue, Wed & Fri-Sun, to 9.30pm Thu; Ⓜ Arts et Métiers) The Arts & Crafts Museum, dating to 1794 and Europe's oldest science and technology museum, is a must for anyone with kids – or an interest in how things tick or work. Housed inside the sublime 18th-century priory of St-Martin des Champs, some 3000 instruments, machines and working models from the 18th to 20th centuries are displayed across three floors. In the attached church of St-Martin des Champs is Foucault's original pendulum, introduced to the world at the Universal Exhibition in Paris in 1855.

Maison Européenne de la Photographie   Museum

Map p154 (www.mep-fr.org; 5-7 rue de Fourcy, 4e; adult/child €8/4.50; ⏰11am-7.45pm Wed-Sun; Ⓜ St-Paul or Pont Marie) The European House of Photography, housed in the overly renovated Hôtel Hénault de Cantorbe (dating – believe it or not – from the early 18th century), has cutting-edge

Pletzl

LE MARAIS & BASTILLE

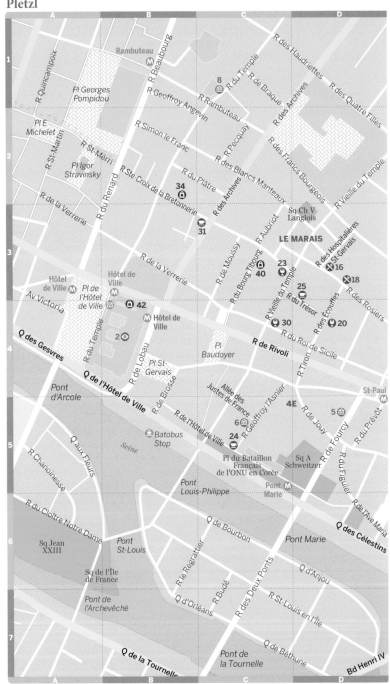

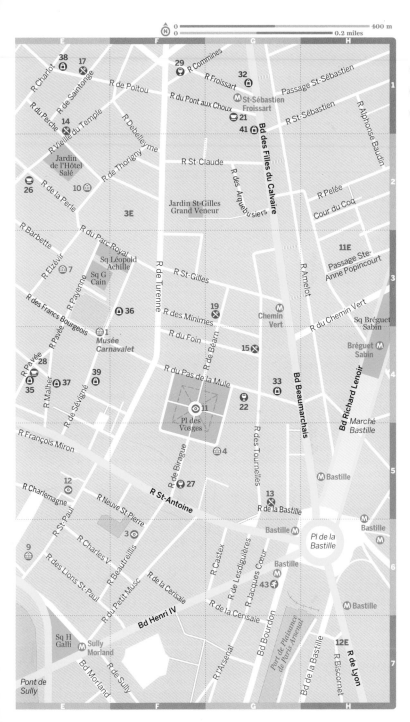

0
N
0

400 m
0.2 miles

38
17
R Charlot
R de Saintonge
R de Poitou

29
R Commines
R Froissart
32

Passage St-Sébastien

R du Perche
R Vieille du Temple
14
R Debelleyme
R de Thorigny

R du Pont aux Choux
21
41
Bd des Filles du Calvaire

M St-Sébastien
Froissart

R St-Sébastien

R Alphonse Baudin

Jardin
de l'Hôtel
Salé
10

R St-Claude

R des Arquebusiers

R Pelée

Cour du Coq

26
R de la Perle

3E

R Barbette
R du Parc-Royal

R Elzévir
7
Sq Léopold
Achille
Sq G
Cain
36

R des Francs Bourgeois
R Payenne
R de Turenne
R St-Gilles

R Pavée

1
Musée
Carnavalet

R des Minimes
19

11E
Passage Ste-
Anne Popincourt

R Amelot

M
Chemin
Vert

R du Chemin Vert

Sq Bréguet
Sabin

R du Foin
R de Béarn
15

Bréguet M
Sabin

28
35
R Malher
37
39

R du Pas de la Mule

33
22

R François Miron

11
Pl des
Vosges

4

Bd Beaumarchais

Bd Richard Lenoir

Marché
Bastille

R de Sévigné

R de Biragues
27
R St-Antoine

R des Tournelles

M Bastille

12
R Charlemagne
R Neuve St-Pierre

13
R de la Bastille

Bastille M

M
Bastille
M

R St-Paul
R Charles V
3
R Beautreillis

Bastille M

Pl de la
Bastille

9
R des Lions St-Paul
R du Petit Musc
R de la Cerisaie

R Castex
R de Lesdiguières
R Jacques Cœur
Bastille M
43

M Bastille

Sq H
Galli
M Sully
Morland

Bd Henri IV

R de la Cerisaie

Bd Bourdon

Port de Plaisance
de Paris Arsenal

Bd de la Bastille

12E
R de Lyon

R Biscornet

Pont de
Sully

Bd Morland
R de Sully
R l'Arsenal

Pletzl

temporary exhibits (usually retrospectives on single photographers), as well as an enormous permanent collection on the history of photography and its connections with France.

There are frequent showings of short films and documentaries on weekend afternoons. The Japanese garden at the entrance is a delight.

Musée de la Magie   Museum
Map p154 (www.museedelamagie.com; 11 rue St-Paul, 4e; adult/child €9/7; ⊙2-7pm Wed, Sat & Sun; MSt-Paul) The ancient arts of magic, optical illusion and sleight of hand are explored in this museum, in the 16th-century *caves* (cellars) of the Marquis de Sade's former home. Admission includes a magic show, and a combination ticket covering admission to the adjoining Musée des Automates – a collection of antique wind-up toys – is also available (€12/9).

Musée d'Art et d'Histoire du Judaïsme   Museum
Map p154 (www.mahj.org; 71 rue du Temple, 4e; adult/child €8/free; ⊙11am-6pm Mon-Fri, 10am-6pm Sun; MRambuteau) To delve into the historic heart of the Marais' long-established Jewish community in Pletzl (from the Yiddish for 'little square'), visit this fascinating museum inside Hôtel de St-Aignan, dating from 1650. The museum traces the evolution of Jewish communities from the Middle Ages to the present, with particular emphasis on French Jewish history. Highlights include documents relating to the Dreyfus Affair; and works by Chagall, Modigliani and Soutine. Creative workshops for children, adults and families complement excellent temporary exhibitions.

Musée Picasso   Art Museum
Map p154 (☏01 42 71 25 21; www.museepicassoparis.fr; 5 rue de Thorigny, 3e; admission €11; ⊙11.30am-6pm Tue-Sun, to 9pm 3rd Sat of month; MSt-Paul or Chemin Vert) One of Paris' most beloved art collections reopened

AA WORLD TRAVEL LIBRARY/ALAMY ©

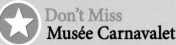

Don't Miss
Musée Carnavalet

This engaging history museum, spanning Gallo-Roman times to modern day, is in two *hôtels particuliers* (private mansions): mid-16th-century Renaissance-style Hôtel Carnavalet and late-17th-century Hôtel Le Peletier de St-Fargeau. Some of the nation's most important documents, paintings and other objects from the French Revolution are here.

Don't miss Georges Fouquet's stunning art nouveau jewellery shop from rue Royale, and Marcel Proust's cork-lined bedroom from his bd Haussmann apartment where he wrote his 7350-page literary cycle *À la Recherche de Temps Perdu* (Remembrance of Things Past).

NEED TO KNOW
Map p154 www.carnavalet.paris.fr; 23 rue de Sévigné, 3e; ⊙10am-6pm Tue-Sun; MSt-Paul or Chemin Vert

its doors after a massive renovation and much controversy in late 2014. Housed in the stunning, mid-17th-century Hôtel Salé, the Musée Picasso woos art lovers with 5000 drawings, engravings, paintings, ceramic works and sculptures by the *grand maître* (great master) Pablo Picasso (1881–1973). The extraordinary collection was donated to the French government by the artist's heirs in lieu of paying inheritance tax.

Mémorial de la Shoah   Museum
Map p154 (www.memorialdelashoah.org; 17 rue Geoffroy l'Asnier, 4e; ⊙10am-6pm Sun-Wed & Fri, to 10pm Thu; MSt-Paul) FREE Established in 1956, the Memorial to the Unknown Jewish Martyr has metamorphosed into the Memorial of the Shoah – a Hebrew word meaning 'catastrophe' and synonymous with the Holocaust. Exhibitions relate to the Holocaust and German occupation of parts of France and Paris

157

during WWII. The actual memorial to the victims of the Shoah stands at the entrance.

Place de la Bastille
Square

Map p166 (Ⓜ Bastille) The Bastille, a 14th-century fortress built to protect the city gates, is the most famous monument in Paris that no longer exists. Nothing remains of the prison it became under Cardinal Richelieu, which was mobbed on 14 July 1789, igniting the French Revolution, but you can't miss the 52m-high green-bronze column topped by a gilded, winged Liberty. Revolutionaries from the uprising of 1830 are buried beneath. Now a skirmishly busy roundabout, it's still Paris' most symbolic destination for political protests.

Opéra Bastille
Opera House

Map p166 (www.operadeparis.fr; 2-6 place de la Bastille, 12e; guided tours adult/child €12/6; Ⓜ Bastille) One of the late President Mitterand's pet projects, this 3400-seat venue was intended to strip opera of its elitist airs – hence the notable inauguration date of 13 July 1989, the eve of the 200th anniversary of the storming of the Bastille.

There are 75-minute **guided tours** of the building, which depart at wildly different times depending on the date – you'll need to check in at the **box office** Map p166 (☎ 01 40 01 19 70; 130 rue de Lyon, 12e; ☺ 2.30-6.30pm Mon-Sat; Ⓜ Bastille). Tickets go on sale 10 minutes before tours begin.

Promenade Plantée
Park

Map p166 (12e; ☺ 8am-9.30pm May-Aug, to 5.30pm Sep-Apr; Ⓜ Bastille or Gare de Lyon) The disused 19th-century Vincennes railway viaduct was successfully reborn as the world's first elevated park, planted with a fragrant profusion of cherry trees, maples, rose trellises, bamboo corridors and lavender. Three storeys above ground, it provides a unique aerial vantage point on the surrounding architecture. Access is via staircase – usually at least one per city block – and lift (elevator; although they're invariably out of service). At street

level, the **Viaduc des Arts** (p173) gallery-workshops run along av Daumesnil.

Eating

Candelaria
Taqueria €

Map p160 (www.candelariaparis.com; 52 rue Saintonge; tacos €3.20-3.75, quesadillas & tostadas €3.50, lunch menu €11.50; ☺ noon-midnight Thu-Sat, to 11pm Sun-Wed; Ⓜ Filles du Calvaire) You need to know about this terribly cool taqueria to find it. Made of pure, unadulterated hipness in that brazenly nonchalant manner Paris does so well, clandestine Candelaria serves delicious homemade tacos, quesadillas and tostadas in a laidback setting – squat at the bar in the front or lounge out back around a shared table with bar stools or at low coffee tables.

Marché aux Enfants Rouges
Market €

Map p160 (39 rue de Bretagne, 3e; ☺ 8.30am-1pm & 4-7.30pm Tue-Fri, 4-8pm Sat, 8.30am-2pm Sun; Ⓜ Filles du Calvaire) Built in 1615, Paris' oldest covered market is secreted behind an inconspicuous green metal gate – and for good reason. A glorious maze of 20-odd food stalls selling ready-to-eat dishes from around the globe, it is a great place to come for a meander and munch with locals. Grab a Moroccan couscous or Caribbean platter and consume at communal tables.

L'As du Fallafel
Jewish €

Map p154 (34 rue des Rosiers, 4e; takeaway dishes €5.50-8.50; ☺ noon-midnight Sun-Thu, to 5pm Fri; Ⓜ St-Paul) The lunchtime queue stretching halfway down the street from this place says it all. This Parisian favourite, 100% worth the inevitable wait, is *the* address for kosher, perfectly deep-fried chickpea balls and turkey or lamb shwarma sandwiches. Do as every Parisian does and takeaway.

CheZaline
Delicatessen €

Map p166 (85 rue de la Roquette, 11e; dishes €6.50-9; ☺ 11am-5.30pm Mon-Fri; Ⓜ Voltaire) A former horse-meat butcher's shop (*chevaline,* hence the spin on the name) is now a fabulous deli creating seasonally changing baguettes filled with ingredients like ham and house-made pesto. Other delicacies include salads and homemade terrines. There's a handful of seats (and plenty of parks nearby). Prepare to queue.

Le Clown Bar
Wine Bar €

Map p160 (☎ 01 43 55 87 35; 114 rue Amelot, 11e; mains €15-20; Ⓜ Filles du Calvaire) A historic monument next to the city's winter circus, the Cirque d'Hiver (1852), this unique address is practically a museum with its painted ceilings, mosaics on the wall, zinc bar and purist art decor style. A restaurant for decades, the mythical address was taken over in early 2014 by chef-sommelier duo Sven Chartier and Ewen Lemoigne.

Le Siffleur de Ballons
Wine Bar €

Map p166 (www.lesiffleurdeballons.net; 34 rue de Citeaux, 12e; lunch menu €14, mains €7-16; ⏱ 10.30am-3pm & 5.30-11pm Tue-Fri, 10.30am-11pm Sat; Ⓜ Faidherbe-Chaligny) With Tom Waits on the stereo and cacti atop the register, this contemporary wine bar has a dash of California in its soul. The wines, though, are all French – and all natural – and paired with a quality selection of simple but delicious offerings: *tartines,* soups, lentil salad with truffle oil, cheeses and Iberian charcuterie plates.

Gentle Gourmet Café
Cafe, Vegan €

Map p166 (☎ 01 43 43 48 49; www.gentlegourmetcafe.com; 24 bd de la Bastille, 12e; mains €14-19; ⏱ 11.30am-3pm & 6-11pm Tue-Sun; 🛜 🍴; Ⓜ Bastille) 🌿 If you've been overdoing the *steak-frites* in Paris, head here for a reprieve. All of its dishes are vegan and most are organic (tofu ricotta cannelloni, portobello-mushroom burger in sesame brioche buns, raw lasagne); there are also detox juices and teas. Large windows fill the cafe with natural light, but the best seats are on the terrace.

Breizh Café
Cafe €

Map p154 (www.breizhcafe.com; 109 rue Vieille du Temple, 3e; crêpes & galettes €4-12; ⏱ 11.30am-11pm Wed-Sat, to 10pm Sun; Ⓜ St-Sébastien Froissart) Everything at the Breton Café (*breizh* is 'Breton' in Breton) is 100% authentic, be it the Cancale oysters, the 20 types of cider, or the organic-flour crêpes cooked to perfection.

Chez Nénesse
Bistro €

Map p154 (☎ 01 42 78 46 49; 17 rue Saintonge, 3e; mains €19; ⏱ lunch & dinner Mon-Fri; Ⓜ Filles du Calvaire) 'Old-world bistro' is the atmosphere at this tiny spot with lace curtains and a quality kitchen that cooks classic French dishes that have been around for centuries. Its *salade de canard au vinaigre d'hydromel* (duck salad in honey vinegar) and sweet *medallions de veau au miel* (veal medallions pan fried in honey) are not to be scoffed at.

Au Passage
Bistro €

Map p160 (☎ 01 43 55 07 52; www.restaurant-aupassage.fr; 1bis passage de St-Sébastien, 11e; small plates €4-15; ⏱ noon-3pm Thu & Fri, 7.30pm-1.30am Mon-Sat; Ⓜ St-Sébastien Froissart) Spawned by talented Australian chef James Henry, who went on to open **Bones** (p161), this *petit bar de quartier* (neighbourhood bar) remains raved about. Pick from a good-value, uncomplicated choice selection *of petites assiettes* (small plates designed to be shared) featuring various market produce – cold meats, raw or cooked fish, vegetables and so on. Advance reservations essential.

Derrière
Modern French €€

Map p160 (☎ 01 44 61 91 95; www.derriere-resto.com; 69 rue des Gravilliers, 3e; lunch menus €25, mains €17-24; ⏱ noon-2.30pm & 8-11pm Mon-Sat, noon-4.30pm Sun; Ⓜ Arts et Métiers) Play table tennis, sit on the side of the bed, glass of champers in hand, or lounge between book cases – such is the nature of this restaurant with courtyard seating. Chilled vibe in a trendy 'shoes-off' style aside, Derrière (literally 'behind') is deadly serious in the kitchen. Classic French bistro dishes and more inventive creations are excellent, as is Sunday brunch.

Le Marais & Ménilmontant

500 m
0.25 miles

BELLEVILLE

R des Cascades
R des Pyrénées
R du Transvaal
R des Envierges
24
R Piat
Parc de Belleville
R de Belleville
R Jouye- Rouve
R Lesage
R de Tourtille
Ramponeau
PI A
Allais
Picabia
R du Pressoir
R du Moulin Joly
R de l'Orillon
R de la Fontaine au Roi
20E
Couronnes
Bd de Belleville
R Julien Lacroix
R Étienne Dolet
R de Ménilmontant
Ménilmontant
R des Amandiers
R du Tlemcen
R Duris
R de Panoyaux
Père Lachaise
Bd de Ménilmontant

Cimetière du
Père Lachaise
1
Cimetière du
Père Lachaise
Conservation
Office
Bd de
Ménilmontant
R de la Folie
Regnault
R Durant
Sq de la
Roquette

19E
Belleville
Bd de la Villette
R St-Louis
R du Faubourg du Temple
21
R Darboy
R Moret
R St-Maur
13
23
R Oberkampf
Av Jean Aicard
R des Bluets
Av de la République
R Servan
R St-Maur
R du Chemin Vert
St-Maur
26
Av Parmentier
Sq Maurice
Gardette
St-Ambroise
Bd Voltaire

R St-Maur
R du Buisson
Av Claude
Vellefaux
St-Louis
R Bichat
Q de Jemmapes
Q de Valmy
Canal St-Martin
9
Goncourt
R de la Pierre Levée
Av Parmentier
R Jean-Pierre Timbaud
11E
Parmentier
Bd Jules Ferry
4
R Gambey
12
R de la Folie Méricourt
Bd Richard Lenoir
25
R Ténaux
Bd Richard Lenoir
Besson
Passage
St-Ambroise
Av Parmentier
R St-Sébastien
Richard
Lenoir
Bd Voltaire

R des Vinaigriers
R de Landry
Jacques
Bonsergent
PI J
Strauss
10E
R Beaurepaire
Sq J
Ferry
18
R de Malte
Av de la
République
Bd Voltaire
Bd du Temple
République
Oberkampf
R de Crussol
10
20
R Oberkampf
R Amelot
R du Pont
aux Choux
3
passage
St-Sébastien
17
19
R St-Sébastien

Château
d'Eau
Strasbourg
St-Denis
Bd de
Strasbourg
R du Faubourg St-Martin
R St-Martin
Bd St-Martin
R du Château d'Eau
Bd de Magenta
PI J
Strauss
République
Sq H
Christiné
PI de la
République
R Béranger
15
R Dupuis
R Dupetit Thouars
5
22
Sq du
Temple
Temple
Perrée Forez
R de Bretagne
11
Filles du
Calvaire
27
28
R de Saintonge
R Charlot
R Portefoin
8
R de
Poitou
R du Temple
Filles-du-Calvaire
6
St-Sébastien
Froissart
R des
Fils

Réaumur
Sébastopol
Sq Emile
Chautemps
2
Arts et
Métiers
R Notre Dame de Nazareth
R du Vertbois
R de Turbigo
R Meslay
R Réaumur
3E
R Réaumur
16
R au Maire
R des Gravilliers
7
R Chapon
R de Montmorency
Centre Gai et
Lesbien de Paris
14
Île de France
Rambuteau
4E
R Beaubourg
R Rambuteau
R du Temple
R Pastourelle
R des Archives

Réaumur
Sébastopol
2E
Bd de
Sébastopol
St-Martin
R de Turenne

Le Marais & Ménilmontant

Le 6 Paul Bert
Bistro €€

Map p166 (☎01 43 79 14 32; 6 rue Paul Bert, 12e; 2-/3-course lunch menus €15/19, 4-course dinner menu €44; ⊙noon-2pm Tue, noon-2pm & 7.30-11pm Wed-Sat; Ⓜ Faidherbe-Chaligny) Opened by Bertrand Auboyneau of neighbouring **Bistrot Paul Bert** (p162) and Québecois chef Louis-Philippe Riel, Le 6 serves mindblowing multicourse menus of small(ish) plates. The exquisitely prepared and presented creations from Riel's open kitchen change daily but invariably involve unexpected flavour combinations (quail/turnip, asparagus/monkfish, artichoke/white chocolate).

Bones
Bistro €€

Map p166 (☎09 80 75 32 08; www.bonesparis. com; 43 rue Godefroy Cavaignac, 11e; bar dishes €4-16, 4-/5-course menus €47/55; ⊙kitchen 7-11pm Tue-Sat; Ⓜ Voltaire) Even if you don't score a first-service (7pm to 7.30pm) reservation for red-hot Australian chef James Henry's stripped-back new premises, you have a couple of back-up options. The second service (9.30pm to 10.30pm) is walk-in only. Or you can order Henry's signature small plates (smoked oyster, beef heart, sea-bass carpaccio, house-cured charcuterie) at the lively bar.

Le Petit Marché
Bistro €€

Map p154 (☎01 42 72 06 67; 9 rue de Béarn, 3e; mains €18-26; ⊙noon-4pm & 7.30-midnight; Ⓜ Chemin Vert) A faintly fusion cuisine is what makes this cosy bistro, footsteps from place des Vosges, stand out. Dishes such as raw tuna wrapped in sesame seeds or caramelised duck breast served with roasted bananas lend a welcome Asian kick to a menu that otherwise reassures with old French bistro favourites that have been around for centuries. Also has a summer pavement terrace.

Dessance
Desserts €€

Map p160 (☎01 42 77 23 62; www.dessance. fr; 74 rue des Archives, 3e; desserts à la carte €19, 4-course dessert menu €36-44; ⊙3-11pm Wed-Fri, noon-midnight Sat & Sun; 👶; Ⓜ Arts et Métiers) Dining at Dessance is unique. Only desserts are served – with an astonishing eye for detail and creative zeal for marrying unexpected ingredients (yes, broccoli, beetroot and roquette with chocolate and caramel). Whether you opt for the four-dessert menu or à la carte, a sweet *amuse-bouche* (appetiser) kicks off the experience and a plate of mini *gourmandises* (sweet things) ends it.

Broken Arm
Cafe €€

Map p160 (📱01 44 61 53 60; 2 rue Perrée, 3e; ⏰9am-6pm Tue-Sat, lunch noon-3.30pm; 📶; Ⓜ️Temple or Arts et Métiers) Kick off with a freshly squeezed apple, kiwi and mint juice and congratulate yourself on scoring a table – inside or out – at this overpoweringly hipster address where the chic folk of the Marais lunch after making an appearance in the adjoining concept store. The menu is limited but packed with goodness: excellent salads, cold platters and cakes.

Blue Valentine
Modern French €€

Map p160 (📱01 43 38 34 72; http://bluevalentine-restaurant.com; 13 rue de la Pierre Levée, 11e; 2-/3-course menu €29/36, 8-course tasting menu €54; ⏰noon-2.30pm & 7.30-11pm Wed-Sun, bar 7pm-2am; Ⓜ️République) This thoroughly modern bistro with retro decor in the increasingly gourmet 11e was a hit the moment it opened in late 2013. A hip crowd flocks here for well-crafted cocktails and Japanese chef Saito Terumitsu's exquisite dishes flavoured with edible flowers and a profusion of herbs. The menu is small – just three dishes to choose from per course – but memorable.

Yard
Modern French €€

Map p166 (📱01 40 09 70 30; 6 rue de Mont Louis, 11e; 3-course lunch menu €18, mains €15-18; ⏰noon-2.30pm Mon, noon-2.30pm & 8-10.30pm Tue-Fri; Ⓜ️Philippe Auguste) Opening to an atmospheric terrace near Père Lachaise cemetery, this bistro built on a former construction yard has been resurrected by chefs Shaun Kelly (previously of **Au Passage**) and Elenie Sapera (of **Bones** (p161)) working the open kitchen and tapas bar. Daily changing menus incorporate seasonal dishes such as spring lamb with leeks. Book ahead for dinner.

À la Biche au Bois
Traditional French €€

Map p166 (📱01 43 43 34 38; 45 av Ledru-Rollin, 12e; 7-10.45pm Mon, noon-2.30pm & 7-10.45pm Tue-Sat; ⏰3-course lunch menu €29.80, mains €17-22.50; Ⓜ️Gare de Lyon) Game, especially *la biche,* is the speciality of the convivial 'doe in the woods', but dishes like foie

gras and *coq au vin* also add to the ambience of being out in the countryside, as do the green awning and potted plants out front. The cheeses and wines are excellent, but top honours, game aside, go to the sensational *frites*.

Chez Janou
Provençal €€

Map p154 (📱01 42 72 28 41; www.chezjanou.com; 2 rue Roger Verlomme, 3e; mains €15-25; ⏰lunch & dinner daily; Ⓜ️Chemin Vert) Push your way in, order a kir from the jam-packed bar while you wait for a table, and revel in the buzz of this busy spot. Cuisine is as close as you get to Provençal in Paris, with all the southern classics like *brandade de morue* (salt-cod puree with potatoes), ratatouille and lavender-scented *crème brûlée*.

Bistrot Paul Bert
Bistro €€

Map p166 (📱01 43 72 24 01; 18 rue Paul Bert, 11e; 3-course lunch/dinner menus €19/38; ⏰noon-2pm & 7.30-11pm Tue-Sat; Ⓜ️Faidherbe-Chaligny) When food writers list Paris' best bistros, one of the names that consistently pop up is Paul Bert. The timeless vintage decor and perfectly executed classic dishes like *steak-frites* and hazelnut-cream Paris-Brest pastry merit booking ahead. Look out for its siblings **L'Écailler du Bistrot** Map p166 (📱01 43 72 76 77; 22 rue Paul Bert, 11e; mains €17-34, seafood platter €65; ⏰noon-2.30pm & 7.30-11pm Tue-Sat; Ⓜ️Faidherbe-Chaligny) (seafood) and **Le 6 Paul Bert** (p161) (small plates) in the same street.

Chez Paul
Bistro €€

Map p166 (📱01 47 00 34 57; www.chezpaul.com; 13 rue de Charonne, 11e; 2-/3-course lunch menus €18/21, mains €16-26; ⏰noon-3pm & 7pm-12.30am Mon-Fri, noon-12.30am Sat & Sun; Ⓜ️Ledru-Rollin) This is Paris as your grandmother would have known it: chequered red-and-white napkins, faded photographs on the walls, old red banquettes and traditional French dishes handwritten on a yellowing menu. Stick with the simplest of dishes and make sure you've booked ahead.

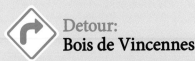

Detour:
Bois de Vincennes

A fabulous place to escape the endless stretches of Parisian concrete, the Bois de Vincennes also contains a handful of notable sights. Metro lines 1 (St-Mandé, Château de Vincennes) and 8 (Porte Dorée, Porte de Charenton) will get you to the eastern edges of the park. Pick up picnic supplies on rue de Midi, Vincennes' main shopping street.

Château de Vincennes (www.chateau-vincennes.fr; av de Paris, Vincennes; adult/child €8.50/free; ◷10am-6pm mid-May–mid-Sep, to 5pm mid-Sep–mid-May; Ⓜ Château de Vincennes) Originally a meagre 12th-century hunting lodge, this castle was expanded several times throughout the centuries until it reached its present size under Louis XIV. Notable features include the beautiful 52m-high keep (1370) and the royal chapel (1552), both of which are open to visits. Note that the chapel is only open between 11am and noon, and 2.30pm and 4pm.

Parc Zoologique de Paris (Zoo de Vincennes; http://parczoologiquedeparis.fr; cnr Daumesnil & rte de la Ceinture du Lac, 12e; adult/child €22/16.50; ◷10am-6pm Mon-Fri, 9.30am-7.30pm Sat & Sun mid-Mar–mid-Oct, 10am-5pm daily mid-Oct–mid-Mar; Ⓜ Porte Dorée) Reopened in 2014 after nearly a decade of renovations, Paris' largest, now state-of-the-art zoo focusses on the conservation of species and habitats, with camouflaged vantage points (no peering through fences). Its biozones include Patagonia, with sea lions to cougars; the savannah of Sahel-Sudan, with lions, white rhinos and giraffes; forested Europe, with wolves, lynx and wolverines; a Guiana rainforest with jaguars, monkeys and anacondas; and Madagascar, home to lemurs. Other highlights include Australian marsupials and manatees (sea cows).

Parc Floral de Paris (www.parcfloraldeparisjeux.com; Esplanade du Château de Vincennes or rte de la Pyramide; adult/child €5.50/2.75; ◷9.30am-8pm Apr-Sep, shorter hours rest of year; Ⓜ Château de Vincennes) This magnificent botanical park is one of the highlights of the Bois de Vincennes. Natural landscaping and a magnificent collection of plants will keep garden lovers happy, while Paris' largest play area (giant climbing webs and slides, jungle gyms, sandboxes etc) will absolutely thrill families. Open-air concerts are staged throughout summer, making it a first-rate picnic destination.

Bofinger
Brasserie €€

Map p154 (☏ 01 42 72 87 82; www.bofingerparis.com; 5-7 rue de la Bastille, 4e; menus €36.50-59, mains €22.50-46; ◷noon-3pm & 6.30pm-midnight; Ⓜ Bastille) Founded in 1864, Bofinger is reputedly Paris' oldest brasserie, though its polished art nouveau brass, glass and mirrors flags redecoration a few decades later. Specialities include Alsatian-inspired dishes such as *choucroute* (sauerkraut), oysters and seafood dishes. Ask for a seat downstairs and under the *coupole* (stained-glass dome)

Clamato
Seafood €€

Map p166 (www.septime-charonne.fr; 80 rue de Charonne, 11e; tapas €6-19; ◷7-11pm Mon-Fri, noon-11pm Sat & Sun; Ⓜ Charonne) Arrive early: unlike its raved-about sister restaurant and next-door neighbour **Septime** (p164), Clamato doesn't take reservations and you seriously don't want to miss out on Bertrand Grébaut and Théo Pourriat's seafood tapas. The menu changes daily but might include mussels with onion confit and saffron, baked razor clams with crushed peanuts and herb butter or octopus carpaccio with grapefruit pulp.

Le Cotte Rôti   Neobistro €€

Map p166 (☏01 43 45 06 37; 1 rue de Cotte, 12e; 2-/3-course lunch menus, 3-course dinner menu €39; ⏰noon-2.30pm & 8-11pm Tue-Fri, 8-11pm Sat; Ⓜ Ledru-Rollin) Contemporary cooking by Nicolas Michel and a chic charcoal-hued dining space ensure this under-the-radar restaurant won't remain so for long. *Menu* choices are explained to you in detail; mainstays include Michel's signature *épaule d'agneau confite* (shoulder of lamb cooked slowly in its own fat) and stunning desserts like pistachio soufflé. Be sure to book.

Chez Marianne   Jewish €€

Map p154 (2 rue des Hospitalières St-Gervais, 4e; mains €18-25; ⏰noon-midnight; Ⓜ St-Paul) Heaving at lunchtime, Chez Marianne translates as elbow-to-elbow eating beneath age-old beams on copious portions of felafel, hummus, aubergine puree and 25-odd other *zakouski* (hors d'œuvres; €14/16/18 for plate of four/five/six). Fare is Sephardic rather than Ashkenazi (the norm at most Pletzl eateries), not Beth Din kosher. A hole-in-the-wall window sells felafel in pita (€7) to munch on the move.

Septime   Modern French €€€

Map p166 (☏01 43 67 38 29; 80 rue de Charonne, 11e; menus lunch €28-55, dinner €58; ⏰7-10pm Mon, 12.15-2pm & 7-10pm Tue-Fri; Ⓜ Charonne) Reading the menu at newly Michelin-starred Septime won't get you far, as it looks mostly like an obscure shopping list (hanger steak/chicory/roots, chicken's egg/foie gras/*lardo*). And that's if you even get a menu – if you order the excellent five-course meal (available for both lunch and dinner), you won't even know what's being served until it arrives. Reserve in advance.

The alchemists in Bertrand Grébaut's kitchen are capable of producing some truly beautiful creations, and the blue-smocked waitstaff go out of their way to ensure that the culinary surprises are all pleasant ones.

For a pre- or post-meal drink, drop by its wine bar **Septime La Cave** Map p166 (www.septime-charonne.fr; 3 rue Basfroi, 11e; ⏰4-11pm Tue-Sat; Ⓜ Charonne). And for stunning seafood tapas, try its sister restaurant **Clamato** (p163).

Le Train Bleu   Brasserie €€€

Map p166 (☏01 43 43 09 06; www.le-train-bleu.com; 1st fl, Gare de Lyon, 26 place Louis Armand, 12e; menu €60-102, mains €27-46; ⏰kitchen 11.30am-3pm & 7-11pm, bar 7.30am-11pm Mon-Sat, 9am-11pm Sun; 🛜♿; Ⓜ Gare de Lyon) In all probability you've never – ever – seen a railway-station restaurant as sumptuous as this heritage-listed belle époque showpiece. This is a top-end spot to dine on such fare as foie gras with a confiture of red onions, grapes and hazelnuts, Charolais beef tartare, prepared at your table, and the house-made *baba au rhum*.

Le Chateaubriand   Neobistro €€€

Map p160 (☏01 43 57 45 95; 129 av Parmentier, 11e; menus €60-120; ⏰7.30-10.30pm Tue-Sat; Ⓜ Goncourt) Le Chateaubriand is an elegantly tiled, art deco dining room with strikingly imaginative cuisine. Basque chef Iñaki Aizpitarte is well travelled and his dishes show that global exposure again and again in its odd combinations (watermelon and mackerel, milk-fed veal with langoustines and truffles). Advance reservations are absolutely essential; if you don't have one, try your luck but only after 9.30pm.

🍷 Drinking & Nightlife

A lively mix of gay-friendly (and gay-only) cafe society and bourgeois arty spots, with an interesting sprinkling of eclectic bars and relatively raucous pubs, the Marais is a spot par excellence when it comes to a night out. Rue Oberkampf is the essential hub of the Ménilmontant bar crawl, springing from a few cafes to being the epicentre of a vibrant, rapidly expanding bar scene. But as Oberkampf commercialises, the arty/edgy crowd is moving steadily outwards, through cosmopolitan Belleville and towards La Villette.

Bastille invariably draws a crowd, particularly to heaving rue de Lappe.

Le Baron Rouge   Wine Bar

Map p166 (1 rue Théophile Roussel, 12e; ☺10am-2pm & 5-10pm Tue-Fri, 10am-10pm Sat, 10am-4pm Sun; Ⓜ Ledru-Rollin) Just about the ultimate Parisian wine-bar experience, this place has barrels stacked against the bottle-lined walls. As unpretentious as you'll find, it's a local meeting place where everyone is welcome and it's especially busy on Sunday after the **Marché d'Aligre** (p174) wraps up. All the usual suspects – cheese, charcuterie and oysters – will keep your belly full.

Le Cap Horn   Bar

Map p154 (8 rue de Birague, 4e; ☺10-1am; Ⓜ St-Paul or Chemin Vert) On summer evenings the ambience at this laid-back, Chilean bar is electric. The crowd spills onto the pavement, parked cars doubling as table tops for well-shaken pina coladas, punch cocos and cocktails made with pisco,

a fiery Chilean grape eau-de-vie. Find it steps from place des Vosges.

Le Mary Céleste   Cocktail Bar

Map p154 (www.lemaryceleste.com; 1 rue Commines, 3e; cocktails €12-13, tapas €8-12; ☺6pm-2am; Ⓜ Filles du Calvaire) Predictably there's a distinct nautical feel to this fashionable, uber-cool cocktail bar in the Marais. Snag a stool at the central circular bar or play savvy and reserve one of a handful of tables (in advance online). Cocktails are creative and the perfect partner to a dozen oysters or your pick of a dozen-odd, tapas-style 'small plates' designed to be shared.

Le Pure Café   Cafe

Map p166 (www.purecafe.fr; 14 rue Jean Macé, 11e; ☺7am-2am Mon-Fri, 8am-2am Sat, 9am-midnight Sun; Ⓜ Charonne) A classic Parisian haunt, this rustic, cherry-red corner cafe featured in the art-house film *Before Sunset*, but it's still a refreshingly unpretentious spot for a drink, cheese or charcuterie platters, fusion cuisine or Sunday brunch.

Chez Marianne

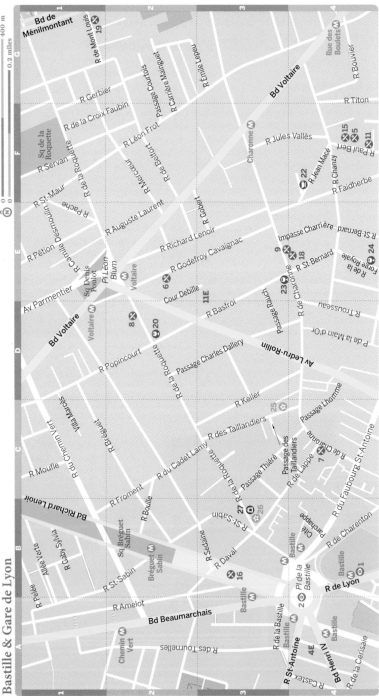

LE MARAIS & BASTILLE

Bastille & Gare de Lyon

400 m

0.2 miles

Bd de Ménilmontant

R de Mont Louis 19

R Gerbier

R de la Croix Faubin

Sq de la Roquette

R Servan

R St-Maur

R de la Roquette

R Pache

R Pétion

R Camille Desmoulins

Av Parmentier

R Léon Frot

R Merlin

R Narcisse

R de Belfort

Passage Courtois

R Carrière Mainguet

R Émile Lepeu

Bd Voltaire

R Titon

R Jules Vallès 15 5

R Chanzy 11

R Paul Bert

R Jean Macé

R Faidherbe

22

R St-Bernard

Impasse Charrière 24

R de la Forge Royale

R St-Bernard 9 18

R de Charonne

Charonne

R Auguste Laurent

R Richard Lenoir

R Godefroy Cavaignac 6

Pl Léon Blum

Sq Denis Poulot

Voltaire

Cour Debille

11E

R Basfroi

Passage Rauch

23

R Trousseau

P de la Main d'Or

Voltaire

Bd Voltaire

8 20

R Popincourt

R de la Roquette

Passage Charles Dallery

Av Ledru-Rollin

R Gobert

R Moufle

R du Chemin Vert

Villa Marcès

R Bréguet

R Froment

R Boulle

R du Cadet Lamy

R de la Roquette

Passage Thiéré

R des Taillandiers

R Keller 25

Passage des Taillandiers

Passage Lhomme

R de Lappe

7

R de Charonne

R du Faubourg St-Antoine

Bd Richard Lenoir

Allée Verte

R Gaby Sylvia

R Pelée

R St-Sabin

Sq Bréguet Sabin

Bréguet Sabin

R Sédaine

R St-Sabin 27 26

R Daval 16

Cité Parchappe

R de Charenton

Bastille

Bastille

Chemin Vert

R Amelot

R des Tournelles

Bd Beaumarchais

Bastille

R de la Bastille

Pl de la Bastille 2

Bastille

Bastille 1

R de Lyon

R St-Antoine

R Castex

Bd Henri IV

4E

R de la Cerisaie

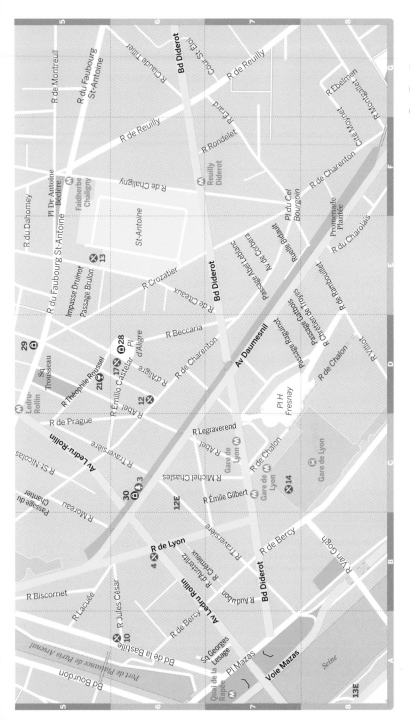

R de Montreuil

R du Faubourg St-Antoine

Bd Diderot

Cour-St-Éloi

R Claude Tillier

R de Reuilly

R Ebelmen

R Montgallet

Cité Moynet

R du Dahomey

Pl Dr Antoine Béclère

Faidherbe Chaligny

R de Reuilly

R Rondelet

R Etard

Reuilly Diderot

R de Charenton

R du Faubourg St-Antoine

R de Chaligny

St-Antoine

Pl du Cel Bourgoin

Promenade Plantée

R du Charolais

13

Impasse Druinot

Passage Brûlon

R Crozatier

R de Citeaux

Bd Diderot

R Beccaria

Passage Abel Leblanc

Av de Corbera

Ruelle Bidault

R de Rambouillet

29

Sq Trousseau

28

Pl d'Aligre

R de Charenton

Av Daumesnil

Passage Gatbois

Passage Ramoud

R Chrétien de Troyes

R de Chalon

P Yvillot

Ledru-Rollin

R Théophile Roussel

21

17

R Emilio Castelar

R d'Aligre

12

R Abel

R de Prague

Av Ledru-Rollin

R Traversière

R Legraverend

R Abel

R Michel Chasles

Gare de Lyon

Pl H Fresnay

R de Chalon

Gare de Lyon

R St-Nicolas

Passage du Chantier

R Moreau

Gare de Lyon

14

Gare de Lyon

30

3

12E

R Émile Gilbert

R de Bercy

P Van Gogh

R Biscornet

R Lacuée

R de Lyon

4

R d'Austerlitz

R de Crétinieux

R Traversière

Bd Diderot

10

R Jules César

Av Ledru Rollin

R de Bercy

Sq Georges Lesage

Pl Mazas

Voie Mazas

Seine

Bd Bourdon

Port de Plaisance de Paris Arsenal

Bd de la Bastille

Quai de la Rapée

13E

167

Bastille & Gare de Lyon

⊙ Sights
1 Opéra Bastille....................................B4
2 Place de la Bastille.........................A4
3 Promenade Plantée........................C6

✪ Eating
4 À la Biche au Bois B6
5 Bistrot Paul Bert F4
6 Bones..E2
7 Chez Paul..C4
8 CheZaline..D2
9 Clamato...E3
10 Gentle Gourmet Café A6
11 Le 6 Paul Bert..................................F4
12 Le Cotte Rôti....................................D6
13 Le Siffleur de Ballons.....................E5
14 Le Train Bleu....................................C7
15 L'Écailler du Bistrot F4
16 Marché Bastille...............................B3
17 Marché d'Aligre...............................D6

18 Septime E4
19 Yard G1

⊙ Drinking & Nightlife
20 La Fée Verte.....................................D2
21 Le Baron Rouge...............................D5
22 Le Pure Café.....................................F4
23 Septime La Cave.............................E3
24 Twenty One Sound Bar...................E4

⊙ Entertainment
25 Badaboum...C3
26 Le Balajo...B3
Opéra Bastille Box Office ....(see 1)

⊙ Shopping
27 La Manufacture de Chocolat B3
28 Marché aux Puces d'Aligre............D6
29 My Crazy Pop....................................D5
30 Viaduc des Arts................................C6

La Fée Verte   Bar
Map p166 (108 rue de la Roquette, 11e; ⊙8am-2am Mon-Sat, 9am-2am Sun; � >; Ⓜ Voltaire) You guessed it, the 'Green Fairy' specialises in absinthe (served traditionally with spoons and sugar cubes), but this fabulously old-fashioned neighbourhood cafe and bar also serves terrific food.

Le Pick-Clops   Bar
Map p154 (16 rue Vieille du Temple, 4e; ⊙8am-2am Mon-Sun; ⊙; Ⓜ Hôtel de Ville or St-Paul) This buzzy bar-cafe – all shades of yellow and lit by neon – has Formica tables, ancient bar stools and plenty of mirrors. Attracting a friendly flow of locals and passersby, it's a great place for morning or afternoon coffee, or that last drink alone or with friends.

Le Loir dans La Théière   Cafe
Map p154 (3 rue des Rosiers, 4e; ⊙9am-7.30pm; Ⓜ St-Paul) Its cutesy name (Dormouse in the Teapot) notwithstanding, this is a wonderful old space filled with retro toys, comfy couches and scenes of *Through the Looking Glass* on the walls. Its dozen different types of tea poured in the company of excellent savoury tarts and crumble-type desserts ensure a constant queue on the street outside. Breakfast and brunch, too.

Aux Deux Amis   Cafe, Bar
Map p160 (☎01 58 30 38 13; 45 rue Oberkampf, 11e; ⊙8am-2am Tue-Sat; Ⓜ Oberkampf) From the well-worn, tiled floor to the day's menu scrawled in marker on the vintage mirror behind the bar (two-/three-course lunch menu €18/22), Aux Deux Amis is the quintessential Parisian neighbourhood bar. It's perfect for a coffee any time and come dusk it serves tapas-style dishes. Friday brings the house special-ity – *tartare de cheval* (hand-chopped horsemeat seasoned with a secret mix of herbs).

Zéro Zéro   Bar
Map p160 (www.radiozerozero.com; 89 rue Amelot, 11e; ⊙7.30pm-midnight Mon-Sat; Ⓜ St-Sébastien Froissart) Zéro Zéro screams Berlin with its banquet seating and tag-covered walls (and ceiling, and windows, and bar...). Electro and house is the sound and the house cocktail, a potent rum-and-ginger concoction, ensures a wild party spirit.

Andy Wahloo   Cocktail Bar
Map p160 (http://andywahloo-bar.com; 69 rue des Gravilliers, 3e; ⊙7pm-1.45am Tue-Sat; Ⓜ Arts et Métiers) Casablanca meets pop-artist Andy Warhol in this cool cocktail lounge at home in a former *fabrique de chemises* (shirt factory). Its clever name

means 'I have nothing' in Arabic and is a major misnomer: think acid-yellow coloured decor, sweet cocktails, pushy staff and loud house music. Its courtyard is paradise for smokers and pullers.

Panic Room
Bar

Map p160 (www.panicroomparis.com; 101 rue Amelot, 11e; ⏰6.30pm-2am Mon-Sat; Ⓜ St-Sébastien Froissart) This brazenly wild bar is not quite as terrifying as its name suggests. A wildly flavoured cocktail – such as gin shaken with strawberries and basil, or a cognac-based creation mixing cucumber, coriander and ginger – is the thing to sip here, especially during happy hour (6.30pm to 9pm). Check its website for DJ sets, gigs and happenings.

Café La Fusée
Bar

Map p108 (168 rue St-Martin, 3e; ⏰8am-2am daily; Ⓜ Rambuteau or Étienne Marcel) A short walk from the Pompidou, the Rocket is a lively, laid-back indie hang-out with a red-and-white striped awning strung with fairy lights outside, and paint-peeling, tobacco-coloured walls indoors. You can grab simple meals here (€8 to €13), and it's got a decent wine selection by the glass.

Le Barav
Wine Bar

Map p160 (📞01 48 04 57 59; www.lebarav.fr; 6 rue Charles-François Dupuis, 3e; ⏰noon-3pm Mon-Fri, 6pm-12.30am Tue-Sat; Ⓜ Temple) This hipster *bar à vin*, smart in the trendy Haut Marais, oozes atmosphere – and one of the city's loveliest pavement terraces. Its extensive wine list is complemented by tasty food.

Boot Café
Cafe

Map p154 (19 rue du Pont aux Choux, 3e; ⏰8.30am-7.30pm Tue-Fri, 10am-6pm Sat; Ⓜ Filles du Calvaire) The charm of this three-table ode to good coffee is its façade - which must win the prize for 'most photographed'. An old cobbler's shop, the original washed-blue façade and 'Cordonnerie' lettering have been beautifully preserved, as has the fantastic red boot sign above. Excellent coffee, roasted in Paris, to boot.

Café Charbon
Bar

Map p160 (www.lecafecharbon.com; 109 rue Oberkampf, 11e; ⏰9am-2am; 📶; Ⓜ Parmentier) With its post-industrial belle époque ambience, the Charbon was the first of the hip cafes and bars to catch on in Ménilmontant. It's always crowded and worth heading to for the distressed decor with high ceilings, chandeliers and perched DJ booth.

La Belle Hortense
Literary Bar

Map p154 (www.cafeine.com; 31 rue Vieille du Temple, 4e; ⏰5pm-2am; Ⓜ Hôtel de Ville or St-Paul) This creative wine bar named after a Jacques Roubaud novel fuses shelf after shelf of good books to read with an excellent wine list and enriching weekly agenda of book readings, signings and art events. A zinc bar and original 19th-century ceiling set the mood perfectly.

La Chaise au Plafond
Cafe

Map p154 (10 rue du Trésor, 4e; ⏰9am-2am; Ⓜ Hôtel de Ville or St-Paul) The Chair on the Ceiling is a peaceful, bohemian cafe-bar with wooden tables outside, a fine wine

Coffee Revolution

Coffee has always been Parisians' drink of choice to kick-start the day. So it's surprising, particularly given France's fixation on quality, that Parisian coffee has lagged behind world standards, with burnt, poor-quality beans and unrefined preparation methods. But the city is in the throes of a coffee revolution, with local roasteries like **Belleville Brûlerie** (p173) and **Coutume** (p247) priming cafes citywide for outstanding brews made by professional baristas, often using cutting-edge extraction techniques. Caffeine fiends are now spoilt for choice and while there's still plenty of substandard coffee in Paris, you don't have to go far to avoid it.

list and a food menu that venerates local producers: vegetables, eggs for its all-day brunch, apples for a juice not to be missed and so on, arrive fresh each day from an organic farm 30km outside Paris.

La Perle — Cafe, Bar

Map p154 (http://cafelaperle.com; 78 rue Vieille du Temple, 3e; ⊙9am-2am; MSt-Paul or Chemin Vert) This party bar is where bobos (bohemian bourgeois) come to slum it over *un rouge* (glass of red wine) in the Marais until the DJ arrives to liven things up. Unique trademarks: the (for real) distressed look of the place and the model locomotive over the bar.

Café Martini — Bar

Map p154 (www.cafemartini.fr; 9 rue du Pas de la Mule, 4e; ⊙6pm-midnight; MChemin Vert) Skip the unmemorable cafe-bars on place des Vosges and nip around the corner to this cosy den with wood-panelling, beams and a buzzing after-work crowd – the saggy sofa is the hot spot! Spoil yourself with smoothies, thick-enough-to-spoon *chocolat chaud à l'ancienne,* copious cheese/cold meat platters and happy hour cocktails.

Open Café — Cafe

Map p154 (www.opencafe.fr; 17 rue des Archives, 4e; ⊙11am-2am; MHôtel de Ville) A gay venue for all types at all hours, this spacious bar-cafe with twinkling disco balls strung from the starry ceiling has bags of appeal – not least, a big buzzing pavement terrace, a kitchen serving breakfast (€8.70), all-day *tartines* (€6.70), and a four-hour happy hour kicking in daily at 6pm.

Twenty One Sound Bar — Club

Map p166 (20 rue de la Forge Royale, 11e; ⊙8pm-2am Tue-Thu, from 9pm Fri & Sat; MFaidherbe-Chaligny) Stark steel and concrete amp up the acoustics at this hip-hop haven, with renowned (sometimes legendary) DJs mixing on the decks and regular drinks specials.

Scream Club — Club

Map p160 (www.scream-paris.com; 18 rue du Faubourg du Temple, 11e; admission €15; ⊙midnight-7am Sat; MBelleville or Goncourt) What started out as a summer party is now a permanent fixture on the city's gay scene (marketed as Paris' biggest gay party). The Saturday-night *soirée gay* brings clubbers together on two dance

Café Martini

LE MARAIS & BASTILLE DRINKING & NIGHTLIFE

floors – one dedicated to pop, the other to sets by an international DJ – and an ooh la la! *espace cruising*.

3w Kafé
Gay Bar

Map p154 (8 rue des Écouffes, 4e; ☺8pm-3am Wed & Thu, to 5.30am Fri & Sat; ⓂSt-Paul) The name of this flagship cocktail bar-pub on a street with several lesbian bars means 'women with women'. It's relaxed and there's no ban on men (they must be accompanied by a woman). On weekends there's dancing downstairs with a DJ and themed evenings take place regularly. Check its Facebook page for events.

Le Tango
Club

Map p160 (www.boiteafrissons.fr; 13 rue au Maire, 3e; admission €6-9; ☺10.30pm-5am Fri & Sat, 6-11pm Sun; ⓂArts et Métiers) Billing itself as a *boîte à frissons* (club of thrills), Le Tango hosts a mixed and cosmopolitan, gay and lesbian crowd in a historic 1930s dancehall. Its atmosphere and style is retro and festive, with waltzing, salsa and tango getting going from the moment it opens. From about 12.30am onwards DJs play. Sunday's gay tea dance is legendary.

La Caféothèque
Cafe

Map p154 (www.lacafeotheque.com; 52 rue de l'Hôtel de Ville, 4e; ☺9.30am-7.30pm; ⓦ; ⓂSt-Paul or Hôtel de Ville) From the industrial grinder to elaborate tasting notes, this maze of a coffee house is serious. Grab a pew, pick your bean, and get it served just the way you like it (espresso, ristretto, latte etc). The coffee of the day (€3) keeps well-travelled tastebuds on their toes, as does the €10 *dégustation* (tasting) of three different *crus*.

☆ Entertainment

Le Nouveau Casino
Live Music

Map p160 (www.nouveaucasino.net; 109 rue Oberkampf, 11e; ☺Tue-Sun; ⓂParmentier) This club-concert annexe of **Café Charbon** (p169) has made a name for itself amid the bars of Oberkampf with its live music concerts (usually Tuesday, Thursday and

Gay & Lesbian Paris

Le Marais, especially around the intersection of rue Ste-Croix de la Bretonnerie and rue des Archives, and eastwards to rue Vieille du Temple, has been Paris' main centre of gay nightlife for decades. The lesbian scene centres on a few cafes and bars, especially along rue des Écouffes. The **Centre Gai et Lesbien de Paris** (CGL; Map p160; ☎01 43 57 21 47; www.centrelgbtparis.org; 63 rue Beaubourg, 3e; ☺centre & bar 3.30-8pm Mon-Fri, 1-7pm Sat, library 6-8pm Mon-Wed, 3.30-6pm Fri, 5-7pm Sat; ⓂRambuteau or Arts et Métiers) is gay and lesbian travellers' single best source of information in Paris, with a sociable bar.

Friday) and lively club nights on weekends. Electro, pop, deep house, rock – the program is eclectic, underground and always up to the minute. Check the website for listings.

La Java
World Music

Map p160 (www.la-java.fr; 105 rue du Faubourg du Temple, 11e; ⓂGoncourt) Built in 1922, this is the dance hall where Édith Piaf got her first break, and it now reverberates to the sound of live salsa, rock and world music. Live concerts usually take place during the week at 8pm or 9pm. Afterwards a festive crowd gets dancing to electro, house, disco and Latino DJs.

Le Balajo
Live Music

Map p166 (www.balajo.fr; 9 rue de Lappe, 11e; ☺vary; ⓂBastille) A mainstay of Parisian nightlife since 1936, this ancient ballroom is devoted to salsa classes and Latino music during the week, with an R&B slant on weekends. But the best time to visit is for its old-fashioned *musette* (accordion music) gigs on Monday afternoon from 2pm to 7pm.

Le Carreau du Temple — Cultural Centre

Map p160 (☎01 83 81 93 30; www.lecarreaudu-temple.eu; 4 rue Eugène Spuller, 3e; ⊙ticket office 2-6pm Mon-Sat; MTemple) The quarter's old covered market with drop-dead-gorgeous art-nouveau ironwork is now the city's most architecturally appealing cultural centre and entertainment venue. The place where silks, lace, leather and other materials were sold in the 19th century is now a vast stage for exhibitions, concerts, sports classes and theatre. Check the program online.

Le Vieux Belleville — Live Music

Map p160 (www.le-vieux-belleville.com; 12 rue des Envierges, 20e; ⊙11am-3pm Mon-Fri, 8pm-2am Thu-Sat; MPyrénées) This old-fashioned bistro and *musette* at the top of Parc de Belleville is an atmospheric venue for performances of *chansons* featuring accordions and an organ grinder three times a week. It's a lively favourite with locals, so booking ahead is advised.

Badaboum — Live Music

Map p166 (www.badaboum-paris.com; 2bis rue des Taillandiers, 11e; ⊙cocktail bar 7pm-2am Wed-Sat, club & concerts vary; MBastille or Ledru-Rollin) Formerly La Scène Bastille and freshly refitted, the onomatopoeically named Badaboum hosts a mixed bag of concerts on its up-close-and-personal stage but focusses on electro, funk and hip-hop. Great atmosphere, super cocktails and a secret room upstairs.

Cirque d'Hiver Bouglione — Circus

Map p160 (☎01 47 00 28 81; www.cirquedhiver.com; 110 rue Amelot, 11e; ⊙Oct-Mar; MFilles du Calvaire) Clowns, trapeze artists and acrobats have entertained children of all ages at the city's circus in Le Marais since 1852. The season runs October to March, and performances last around 2½ hours.

Satellit Café — World Music

Map p160 (☎01 47 00 48 87; www.satellit-cafe.com; 44 rue de la Folie Méricourt, 11e; ⊙Tue-Sun; MOberkampf or St-Ambroise) A great venue for world music and not as painfully trendy as some others in Paris – come to hear everything from blues and flamenco to African and Bollywood. Sunday is salsa. Check its Facebook page for events and opening times.

🔒 Shopping

The lower Marais has long been fashionable but the Haut Marais (upper, ie northern Marais) continues its rapid evolution as a hub for up-and-coming fashion designers, art galleries and vintage, accessories and home-wares boutiques plus exhibitions, events and pop-up shops, alongside

Mariage Frères

long-established enterprises enjoying a renaissance.

Belleville Brûlerie — Coffee

(☏ 09 83 75 60 80; http://cafesbelleville.com; 10 rue Pradier, 19e; 300g packet €13-16; ⏱ 11.30am-6.30pm Sat; Ⓜ Belleville) With its understated steel-grey façade, this ground-breaking roastery in Belleville is easy to miss. Don't! These are the guys who brought good coffee to Paris and its beans go into some of the best espressos and cappucinos in town. Taste the week's selection, compare tasting notes, and buy a bag to take home. Online shop, too.

Paris Rendez-Vous — Concept Store

Map p154 (29 rue de Rivoli, 4e; ⏱ 10am-7pm Mon-Sat; Ⓜ Hôtel de Ville) Only the city of Paris could be so chic as to have its own designer line of souvenirs, sold in its own uber-cool concept store inside the Hôtel de Ville. Shop here for everything from clothing and homewares to Paris-themed books, toy sailing boats and signature Jardin du Luxembourg's Fermob chairs. *Quel style!*

L'Éclair de Génie — Cakes

Map p154 (www.leclairdegenie.com; 14 rue Pavée, 4e; ⏱ 11am-7pm Mon-Fri, 10am-7.30pm Sat & Sun; Ⓜ St-Paul) A thrill to visit, this luminous boutique is an ode to sweet éclairs and chocolate truffles. Éclairs created by *pâtissier* (pastry chef) Christophe Adam are displayed like art beneath glass, with dazzling effect. Pick your flavours, pay at the back of the boutique, pick up your goodie bag and pinch yourself that you've just paid between €5 and €7 for one tiny éclair. It's worth it.

Fleux — Design, Homewares

Map p154 (www.fleux.com; 39 & 52 rue Sainte Croix de la Bretonnerie, 4e; ⏱ 10.45am-7.30pm Mon-Fri, 10.30am-8pm Sat, 1.30-7.30pm Sun; Ⓜ Hôtel de Ville) Innovative designs for the home by European designers fill this twinset of big white mazes. Products range from super chic to kitsch, clever and plain crazy. Its e-boutique stocks about 10% of what you see on the shop floor, but Fleux can post most Paris purchases home for you (at a price, *bien sûr*).

Merci — Concept Store

Map p154 (www.merci-merci.com; 111 bd Beaumarchais, 3e; ⏱ 10am-7pm Mon-Sat; Ⓜ St-Sébastien Froissart) A Fiat Cinquecento marks the entrance to this unique concept store which donates all its profits to a children's charity in Madagascar. Shop for fashion, accessories, linens, lamps and nifty designs for the home; and complete the experience with a coffee in its hybrid used-book-shop-cafe or lunch in its stylish basement.

La Manufacture de Chocolat — Food, Drink

Map p166 (www.lechocolat-alainducasse.com; 40 rue de la Roquette, 11e; ⏱ 10.30am-7pm Tue-Sat; Ⓜ Bastille) If you dine at superstar chef Alain Ducasse's restaurants, the chocolate will have been made here at Ducasse's own chocolate factory – the first in Paris to produce 'bean-to-bar' chocolate – which he set up with his former executive pastry chef Nicolas Berger. Deliberate over ganaches, pralines and truffles and no fewer than 44 flavours of chocolate bar.

You can also buy Ducasse's chocolates at his Left Bank boutique, **Le Chocolat Alain Ducasse** Map p230 (www.lechocolat-alainducasse.com; 26 rue St-Benoît, 6e; ⏱ 10.30am-7.30pm Tue-Sat; Ⓜ St-Germain des Prés).

Mariage Frères — Tea

Map p154 (www.mariagefreres.com; 30, 32 & 35 rue du Bourg Tibourg, 4e; pot of tea €10; ⏱ daily; Ⓜ Hôtel de Ville) Founded in 1854, this is Paris' first and arguably finest teashop. Choose from more than 500 varieties of tea sourced from some 35 countries.

Viaduc des Arts — Arts, Crafts

Map p166 (www.viaducdesarts.fr; 1-129 av Daumesnil, 12e; ⏱ vary; Ⓜ Bastille or Gare de Lyon) Located beneath the red-brick arches of the **Promenade Plantée** (p158) is the Viaduc des Arts, where traditional artisans and contemporary designers carry out antique renovations and create new

Best Bastille Markets

Fabulous markets in this part of Paris include the following:

Marché Bastille (Map p166; bd Richard Lenoir, 11e; ⏰7am-2.30pm Thu & Sun; Ⓜ Bastille or Richard Lenoir) If you only get to one open-air street market in Paris, this one – stretching between the Bastille and Richard Lenoir metro stations – is among the very best.

Marché d'Aligre (Map p166; http://marchedaligre.free.fr; rue d'Aligre, 12e; ⏰8am-1pm & 4-7.30pm Tue-Sat, 8am-1.30pm Sun; Ⓜ Ledru-Rollin) All the staples of French cuisine can be found in this chaotic marketplace: cheese, coffee, chocolate, wine, charcuterie, even Tunisian pastries. It's a fantastic place to put together a DIY lunch; offerings in the covered **Marché Beauvau**, in the centre of place d'Aligre, are a bit more gourmet. The morning **Marché aux Puces d'Aligre** Map p166 (place d'Aligre, 12e; ⏰8am-1pm Tue-Sun; Ⓜ Ledru-Rollin) flea market takes place here.

items using traditional methods. Artisans include furniture and tapestry restorers, interior designers, cabinet makers, violin- and flute-makers, embroiderers and jewellers.

Violette et Léonie   Fashion
Map p160 (www.violetteleonie.com; 114 rue de Turenne, 3e; ⏰1-7.30pm Mon, 11am-7.30pm Tue-Sat, 2-7pm Sun; Ⓜ Filles du Calvaire) So chic and of such high quality that it really does not seem like second-hand, Violette et Léonie is a first-class *depôt-vente* boutique specialising in vintage. Shop *sur place* in its wonderfully spacious concept store or online.

Bonton   Children's Fashion
Map p154 (www.bonton.fr; 5 bd des Filles du Calvaire, 3e; ⏰10am-7pm Mon-Sat; Ⓜ Filles du Calvaire) Chic and stylish, this concept store stocks vintage-inspired fashion, furnishings and knick-knacks for babies, toddlers and children. Don't leave without donning an old-fashioned, floppy sunhat or pair of oversized sunglasses and getting your photo snapped in its retro photo booth. Parents note: loo with changing mat in the basement.

Village St-Paul   Crafts, Antiques
Map p154 (rue St-Paul, des rue Jardins St-Paul & rue Charlemagne, 4e; Ⓜ St-Paul) Wander around Village St-Paul, a hidden enclave with tiny boutiques, galleries , cafes and restaurants. Sometimes there is a farmers market or fair.

Rougier & Plé   Fine Arts
Map p160 (www.rougier-ple.fr; 13 bd des Filles du Calvaire, 3e; ⏰11am-7pm Tue-Sat, 2.30-7pm Sun & Mon; Ⓜ Filles du Calvaire) The city's oldest *beaux arts* (fine arts) shop, in business since 1854, sells paper, pens, arts and crafts materials – everything imaginable, in fact, for *le plaisir de crée* (the pleasure of creation).

Chocolaterie Joséphine Vannier   Chocolate
Map p154 (www.chocolats-vannier.com; 4 rue du Pas de la Mule, 4e; ⏰11am-1pm & 2-7pm Tue-Sat, 2.30-7pm Sun; Ⓜ Chemin Vert) Miniature piano keyboards, violins, chic ballerina slippers or a pair of jogging shoes...you name it, *chocolatier* Joséphine Vannier creates it out of chocolate in her shop steps from place des Vosges.

Losco
Accessories

Map p154 (www.losco.fr; 20 rue de Sévigné, 4e; 🕐11am-1pm Wed-Fri, 2-7pm Sun-Fri, 11am-7pm Sat; Ⓜ St-Paul) This artisan *ceinturier* epitomises the main draw of shopping in Paris – stumbling upon tiny boutique-workshops selling 101 quality variations of one single item, in this case *ceintures* (belts). Pick leather type (lizard, python, croc etc), length and buckle to suit just you. Expect to pay anything upwards of €160.

L'Éclaireur
Concept Store

Map p154 (www.leclaireur.com; 40 rue de Sévigné, 4e; 🕐11am-7pm Mon-Sat; Ⓜ St-Paul) Part art space, part lounge and part deconstructionist fashion statement, this shop for women is known for having the next big thing first. The nearby **menswear store** Map p154 (www.leclaireur.com; 12 rue Malher, 4e; Ⓜ St-Paul) on rue Malher fills an equally stunning, old warehouse-turned-art space.

My Crazy Pop
Food

Map p166 (15 rue Trousseau, 11e; 🕐11am-7pm Tue-Fri, to 8pm Sat; Ⓜ Ledru-Rollin) Wasabi, Parmesan, barbecue and olive tapenade are among the amazing savoury flavours at this popcorn shop (a French first); sweet styles include gingerbread praline, salted-butter caramel and orange and cinnamon. Wander through to the viewing window at the back to watch the kernels being popped using heat and pressure only (no oil).

L'Habilleur
Fashion, Accessories

Map p154 (www.lhabilleur.fr; 44 rue de Poitou, 4e; 🕐noon-7.30pm Mon-Sat; Ⓜ St-Sébastien Froissart) Discount designer wear – 50% to 70% off original prices – is the lure of this veteran boutique. It generally stocks last season's collections.

Boutique Obut
Games, Hobbies

Map p160 (www.labouleobut.com; 60 av de la République, 11e; 🕐10am-noon & 12.30-6.30pm Tue-Sat; Ⓜ Parmentier) This is the Parisian mecca for fans of *pétanque* or the similar (though more formal) game of boules, a form of bowls played with heavy steel balls wherever a bit of flat and shady ground can be found. It will kit you out with all the equipment necessary to get a game going and even has team uniforms.

Bercy Village
Mall

(www.bercyvillage.com; cour St-Émilion, 12e; 🕐shops 11am-9pm Mon-Sat, restaurants & bars 11am-2am daily; Ⓜ Cour St-Émilion) Set in the former Bercy wine warehouses, this popular outdoor mall has an 18-screen cinema, restaurants, bars and a string of stores catering to the needs of Parisian families: home design, clever kitchen supplies, quality toy stores and more.

🏃 Sports & Activities

Nomadeshop
Skating

Map p154 (📞01 44 54 07 44; www.nomade-shop.com; 37 bd Bourdon, 4e; half/full day from €5/8; 🕐11am-1.30pm & 2.30-7.30pm Tue-Fri, 10am-7pm Sat, noon-6pm Sun; Ⓜ Bastille) Paris' 'Harrods for roller-heads' rents and sells equipment and accessories, including wheels, helmets, elbow and knee guards. The shop is also the departure point for Sunday's 'Randonnée en Rollers' around Paris, kicking off at 2.30pm (and lasting three hours), organised by skating club **Rollers & Coquillages** Map p154 (www.rollers-coquillages.org) FREE .

The Islands

Paris' geographic and historic heart is situated here in the Seine. The city's watery beginnings took place on the Île de la Cité, the larger of the two inner-city islands. Today, all distances in France are measured from Point Zéro, marked by a bronze star outside Notre Dame. The island is also home to the beautiful Sainte-Chapelle; the Conciergerie, where Marie Antoinette was imprisoned; a colourful flower market; and some picturesque parks such as place Dauphine and square du Vert Galant.

To the east, the tranquil Île St-Louis is graced with elegant mansions that are among the city's most exclusive residential addresses, along with a handful of intimate hotels and exquisite boutiques.

Connecting the two islands, the Pont St-Louis is an impossibly romantic spot at sunset. After nightfall, the Seine dances with the watery reflections of streetlights, headlamps, stop signals and the dim glow of curtained windows.

The Pont au Double linking Île de la Cité with the Left Bank **177**

The Islands Highlights

Notre Dame (p182)

Revel in the crowning glory of medieval Gothic architecture at the Cathédrale de Notre Dame de Paris and its brilliantly bestial rooftop walk where you'll find yourself face-to-face with the most frightening of the cathedral's fantastic gargoyles, as well as the 13-tonne bell Emmanuel in the South Tower and a spectacular view of Paris from the Galerie des Chimères (Gargoyles Gallery).

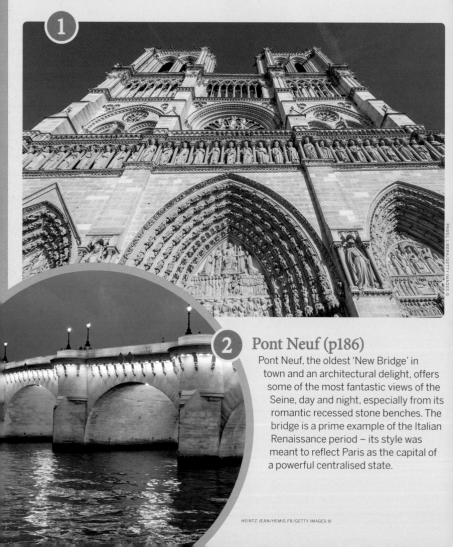

PAVEL LIBERA/GETTY IMAGES ©

Pont Neuf (p186)

Pont Neuf, the oldest 'New Bridge' in town and an architectural delight, offers some of the most fantastic views of the Seine, day and night, especially from its romantic recessed stone benches. The bridge is a prime example of the Italian Renaissance period – its style was meant to reflect Paris as the capital of a powerful centralised state.

HEINTZ JEAN/HEMIS.FR/GETTY IMAGES ©

Conciergerie (p186)

Learn how Marie Antoinette and thousands of others lived out their final days before being beheaded at the Conciergerie. Here you can also admire the city's best example of the Rayonnant Gothic style in the 14th-century Cavalrymen's Hall, the largest surviving medieval hall in Europe, and the adjacent Tour de l'Horloge (Clock Tower). Built in 1353, it's held a public clock aloft since 1370.

RACHEL LEWIS/GETTY IMAGES ©

EDUCATION IMAGES/UIG/GETTY IMAGES ©

CARLO BOLLO/ALAMY ©

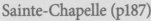

Sainte-Chapelle (p187)

Tucked away within the walls of the Palais de Justice (Law Courts), Sainte-Chapelle is Paris' most exceptional Gothic building. Try to time your visit for a bright day, when sunlight streams through the glass. A *billet jumelé* combination ticket with the nearby Conciergerie is the best way to skip the long ticket queues. To experience the setting at its most ethereal, take in a classical concert here.

Berthillon (p188)

It's largely undisputed that Paris' best ice cream comes from Île St-Louis-based *glacier* (ice-cream maker) Berthillon. Buy a scoop of fresh-fruit sorbet, creamy coffee, *nougat au miel* (honey nougat) or luscious *noisette* (hazelnut) and wander, cone in hand, along the Seine or rue St-Louis en l'Île – or linger on Pont St-Louis and watch the buskers and street entertainers perform.

The Islands Walk

The Île de la Cité and the Île St-Louis might be tiny but there's plenty to take in on this walk, from Roman remains to the twin Gothic splendours Notre Dame cathedral and Sainte-Chapelle, as well as Paris' oldest market – and its best ice cream.

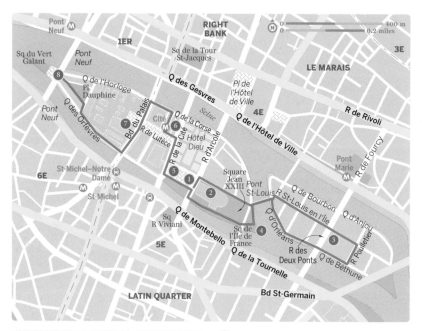

WALK FACTS
- **Start** Point Zéro
- **Finish** Pont Neuf
- **Distance** 3km
- **Duration** 1½ hours

1 Point Zéro

Where better to start your exploration of the islands than **Point Zéro** – the point from which all distances in France are measured, marked by a bronze star on the place du Parvis Notre Dame.

2 Notre Dame

Unthinkably, the glorious **Notre Dame** (p182), was slated for demolition following damage during the French Revolution. Salvation came with the popularity of Victor Hugo's 1831 novel, *The Hunchback of Notre Dame*, which sparked a petition to save it.

3 Berthillon

Turn left (north) then right on rue du Cloître Notre Dame. Cross Pont St-Louis to the Île St-Louis and walk along rue St-Louis en l'Île past charming shops to **Berthillon** (p188). Although shops and cafes all over the islands and beyond sell these exquisite sorbets and ice creams, you can't beat buying it here from the company's own premises.

4 Mémorial des Martyrs de la Déportation

Pass the baroque church **Église St-Louis en l'Île** and turn right on rue Poulletier then right again and follow the river back to Pont St-Louis. Back on the Île de la Cité, the **Mémorial des Martyrs de la Déportation** (p187) sits on the island's eastern tip. Up ahead, one of the best views of Notre Dame is from **square Jean XXIII**, the little park behind the cathedral, where you can appreciate the forest of ornate flying buttresses.

5 Crypte Archéologique

Continue west along Notre Dame's southern side past the **statue of Charlemagne**, emperor of the Franks. Beneath your feet, the **Crypte Archéologique** (p183) reveals the Île de la Cité's history from the Gallo-Roman town of Lutetia to the 20th century.

6 Marché aux Fleurs Reine Elizabeth II

Head north on rue de la Cité and turn right opposite the **Préfecture de Police de Paris**, the city's police headquarters, then cut through the flower market, the **Marché aux Fleurs Reine Elizabeth II** (p193), alive with birdsong on Sunday from the bird market.

7 Sainte-Chapelle

Follow the river around to turn left into bd du Palais; on your right is the **Conciergerie** (p186), a 14th-century royal palace used as a prison during the French Revolution before inmates were tried next door in the **Palais de Justice** (Law Courts). Within the Palais de Justice is the Gothic jewel **Sainte-Chapelle** (p187); you can see the chapel's exterior by the law courts' magnificently gilded 18th-century gate facing rue de Lutèce.

8 Pont Neuf

Walk west around the island's southern side to rue de Harlay and cut across **place Dauphine** to **Pont Neuf** (p186). Steps lead from the bridge down to the pretty **square du Vert Gallant** (p195), perched at the Île de la Cité's western tip, which is an idyllic spot to rest your feet.

The Best...

PLACES TO EAT

Berthillon Premium all-natural ice cream and sorbets in some 70 flavours. (p188)

Le Tastevin Traditional lace-curtained decor and timeless French cuisine such as *escargots* (snails). (p190)

Mon Vieil Ami Vegetables are the star at neobistro 'My Old Friend'. (p190)

PLACES TO DRINK

Café St-Régis A deliciously Parisian hang-out any time of day. (p189)

Taverne IV Authentic wine bar serving cheese and charcuterie platters. (p192)

La Charlotte de l'Isle Tiny, delightful *salon de thé* (tearoom). (p193)

PLACES TO ROMANCE

Tours de Notre Dame Hidden corners, stairwells and the rooftop. (p183)

Pont St-Louis Buskers by day and beautiful sunset views.

Pont Neuf Semicircular stone benches perfect for watching the riverboats pass beneath. (p186)

Square du Vert Galant Romantically situated on the tip of the Île de la Cité. (p195)

Mon Vieil Ami restaurant (p190)

Don't Miss
Notre Dame

Notre Dame, the most visited unticketed site in Paris with upwards of 14 million people crossing its threshold annually, is a masterpiece of French Gothic architecture and the focus of Catholic Paris for seven centuries. Its vast stained-glass lit interior has wow factor aplenty, but it is the sky-high meander around its gargoyle-guarded rooftop and extraordinary sculpted façade – best photographed in the afternoon sun – that most visitors swoon over.

Map p188

☎ 01 53 10 07 00

www.cathedraledeparis.com

6 place du Parvis Notre Dame, 4e

cathedral free, towers adult/child €8.50/free, treasury €2/1

⊙ cathedral 7.45am-6.45pm Mon-Sat, to 7.15pm Sun, towers 10am-6.30pm, to 11pm Fri & Sat Jul & Aug

Ⓜ Cité

Architecture

Built on a site occupied by earlier churches and, a millennium before that, a Gallo-Roman temple, Notre Dame was begun in 1163 and largely completed by the early 14th century. The cathedral was badly damaged during the Revolution, prompting architect Eugène Emmanuel Viollet-le-Duc to oversee extensive renovations between 1845 and 1864. Enter the magnificent forest of ornate **flying buttresses** that encircle the cathedral chancel and support its walls and roof.

Notre Dame is known for its sublime balance, though if you look closely you'll see all sorts of minor asymmetrical elements introduced to avoid monotony, in accordance with standard Gothic practice. These include the slightly different shapes of each of the three main **portals**, whose statues were once brightly coloured to make them more effective as a *Biblia pauperum* – a 'Bible of the poor' to help the illiterate faithful understand Old Testament stories, the Passion of the Christ and the lives of the saints.

Rose Windows

Entering the cathedral, its grand dimensions are immediately evident: the interior alone is 130m long, 48m wide and 35m high and can accommodate more than 6000 worshippers.

The most spectacular interior features are three rose windows. The most renowned is the 10m-wide window over the western façade above the 7800-pipe organ, and the window on the northern side of the transept (virtually unchanged since the 13th century).

Treasury

In the southeastern transept, the trésor contains artwork, liturgical objects and first-class relics. Among these is the **Ste-Couronne** (Holy Crown), purportedly the wreath of thorns placed on Jesus' head before he was crucified. It is exhibited between 3pm and 4pm on the first Friday of each month, 3pm to 4pm every Friday during Lent, and 10am to 5pm on Good Friday.

Towers

A constant queue marks the entrance to the **Tours de Notre Dame** Map p188 (Notre Dame Towers; rue du Cloître Notre Dame, 4e; adult/child €8.50/free; ⊙10am-6.30pm, to 11pm Fri & Sat Jul & Aug, to 5.30pm daily Oct-Mar; MCité). Climb the 422 steps to the top of the western façade of the **North Tower** where you'll find yourself face-to-face with the cathedral's most frightening of its fantastic gargoyles, as well as the 13-tonne bell **Emmanuel** in the **South Tower**, and a spectacular view of Paris from the **Galerie des Chimères** (Gargoyles Gallery).

Crypt

Under the square in front of Notre Dame lies the **Crypte Archéologique** Map p188 (Archaeological Crypt; 1 place du Parvis Notre Dame, 1er; adult/child €6/4.50; ⊙10am-6pm; MCité) a 117m-long and 28m-wide area displaying *in situ* the remains of structures built on this site during the Gallo-Roman period.

The Heart of Paris

Notre Dame really is the heart of the city, so much so that distances from Paris to every part of metropolitan France are measured from **place du Parvis Notre Dame**, the square in front of it across which Charlemagne (AD 742–814), emperor of the Franks, rides his steed. A bronze star across the street from the cathedral's main entrance marks the location of **Point Zéro des Routes de France** Map p188.

Music at Notre Dame

Music has been a sacred part of Notre Dame's soul since birth and there's no better day to revel in the cathedral's rousing musical heritage than on Sunday at a Gregorian or polyphonic Mass (10am and 6.30pm, respectively) or a free organ recital (4.30pm). October to June, the cathedral stages evening concerts; find the program online at www.musique-sacree-notredamedeparis.fr.

Notre Dame

TIMELINE

1160 Maurice de Sully becomes bishop of Paris. Mission: to grace growing Paris with a lofty new cathedral.

1182–90 The **choir with double ambulatory ❶** is finished and work starts on the nave and side chapels.

1200–50 The **west façade ❷**, with rose window, three portals and two soaring towers, goes up. Everyone is stunned.

1345 Some 180 years after the foundation stone was laid, the Cathédrale de Notre Dame is complete. It is dedicated to notre dame (our lady), the Virgin Mary.

1789 Revolutionaries smash the original **Gallery of Kings ❸**, pillage the cathedral and melt all its bells except the great bell Emmanuel. The cathedral becomes a Temple of Reason then a warehouse.

1831 Victor Hugo's novel *The Hunchback of Notre Dame* inspires new interest in the half-ruined Gothic cathedral.

1845–50 Architect Viollet-le-Duc undertakes its restoration. Twenty-eight new kings are sculpted for the west façade. The heavily decorated **portals ❹** and **spire ❺** are reconstructed. The neo-Gothic **treasury ❻** is built.

1860 The area in front of Notre Dame is cleared to create the parvis, an alfresco classroom where Parisians can learn a catechism illustrated on sculpted stone portals.

1935 A rooster bearing part of the relics of the Crown of Thorns, St Denis and St Geneviève is put on top of the cathedral spire to protect those who pray inside.

1991 The architectural masterpiece of Notre Dame and its Seine-side riverbanks become a Unesco World Heritage Site.

2013 Notre Dame celebrates 850 years since construction began with a bevy of new bells and restoration works.

Virgin & Child
Spot all 37 artworks representing the Virgin Mary. Pilgrims have revered the pearly-cream sculpture of her in the sanctuary since the 14th century. Light a devotional candle and write some words to the *Livre de Vie* (Book of Life).

North Rose Window
See prophets, judges, kings and priests venerate Mary in vivid blue and violet glass, one of three beautiful rose blooms (1225–70), each almost 10m in diameter.

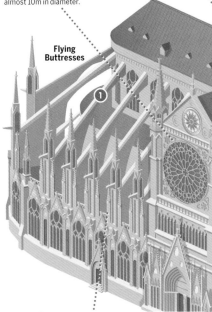

Flying Buttresses

Choir Screen
No part of the cathedral weaves biblical tales more evocatively than these ornate wooden panels, carved in the 14th century after the Black Death killed half the country's population. The faintly gaudy colours were restored in the 1960s.

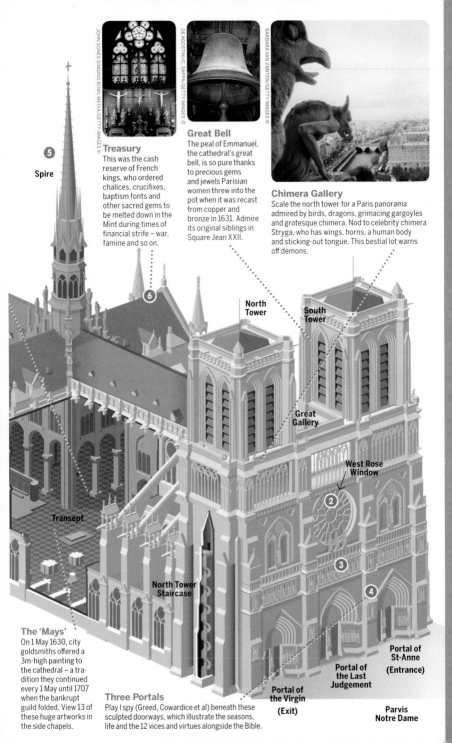

Spire

❺

Treasury
This was the cash reserve of French kings, who ordered chalices, crucifixes, baptism fonts and other sacred gems to be melted down in the Mint during times of financial strife – war, famine and so on.

Great Bell
The peal of Emmanuel, the cathedral's great bell, is so pure thanks to precious gems and jewels Parisian women threw into the pot when it was recast from copper and bronze in 1631. Admire its original siblings in Square Jean XXII.

Chimera Gallery
Scale the north tower for a Paris panorama admired by birds, dragons, grimacing gargoyles and grotesque chimera. Nod to celebrity chimera Stryga, who has wings, horns, a human body and sticking-out tongue. This bestial lot warns off demons.

❻

North Tower

South Tower

Great Gallery

West Rose Window

❷

Transept

North Tower Staircase

❸

❹

The 'Mays'
On 1 May 1630, city goldsmiths offered a 3m-high painting to the cathedral – a tradition they continued every 1 May until 1707 when the bankrupt guild folded. View 13 of these huge artworks in the side chapels.

Three Portals
Play I spy (Greed, Cowardice et al) beneath these sculpted doorways, which illustrate the seasons, life and the 12 vices and virtues alongside the Bible.

Portal of the Virgin
(Exit)

Portal of the Last Judgement

Portal of St-Anne
(Entrance)

Parvis Notre Dame

The Islands

Getting There & Away

- **Metro** The closest stations are Cité (line 4) and Pont Marie (line 7).

- **Bus** Bus 47 links Île de la Cité with the Marais and Gare de l'Est; bus 21 with Opéra and Gare St-Lazare. On Île St-Louis it's bus 67 to Jardin des Plantes and place d'Italie, and bus 87 through the Latin Quarter to École Militaire and Champ de Mars.

- **Bicycle** Île de la Cité has a trio of handy Vélib' stations: one at place Louis Lépine by the Cité metro station; others at 1 quai aux Fleurs and 5 rue d'Arcole, both by Cathédrale de Notre Dame.

◉ Sights

Île de la Cité was the site of the first settlement in Paris (c 3rd century BC) and later the centre of Roman Lutetia. The island remained the hub of royal and ecclesiastical power, even after the city spread to both banks of the Seine in the Middle Ages. Smaller Île St-Louis was actually two uninhabited islets called Île Notre Dame (Our Lady Isle) and Île aux Vaches (Cows Island) in the early 17th century – until a building contractor and two financiers worked out a deal with Louis XIII to create one island and build two stone bridges to the mainland.

Conciergerie · Monument

Map p188 (www.monuments-nationaux.fr; 2 bd du Palais, 1er; adult/child €8.50/free; joint ticket with Sainte-Chapelle €12.50; ◷9.30am-6pm; M Cité) A royal palace in the 14th century, the Conciergerie later became a prison. During the Reign of Terror (1793–94) alleged enemies of the Revolution were incarcerated here before being brought before the Revolutionary Tribunal next door in the **Palais de Justice**. Top-billing exhibitions take place in the beautiful, Rayonnant Gothic **Salle des Gens d'Armes**, Europe's largest surviving medieval hall.

Pont Neuf · Bridge

Map p188 (M Pont Neuf) Paris' oldest bridge has linked the western end of Île de la Cité with both river banks since 1607, when the king inaugurated it by crossing the bridge on a white stallion. The occasion is commemorated by an equestrian **statue of Henry IV**, known to his subjects as the Vert Galant ('jolly

The Conciergerie
DANIEL THIERRY/GETTY IMAGES ©

FRENCH CONNECTION/ALAMY ©

 Don't Miss
Sainte-Chapelle

Try to save Sainte-Chapelle for a sunny day, when Paris' oldest, finest stained glass is at its dazzling best. Enshrined within the **Palais de Justice** (Law Courts), this gem-like Holy Chapel is Paris' most exquisite Gothic monument. Ste-Chapelle was built in just six years (compared with nearly 200 years for Notre Dame) and consecrated in 1248.

The chapel was conceived by Louis IX to house his personal collection of holy relics, including the famous Holy Crown (now in Notre Dame).

Peek at its exterior from across the street, by the law courts' magnificently gilded 18th-century gate facing rue de Lutèce.

NEED TO KNOW

Map p188 ☏01 53 40 60 80, concerts 01 42 77 65 65; http://sainte-chapelle.monuments-nationaux.fr; 8 bd du Palais, 1er; adult/child €8.50/free, joint ticket with Conciergerie €12.50; ⏱9.30am-6pm daily, to 9.30pm Wed mid-May–mid-Sep, 9am-5pm daily Nov-Feb; Ⓜ Cité

rogue' or 'dirty old man', perspective depending).

View the bridge's seven arches, decorated with humorous and grotesque figures of barbers, dentists, pickpockets, loiterers etc, from a spot along the river or afloat.

Mémorial des Martyrs de la Déportation
Monument

Map p188 (square de l'Île de France, 4e; ⏱10am-noon & 2-7pm Apr-Sep, to 5pm Oct-Mar; RER St-Michel–Notre Dame) The Memorial to the Victims of the Deportation, erected in 1962, remembers the 160,000 residents of France (including 76,000 Jews, of whom 11,000 were children) deported

THE ISLANDS EATING

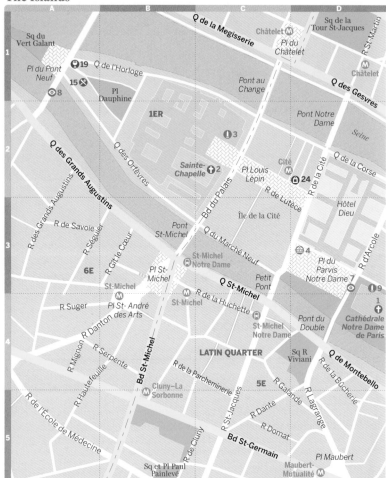

to and murdered in Nazi concentration camps during WWII. A single barred 'window' separates the bleak, rough-concrete courtyard from the waters of the Seine. Inside lies the **Tomb of the Unknown Deportee**.

Église St-Louis en l'Île   Church
Map p188 (19bis rue St-Louis en l'Île; ⏰9am-1pm & 2-7.30pm Tue-Sat, to 7pm Sun; Ⓜ Pont Marie) The French baroque Église St-Louis en l'Île was built between 1664 and 1726.

Eating

The Île St-Louis' most famous foodstuff is Berthillon ice cream, which is sold at outlets around the island including Berthillon's own premises.

Berthillon   Ice Cream €
Map p188 (31 rue St-Louis en l'Île, 4e; 2-/3-/4-ball cone or tub €2.50/5.50/7; ⏰10am-8pm Wed-Sun; Ⓜ Pont Marie) Berthillon is to ice cream what Château Lafite Rothschild is to wine and Valrhona is to chocolate.

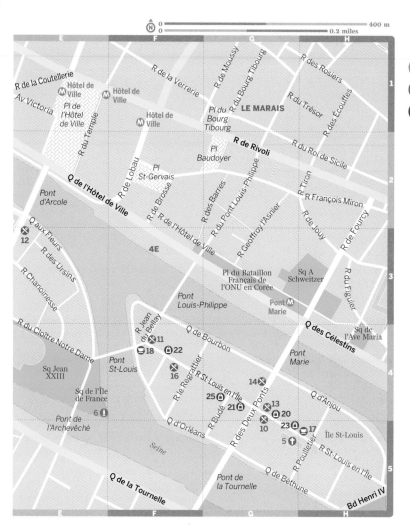

Among its 70-odd flavours, the fruit-flavoured sorbets are renowned, as are its rich chocolate, coffee, *marrons glacés* (candied chestnuts) and Agenaise (Armagnac and prunes). Watch for seasonal flavours like roasted pineapple and basil, or ginger and caramel. Eat in or take away.

Café Saint Régis   Cafe €

Map p188 (http://cafesaintregisparis.com; 6 rue du Jean de Bellay, 4e; salads & mains €14.50-28; 7am-2am; ; M Pont Marie) Hip and

historical with an effortless dose of retro vintage thrown in, Le Saint Régis – as those in the know call it – is a deliciously Parisian hang-out any time of day. From pastries for breakfast to a mid-morning pancake, brasserie lunch or early-evening oyster platter, Café St-Regis gets it just right. Come midnight it morphs into a late-night hot spot.

Sunday brunch jostles with Happy Hour (7pm to 9pm daily) for best crowd-packed moment. Magazines and newspapers to read, charismatic wait

The Islands

staff in long white aprons, and a lovely white ceramic-tiled interior top off the appealing ensemble.

Huré   Boulangerie €

Map p188 (www.hure-createur.fr; 1 rue d'Arcole, 4e; takeaway lunch menus €8.50-9.30, sandwiches €4-6; ⏰6.30am-8pm Mon-Sat; Ⓜ St-Michel, Notre Dame or Châtelet) Feisty savoury tarts and quiches, jumbo salads bursting with fresh veggies, giant cookies and cakes every colour and flavour of the rainbow: assuming it's a light lunch al fresco you're after, you'll be hard-pushed to find a better *boulangerie* (bakery) in spitting distance of Notre Dame than this. Simply look for the mountains of giant meringues piled high on the counter and queue stretching half-way down the street.

Les Voyelles   Modern French €€

Map p188 (📞01 46 33 69 75; www.les-voyelles. com; 74 quai des Orfèvres, 4e; plat du jour €12, 2-/3-course menus €17/22.50; ⏰8am-midnight Tue-Sat; Ⓜ Pont Neuf) This new kid on the block is worth the short walk from Notre Dame. The Vowels – spot the letters casually scattered between books and beautiful objects on the shelves lining the intimate 'library' dining room – is thoroughly contemporary, with a menu ranging from finger food to full-blown

dinner to match. Its pavement terrace is Paris gold.

Le Tastevin   Traditional French €€€

Map p188 (📞01 43 54 17 31; www.letastevin-paris.com; 46 rue St-Louis en l'Île, 4e; mains €27-34.50, menus from €33; ⏰noon-2pm & 7-11.15pm Tue-Sun; Ⓜ Pont Marie) With its old-fashioned lace curtains, wood panelling and beamed ceiling, this posh old-style address in a 17th-century building smacks of charm. Its excellent cuisine is equally traditional: think *escargots* (snails), foie gras, sole, or *ris de veau* (calf sweetbreads) with morels and tagliatelli.

Mon Vieil
Ami   Traditional French €€€

Map p188 (📞01 40 46 01 35; www.mon-vieil-ami.com; 69 rue St-Louis en l'Île, 4e; plat du jour €15.50, menu €47.50; ⏰noon-2.30pm & 7-11pm; Ⓜ Pont Marie) Alsatian chef Antoine Westermann is the creative talent behind this sleek black neobistro where guests are treated like old friends (hence the name) and vegetables get royal treatment. The good-value lunchtime *plat du jour* (dish of the day) is a perfect reflection of the season. Dinner is served from 6.30pm – handy for those seeking an early meal.

MARIA PAVLOVA/GETTY IMAGES ©

Saved by the Hunchback of Notre Dame

The damage inflicted on Notre Dame during the French Revolution saw it fall into ruin, and it was destined for demolition. Salvation came with the widespread popularity of Victor Hugo's 1831 novel, *The Hunchback of Notre Dame,* which sparked a petition to save it.

The novel opens in 1482 on the Epiphany (6 January), the day of the 'Feast of Fools', with the eponymous hunchback, Quasimodo, the deafened bell-ringer at Notre Dame, crowned the King of Fools. Much of the ensuing action (such as the scene where the dancer Esmeralda is being led to the gallows and Quasimodo swings down by a bell rope to rescue her) takes place in and around the cathedral, which effectively becomes another 'character' in the novel.

Subsequently, in 1845, architect Eugène Emmanuel Viollet-le-Duc began the cathedral's grand-scale renovations. Likewise, Hugo's novel has gone on to achieve immortality of its own, with numerous film, TV, theatre and ballet adaptations, including the hugely successful 1996 Disney animation incorporating faithfully recreated architectural detail.

Les Fous de l'Île   Brasserie €€
Map p188 (☎01 43 25 76 67; www.les-fousdelile.com; 33 rue des Deux Ponts, 4e; 2-/3-course menus lunch €19/25, dinner €23/28; ☺10am-2am; ⓜPont Marie) This typical brasserie is a popular family address with a lovely open kitchen and an unusual cockerel theme throughout. Hearty fare like *cassoulet* (traditional Languedoc stew with beans and meat) and lighter Spanish-inspired tapas dishes are served between noon and 11pm. Sunday brunch (€24, €29 with a cocktail), served noon to 4pm, buzzes.

Buskers

Paris' eclectic gaggle of clowns, mime artists, living statues, acrobats, roller-bladers, buskers and other street entertainers cost substantially less than a theatre ticket (a few coins in the hat is appreciated). Some excellent musicians audition to perform aboard the metro and in the corridors. Outside, you can be sure of a good show at countless spots around the city. Two of the best are Pont St-Louis, the bridge between the Île de la Cité and Île St-Louis, and Pont au Double, the pedestrian bridge linking the Île de la Cité near Notre Dame with the Left Bank.

 Drinking & Nightlife

Drinking venues on the islands are as scarce as hens' teeth. They do exist but use them as a starting point as very few places stay open after the witching hour of midnight.

Taverne Henri IV   Wine Bar
Map p188 (13 place du Pont Neuf, 1er; ⊙11.30am-11pm Mon-Sat, closed Aug; MPont Neuf) One of the few places to drink on Île de la Cité, this wine bar dates to 1885 and lures a fair few legal types from the nearby Palais de Justice (not to mention celeb writers and actors, as the autographed snaps testify). A tasty choice of *tartines* (open sandwiches), *charcuterie* (cold cooked meats) and cheese platters complement its extensive wine list.

La Charlotte de l'Isle   Tearoom

Map p188 (www.lacharlottedelisle.fr; 24 rue
St-Louis en l'Île, 4e; ⏱11am-7pm Wed-Sun;
MPont Marie) This tiny place is a particularly lovely *salon de thé* (tearoom) with
a quaint fairy-tale theme, old-fashioned
glass sweet jars on the shelf and a fine
collection of tea to taste *in situ* or buy to
sip at home. Hot chocolate, chocolate
sculptures, cakes and pastries are other
sweet reasons to come here.

Le Flore en l'Île   Cafe

Map p188 (42 quai d'Orléans, 4e; ⏱8am-1am;
MPont Marie) A tourist crowd piles into this
excellent and elegant old-world people-
watching spot with prime views of the
buskers on Pont St-Louis.

🔒 Shopping

Île de St-Louis is a shopper's delight
for crafty boutiques and tiny specialist
stores; Île de la Cité for souvenirs and
tourist kitsch.

Marché aux Fleurs Reine
Elizabeth II   Market

Map p188 (place Louis Lépin, 4e; ⏱8am-7.30pm
Mon-Sat; MCité) Blooms have been sold
at this flower market since 1808, making
it the oldest market of any kind in Paris.
On Sunday, between 9am and 7pm, it
transforms into a twittering bird market,
Marché aux Oiseaux Map p188 (⏱9am-
7pm).

38 Saint Louis   Cheese

Map p188 (38 rue St-Louis en l'Île, 4e; ⏱9am-
9.30pm Tue-Sat, to 7pm Sun & Mon; MPont
Marie) Saturday wine tastings, artisan
fruit chutneys, grape juice and prepared

PAWEL LIBERA/GETTY IMAGES ©

Bouquinistes

Lining both banks of the Seine through the centre of Paris (not on the islands themselves), the open-air *bouquiniste* stalls selling secondhand, often out-of-print, books, rare magazines, postcards and old advertising posters are a definitive Parisian sight. Trading here since the 16th century, the name comes from *bouquiner*, meaning 'to read with appreciation'. At night, *bouquinistes'* dark-green metal stalls are folded down and locked like suitcases. Many open only from spring to autumn (and many shut in August), but even in the depths of winter, you'll still find somewhere to unearth antiquarian treasures.

dishes to go: there is far more to this thoroughly modern *fromagerie* (cheese shop) than its old-fashioned façade and absolutely superb selection of first-class French *fromage* (cheese). The shop is run by a young, dynamic duo, driven by food. Buy a wooden box filled with vacuum-packed cheese to take home.

Il Campiello   Crafts
Map p188 (www.ilcampiello.com; 88 rue St-Louis en l'Île, 4e; ⏱11am-7pm; Ⓜ Pont Marie) Venetian carnival masks – intricately crafted from papier mâché, ceramics and leather – are the speciality of this exquisite shop, which also sells jewellery made from Murano glass beads. It was established by a native of Venice, to which the Île St-Louis bears more than a passing resemblance.

Librairie Ulysse   Books
Map p188 (www.ulysse.fr; 26 rue St-Louis en l'Île, 4e; ⏱2-8pm Tue-Fri; Ⓜ Pont Marie) You can barely move in between this shop's anti-

Seine-ful Pursuits

The Seine is more than just the line dividing the Right Bank from the Left. The river's award-winning role comes in July and August, when some 5km of its banks are transformed into **Paris Plages** (www.paris.fr), 'beaches' with real sand, water fountains and sprays. The banks between the Pont Alexandre III and the Pont d'Austerlitz have been listed as a Unesco World Heritage Site since 1991, but the choicest spot is the delightful **Square du Vert Gallant**, the little park at the tip of the Île de la Cité named after that rake Henri IV.

quarian and new travel guides, *National Geographic* back editions and maps. Opened in 1971 by the intrepid Catherine Domaine, this was the world's first travel bookshop. Hours vary, but ring the bell and Catherine will open up if she's around.

Clair de Rêve   Toys
Map p188 (www.clairdereve.com; 35 rue St-Louis en l'Île, 4e; ⏰11am-1pm & 2-7pm Mon-Sat; Ⓜ Pont Marie) This shop is all about wind-up toys, music boxes and puppets – mostly marionettes, which sway and bob suspended from the ceiling.

Première Pression Provence   Food
Map p188 (51 rue St-Louis en l'Île, 4e; ⏰11am-1pm & 2-7pm Mon-Sat; Ⓜ Pont Marie) Its name evokes the first pressing of olives to make olive oil in the south of France and that is precisely what this gourmet boutique sells – be it as oil or in any number of spreads and sauces (pesto, tapenade etc).

Latin Quarter

So named because university students here used Latin until the French Revolution, the Latin Quarter is renowned worldwide as an intellectual incubator and remains the centre of academic life in Paris.

The quarter centres on the Sorbonne's main university campus, which is graced by fountains and lime trees. In the surrounding area you'll encounter students and professors lingering at late-night bookshops and secondhand record shops on and around the 'boul Mich' (bd St-Michel). You'll also encounter them researching in its museums like the Musée National du Moyen Âge (aka Cluny); at the library within its exquisite art deco–Moorish mosque; in its botanic gardens, the Jardin des Plantes; or simply relaxing in its pigeon-filled squares and gardens.

To really take the area's pulse, head to its liveliest commercial street, rue Mouffetard, a colourful jumble of student bars, cheap eateries, market stalls and inexpensive clothing and homewares shops.

The Pantheon (p208)

Latin Quarter Highlights

Institut du Monde Arabe (p207)

Inspired by traditional latticed-wood windows, this stunning building blends modern and traditional Arab and Western elements, including thousands of *mushrabiyah* (or *mouchearabies*): photo-electrically sensitive apertures built into the glass walls that allow you to see out without being seen. The apertures are opened and closed by electric motors in order to regulate the amount of light and heat that reaches the building's interior.

Jardin des Plantes (p202)

Paris' sprawling botanical gardens incorporate a winter garden, tropical greenhouses and an alpine garden with 2000 plants, as well as the École de Botanique (School of Botany) gardens, used by students and green-fingered Parisians. It also encompasses a zoo – the Ménagerie du Jardin des Plantes – and the Musée National d'Histoire Naturelle, France's natural-history museum with a trio of museums including the kid-friendly Grande Galerie de l'Évolution.

TRISH PUNCH/GETTY IMAGES ©

Musée National du Moyen Âge (p203)

France's fascinating medieval history museum, the Musée National du Moyen Âge, doesn't attract the same volume of tourists as other major sights, so any time is generally good to visit. Audioguides are typically included in the admission price; for medieval history buffs wanting to delve even deeper, the museum's document centre (open by appointment) has thousands of references.

MARK HARMEL/ALAMY ©

SMPPHOTOGRAPHY/GETTY IMAGES ©

GARDEL BERTRAND/GETTY IMAGES ©

Panthéon (p208)

Let your soul soar inside the Panthéon. Built as a church and completed the year the Revolution broke out, this sublime neoclassical structure now serves as a mausoleum for *les grands hommes de l'époque de la liberté française* (great men of the era of French liberty), though in 1995 it welcomed its first woman, Nobel Prize-winner Marie Curie, who was reburied here along with her husband, Pierre.

Shakespeare & Company (p216)

Not merely a bookshop but the stuff of legends, the original shop at 12 rue l'Odéon (closed by the Nazis in 1941) was run by Sylvia Beach and became the meeting point for Hemingway's 'Lost Generation'. George Whitman opened the present incarnation in 1951, and today Whitman's daughter, Sylvia Beach Whitman, maintains Shakespeare & Company's serendipitous magic.

Latin Quarter Walk

This walk through Paris' academic heartland contains lessons in Arab arts, horticulture and natural history at the city's botanic gardens, literary history at the haunts of writers including Hemingway and George Orwell, French medieval history and more.

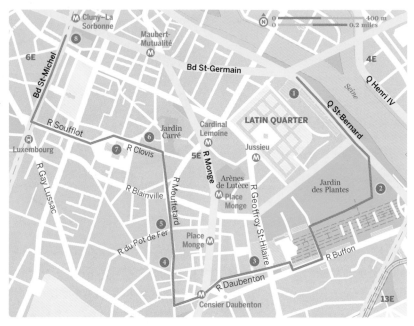

WALK FACTS
- **Start** Institute du Monde Arabe
- **Finish** Musée National du Moyen Age
- **Distance** 3km
- **Duration** Two hours

1 Institut du Monde Arabe
Even from the outside, the **Institut du Monde Arabe** (p207) is extraordinary. The building confirmed French architect Jean Nouvel's reputation is a masterpiece of 1980s architecture, melding contemporary and traditional Arab and Western elements to reflect the Arabic arts displayed inside.

2 Jardin des Plantes
Turn right from the Institut du Monde Arabe, follow the river for 400m before entering the green oasis of Paris' botanic gardens, the **Jardin des Plantes** (p202). In the southwest corner is the **Musée National d'Histoire Naturelle** (p202).

3 Mosquée de Paris
Across rue Geoffroy St-Hilaire from the Musée National d'Histoire Naturelle, you'll see the 26m-high minaret topping Paris' magnificently tiled art deco Moorish mosque, the **Mosquée de Paris** (p207). (Take an idyllic break with a sweet mint tea and North African pastry in its tearoom.)

④ Rue Mouffetard

Head west from the Mosquée de Paris along rue Daubenton. Cross rue Monge and continue to the end, then turn right up **rue Mouffetard** (p210) This old Roman road is thronged with market stalls (except Mondays) as well as food shops and bars (look up: several have murals above).

⑤ Rue du Pot de Fer

In 1928 George Orwell stayed in a cheap boarding house above **6 rue du Pot de Fer** while working as a dishwasher. Read about it and the street, which he called 'rue du Coq d'Or' (Street of the Golden Rooster), in *Down and Out in Paris and London*.

⑥ Église St-Étienne du Mont

Beyond **place de la Contrescarpe** rue Mouffetard's northern continuation is rue Descartes. Follow it north before turning left on rue Clovis. On your right, **Église St-Étienne du Mont** (p208) contains Paris' only surviving rood screen (1535), separating the chancel from the nave (the other rood screens were removed during the late Renaissance because they prevented the faithful in the nave from seeing the priest celebrate Mass).

⑦ Panthéon

Still on rue Clovis, the domed, neoclassical **Panthéon** (p208) rises on your left. Originally built as a church, it's now a mausoleum for France's finest intellectuals.

⑧ Musée National du Moyen Age

West of the Panthéon, turn right on bd St-Michel. To your right, place de la Sorbonne links bd St-Michel and the Chapelle de la Sorbonne, the prestigious **Sorbonne** (p209) university's domed church, built in the early 17th century. Just a few metres ahead on your right is the Middle Ages museum the **Musée National du Moyen Age** (p203).

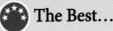

The Best...

PLACES TO EAT

L'AOC Nothing but the finest ingredients and wines. (p210)

L'Agrume Watch chefs turn seasonal produce into sensational meals. (p212)

La Tour d'Argent Centuries-old establishment overlooking Notre Dame (p213)

Le Coupe-Chou Seductive French fare in a romantic candlelit setting. (p212)

Les Papilles Rustic bistro with wonderful wines. (p211)

PLACES TO DRINK

Café de la Nouvelle Mairie Local wine bar hidden away on a small square round the corner from the Panthéon. (p214)

Le Verre à Pied Classic cafe that's scacely changed since 1870. (p214)

Le Pub St-Hilaire Fun-loving student pub. (p214)

JAZZ CLUBS

Café Universel Adventurous program that includes jam sessions. (p215)

Le Caveau des Oubliettes Jazz in a 12th-century dungeon. (p215)

Le Petit Journal St-Michel Sophisticated jazz venue across from the Jardin du Luxembourg. (p215)

Bustling street life in the Latin Quarter
PAWEL LIBERA/GETTY IMAGES ©

Latin Quarter

Getting There & Away

● **Metro** The most central metro stations are St-Michel by the Seine; Cluny–La Sorbonne or Maubert-Mutualité on bd St-Germain; and Censier Daubenton or Gare d'Austerlitz by the Jardin des Plantes.

● **Bus** Convenient bus stops include the Panthéon for the 89 to Jardin des Plantes and 13e; bd St-Michel for the 38 to Centre Pompidou, Gare de l'Est & Gare du Nord; and rue Gay Lussac for the 27 to Île de la Cité and Opéra.

● **Bicycle** Handy Vélib' stations include 42 rue St-Severin, 5e, by bd St-Michel; 40 rue Boulangers, 5e, near Cardinal Lemoine metro station; and 27 rue Lacépède, 5e, near Place Monge.

● **Boat** Opposite Notre Dame on quai de Montebello, and at the Jardin des Plantes on quai St-Bernard.

Sights

Jardin des Plantes Gardens
Map p204 (www.jardindesplantes.net; place Valhubert & 36 rue Geoffroy-St-Hilaire, 5e; ⏱7.30am-7.45pm Apr-Oct, 8am-5.15pm Nov-Mar; Ⓜ Gare d'Austerlitz, Censier Daubenton or Jussieu) **FREE** Founded in 1626 as a medicinal herb garden for Louis XIII, Paris' 24-hectare botanic gardens – visually defined by the double alley of plane trees that run the length of the park – are an idyllic spot to stroll around, break for a picnic (watch out for the automatic sprinklers!) and escape the city concrete for a spell. Upping its appeal are three museums from the Muséum National d'Histoire Naturelle and a small **zoo** (p206).

Muséum National d'Histoire Naturelle Museum
Map p204 (www.mnhn.fr; place Valhubert & 36 rue Geoffroy St-Hilaire, 5e; Ⓜ Gare d'Austerlitz, Censier Daubenton or Jussieu) Despite the name, the Natural History Museum is not a single building, but a collection of sites throughout France. Its historic home is in the Jardin des Plantes, and it's here you'll find the greatest number of branches: taxidermied animals in the excellent **Grande Galerie de l'Évolution** Map p204 (adult/child €7/free; ⏱10am-6pm Wed-Mon), fossils and dinosaur skeletons in the **Galerie d'Anatomie Comparée et de Paléontologie** Map p204 (adult/child €7/free; ⏱10am-5pm Wed-Mon) and meteorites and crystals in the **Galerie de Minéralogie et de Géologie** Map p204.

Created in 1793, the National Museum of Natural History became a site of significant scientific research in the 19th century.

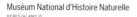

Muséum National d'Histoire Naturelle
HEMIS/ALAMY ©

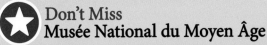

Don't Miss
Musée National du Moyen Âge

The National Museum of the Middle Ages holds a series of sublime treasures, from medieval statuary, stained glass and objets d'art to its celebrated series of tapestries, *The Lady with the Unicorn* (1500). Throw in the extant architecture – an ornate 15th-century mansion (the Hôtel de Cluny), and the much older *frigidarium* (cold room) of an enormous Roman-era bathhouse – and you have one of Paris' top small museums. Outside, four medieval gardens grace the northeastern corner; more bathhouse remains are to the west.

It's believed that the unicorn tapestries – representing the five senses and an enigmatic sixth, perhaps the heart – were originally commissioned by the Le Viste family in Paris. Discovered in 1814 in the Château de Boussac, they were acquired by the museum in 1882 and have since provided inspiration to many, from Prosper Mérimée and George Sand to, most recently, Tracy Chevalier.

NEED TO KNOW

Map p204 www.musee-moyenage.fr; 6 place Paul Painlevé, 5e; adult/child €8/free; ⊗9.15am-5.45pm Wed-Mon; Ⓜ Cluny–La Sorbonne

Of the three museums here, the four-floor Grande Galerie de l'Évolution is a particular winner if you're travelling with kids: life-sized elephants, tigers and rhinos play safari, and imaginative exhibits on evolution, extinction and global warming fill 6000 sq metres.

The temporary exhibits are generally superb. Within this building is a separate attraction – the **Galerie des Enfants** Map p204 (adult/child €9/7) – which is a hands-on science museum tailored to children from ages six to 12.

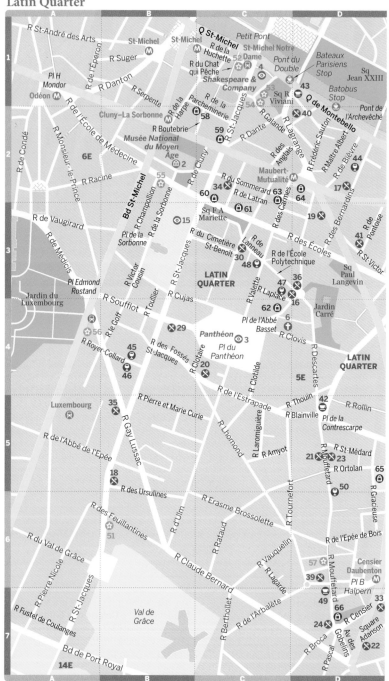

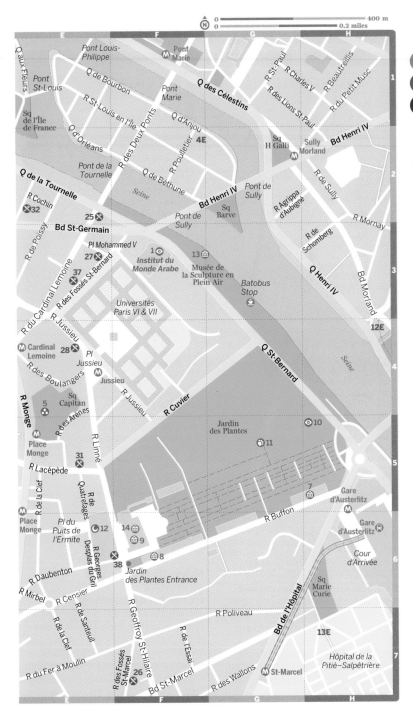

N

0 — 400 m
0 — 0.2 miles

Q aux Fleurs

Pont Louis-Philippe

Pont St-Louis

Q de Bourbon

R St-Louis en l'Île

Pont Marie

M Pont Marie

Q des Célestins

R St-Paul

R Charles V

R des Lions St-Paul

R Beautreillis

R du Petit Musc

Sq de l'Île de France

Q d'Orléans

R des Deux-Ponts

Q d'Anjou

R Poulletier

4E

Sq H Galli

Sully Morland

Bd Henri IV

Pont de la Tournelle

Q de Béthune

Seine

Bd Henri IV

Pont de Sully

R Agrippa d'Aubigné

R de Sully

Q de la Tournelle

R Cochin

X 32

Pont de Sully

Sq Barve

R de Schomberg

R Mornay

25 X

Bd St-Germain

R de Poissy

Pl Mohammed V

27 X

37

R des Fossés St-Bernard

R du Cardinal Lemoine

1 Institut du Monde Arabe

13 Musée de la Sculpture en Plein Air

Q Henri IV

Bd Morland

Universités Paris VI & VII

Batobus Stop

12E

R Jussieu

M Cardinal Lemoine

28 X

Pl Jussieu

R des Boulangers

Jussieu

R Jussieu

R Cuvier

Q St-Bernard

Seine

R Monge

5

Sq Capitan

R des Arènes

R Linné

Jardin des Plantes

10

11

M Place Monge

31 X

R Lacépède

R de la Clef

R de Quatrefages

R Buffon

7

Gare d'Austerlitz

M

M Place Monge

Pl du Puits de l'Ermite

12

14

9

8

38

Jardin des Plantes Entrance

Gare d'Austerlitz

Cour d'Arrivée

R Daubenton

R Georges Desplas du Gril

Sq Marie Curie

R Mirbel

R Censier

R de Santeuil

R Geoffroy St-Hilaire

R Poliveau

Bd de l'Hôpital

13E

R de la Clef

R de l'Essai

Hôpital de la Pitié–Salpêtrière

R du Fer à Moulin

R des Fossés St-Marcel

26

Bd St-Marcel

R des Wallons

M St-Marcel

Latin Quarter

Ménagerie du Jardin des Plantes
Zoo

Map p204 (www.mnhn.fr; 57 rue Cuvier, 5e; adult/child €11/9; ⏰9am-6.30pm Apr-Oct, shorter hours rest of year; Ⓜ Gare d'Austerlitz, Censier Daubenton or Jussieu) Like the Jardin des Plantes in which it's located, this 1000-animal zoo is more than a tourist attraction, also doubling as a research centre for the reproduction of rare and endangered species. During the Prussian siege of 1870, the animals of the day were endangered, when almost all were eaten by starving Parisians.

Musée de la Sculpture en Plein Air
Museum

Map p204 (quai St-Bernard, 5e; Ⓜ Gare d'Austerlitz) FREE Along quai St-Bernard, this open-air sculpture museum (also known as the Jardin Tino Rossi) has more than 50 late-20th-century unfenced sculptures, and makes a great picnic spot. A salad beneath a César or a baguette beside a Brancusi is a pretty classy way to see the Seine up close.

COURTESY OF INSTITUT DU MONDE ARABE/FESSY ©

Don't Miss
Institut du Monde Arabe

The Arab World Institute was jointly founded by France and 18 Middle Eastern and North African nations in 1980, with the aim of promoting cross-cultural dialogue. In addition to hosting concerts, film screenings and a research centre, the stunning landmark is also home to a new museum and temporary exhibition space.

NEED TO KNOW

Map p204 Arab World Institute; www.imarabe.org; 1 place Mohammed V, 5e; adult/child €8/4; ⊙10am-6pm Tue-Thu, to 9.30pm Fri, to 7pm Sat & Sun; Ⓜ Jussieu

Mosquée de Paris   Mosque
Map p204 (☏01 45 35 97 33; www.la-mosquee.com; 2bis place du Puits de l'Ermite, 5e; adult/child €3/2; ⊙mosque 9am-noon & 2-6pm Sat-Thu; Ⓜ Censier Daubenton or Place Monge) Paris' central mosque, with striking 26m-high minaret, was completed in 1926 in an ornate art deco Moorish style. You can visit the interior to admire the intricate tile work and calligraphy. A separate entrance leads to the wonderful North African–style **hammam** Map p204 (☏01 43 31 38 20; www.la-mosquee.com; 39 rue Geoffroy St-Hilaire, 5e; admission/spa package €18/from €43; ⊙10am-9pm Wed-Mon; Ⓜ Censier Daubenton or Place Monge), **restaurant** (p212) and

salon de thé (tearoom), and a small souk (actually more of a gift shop). Visitors must be modestly dressed.

Arènes de Lutèce   Ruins
Map p204 (www.arenesdelutece.com; 49 rue Monge, 5e; ⊙9am-9.30pm Apr-Oct, 8am-5.30pm Nov-Mar; Ⓜ Place Monge) FREE The 2nd-century Roman amphitheatre Lutetia Arena once sat 10,000 people for gladiatorial combats and other events. Found by accident in 1869 when rue Monge was under construction, it's now used by locals playing football and, especially, boules.

BRUNO DE HOGUES/GETTY IMAGES ©

Don't Miss
Panthéon

Overlooking the city from its Left Bank perch, the Panthéon's stately neoclassical dome stands out as one of the most recognizable icons in the Parisian skyline. Originally a church and now a mausoleum, it has served since 1791 as the resting place of some of France's greatest thinkers, including Voltaire, Rousseau, Braille and Hugo. An architectural masterpiece, the interior is impressively vast (if slightly soulless) and certainly worth a wander. The dome is closed for renovations through 2015 (other structural work will continue through 2022).

NEED TO KNOW
Map p204 www.monum.fr; place du Panthéon, 5e; adult/child €7.50/free; ⏱10am-6.30pm Apr-Sep, to 6pm Oct-Mar; Ⓜ Maubert-Mutualité, Cardinal Lemoine or RER Luxembourg

Église St Étienne du Mont   Church
Map p204 (www.saintetiennedumont.fr; 1 place Ste-Geneviève, 5e; ⏱8.45am-7.30pm Tue-Fri, 8.45am-noon & 2-7.45pm Sat & Sun; Ⓜ Cardinal Lemoine) FREE The Church of Mount St Stephen, built between 1492 and 1655, contains Paris' only surviving rood screen (1535), separating the chancel from the nave; the others were removed during the late Renaissance because they prevented the faith-ful in the nave from seeing the priest celebrate Mass.

In the nave's southeastern corner, the tomb of Ste Geneviève lies in a chapel. The patron of Paris, Ste Geneviève was born at Nanterre in AD 422 and turned away Attila the Hun from Paris in AD 451. A highly decorated reliquary near her tomb contains all that is left of her earthly remains – a finger bone.

Sorbonne
University

Map p204 (12 rue de la Sorbonne, 5e; M Cluny–La Sorbonne or RER Luxembourg) The crème de la crème of academia flock to this distinguished university, one of the world's most famous. Today, 'La Sorbonne' embraces most of the 13 autonomous universities – 35,500-odd students in all – created when the University of Paris was reorganised after the student protests of 1968. Until 2015, when an ambitious, 10-year modernisation program costing €45 million reaches completion, parts of the complex will be under renovation. Visitors are not permitted to enter.

✕️ Eating

First-time visitors often think the touristy, restaurant-filled maze of tiny streets between the Seine and bd St-Germain in the 5e constitutes the Latin Quarter. But this neighbourhood encompasses so much more: there are wonderful bistros, restaurants, pubs, cafes, wine bars and squares tucked throughout the entire *arrondissement* (city district).

Petits Plats de Marc
Tearoom €

Map p204 (6 Rue de l'Arbalète, 5e; quiches €7, lunch menus €10-14; ⊙9.30am-3.30pm Tue & Wed, 9am-7pm Thu-Sun; 🛜; M Censier Daubenton) This tiny pit stop off rue Mouffetard is wonderfully cosy and a change from the usual humdrum tourist stops; the homemade soups, quiches, pastries and salads are delicious and easy on the wallet. Tea and coffee is served throughout the day.

Boulangerie Bruno Solques
Patisserie €

Map p204 (243 rue St-Jacques, 5e; ⊙6.30am-1:30pm & 3.30-8pm Mon-Fri; 🚼; M Place Monge or RER Luxembourg) Inventive *pâtissier* (pastry chef) Bruno Solques crafts oddly shaped flat tarts with mashed fruit, fruit-filled brioches and subtly spiced gingerbread. This small, bare-boards shop is also filled with wonderfully rustic breads. It's on the pricey side but worth it – kids from the school across the way can't get enough.

Le Pot O'Lait
Crêperie €

Map p204 (www.lepotolait.com; 41 rue Censier, 5e; lunch menus €10 & 12.90, crêpes €3-11.50; ⊙noon-2.30pm & 7.30-10.30pm Tue-Sat; 🚼; M Censier Daubenton) A bright, contemporary spot, the Milk Can is the business when it comes to *galettes* (savoury buckwheat crêpes) – try smoked salmon or goat's cheese and bacon – and sweet crêpes (pistachio ice cream, zesty orange, hot chocolate and whipped cream). Salads are spectacular; kids will love the ice-cream sundaes.

Boulangerie Eric Kayser
Boulangerie €

Map p204 (www.maison-kayser.com; 8 rue Monge, 5e; ⊙6.45am-8.30pm Wed-Mon; M Maubert–Mutualité) The original branch of Eric Kayser, which has now become a household name in Paris. It's one of the best bakeries that's reasonably close to the Seine and the islands. A few doors down (at No 12) is a second shop, with seating, coffee and light, flaky pastries.

La Salle à Manger
Traditional French €

Map p204 (📞01 55 43 91 99; 138 rue Mouffetard, 5e; mains €10-14; ⊙8.30am-6.30pm; M Censier Daubenton) With a sunny pavement terrace beneath trees enviably placed at the foot of foodie street rue Mouffetard, the 'Dining Room' is prime real estate. Its 360-degree outlook – market stalls, fountain, church and garden with playground for tots – couldn't be prettier, and its salads, *tartines* (open-faced sandwiches), tarts and pastries ensure packed tables at breakfast, lunch and weekend brunch.

Le Comptoir du Panthéon
Cafe, Brasserie €

Map p204 (📞01 43 54 75 56; 5 rue Souflot, 5e; salads €11-13, mains €12.40-15.40; ⊙7am-1.45am; 🛜; M Cardinal Lemoine or RER Luxembourg) Enormous, creative meal-size salads are the reason to pick this as a dining spot. Magnificently placed across from the domed Panthéon on the shady side of the street, its pavement terrace is big, busy and oh so Parisian – turn your head away from Voltaire's burial place and the Eiffel Tower pops into view.

Chez Nicos Crêperie €

Map p204 (44 rue Mouffetard, 5e; crêpes €3-6; noon-2am; [⚲]; [M]Place Monge) The signboard outside crêpe artist Nicos' unassuming little shop chalks up dozens of fillings but ask by name for his masterpiece, 'La Crêpe du Chef', stuffed with aubergines, feta, mozzarella, lettuce, tomatoes and onions. There's a handful of tables inside; otherwise get it wrapped up in foil and head to a nearby park.

Le Jardin des Pâtes Pasta €

Map p204 ([☎]01 43 31 50 71; 4 rue Lacépède, 5e; pasta €10.50-14; ⦿noon-2.30pm & 7.30-10.30pm; [⚲]; [M]Place Monge) ⚑ A crisp white-and-green façade handily placed next to a Vélib' station flags the Pasta Garden, a simple, smart 100% *bio* (organic) place where pasta comes in every guise imaginable – barley, buckwheat, rye, wheat, rice, chestnut and so on. Try the *pâtes de chataignes* (chestnut pasta) with

Gelati d'Alberto Ice Cream

Map p204 (45 rue Mouffetard, 5e; ⦿noon-midnight; [M]Place Monge) Excellent Italian gelato in 36 flavours – a small gets you two scoops, shaped to resemble a flower.

58 Qualité Street Deli €

Map p204 (58 rue de la Montagne Ste-Geneviève, 5e; mains €8.50-18, sandwiches €4.90; ⦿noon-11pm Mon-Sat; [M]Maubert-Mutualité or Cardinal Lemoine) An inviting red-walled deli, this is a handy address if you're after a light meal or an off-hours pick-me-up. There's a handful of main courses (*tartiflette, pot au feu*) prepared in the open 'kitchen' – although truthfully the cooking equipment is pretty limited – along with simple but quality sandwiches to take away and charcuterie and cheese plates to savour over a glass of wine. Cash only.

Les Pipos Wine Bar €€

Map p204 ([☎]01 43 54 11 40; www.les-pipos.com; 2 rue de l'École Polytechnique, 5e; mains €13.90-26.90; ⦿8am-2am Mon-Sat; [M]Maubert-Mutualité) A feast for the eyes and the senses, this *bar à vins* is above all worth a visit for its food. The bistro standards (boeuf bourguignon) and *charcuteries de terroir* (regional cold meats and sausages) are mouth-watering, as is the cheese board, which includes all the gourmet names (bleu d'Auvergne, St-Félicien, St-Marcellin). No credit cards.

L'AOC Traditional French €€

Map p204 ([☎]01 43 54 22 52; www.restoaoc.com; 14 rue des Fossés St-Bernard, 5e; 2-/3-course lunch menus €21/29, mains €19-36; ⦿noon-2.30pm & 7.30-10.30pm Tue-Sat; [M]Cardinal Lemoine) '*Bistrot carnivore*' is the strapline of this ingenious restaurant concocted around France's most respected culinary products. The concept is Appellation d'Origine Contrôlée (AOC), meaning everything has been reared or produced according to strict guidelines. The result? Only the best! Choose between meaty favourites (steak tartare) or the rotisserie

---

Rue Mouffetard

Originally a Roman road, the sloping, cobbled rue Mouffetard acquired its name in the 18th century, when the now-underground River Bievre became the communal waste-disposal for local tanners and wood-pulpers. The odours gave rise to the name Moffettes (literally 'skunk'), which evolved into Mouffetard.

Today the aromas on 'La Mouffe', as it's nicknamed by locals, are infinitely more enticing. Grocers, butchers, fishmongers and other food purveyors set their goods out on street stalls during the **Marché Mouffetard** (Map p204; ⦿8am-7.30pm Tue-Sat, to noon Sun; [M]Censier Daubenton).

duck breast, nutmeg, crème fraîche and mushrooms.

menu, ranging from roast chicken to suckling pig.

Les Papilles
Bistro €€

Map p204 (01 43 25 20 79; www.lespapilles-paris.com; 30 rue Gay Lussac, 5e; 2-/3-course menus from €22/31; noon-2.30pm & 7-10pm Tue-Sat; Raspail or RER Luxembourg) This hybrid bistro, wine cellar and *épicerie* (specialist grocer) with sunflower-yellow façade is one of those fabulous Parisian dining experiences. Meals are served at simply dressed tables wedged beneath bottle-lined walls, and fare is market-driven: each weekday cooks up a different *marmite du marché* (market casserole). But what really sets it apart is its exceptional wine list.

Le Petit Pontoise
Bistro €€

Map p204 (01 43 29 25 20; 9 rue de Pontoise, 5e; mains €21-30; noon-2.30pm & 7.30-10.30pm; Maubert-Mutualité) Sit at a wooden table behind the lace curtains hiding you from the world and indulge in fantastic old-fashioned classics like *rognons de veau à l'ancienne* (calf kidneys), *boudin campagnard* (black pudding) and sweet apple purée or roast quail with dates. Dishes – like the decor – might seem simple, but you'll leave pledging to return.

Le Pré Verre
Bistro €€

Map p204 (01 43 54 59 47; www.lepreverre.com; 25 rue Thénard, 5e; lunch menu €14.50, mains €20; noon-2.30pm & 7.30-10.30pm Tue-Sat; ; Maubert-Mutualité) Noisy, busy and buzzing, the Delacourcelle brothers' jovial bistro plunges diners into the heart of a Parisian's Paris. At lunchtime join the flock and go for the fabulous-value *formule déjeuner* (lunch menu), which might be curried chickpea soup, guinea-fowl thigh spiced with ginger on a bed of red and green cabbage, a glass of wine and loads of ultracrusty, ultrachewy baguette (the best).

Desserts mix Asian spices with traditional French equally well, thanks to chef Philippe's extended sojourns in China, Malaysia, Japan and India. Marc is the man behind the interesting

Love Locks

Stretching from the Latin Quarter's quai de la Tournelle to the eastern tip of the Île de la Cité, the **Pont de l'Archevêché** footbridge is one of many Parisian bridges covered in padlocks. Inscribed with initials and sometimes adorned with ribbons, the locks are attached by couples who then throw the key into the Seine as a symbol of eternal love. Although it sounds romantic, there are now so many padlocks that several bridge railings and grates have been permanently damaged by the sheer weight. One of Mme Hidalgo's first high-profile acts as Paris mayor was to remove the locks on the adorned **Pont des Arts** (west of the Île de la Cité), but just weeks after the initial cleanup the locks were back, causing a section of railing to collapse – a signal to couples that it may be time to find a new way to express their love. Flowers, perhaps?

wine list, which features France's small independent *vignerons* (wine producers).

Dans Les Landes
Gascogne €€

Map p204 (01 45 87 06 00; www.dansles-landesmaisaparis.com; 119bis rue Monge, 5e; tapas €8-16; noon-11pm; Censier Daubenton) Treat yourself to a trip to the Basque Country: Gascogne chef Julien Duboué presents his artful, tapas-size take on southwestern cuisine, with whimsical dishes that range from smoked duck with polenta and chili-smothered *xistoria* (Basque sausages) to truffled artichoke dip, duck neck confit and jars of foie gras. One of the few places in Paris to carry Basque wines.

L'Agrume
Neobistro €€

Map p204 (☎01 43 31 86 48; www.restaurant-lagrume.fr; 15 rue des Fossés St-Marcel, 5e; 2-/3-course lunch menus €22/25, dinner menu €45; ☺noon-2.30pm & 7.30-10.30pm Tue-Sat; Ⓜ Censier Daubenton) Snagging a table at L'Agrume (meaning 'Citrus Fruit') can be tough; reserve several days ahead. The reward is watching chefs work with seasonal products in the open kitchen while you dine – at a table, bar stool or *comptoir* (counter) – at this pocket-size contemporary bistro on a little-known street on the Latin Quarter's southern fringe.

Le Coupe-Chou
French €€

Map p204 (☎01 46 33 68 69; www.lecoupechou.com; 9 & 11 rue de Lanneau, 5e; 2-/3-course menus €27/33; ☺noon-2.30pm & 7.30-10.30pm; Ⓜ Maubert-Mutualité) This maze of candlelit rooms inside a vine-clad 17th-century townhouse is overwhelmingly romantic. Ceilings are beamed, furnishings are antique, and background classical music mingles with the intimate chatter of diners. As in the days when Marlene Dietrich dined here, advance reservations are essential.

Terroir Parisien
Bistro €€

Map p204 (☎01 44 31 54 54; www.yannick-alleno.com; 20 rue St-Victor, 5e; mains €19-25; ☺noon-2.30pm & 7-10.30pm; Ⓜ Maubert-Mutualité or Cardinal Lemoine) A good concept (a focus on local dishes and ingredients) and an airy, modern interior give Terroir Parisien a nice one-two punch. You can expect contemporary interpretations of typically Parisian fare, such as deconstructed onion soup or a perfect disk of blood sausage over creamy puréed potatoes. A few quick bites (eg croque monsieur) are also served. Do note that portions are small.

Mosquée de Paris
North African €€

Map p204 (☎01 43 31 38 20; www.la-mosquee.com; 39 rue Geoffroy St-Hilaire, 5e; mains €15-26; ☺noon-2.30pm & 7.30-10.30pm; Ⓜ Censier Daubenton or Place Monge) Dig into one of nine types of couscous, or choose a heaping *tajine* or meaty grill at this richly decorated, authentic-as-it-gets North African restaurant tucked within the walls of the city's art deco–Moorish mosque, or sip a sweet mint tea and nibble on a *pâtisserie orientale* between trees and chirping

Al fresco dining, Latin Quarter

birds in the courtyard of the **tearoom** (🕙9am-11.30pm).

Feeling decadent? Book a *formule orientale* (€63), which includes a body scrub, 10-minute massage and a lounge in the hammam (p207) as well as lunch, mint tea and sweet pastry.

Restaurant Variations   Bistro €€

(☎01 43 31 36 04; www.restaurantvariations.com; 18 rue des Wallons, 13e; lunch menus €16.50-19, dinner menus €24-44; 🕙noon-2pm Mon-Fri, 7-10pm Mon-Sat; Ⓜ St-Marcel) In a pin-drop-quiet back street you'd never stumble on by chance, this light-filled restaurant is a diamond find. It's framed by huge glass windows and artfully decorated with large-scale photographs; square white plates showcase the colours and textures of brothers Philippe and Pierre Tondetta's Italian-accented offerings such as rack of lamb accompanied by polenta with olives and aged parmesan.

Anahuacalli   Mexican €€

Map p204 (☎01 43 26 10 20; www.anahuacalli.fr; 30 rue des Bernardins, 5e; mains €17-22; 🕙7.30-10.30pm daily, noon-2.30pm Sun; Ⓜ Maubert-Mutualité) Mexican food is riding a wave of popularity in Paris and this upmarket restaurant – behind a discreet rosemary-coloured façade, with a sparingly decorated interior lined with mirrors and statuettes – offers some of the best. Authentic enchiladas, tamales and mole poblano are all elegantly presented; fish aficionados should try the *pescado à la veracruzana* (fish of the day flambéed with tequila).

Sola   Fusion €€€

Map p204 (☎dinner 01 43 29 59 04, lunch 09 65 01 73 68; www.restaurant-sola.com; 12 rue de l'Hôtel Colbert, 5e; lunch/dinner €48/98; 🕙noon-2pm & 7-10pm Tue-Sat; Ⓜ St-Michel) For serious gourmands, Sola is arguably the Latin Quarter's proverbial brass ring. Pedigreed chef Hiroki Yoshitake combines French technique with Japanese sensibility, resulting in gorgeous signature creations (such as miso-marinated foie gras on *feuille de brick* (filo pastry)

served on a slice of tree trunk). The artful presentations and attentive service make this a great choice for a romantic meal – go for the full experience and reserve a table in the Japanese dining room downstairs.

La Tour d'Argent   Gastronomic €€€

Map p204 (☎01 43 54 23 31; www.latourdargent.com; 15 quai de la Tournelle, 5e; lunch menus €65, dinner menus €170-190; 🕙noon-2.30pm & 7.30-10.30pm Tue-Sat; Ⓜ Cardinal Lemoine or Pont Marie) The venerable 'Silver Tower' is famous for its *caneton* (duckling), rooftop garden with glimmering Notre Dame views and a fabulous history harking back to 1582 – from Henry III's inauguration of the first fork in France to inspiration for the winsome animated film *Ratatouille*. Its wine cellar is one of Paris' best; dining is dressy and exceedingly fine.

Le Buisson Ardent   Modern French €€€

Map p204 (☎01 43 54 93 02; www.lebuissonardent.fr; 25 rue Jussieu, 5e; lunch/dinner menu €28/41; 🕙noon-2.30pm & 7.30-10.30pm; Ⓜ Jussieu) Housed in a former coach house, this time-worn bistro (murals in the front room date to the 1920s) serves classy, exciting French fare, from sea bass with grilled fennel and chorizo to spare ribs with olive paste, polenta and onion jam.

Moissonnier   Lyonnais €€€

Map p204 (☎01 43 29 87 65; 28 rue des Fossés St-Bernard, 5e; lunch mains €17-26, 4-/6-course dinner menus €75/115; 🕙noon-2.30pm & 7.30-10.30pm Tue-Sat; Ⓜ Cardinal Lemoine) It's Lyon, not Paris, that French gourmets venerate as the French food capital. Take one bite of a big, fat *andouillette* (pig-intestine sausage), *tablier de sapeur* (breaded, fried stomach), traditional *quenelles* (dumplings) or *boudin noir aux pommes* (black pudding with apples) and you'll realise why. A perfect reflection of one of France's most unforgettable regional cuisines.

Café de la Nouvelle Mairie
Wine Bar €€

Map p204 (19 rue des Fossés St-Jacques, 5e; mains €14-16; ⏰8am-midnight Mon-Fri; ⓂCardinal-Lemoine) Shhhh...just around the corner from the Panthéon but hidden away on a small, fountained square, the narrow wine bar Café de la Nouvelle Mairie is a neighbourhood secret, serving blackboard-chalked natural wines by the glass and delicious seasonal bistro fare from oysters and ribs (*à la française*) to grilled lamb sausage over lentils.

Drinking & Nightlife

Le Verre à Pied
Cafe

Map p204 (http://leverreapied.fr; 118bis rue Mouffetard, 5e; ⏰9am-9pm Tue-Sat, 9.30am-4pm Sun; ⓂCensier Daubenton) This *café-tabac* is a pearl of a place where little has changed since 1870. Its nicotine-hued mirrored wall, moulded cornices and original bar make it part of a dying breed, but the place oozes the charm, glamour and romance of an old Paris everyone loves, including stall holders from the rue Mouffetard market who yo-yo in and out.

Le Pub St-Hilaire
Pub

Map p204 (2 rue Valette, 5e; ⏰3pm-2am Mon-Thu, 3pm-4am Fri, 4pm-4am Sat, 4pm-midnight Sun; ⓂMaubert-Mutualité) 'Buzzing' fails to do justice to the pulsating vibe inside this student-loved pub. Generous happy hours last several hours and the place is kept packed with a trio of pool tables, board games, music on two floors, hearty bar food and various gimmicks to rev up the party crowd (a metre of cocktails, 'be your own barman' etc).

Curio Parlor Cocktail Club
Cocktail Bar

Map p204 (www.curioparlor.com; 16 rue des Bernardins, 5e; ⏰7pm-2am Mon-Thu, to 4am Fri-Sun; ⓂMaubert-Mutualité) Run by the same switched-on, chilled-out team as the Experimental Cocktail Club (p116), this hybrid bar-club looks to the interwar *années folles* (crazy years) of 1920s Paris, London and New York for inspiration. Its racing-green façade with a simple brass plaque on the door is the height of discretion.

Go to its Facebook page to find out which party is happening when.

Café Panis
Cafe

Map p204 (21 quai de Montebello, 5e; ⏰7am-midnight; 🛜; ⓂSt-Michel) Snag a sunlit table to write your postcards home at this busy, timeless cafe facing Notre Dame. Coffee, tea and inexpensive French comfort food – croque monsieur, *magret de canard* (duck breast) – make it an excellent place to linger and refuel.

Café Delmas
Cafe

Map p204 (www.cafedelmasparis.com; 2 place de la Contrescarpe, 5e; ⏰8am-2am Sun-Thu, to 4am Fri & Sat; 🛜; ⓂPlace Monge) Enviably situated on tree-studded place de la Contrescarpe, the Delmas is a hot spot for chilling over *un café*/cappuccino or all-day breakfast. Cosy up beneath overhead heaters outside to soak up the street atmosphere or snuggle up between books in the library-style interior – awash with students from the nearby universities.

Le Vieux Chêne
Bar

Map p204 (69 rue Mouffetard, 5e; ⏰4pm-2am Sun-Thu, to 5am Fri & Sat; ⓂPlace Monge) This rue Mouffetard institution is reckoned to be Paris' oldest bar. Indeed, a revolutionary circle met here in 1848 and it was a popular *bal musette* (dancing club) in the late 19th and early 20th centuries. These days it's a student favourite, especially during happy hour (4pm to 9pm Tuesday to Sunday, and from 4pm until closing on Monday).

Le Crocodile
Bar

Map p204 (6 rue Royer-Collard, 5e; ⏰6pm-2am Mon-Sat; ⓂOdéon or RER Luxembourg) This green-shuttered bar has been dispensing affordable cocktails (more than 200 on the list) since 1966. The '70s were 'epic' here, and the dream kicks on well into the new millennium. Arrive late for a truly eclectic crowd, including lots of students, and an atmosphere that can go from quiet tippling to raucous revelry. Hours can vary.

Le Piano Vache
Bar

Map p204 (www.lepianovache.com; 8 rue Laplace, 5e; ⏰noon-4pm Mon-Fri, 7pm-2am Mon-Sat; Ⓜ Maubert-Mutualité) Down the hill from the Panthéon, this bar is covered in aged posters above old couches and drenched in 1970s and '80s rock ambience. Effortlessly underground and a real student fave, it has bands and DJs playing mainly rock, plus some goth, reggae and pop.

Le Pantalon
Bar

Map p204 (7 rue Royer-Collard, 5e; ⏰5.30pm-2am; Ⓜ Cluny–La Sorbonne or RER Luxembourg) Ripped vinyl seats, coloured-glass light fittings and old stickers plastered on the walls make this rockin' little bar a favourite hang-out for those with little change but lots of heart.

⭐ Entertainment

Café Universel
Jazz, Blues

Map p204 (☎01 43 25 74 20; http://cafeuni-versel.com; 267 rue St-Jacques, 5e; ⏰9pm-2am Mon-Sat; 📶; Ⓜ Censier Daubenton or RER Port Royal) FREE Café Universel hosts a brilliant array of live concerts with everything from bebop and Latin sounds to vocal jazz sessions. Plenty of freedom is given to young producers and artists, and its convivial relaxed atmosphere attracts a mix of students and jazz lovers. Concerts are free, but tip the artists when they pass the hat around.

Le Champo
Cinema

Map p204 (www.lechampo.com; 51 rue des Écoles, 5e; Ⓜ St-Michel or Cluny–La Sorbonne) This is one of the most popular of the many Latin Quarter cinemas, featuring classics and retrospectives looking at the films of such actors and directors as Alfred Hitchcock,

Jacques Tati, Alain Resnais, Frank Capra, Tim Burton and Woody Allen. One of the two *salles* (cinemas) has wheelchair access.

Le Caveau des Oubliettes
Jazz, Blues

Map p204 (☎01 46 34 24 09; www.caveaudes-oubliettes.fr; 52 rue Galande, 5e; ⏰5pm-4am; Ⓜ St-Michel) From the 16th-century ground-floor pub, descend to the 12th-century dungeon for jazz, blues and funk concerts and jam sessions (from 10pm).

Le Petit Journal St-Michel
Jazz, Blues

Map p204 (☎01 43 26 28 59; www.petitjournal saintmichel.com; 71 bd St-Michel, 5e; admission incl 1 drink €20, with dinner €49-53; ⏰Mon-Sat; Ⓜ Cluny–La Sorbonne or RER Luxembourg) Classic jazz concerts kick off at 9.15pm in the atmospheric downstairs cellar of this sophisticated jazz venue across from the Jardin du Luxembourg. Everything ranging from Dixieland and vocals to big band and swing sets patrons' toes tapping. Dinner is served at 8pm.

Caveau de la Huchette
Jazz, Blues

Map p204 (☎01 43 26 65 05; www.caveaude-lahuchette.fr; 5 rue de la Huchette, 5e; Sun-Thu €13, Fri & Sat €15, under 25yr €10; ⏰9.30pm-2.30am Sun-Wed, to 4am Thu-Sat; Ⓜ St-Michel) Housed in a medieval *caveau* (cellar) used as a courtroom and torture chamber during the Revolution, this club is where virtually all the jazz greats have played since the end of WWII. It attracts its fair share of tourists, but the atmosphere can be more electric than at the more serious jazz clubs. Sessions start at 10pm.

L'Epée de Bois
Cinema

Map p204 (100 rue Mouffetard, 5e; Ⓜ Censier Daubenton) Even locals find it easy to miss the small doorway leading to rue Mouf-fetard's little cinema, which screens art-house flicks such as Julie Delpy–directed films.

GARDEL BERTRAND/GETTY IMAGES ©

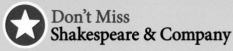

Don't Miss
Shakespeare & Company

This bookshop is the stuff of legends. A kind of spell descends as you enter, weaving between nooks and crannies overflowing with new and secondhand English-language books. The original shop (12 rue l'Odéon, 6e; closed by the Nazis in 1941) was run by Sylvia Beach and became the meeting point for Hemingway's 'Lost Generation'. Readings by emerging and illustrious authors take place at 7pm on most Mondays; it also hosts workshops and festivals.

American-born George Whitman opened the present incarnation in 1951, attracting a beat-poet clientele, and scores of authors have since passed through its doors. In 2006 Whitman was awarded the Officier des Arts et Lettres by the French Minister of Culture, recognising 'significant contribution to the enrichment of the French cultural inheritance'. Whitman died in 2011, aged 98; he is buried in division 73 of Cimetière du Père Lachaise. Today his daughter, Sylvia Beach Whitman, maintains Shakespeare & Company's serendipitous magic. It's fabled for nurturing writers, and at night its couches turn into beds where writers stay in exchange for stacking shelves.

NEED TO KNOW
Map p204 www.shakespeareandcompany.com; 37 rue de la Bûcherie, 5e; ⏱10am-11pm Mon-Fri, from 11am Sat & Sun; MSt-Michel

Église St-Julien le Pauvre Classical
Map p204 (☎01 42 26 00 00; www.concertin-paris.com; 1 rue St-Julien le Pauvre, 5e; MSt-Michel) Piano recitals (Chopin, Liszt) are staged on two evenings a week in one of the oldest churches in Paris.

🔒 Shopping

Fromagerie Laurent Dubois
Food, Drink

Map p204 (www.fromageslaurentdubois.fr; 47ter bd St-Germain, 5e; ⏰8.30am-7.30pm Tue-Sat, to 1pm Sun; M Maubert-Mutualité) One of the best *fromageries* (cheese shops) in Paris, this cheese-lover's nirvana is filled with to-die-for delicacies such as St-Félicien with Périgord truffles. Rare, limited-production cheeses include blue Termignon and Tarentaise goat's cheese. All are appropriately cellared in warm, humid or cold environments. There's also a 15e **branch** (www.fromageslaurentdubois.fr; 2 rue de Lourmel, 15e; ⏰9am-1pm & 4-7.45pm Tue-Fri, 8.30am-7.45pm Sat, 9am-1pm Sun; M Dupleix).

Magie
Games, Hobbies

Map p204 (📞01 43 54 13 63; www.mayette. com; 8 rue des Carmes, 5e; ⏰1-8pm Mon-Sat; M Maubert-Mutualité) One of a kind, this 1808-established magic shop is said to be the world's oldest. Since 1991 it's been in the hands of world-famous magic pro Dominique Duvivier. Professional and hobbyist magicians flock here to discuss king sandwiches, reverse assemblies, false cuts and other card tricks with him and his daughter, Alexandra.

   If you want to learn the tricks of the trade, Duvivier has magic courses up his sleeve.

Abbey Bookshop
Books

Map p204 (📞01 46 33 16 24; 29 rue de la Parcheminerie, 5e; ⏰10am-7pm Mon-Sat; M St-Michel or Cluny–La Sorbonne) In a heritage-listed townhouse, this welcoming Canadian-run bookshop serves free coffee (sweetened with maple syrup) to sip while you browse tens of thousands of new and used books, and organises literary events and countryside hikes.

Au Vieux Campeur
Outdoor Equipment

Map p204 (www.auvieuxcampeur.fr; 48 rue des Écoles, 5e; ⏰11am-7.30pm Mon-Wed, Fri & Sat, to 9pm Thu; M Maubert-Mutualité or Cluny–La Sorbonne) This outdoor store seems to have colonised the Latin Quarter, with some 25 different outlets scattered about, each devoted to your favourite sport: climbing, skiing, diving, biking and so on. While it's a great resource if you need any gear, the many boutiques make shopping something of a treasure hunt – especially as many outlets change what they sell with the seasons.

Marché Maubert
Market

Map p204 (place Maubert, 5e; ⏰7am-2.30pm Tue, Thu & Sat; M Maubert-Mutualité) The Left Bank's bourgeois bohemian soul lives on at this colourful street market. Expect the usual line of tempting market fare, though it doesn't come cheap.

Marché Monge
Market

Map p204 (place Monge, 5e; ⏰7am-2pm Wed, Fri & Sun; M Place Monge) The open-air Marché Monge is laden with cheeses, baked goods and many other temptations.

Album
Comics

Map p204 (www.album.fr; 67 bd St-Germain, 5e; ⏰10am-8pm Mon-Sat, noon-7pm Sun; M Cluny–La Sorbonne) Album specialises in *bandes dessinées* (comics and graphic novels), which have an enormous following in France, with everything from Tintin and Babar to erotic comics and the latest Japanese manga. Serious comic collectors – and anyone excited by Harry Potter wands, Star Wars, Superman and other superhero figurines and T-shirts (you know who you are!) – shouldn't miss it.

Crocodisc
Music

Map p204 (www.crocodisc.com; 40 & 42 rue des Écoles, 5e; ⏰11am-7pm Tue-Sat; M Maubert-Mutualité) Music might be more accessible than ever before thanks to iPods, iPads and phones, but for many it will never replace rummaging through racks for treasures. New and secondhand CDs and vinyl discs at 40 rue des Écoles span world music, rap, reggae, salsa, soul and disco, while No 42 has pop, rock, punk, new wave, electro and soundtracks.

   Its nearby sister shop **Crocojazz** Map p204 (64 rue de la Montagne Ste-Geneviève, 5e; ⏰11am-1pm & 2-7pm Tue-Sat; M Maubert-Mutualité) specialises in jazz, blues, gospel and timeless crooners, with books and DVDs as well as recordings.

St-Germain, Les Invalides & Montparnasse

Despite gentrification since its early-20th-century bohemian days, there remains a startling cinematic quality to this soulful part of the Left Bank where artists, writers, actors and musicians cross paths and where *la vie germanopratine* (St-Germain life) is *belle*.

West towards the Eiffel Tower the Invalides area is an elegant if staid *quartier* (quarter) bordered by the smooth lawns of Esplanade des Invalides.

To the south, the Tour Montparnasse is an unavoidable sight, but its observation deck is an unrivalled spot to get to grips with the lie of the land. At its feet are the cafes, brasseries and backstreets where some of the early 20th century's most seminal artists and writers hung out – albeit now swathed by urban grit. The area's tree-filled cemetery is a peaceful spot to escape – and to visit famous graves of many of those same visionaries.

Hôtel des Invalides (p236)

CALLE MONTES/GETTY IMAGES ©

St-Germain, Les Invalides & Montparnasse Highlights

Musée d'Orsay (p224)

Revel in a wealth of impressionist masterpieces and art nouveau architecture in resplendently renovated surrounds at the glorious Musée d'Orsay, the home of France's national collection from the impressionist, postimpressionist and art nouveau movements, with world-famous works on display. Entry to the Musée d'Orsay is cheaper in the late afternoon, so it's an ideal time to check out its breathtaking collections.

1

JOELLE ICARD/GETTY IMAGES ©

Les Catacombes (p243)

2

Venture into the spine-prickling, subterranean tunnels of Paris' creepy ossuary, Les Catacombes, to ogle the freakishly large number of bones and skulls surrounding you. Millions of Parisians' remains are neatly packed along the walls of these underground corridors. During WWII these tunnels were used as a headquarters for the Resistance, and today they're the city's most macabre tourist attraction.

RUNE JOHANSEN/GETTY IMAGES ©

WIN-INITIATIVE/GETTY IMAGES ©

Hôtel des Invalides (p236)

The monumental Hôtel des Invalides was built in the 17th century to house infirm war veterans. At the southern end of the esplanade, laid out between 1704 and 1720, is the final resting place of Napoleon. Also here is France's largest military museum, as well as the Musée des Plans-Reliefs, with scale models of towns, fortresses and châteaux across France.

FREDERIC SOLTAN/CORBIS ©

BRIAN JANNSEN/ALAMY ©

Les Deux Magots (p245)

Sartre, de Beauvoir, Hemingway, Camus, Picasso, Joyce and Brecht are just some of the luminaries who frequented classic Parisian cafe Les Deux Magots, which has awarded its own Prix des Deux Magots literary prize since 1933. Its corner position on bd St-Germain provides primo people watching. If you're feeling decadent, order its famous hot chocolate, served in porcelain jugs.

Musée Rodin (p234)

Indulge in an exquisitely Parisian moment in the sculpture-filled gardens of the Musée Rodin. The collection of the master sculptor's works are displayed not only in his former workshop and showroom, the *hôtel particulier* Hôtel Biron (1730), but also beyond the doors of the mansion in its rose-covered garden – one of the most peaceful places in central Paris.

St-Germain, Les Invalides & Montparnasse Walk

Graceful gardens, monumental museums and centuries-old churches all feature on this walk, as well as time to linger along the neighbourhood's elegant streets.

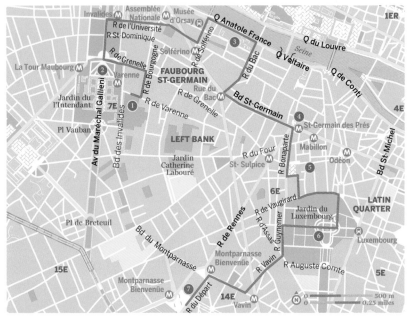

WALK FACTS

- **Start** Musée Rodin
- **Finish** Tour Montparnasse
- **Distance** 6.5km
- **Duration** Three hours

1 Musée Rodin

Sculptor Rodin's former workshop and showroom is the 18th-century Hôtel Biron. Even if you don't have time to visit the mansion itself, at least stop to see the **Musée Rodin's** (p234) sculpture-filled gardens (reduced garden-only entry is available).

2 Hôtel des Invalides

Head east on rue de Varenne and take your first left on rue de Bourgogne – on your left, you can see baguettes being baked through the viewing window of *boulangerie* **Besnier** (p240). Turn left onto rue de Grenelle and continue to place des Invalides. The **Hôtel des Invalides** (p236) complex, with the **Musée de l'Armée** military museum, and **Napoleon's tomb** are to your left. Turn right and stroll along av du Maréchal Gallieni through the grand lawns of the Esplanade des Invalides.

3 Musée d'Orsay

From the Esplanade des Invalides, turn right on rue de l'Université, passing the **Assemblée Nationale** – the French Parliament's lower house – on your left. Turn left on rue de Solférino, and right around the **Musée d'Orsay** (p224) on the riverfront. Not only does the d'Orsay contain breathtaking artworks and artefacts from the art nouveau era, but the former railway station in which it's housed, the Gare d'Orsay, is also an art nouveau architectural wonder.

4 Église St-Germain des Prés

At the Gare d'Orsay's eastern end, turn right on rue du Bac. On your right at No 46, duck into the 1831-established taxidermist **Deyrolle**, which is overrun with stuffed creatures including lions, tigers, zebras and storks. Continue south to bd St-Germain and turn right until you reach Paris' oldest church, **Église St-Germain des Prés** (p228), dating from the 11th century. Opposite the church is fêted literary café **Les Deux Magots** (p245).

5 Église St-Sulpice

Follow rue Bonaparte south of the Église St-Germain des Prés to another landmark church, the **Église St-Sulpice** (p228). Fronted by dramatic Italianate columns, highlights inside include frescoes by Eugène Delacroix in the Chapelle des Stes-Agnes, and the Rose Line (to the right of the middle of the nave), featured in a pivotal scene of *The Da Vinci Code*.

6 Jardin du Luxembourg

From Église St-Sulpice, head south on to rue Férou. Cross rue de Vaugirard and enter the enchanting **Jardin du Luxembourg** (p226) near the early 17th-century **Palais du Luxembourg** (p227), which now houses the French Sénat (upper house).

7 Tour Montparnasse

Stroll through the gardens to the octagonal pond. Turn right at the pond and exit the gardens at rue Guynemer, turning left. Cross rue d'Assas and take rue Vavin until turning right on bd du Montparnasse – up ahead you can't miss the towering **Tour Montparnasse** (p232) skyscraper, which has sensational views from its observation terrace.

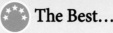 The Best...

PLACES TO EAT

Bouillon Racine An art nouveau jewel with traditional French fare. (p235)

Huîterie Regis Small but supremely stylish oyster bar. (p235)

Ze Kitchen Galerie Not just a Michelin-starred restaurant but a smart art gallery too. (p237)

David Toutain Mystery degustation courses showcase creative highend cooking. (p241)

PLACES TO DRINK

Les Deux Magots A literary stalwart, whose former regulars included Hemingway. Their hot chocolate is a must. (p245)

Au Sauvignon Authentic *bar à vin* (wine bar) with an original zinc bar. (p246)

Brasserie O'Neil Paris' original microbrewery, serving thin-crusted *flammekueches* (Alsatian pizzas). (p246)

CHURCHES

Église St-Germain des Prés Built in the 11th century, this is Paris' oldest church. (p228)

Église St-Sulpice Frescoes by Eugène Delacroix and a starring role in *The Da Vinci Code*. (p228)

Bouillon Racine (p235)
LONELY PLANET/GETTY IMAGES ©

Don't Miss
Musée d'Orsay

The home of France's national collection from the impressionist, postimpressionist and art-nouveau movements is, appropriately, the glorious former Gare d'Orsay. The railway station is itself an art-nouveau masterpiece designed by competition-winning architect Victor Laloux. Transforming the languishing building into the country's premier showcase for art from 1848 to 1914 was the grand project of President Valéry Giscard d'Estaing, who signed off on it in 1977. The museum opened its doors in 1986, with a roll call of instantly recognisable works from French and international masters.

Map p238

www.musee-orsay.fr

62 rue de Lille, 7e

adult/child €11/free

⊙9.30am-6pm Tue, Wed & Fri-Sun, to 9.45pm Thu

Ⓜ Assemblée Nationale or RER Musée d'Orsay

The Building

Even on its completion, just in time for the 1900 Exposition Universelle, painter Edouard Detaille declared that the new station looked like a Palais des Beaux Arts. But although it had all the mod-cons of the day – including luggage lifts and passenger elevators – by 1939 the increasing electrification of the rail network meant the Gare d'Orsay's platforms were too short for mainline trains, and within a few years all rail services ceased.

The station was used as a mailing centre during WWII, and in 1962 Orson Welles filmed Kafka's *The Trial* in the then-abandoned building. Fortunately, it was saved from being demolished and replaced with a hotel complex by a Historical Monument listing in 1973, before the government set about establishing the palatial museum.

The Paintings

Top of every visitor's must-see list is the world's largest collection of impressionist and postimpressionist art. Just some of its highlights include Manet's *On The Beach* and *Woman With Fans*; Monet's gardens at Giverny and *Rue Montorgueil, Paris, Festival of June 30, 1878*; Cézanne's card players, *Green Apples* and *Blue Vase*; Renoir's *Ball at the Moulin de la Galette* and *Young Girls at the Piano*; Degas' ballerinas; Toulouse-Lautrec's cabaret dancers; Pissarro's *The Harvest*; Sisley's *View of the Canal St-Martin*; and Van Gogh's self-portraits, *Bedroom in Arles* and *Starry Night over the Rhône*. One of the museum's newest acquisitions is James Tissot's 1868 painting *The Circle of the Rue Royale*, classified as a national treasure.

Decorative Arts

Household items such as hat and coat stands, candlesticks, desks, chairs, bookcases, vases, pot-plant holders, freestanding screens, wall mirrors, water pitchers, plates, goblets, bowls and even soup terrines become works of art in the hands of their creators from the era, incorporating exquisite design elements and motifs.

Sculptures

The cavernous former station is a magnificent setting for sculptures, including works by Degas, Gaugin, Claudel, Renoir and Rodin.

Graphic Arts

Drawings, pastels and sketches from major artists are another of the d'Orsay's lesser-known highlights. Look for Seurat's *The Black Bow* (c 1882), which uses crayon on paper to define forms by contrasting between black and white, and Paul Gaugin's poignant self-portrait (c 1902-1903), drawn near the end of his life.

Guided Tours

For a thorough introduction to the museum, 90-minute 'Masterpieces of the Musée d'Orsay' guided tours (€6) in English generally run at least once a day from Tuesday to Saturday – check the website for seasonal departure times. Kids under 13 aren't permitted on tours.

Money-saving Tips

A combined ticket with the Musée de l'Orangerie is €16 (visit both museums within four days); one with the Musée Rodin is €15 (visit both on the same day). Musée d'Orsay admission drops to €8.50 after 4.30pm (6pm Thursday).

Dining

Designed like a fantasy underwater world, **Café Campana** Map p238 (dishes €9-18; ⏲10am-5pm Tue, Wed & Fri-Sun, to 9pm Thu; M Assemblée Nationale or RER Musée d'Orsay) serves a short, stylish menu. Time has scarcely changed the museum's – originally the station's – sumptuous **Restaurant Musée d'Orsay** Map p238 (📞01 45 49 47 03; 2-/3-course lunch menus €22/32, mains €16-25; ⏲9.30am-5.45pm Tue-Wed & Fri-Sun, to 9.30pm Thu; M Assemblée Nationale or RER Musée d'Orsay).

Don't Miss
Jardin du Luxembourg

The merest ray of sunshine is enough to draw Parisians outdoors, but this inner-city oasis of formal terraces, chestnut groves and lawns has a special place in the hearts of Parisians. Napoléon dedicated the 23 gracefully laid-out hectares of the Luxembourg Gardens to the children of Paris, and many residents spent their childhood prodding little wooden sailboats with long sticks on the octagonal pond, watching puppets perform Punch & Judy–type shows, and riding the carousel (merry-go-round). All those activities are still here today, as well as modern play equipment, tennis courts and other games venues.

Map p230

numerous entrances

⊙ hours vary

Ⓜ St-Sulpice, Rennes or Notre Dame des Champs, or RER Luxembourg

Grand Bassin

All ages love the octagonal **Grand Bassin** Map p230, a serene ornamental pond where adults can lounge and kids can prod 1920s **toy sailboats** (per 30min €3; ⏱Apr-Oct) with long sticks. Nearby, littlies can take **pony rides** (rides €3.50; ⏱Apr-Oct) or romp around the **playgrounds** Map p230 (adult/child €1.20/2.50) – the green half is for kids aged seven to 12 years, the blue half for under-sevens.

Puppet Shows

You don't have to be a kid or speak French to be delighted by marionette shows, which have entertained audiences in France since the Middle Ages. The lively puppets perform in the Jardin du Luxembourg's little **Théâtre du Luxembourg** Map p230 (www.marionnettesduluxembourg.fr; tickets €4.80; ⏱usually 3.30pm Wed, 11am & 3.30pm Sat & Sun, daily during school holidays; Ⓜ Notre Dame des Champs). Show times can vary; check the program online and arrive half an hour ahead.

Orchards

Dozens of apple varieties grow in the **orchards** Map p230 in the gardens' south. Bees have produced honey in the nearby apiary, the **Rucher du Luxembourg** Map p230, since the 19th century. The annual Fête du Miel (Honey Festival) offers two days of tasting and buying its sweet harvest in late September in the ornate **Pavillon Davioud** Map p230 (55bis rue d'Assas).

Palais du Luxembourg

The gardens are the backdrop to the **Palais du Luxembourg** Map p230 (rue de Vaugirard; Ⓜ Rennes or RER Luxembourg), built in the 1620s for Marie de Médici, Henri IV's consort, to assuage her longing for the Pitti Palace in Florence.

Since 1958 the palace has housed the French **Sénat** Map p230 (Senate; ☎01 44 54 19 49; www.senat.fr; rue de Vaugirard; adult/18-25yr €8/6). It's occasionally visitable by guided tour.

East of the palace is the Italianate **Fontaine des Médici** Map p230, an ornate fountain built in 1630. During Baron Haussmann's 19th-century reshaping of the roads, it was moved 30m and the pond and dramatic statues of the giant bronze Polyphemus discovering the white-marble lovers Acis and Galatea were added.

Musée du Luxembourg

Prestigious temporary art exhibitions, such as 'Cézanne et Paris', take place in the **Musée du Luxembourg** Map p230 (www. museeduluxembourg.fr; 19 rue de Vaugirard, 6e; most exhibitions adult/child around €13.50/9; ⏱10am-7.30pm Tue-Thu & Sat-Sun, to 10pm Fri & Mon; Ⓜ Rennes or RER Luxembourg). It was the first French museum to be opened to the public, in 1750, before relocating here in 1886; following closures, it has mounted exhibitions regularly since 1979.

Around the back of the museum, lemon and orange trees, palms, grenadiers and oleanders shelter from the cold in the palace's **orangery** Map p230. Nearby, the heavily guarded **Hôtel du Petit Luxembourg** was where Marie de Médici lived while Palais du Luxembourg was being built. The president of the Senate has called it home since 1825.

Picnicking

Kiosks and cafes are dotted throughout the park. If you're planning on picnicking, forget bringing a blanket – the elegantly manicured lawns are off-limits apart from a small wedge on the southern boundary. Instead, do as Parisians do, and corral one of the iconic 1923-designed green metal chairs and find your own favourite part of the park.

St-Germain, Les Invalides & Montparnasse

Getting There & Away

○ **Metro** Get off at metro stations St-Germain des Prés, Mabillon or Odéon for its busy bd St-Germain heart. Montparnasse Bienvenüe is the transport hub for Montparnasse and the 15e. Bibliothèque and Place d'Italie are the main stops in Place d'Italie and Chinatown.

○ **Bus** Buses stop on bd St-Germain for the 86 to Odéon and Bastille; rue de Rennes for the 96 to place Châtelet, Hôtel de Ville, St-Paul (Le Marais) and Ménilmontant; and by the Musée d'Orsay for the 73 to place de la Concorde, av des Champs-Élysées and La Défense.

○ **Bicycle** Handy Vélib' stations include 141 bd St-Germain, 6e; opposite 2 bd Raspail, 6e; and 62 rue de Lille, 7e.

○ **Boat** St-Germain des Prés and Musée d'Orsay.

Sights

Église St-Germain des Prés
Church

Map p230 (www.eglise-sgp.org; 3 place St-Germain des Prés, 6e; ⏱8am-7.45pm Mon-Sat, 9am-8pm Sun; Ⓜ St-Germain des Prés) Paris' oldest standing church, the Romanesque St Germanus of the Fields, was built in the 11th century on the site of a 6th-century abbey and was the dominant place of worship in Paris until the arrival of Notre Dame. It's since been altered many times, but the **Chapelle de St-Symphorien** (to the right as you enter) was part of the original abbey and is believed to be the resting place of St Germanus (AD 496–576), the first bishop of Paris.

Église St-Sulpice
Church

Map p230 (http://pss75.fr/saint-sulpice-paris; place St-Sulpice, 6e; ⏱7.30am-7.30pm; Ⓜ St-Sulpice) In 1646 work started on the twin-towered Church of St Sulpicius, lined inside with 21 side chapels, and it took six architects 150 years to finish. What draws most visitors isn't its striking Italianate façade with two rows of superimposed columns, its Counter-Reformation-influenced neoclassical decor or even its frescoes by Eugène Delecroix but its setting for a murderous scene in Dan Brown's *The Da Vinci Code*.

You can hear the monumental, 1781-built organ during 10.30am Mass on Sunday or the occasional Sunday-afternoon concert.

Musée de la Monnaie de Paris
Museum

Map p230 (📞01 40 46 56 66; www.monnaiede-paris.fr; 11 quai de Conti, 6e; Ⓜ Pont Neuf) Due to have reopened after extensive renovations

Église St-Germain des Prés
ARPAD BENEDEK/GETTY IMAGES ©

0 — 1 km
0 — 0.5 mile

TRIANGLE D'OR
8E
16E — Jardins du Trocadéro
2E RIGHT BANK
3E
1ER
11E
LE MARAIS

See Les Invalides Map p238
Jardin des Tuileries
FAUBOURG ST-GERMAIN
Parc du Champ de Mars
See St-Germain Map p230
Jardin du l'Intendant 7E
4E
Seine
LEFT BANK
6E
Jardin du Luxembourg
12E
Sq St-Lambert
15E
5E
LATIN QUARTER
Jardin des Plantes
Cimetière du Montparnasse
Observatoire de Paris
See Montparnasse Map p244
Sq René Le Gall
Parc Georges Brassens
13E
Parc de Choisy
Sq du Sermerat de Koufra
Parc Montsouris

by the time you're reading this, the Parisian Mint Museum traces the history of French coinage from antiquity onwards, with displays that help bring to life this otherwise niche subject. It's housed in the 18th-century royal mint, the Monnaie de Paris, which is still used by the Ministry of Finance to produce commemorative medals and coins.

Musée des Lettres et Manuscrits   Museum

Map p230 (MLM; www.museedeslettres.fr; 222 bd St-Germain, 7e; adult/child €7/5; ⊙10am-7pm Tue-Wed & Fri-Sun, to 9.30pm Thu; MRue du Bac) Grouped into five themes – history, science, music, art and literature – the handwritten and annotated letters and works on display at this captivating museum provide a powerful emotional connection to their authors. They include Napoléon, Charles de Gaulle, Marie Curie, Albert Einstein, Mozart, Beethoven, Piaf, Monet, Toulouse-Lautrec, Van Gogh, Victor Hugo, Hemingway and F Scott Fitzgerald; there are many, many more. It's thoroughly absorbing – allow at least

a couple of hours. Temporary exhibitions also take place regularly.

Les Berges de Seine   Promenade

Map p238 (http://lesberges.paris.fr; btwn Musée d'Orsay & Pont de l'Alma, 7e; ⊙information point noon-7pm Sun-Thu, 10am-10pm Fri & Sat; MSolférino, Assemblée Nationale or Invalides) A breath of fresh air, this 2.3km-long riverside promenade is Parisians' latest spot to run, cycle, skate, play board games or take part in a packed program of events. Equally, it's simply a great place to hang out – in a Zzz shipping-container hut (free by reservation at the information point just west of the Musée d'Orsay), on the archipelago of floating gardens, or at the burgeoning restaurants and bars (some floating too aboard boats and barges).

Bibliothèque Nationale de France   Library

(☎01 53 79 59 59; www.bnf.fr; 11 quai François Mauriac, 13e; temporary exhibitions adult/child from €9/free; ⊙exhibitions 10am-7pm Tue-Sat, 1-7pm Sun, closed early-late Sep; MBibliothèque) With four glass towers shaped like

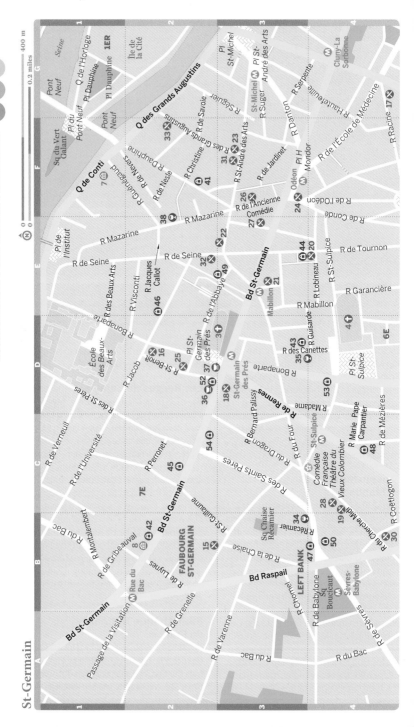

St-Germain

1ER

Seine

Pont Neuf

Q de l'Horloge

Pl du Pont Neuf

Pl Dauphine

Île de la Cité

Sq du Vert Galant

Pl du Pont Neuf

Pont Neuf

Pl St-Michel

St-Michel

R de Savoie

R Séguier

Pl St-Michel

St-Suger

R André des Arts

Cluny–La Sorbonne

Q des Grands Augustins

R des Grands Augustins

R Christine

R St-André des Arts

R de l'École de Médecine

R Hautefeuille

R Serpente

R Danton

R Racine 17

Q de Conti

7

R Guénégaud

R de Nevers

R Dauphine

R de Nesle

33

31 23

41

R de Jardinet

Odéon

Mondor

Pl H

R de l'Ancienne Comédie

24

R Mazarine

26

27

R de l'Odéon

R de Conde

Pl de l'Institut

R Mazarine

38

R de Seine

22

R des Beaux Arts

R Visconti

R Jacques Callot

32

49

Bd St-Germain

44 20

École des Beaux Arts

R Bonaparte

R des Beaux Arts

46

R de Seine

R de l'Abbaye

Mabillon

21

R Lobineau

R St-Sulpice

R de Tournon

R Garancière

R Jacob

R St-Benoît

16 25

Pl St-Germain des Prés

37

R Mabillon

R Guisarde

R des Canettes

35 43

4

6E

R de Verneuil

R des Sts-Pères

36 52

18

St-Germain des Prés

R Bonaparte

Pl St-Sulpice

53

R de l'Université

R Perronet

45

54

R Bernard Palissy

R du Four

R du Dragon

R Madame

Comédie Française

St-Sulpice

R Marie Pape Carpantier

R de Mézières

7E

Bd St-Germain

FAUBOURG ST-GERMAIN

R St-Guillaume

R des Saints Pères

Théâtre du Vieux Colombier

48

R du Bac

R Montalembert

R de Gribeauval

42

8

R de Luynes

15

Sq Chaise Récamier

34

R Récamier

R de la Chaise

28

R du Cherche Midi

19

30

R Coëtlogon

Bd St-Germain

Rue du Bac

Passage de la Visitation

R de Grenelle

Bd Raspail

R Chomel

LEFT BANK

47

50

R de Babylone

Sq Boucicaut

Sèvres-Babylone

R de Varenne

R du Bac

R de Sèvres

R du Bac

400 m

0.2 miles

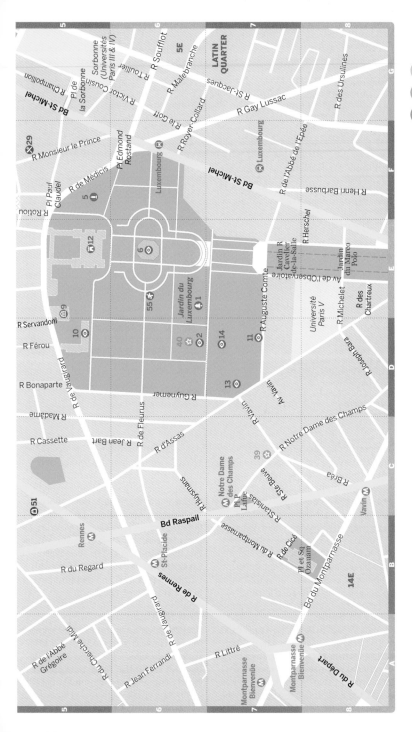

5E

LATIN QUARTER

Sorbonne (Universités Paris III & IV)

R Soufflot
R Malebranche
R St-Jacques
R Gay Lussac
R des Ursulines
R Champollion
Pl de la Sorbonne
R Victor Cousin
R Toullier
Bd St-Michel
R Goff
R Royer-Collard
Luxembourg
R de l'Abbé de l'Epée
R Monsieur le Prince
Pl Edmond Rostand
Luxembourg
Bd St-Michel
R Henri Barbusse
R de Médicis
R Herschel
Pl Paul Claudel
R Rotrou
Jardin R Cavelier de-la-Salle
Jardin du Marco Polo
R Servandoni
Av de l'Observatoire
Université Paris V
R Michelet
R des Chartreux
R Auguste Comte
R Férou
R Bonaparte
Jardin du Luxembourg
R de Vaugirard
R Madame
R Joseph Bara
R Guynemer
Av Vavin
R Cassette
R de Fleurus
R Jean Bart
R d'Assas
R Vavin
R Notre Dame des Champs
Notre Dame des Champs
Pl P Lafue
R Stanislas
R Ste-Beuve
R Bréa
Rennes
R Huysmans
Bd Raspail
St-Placide
R du Montparnasse
R de Cicé
Bd du Montparnasse
Vavin
R de Rennes
R du Regard
Pl et Sq Ozanam
14E
R de l'Abbé Grégoire
R du Cherche Midi
R de Vaugirard
R Jean Ferrandi
R Littré
Montparnasse Bienvenüe
R du Départ
Montparnasse Bienvenüe

29
5
12
6
55
1
9
10
2
14
11
13
40
4
39
51

St-Germain

ST-GERMAIN, LES INVALIDES & MONTPARNASSE SIGHTS

St-Germain

◎ Don't Miss Sights
1 Jardin du Luxembourg..........................E6

◎ Sights
2 Children's Playground...........................D6
3 Église St-Germain des Prés.................D3
4 Église St-Sulpice..................................D4
5 Fontaine des Médici.............................F5
6 Grand Bassin...E6
7 Musée de la Monnaie de Paris............F1
8 Musée des Lettres et Manuscrits........B2
9 Musée du Luxembourg.........................E5
10 Orangery...D5
11 Orchards..D7
12 Palais du Luxembourg.........................E5
13 Pavillon Davioud...................................D7
14 Rucher du Luxembourg........................D7
Sénat..(see 12)

◎ Eating
15 À la Petite Chaise.................................B2
16 Au Pied de Fouet..................................D2
17 Bouillon Racine.....................................G4
18 Brasserie Lipp.......................................D3
19 Cuisine de Bar......................................C4
20 Gérard Mulot...E4
21 Huîterie Regis.......................................E3
22 JSFP Traiteur..E3
23 KGB...F3
24 L'Avant Comptoir..................................F3
25 Le Petit Zinc..D2
26 Le Procope...F3
27 Little Breizh...E3
28 Poilâne...C4
29 Polidor..F5

30 Restaurant Hélène Darroze.................B4
31 Roger la Grenouille...............................F3
32 Semilla...E2
33 Ze Kitchen Galerie...............................F2

◎ Drinking & Nightlife
34 Au Sauvignon..B3
35 Brasserie O'Neil....................................D3
36 Café de Flore...D2
37 Les Deux Magots...................................D2
38 Prescription Cocktail Club...................E2

◎ Entertainment
39 Le Lucernaire..C7
40 Théâtre du Luxembourg.......................D6

◎ Shopping
41 A La Recherche De Jane.......................F2
42 Alexandra Sojfer...................................B2
43 Au Plat d'Étain......................................D3
44 Cire Trudon...E3
45 Fragonard Boutique..............................C2
46 Gab & Jo..E2
47 Hermès...B4
48 JB Guanti...C4
49 La Dernière Goutte...............................E3
50 La Maison du Chocolat.........................B4
51 Le Bain Rose...C5
52 Le Chocolat Alain Ducasse..................D2
53 Pierre Hermé...D4
54 Sonia Rykiel..C2

◎ Sports & Activities
55 Shetland Ponies for Hire......................E6

half-open books, the 1995-opened National Library of France was one of President Mitterand's most ambitious and costliest *grands projets*. Some 12 million tomes are stored on 420km of shelves and the library can accommodate 2000 readers and 2000 researchers. Excellent temporary exhibitions (entrance E) revolve around 'the word' – from storytelling to bookbinding and French heroes. Exhibition admission includes free same-day access to the reference library.

Docks en Seine   Cultural Centre
(Cité de la Mode et du Design; www.paris-docks-en-seine.fr; 36 quai d'Austerlitz, 13e; ◎10am-midnight; Ⓜ Gare d'Austerlitz) Framed by a lurid-lime wave-like glass façade, a transformed Seine-side warehouse now houses the French fashion institute, the Institut Français de la Mode (hence the

docks' alternative name, Cité de la Mode et du Design), mounting fashion and design exhibitions and events throughout the year. Other draws include an entertainment-themed contemporary art museum **Art Ludique-Le Musée** (http://artludique.com; 34 quai d'Austerlitz, 13e, Docks en Seine; adult/child €15/9.50; ◎11am-7pm Mon, 11am-10pm Wed-Fri, 10am-10pm Sat & Sun; Ⓜ Gare d'Austerlitz), along with ultrahip bars, clubs and restaurants and huge riverside terraces.

Tour Montparnasse   Viewpoint
Map p244 (www.tourmontparnasse56.com; rue de l'Arrivée, 15e; adult/child €14.50/9; ◎9.30am-11.30pm daily Apr-Sep, to 10.30pm Sun-Thu, to 11pm Fri & Sat Oct-Mar; Ⓜ Montparnasse Bienvenüe) Spectacular views unfold from this 210m-high smoked-glass and steel office block, built in 1973. (Bonus: it's about the

232

only spot in the city you can't see this startlingly ugly skyscraper, which dwarfs low-rise Paris.) Europe's fastest lift/elevator whisks visitors up in 38 seconds to the indoor observatory on the 56th floor, with multimedia displays. Finish with a hike up the stairs to the 59th-floor open-air terrace (with a sheltered walkway) and bubbly at the terrace's Champagne bar.

Cimetière du Montparnasse
Cemetery

Map p244 (www.paris.fr; bd Edgar Quinet & rue Froidevaux, 14e; ⏰8am-6pm Mon-Fri, 8.30am-6pm Sat, 9am-6pm Sun; M Edgar Quinet or Raspail) Opened in 1824, Montparnasse Cemetery, Paris' second largest after Père Lachaise, sprawls over 19 hectares shaded by 1200 trees, including maples, ash, lime trees and conifers. Among its illustrious 'residents' are poet Charles Baudelaire, writer Guy de Maupassant, playwright Samuel Beckett, sculptor Constantin Brancusi, painter Chaim Soutine, photographer Man Ray, industrialist André Citroën, Captain Alfred Dreyfus of the infamous affair, actress Jean Seberg, and philosopher-writer couple Jean-Paul Sartre and Simone de Beauvoir, as well as legendary singer Serge Gainsbourg.

Le Ballon Air de Paris
Scenic Balloon

(☎01 44 26 20 00; www.ballondeparis.com; Parc André Citroën, 2 rue de la Montagne de la Fage, 15e; adult/child €12/6; ⏰9am-9.30pm, closes earlier Sep-Apr; M Balard or Lourmel) Drift up and up but not away – this helium-filled balloon remains tethered to the ground as it lifts you 150m into the air for spectacular panoramas over Paris. The balloon plays an active environmental role, changing colour depending on the air quality and pollution levels. Confirm ahead; the balloon doesn't ascend in windy conditions.

 # Eating

St-Germain

JSFP Traiteur
Delicatessen €

Map p230 (http://jsfp-traiteur.com; 8 rue de Buci, 6e; dishes €3.40-5.70; ⏰9.30am-8.30pm; ✷; M Mabillon) Brimming with big bowls of salad, terrines, pâté and other prepared delicacies, this deli is a brilliant bet for quality Parisian 'fast food' such as quiches in a variety of flavour combinations (courgette and chive, mozzarella and basil, salmon and spinach...) to take to a nearby park, square or stretch of riverfront.

L'Avant Comptoir
French Tapas €

Map p230 (www.hotel-paris-relais-saint-germain.com; 3 Carrefour de l'Odéon, 6e; tapas €3-7; ⏰noon-midnight; M Odéon) Squeeze in around the zinc bar (there are no seats and it's tiny) and order off the menu suspended from the ceiling to feast on amazing tapas dishes like Iberian ham or salmon tartare croquettes, duck-sausage hot dogs, blood-sausage *macarons*, and prosciutto and artichoke waffles with wines by the glass in a chaotically sociable atmosphere.

Cuisine de Bar
Sandwiches €

Map p230 (www.cuisinedebar.fr; 8 rue du Cherche Midi, 6e; dishes €9.20-13.50; ⏰8.30am-7pm Tue-Sat, 9.30am-3.30pm Sun; ✺; M Sèvres-Babylone) As next-door neighbour to one of Paris' most famous bakers, this isn't your average sandwich bar. Instead, it's an ultrachic spot to lunch between designer boutiques on open sandwiches cut from that celebrated **Poilâne** (p234) bread and fabulously topped with gourmet goodies such as foie gras, smoked duck, gooey St-Marcellin cheese and Bayonne ham.

Au Pied de Fouet
Bistro €

Map p230 (☎01 43 54 87 83; www.aupiedde fouet.com; 50 rue St-Benoît, 6e; mains €9-12.50; ⏰noon-2.30pm & 7-11pm Mon-Sat; M St-Germain des Prés) Wholly classic bistro dishes such as *entrecôte* (steak), *confit de canard* (duck cooked slowly its own fat) and *foie de volailles sauté* (pan-fried chicken livers) at this busy bistro are astonishingly good value. Round off your meal

BLICKWINKEL/ALAMY ©

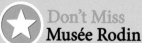

Don't Miss
Musée Rodin

Sculptor, painter, sketcher, engraver and collector Auguste Rodin donated his entire collection to the French state in 1908 on the proviso that they dedicate his former workshop and showroom, the 1730 Hôtel Biron, to displaying his works. They're now installed not only in the mansion itself, but in its rose garden – one of the most peaceful places in Paris and a wonderful spot to contemplate his famous work *The Thinker*.

Other sculptural highlights are *The Gates of Hell*, the 180 figures of which comprise an intricate scene from Dante's *Inferno;* Rodin's marble monument to love, *The Kiss;* and the world's largest collection of works by Rodin's protégé, Camille Claudel. Purchase tickets online to avoid queuing.

NEED TO KNOW

Map p238 www.musee-rodin.fr; 79 rue de Varenne, 7e; adult/child museum incl garden €6/free, garden only €2/free; ⏰10am-5.45pm Tue & Thu-Sun, to 8.45pm Wed; Ⓜ Varenne

with a *tarte Tatin,* wine-soaked prunes or bowl of *fromage blanc* (a cross between yoghurt, sour cream and cream cheese).

Poilâne
Boulangerie €

Map p230 (www.poilane.fr; 8 rue du Cherche Midi, 6e; ⏰7.15am-8.15pm Mon-Sat; Ⓜ Sèvres-Babylone) Pierre Poilâne opened his *boulangerie* upon arriving from Normandy in 1932. Today, his granddaughter Apollonia runs the company, which still makes wood-

fired loaves with stone-milled flour and Guérande sea salt.

Little Breizh
Crêperie €

Map p230 (🕿01 43 54 60 74; www.littlebreizh. fr; 11 rue Grégoire de Tours, 6e; crêpes €4.50-12; ⏰noon-2.30pm & 7-10pm; 🖉🍴; Ⓜ Odéon) As authentic as you'd find in Brittany, but with some innovative twists (such as Breton sardines, olive oil and sundried tomatoes; goats cheese, stewed apple, hazelnuts, rosemary and honey; smoked salmon, dill cream, pink peppercorns and lemon), the crêpes at this sweet spot are infinitely more enticing than those sold on nearby street corners. Hours can fluctuate; book ahead.

Gérard Mulot
Pâtisserie €

Map p230 (www.gerard-mulot.com; 76 rue de Seine, 6e; ⏱6.45am-8pm Thu-Tue; MOdéon or Mabillon) Fruit tarts (peach, lemon, apple), *tarte normande* (apple cake) and *clafoutis* (cherry flan) are among this celebrated pâtisserie's specialties.

Bouillon Racine
Brasserie €€

Map p230 (☎01 44 32 15 60; www.bouillon-racine.com; 3 rue Racine, 6e; weekday lunch menu €16, menus €31-42; ⏱noon-11pm; 🖟; MCluny–La Sorbonne) Situated in a quiet street, this heritage-listed art-nouveau 'soup kitchen', with mirrored walls, floral motifs and ceramic tiling, was built in 1906 to feed market workers. Despite the magnificent interior, the food – inspired by age-old recipes – is by no means an afterthought.

Semilla
Neobistro €€

Map p230 (☎01 43 54 34 50; 54 rue de Seine, 6e; lunch menu €24, mains €20-50; ⏱12.30-2.30pm & 7-10.45pm; MOdéon or Mabillon) Stark concrete, exposed pipes and an open kitchen (in front of which you can book front-row 'chef seats') set the factory-style scene for edgy, modern, daily changing dishes like pork spare ribs with sweet potato and cinnamon, mushrooms in hazelnut butter and trout with passionfruit and ginger. Desserts are outstanding. Be sure to book.

Café Trama
Modern French €€

Map p238 (☎01 45 48 33 71; 83 rue du Cherche Midi, 6e; mains €15-22; ⏱kitchen noon-2.45pm & 7.30-10pm Tue-Sat; MVaneau or St-Placide) Cafe classics come with a contemporary twist at this black-awning-framed local with mellow lighting, chequered tiles, vintage furniture and pavement tables. Try the pan-fried squid with rocket and orange segments, croque monsieur

with truffle salt on premium Poujauran bread, or ginger and basil beef tartare with meat from famed Parisian butcher Hugo Desnoyer, along with all-natural wines.

Huîterie Regis
Oysters €€

Map p230 (☎01 44 41 10 07; http://huitreriere-gis.com; 3 rue de Montfaucon, 6e; dozen oysters from €16; ⏱noon-2.30pm & 6.30-10.30pm Tue-Sun; MMabillon) Hip, trendy, tiny and white, this is *the* spot for slurping oysters on crisp winter days. They come only by the dozen, along with fresh bread and butter, but wash them down with a glass of chilled Muscadet and *voilà*, one perfect lunch. A twinset of tables loiter on the pavement; otherwise it's all inside.

Brasserie Lipp
Brasserie €€

Map p230 (☎01 45 48 53 91; 151 bd St-Germain, 6e; mains €22-38; ⏱11.45am-12.45am; MSt-Germain des Prés) Wait staff in black waistcoats, bow ties and long white aprons serve brasserie favourites like *choucroute garnie* (sauerkraut with pork and potatoes) and *jarret de porc aux lentilles* (pork knuckle with lentils) at this illustrious wood-panelled establishment. (Arrive hungry: salads aren't allowed as meals.) Opened by Léonard Lipp in 1880, the brasserie achieved immortality when Hemingway sang its praises in *A Moveable Feast*.

Polidor
Traditional French €€

Map p230 (☎01 43 26 95 34; www.polidor.com; 41 rue Monsieur le Prince, 6e; menus €22-35; ⏱noon-2.30pm & 7pm-12.30am Mon-Sat, noon-2.30pm & 7-11pm Sun; 🖟; MOdéon) A meal at this quintessentially Parisian *crèmerie-restaurant* is like a trip to Victor Hugo's Paris: the restaurant and its decor date from 1845. *Menus* (fixed-price meals) of tasty, family-style French cuisine ensure a stream of diners eager to sample *bœuf bourguignon, blanquette de veau à l'ancienne* (veal in white sauce) and Polidor's famous *tarte Tatin*. Expect to wait. No credit cards.

PAWEL LIBERA/GETTY IMAGES ©

⭐ Don't Miss
Hôtel des Invalides

Fronted by the 500m-long Esplanade des Invalides lawns, the Hôtel des Invalides was built in the 1670s by Louis XIV to house 4000 *invalides* (disabled war veterans). On 14 July 1789, a mob broke into the building and seized 32,000 rifles before heading on to the prison at Bastille and the start of the French Revolution.

Admission includes entry to all Hôtel des Invalides sights. Hours for individual sites often vary – check the website for updates.

In the **Cour d'Honneur**, the nation's largest collection on the history of the French military is displayed at the **Musée de l'Armée** Map p238 (Army Museum; www.musee-armee. fr; 129 rue de Grenelle, 7e; included in Hôtel des Invalides admission; ⏱10am-6pm Apr-Oct, to 5pm Nov-Mar; M Invalides). South is **Église St-Louis des Invalides**, once used by soldiers, and **Église du Dôme** which, with its sparkling golden dome (1677–1735), is one of the finest religious edifices erected under Louis XIV and was the inspiration for the United States Capitol building. It received the remains of Napoléon in 1840. The extravagant **Tombeau de Napoléon 1er**, in the centre of the church, comprises six coffins fitting into one another like a Russian doll. Scale models of towns, fortresses and châteaux across France fill the esoteric **Musée des Plans-Reliefs**.

Regular classical concerts (some free, others costing up to €9) take place here year-round.

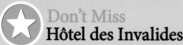

Map p238 www.musee-armee.fr; 129 rue de Grenelle, 7e; adult/child €9.50/free; ⏱7.30am-7pm daily, to 9pm Tue Apr-Sep, hours can vary; M Invalides

Roger la Grenouille
Traditional French €€

Map p230 (☎01 56 24 24 34; 26-28 rue des Grands Augins, 6e; lunch/dinner menus from €22/27; ⏰7-11pm Mon, noon-2pm & 7-11pm Tue-Sat; ⓂSt-Michel) Scattered with frog sculptures, B&W pictures of 1920s Paris and an array of old lamps, time-worn, sepia-coloured institution 'Roger the Frog' serves nine varieties of frogs' legs such as à la Provençale (with tomato) and Normande (cooked in cider and served with apple). If you're squeamish about devouring Roger, alternatives include dishes such as roast sea bass served with braised fennel.

Le Petit Zinc
Brasserie €€

Map p230 (☎01 42 86 61 00; www.petit-zinc.com; 11 rue St-Benoît, 6e; 2-/3-course menus €22.20/29.50; ⏰noon-midnight; 👶; ⓂSt-Germain des Prés) Not a 'little bar', as its name would suggest, but a large, wonderful brasserie serving mountains of fresh seafood and other traditional brasserie specialities in art nouveau splendour (book ahead and dress accordingly).

Ze Kitchen Galerie
Gastronomic €€€

Map p230 (☎01 44 32 00 32; www.zekitchen-galerie.fr; 4 rue des Grands Augustins, 6e; lunch/dinner menus from €41/85; ⏰noon-2.30pm & 7-11pm Tue-Fri, 7-11pm Sat; ⓂSt-Michel) William Ledeuil's passion for Southeast Asia shows in the vibrant dishes he creates in his Michelin-starred glass-box kitchen. Hosting several art exhibitions a year, the restaurant-gallery's menu includes broths loaded with Thai herbs and coconut milk, meat and fish cooked à la plancha and inventive desserts like white-chocolate and wasabi ice cream. Alternatively, try offshoot KGB Map p230 (☎01 46 33 00 85; http://zekitchengalerie.fr; 25 rue des Grands Augustins, 6e; lunch menus €29-36, dinner menus €55-62; ⏰noon-2.30pm & 7.30-11pm Tue-Fri, 7.30-11pm Sat; ⓂSt-Michel) ('Kitchen Galerie Bis').

Paris' Oldest Restaurant & Cafe

À la Petite Chaise Map p230 (☎01 42 22 13 35; www.alapetitechaise.fr; 36 rue de Grenelle, 6e; lunch/dinner menus from €23/36; ⏰noon-2pm & 7-11pm; ⓂSèvres-Babylone) À la Petite Chaise hides behind an iron gate that's been here since it opened in 1680, when wine merchant Georges Rameau served food to the public to accompany his wares. Classical decor and cuisine (onion soup, foie gras, duck, lamb and unexpected delights like truffled asparagus) make it worth a visit above and beyond its history.

Le Procope Map p230 (www.procope.com; 13 rue de l'Ancienne Comédie, 6e; 2-/3-course menus from €29/36; ⏰11.30am-midnight Sun-Wed, to 1am Thu-Sat; 👶; ⓂOdéon) The city's oldest cafe welcomed its first patrons in 1686, and was frequented by Voltaire, Molière and Balzac et al. Its chandeliered interior also has an entrance onto the 1735-built glass-roofed passageway Cour du Commerce St-André. House specialties include coq au vin, calf's head casserole in veal stock, and calf kidneys with violet mustard and homemade ice cream.

Restaurant Hélène Darroze
Modern French €€€

Map p230 (☎01 42 22 00 11; www.helenedarroze.com; 4 rue d'Assas, 6e; lunch/dinner menus from €39/92; ⏰12.30-2.30pm & 7.30-10.30pm Tue-Sat; ⓂSèvres-Babylone) Female star chefs are a rarity in Paris, but Hélène Darroze is a stellar exception (and the inspiration for the character Colette in the winsome animated film Ratatouille). These premises house both her elegant Michelin-starred Salle à Manger restaurant upstairs and relaxed downstairs Salon d'Hélène, where multicourse tasting menus reflect Darroze's native southwestern France, such as wood-grilled foie gras.

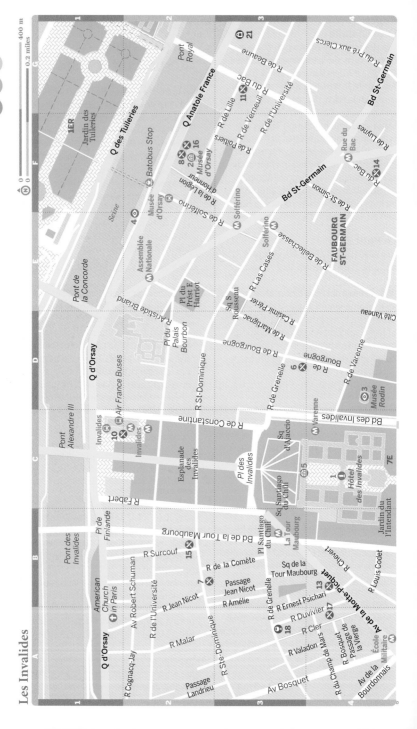

ST-GERMAIN, LES INVALIDES & MONTPARNASSE

Les Invalides

400 m
0.2 miles

1ER
Jardin des
Tuileries

Q des Tuileries

Q Anatole France

Pont
Royal

21

R de Beaune

R du Bac

11

R de Lille

R de Verneuil

R de l'Université

Batobus Stop

8
2
16
Musée
d'Orsay

R de Poitiers

R du Pré aux Clercs

Bd St-Germain

Rue du
Bac

R de Luynes

Musée
d'Orsay

Seine

R de la Légion
d'Honneur

R de Solférino

Solférino

14

R du Bac

Bd St-Germain

R de St-Simon

FAUBOURG
ST-GERMAIN

Assemblée
Nationale

Pont de
la Concorde

R Aristide Briand

Pl du
Prést E
Harriot

R de Bellechasse

Solférino

R Las Cases

Cité Vaneau

Q d'Orsay

Pl du
Palais
Bourbon

Sq S
Rousseau

R Casimir Périer

R de Martignac

R de Bourgogne

R de Varenne

Pont
Alexandre III

Air France Buses

R St-Dominique

R de Grenelle

R de
Bourgogne

6

Musée
Rodin

3

Invalides

10

Invalides

R de Constantine

Varenne

Bd des Invalides

R Fabert

Esplanade
des
Invalides

Pl des
Invalides

Sq
d'Ajaccio

Pl de
Finlande

Pont des
Invalides

American
Church
in Paris

Q d'Orsay

R Cognacq-Jay

Av Robert Schuman

R de l'Université

Sq Santiago
du Chili

5

Hôtel
des Invalides

1

7E

Jardin du
l'Intendant

R Surcouf

15

R de la Comète

Bd de la Tour Maubourg

Pl Santiago
du Chili

La Tour
Maubourg

Sq de la
Tour Maubourg

R Chevert

R Louis Codet

R Jean Nicot

7

Passage
Jean Nicot

R Amélie

R de Grenelle

R Ernest Psichari

13

Av de la Motte-Picquet

R Malar

R Ste-Dominique

R Duvivier

17

R Cler

18

R Valadon

R du Champ de Mars

R Bosquet

Passage de
la Vierge

École
Militaire

Av de la
Bourdonnais

Passage
Landrieu

Av Bosquet

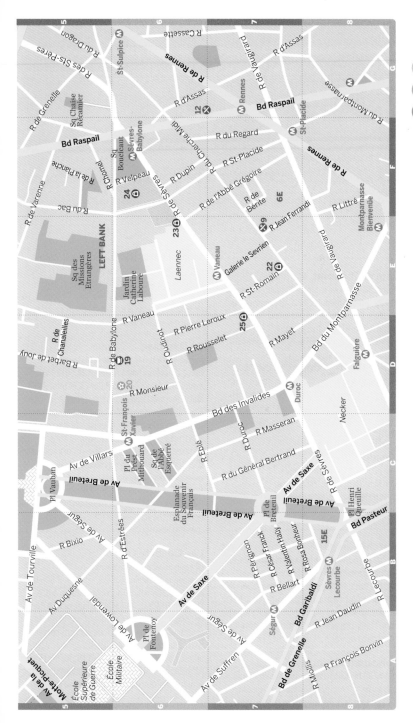

239

Les Invalides

Les Invalides

Pain & Chocolat   Cafe €

Map p238 (16 av de la Motte-Picquet, 7e; mains €10-22, brunch menus €7-22; ◷9am-7pm Tue-Fri, 10am-7pm Sat & Sun; Ⓜ La Tour Maubourg) You'll be glad you forewent that over-priced, underdelivering hotel breakfast when you start the day in proper Parisian style at this delightfully retro cafe. Everything is made on the premises, salads, *tartines* (open sandwiches), egg dishes and cakes, pastries and quiches included. Don't miss the hot chocolate, made from an old family recipe.

Besnier   Boulangerie €

Map p238 (40 rue de Bourgogne, 7e; ◷7am-8pm Mon-Fri Sep-Jul; Ⓜ Varenne) You can watch baguettes being made through the viewing window of this award-winning *boulangerie*.

Marché Raspail   Market €

Map p238 (bd Raspail btwn rue de Rennes & rue du Cherche Midi, 6e; ◷regular market 7am-2.30pm Tue & Fri, organic market 9am-3pm Sun; Ⓜ Rennes) A traditional open-air market on Tuesday and Friday, Marché Raspail is especially popular on Sunday, when it's filled with *biologique* (organic) produce.

Poissonnerie du Bac   Seafood €

Map p238 (www.poissonnerie-paris.fr; 69 rue du Bac, 7e; ◷9am-1pm & 4-7.30pm Tue-Sat, 9.30am-1pm Sun; Ⓜ Rue du Bac) Self-caterers shouldn't miss this superb aquamarine- and cobalt-tiled fishmonger. Even if you don't have access to a kitchen in Paris, the fish, scallops, prawns, crabs and other crustaceans laid out on beds of crushed ice are a visual feast.

La Gauloise   Traditional French €€

(☎01 47 34 11 64; 59 av de la Motte-Picquet, 15e; 2-/3-course lunch menus €24.50/29.50, mains €25-36; ◷noon-2.30pm & 7-11pm; Ⓜ La Motte-Picquet Grenelle) With a name like La Gauloise, you wouldn't expect this venerable, terrace-fronted restaurant to serve anything other than traditional fare, which it does, very well. From the onion soup to the braised stuffed cabbage and duckling with old-fashioned mashed potato, *îles flottantes* for dessert, and Madeleine cakes with coffee, it refines but doesn't reinvent the classics that make French cuisine iconic.

Les Cocottes   Modern French €€

(www.maisonconstant.com; 135 rue Ste-Dominique, 7e; mains €15-29; ◷noon-3.30pm & 6.30-10.30pm Sun-Thu, noon-3.30pm & 6.30-11.30pm Fri & Sat; Ⓜ École Militaire or RER Port de l'Alma) Christian Constant's chic concept space is devoted to *cocottes* (casseroles), with a buoyant crowd feasting on inventive seasonal creations cooked to perfection in little black-enamel, oven-to-table *cocottes* (casserole dishes). Seating is on bar stools around high tables and there are no reservations: arrive by noon or 7.15pm.

Brasserie Thoumieux
Traditional French €€

Map p238 (☎01 47 05 49 75; www.thoumieux. com; 79 rue St-Dominique, 7e; mains €21-45; ⏱noon-midnight; Ⓜ La Tour Maubourg) Founded in 1923, Thoumieux has been worshipped by generations of diners ever since for its menu of duck, veal and snails and its smooth-as-silk service. It's now run by Thierry Costes and multi-award-winning chef Jean-François Piège, who has his twin-Michelin-starred restaurant upstairs, adjacent to the boutique Hôtel Thoumieux.

Restaurant David Toutain
Gastronomic €€€

Map p238 (☎01 45 51 11 10; http://davidtoutain. com; 29 rue Surcouf, 7e; lunch menu €42, lunch & dinner menus $68-98; ⏱noon-2.30pm & 8-10pm Mon-Fri; Ⓜ Invalides) Prepare to be wowed: David Toutain pushes the envelope at his eponymous new restaurant with some of the most creative high-end cooking in Paris today. Mystery degustation courses include unlikely combinations such as smoked eel in green-apple and black-sesame mousse, or candied celery and truffled rice pudding with artichoke praline (stunning wine pairings available).

Chez Françoise
Traditional French €€€

Map p238 (☎01 47 05 49 03; http://chezfrancoise.com; Aérogare des Invalides; 2-/3-course menus from €28/33, oysters per half-dozen €15.50-29; ⏱noon-3pm & 7pm-midnight; Ⓜ Invalides) Buried beneath the enormous Air France building but opening to a retractable-roofed terrace, this old-school 1949-opened restaurant – a favourite with parliamentary workers from the Assemblée Nationale – recalls the early glamour of air travel, when it was established at this former off-site terminal for transiting passengers. Specialities include *entrecôte de bœuf* (rib steak) and sublime oysters.

Les Climats
Traditional French €€€

Map p238 (http://lesclimats.fr; 41 rue de Lille, 7e; 2-/3-course lunch menus €36/42, mains €32-44, bar snacks €7-22; ⏱restaurant noon-2.30pm & 7-10.30pm Tue-Sat, bar noon-2.30pm & 6-11pm; Ⓜ Solférino) Like the neighbouring Musée d'Orsay, this is a magnficent art-nouveau

Fresh produce at Marché Raspail

treasure – a 1905-built former home for female telephone, telegram and postal workers – featuring soaring vaulted ceilings and original stained glass, as well as a garden for summer lunches and a glassed-in winter garden. Exquisite dishes complement its 150-page list of wines, sparkling wines and whiskies purely from Burgundy.

Montparnasse

Marché Edgar Quinet
Market €

Map p244 (bd Edgar Quinet, 14e; ☉7am-2.30pm Wed, 7am-3pm Sat; Ⓜ Edgar Quinet or Montparnasse Bienvenüe) Opposite Tour Montparnasse, this open-air street market teems with neighbourhood shoppers. There's always a great range of cheeses, as well as stalls sizzling up snacks to eat on the run, from crêpes to spicy felafels.

Jeu de Quilles
Bistro €€

Map p244 (☎ 01 53 90 76 22; www.jdequilles.fr; 45 rue Boulard, 14e; mains €25-40; ☉noon-2pm Wed-Sat, 8-10pm Tue-Sat; Ⓜ Mouton-Duvernet)

When your next-door neighbour is the original premises of celebrated butcher Hugo Desnoyer, you have an inside track to serve exceptional meat-based dishes, and chef Benoît Reix does at this brilliant bistro. Creations such as artichoke-paste-encrusted pork or veal carpaccio pair with an extensive selection of natural wines. Reserve ahead: there are just 18 seats and locals love it.

La Closerie des Lilas
Brasserie €€

Map p244 (☎01 40 51 34 50; www.closeriedeslilas.fr; 171 bd du Montparnasse, 6e; restaurant mains €27.50-56.50, brasserie mains €25-33; ☉restaurant noon-2.15pm & 7-11.30pm, brasserie noon-12.30am, piano bar 11am-1.30am; Ⓜ Vavin or RER Port Royal) Brass plaques tell you exactly where Hemingway (who wrote much of *The Sun Also Rises* here) and luminaries like Picasso, Apollinaire, Man Ray, Jean-Paul Sartre and Samuel Beckett stood, sat or fell. The 'Lilac Enclosure' is split into a late-night piano bar, upmarket restaurant and more lovable (and cheaper) brasserie with a hedged-in pavement terrace.

La Rotonde Montparnasse
Brasserie €€

(☎01 43 26 48 26; www.rotondemontparnasse.com; 105 bd du Montparnasse, 6e; 3-course menu €42, mains €14.50-42; ☉6am-2am, menus noon-3pm & 7-11pm; Ⓜ Vavin) Opened in 1911 and recently restored to its former glory, La Rotonde may be awash with the same Les Montparnos history as its famous neighbours like Le Select et al, but the real reason to come is for the superior food. Meat comes from Parisian butcher extraordinaire Hugo Desnoyer, salmon and chicken are organic and brasserie classics are cooked to perfection.

La Closerie des Lilas

PETE SEAWARD/LONELY PLANET ©

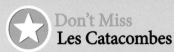

Don't Miss
Les Catacombes

Paris' most macabre sight is its underground tunnels lined with skulls and bones. In 1785 it was decided to rectify the hygiene problems of Paris' overflowing cemeteries by exhuming the bones and storing them in disused quarry tunnels and the Catacombes were created in 1810.

After descending 20m (via 130 narrow, dizzying spiral steps) below street level, you follow the dark, subterranean passages to reach the ossuary itself (2km in all). Exit back up 83 steps onto rue Remy Dumoncel, 14e.

The route through the Catacombes begins at a small, dark-green belle époque building in the centre of a grassy area of av Colonel Henri Roi-Tanguy, adjacent to Place Denfert Rochereau.

You'll traverse 2km of tunnels in all. The surface is uneven and often slippery due to loose stones and mud – sturdy shoes are essential. In the tunnels the temperature is a cool 14° Celsius, there are no toilets and flash photography isn't permitted. A maximum of 200 people are allowed in the tunnels at a time and queues can be huge – arrive early morning to beat the worst of the crowds. Last entry is at 4pm. Bear in mind that it's not suitable for young children (nor anyone faint-hearted).

During WWII these tunnels were used as a headquarters by the Resistance; these days, thrill-seeking cataphiles are often caught (and fined) roaming the tunnels at night.

Bag searches are carried out to prevent visitors 'souveniring' bones. A gift shop selling quirky skull-and-bone-themed items (Jenga, candles, shot glasses) is across the street from the exit.

NEED TO KNOW

Map p244 www.catacombes.paris.fr; 1 av Colonel Henri Roi-Tanguy, 14e; adult/child €8/free; ⊙10am-5pm Tue-Sun; Ⓜ Denfert Rochereau

Montparnasse

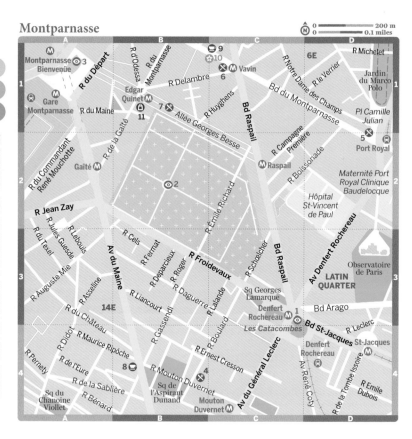

Montparnasse

◎ **Don't Miss Sights**

1 Les Catacombes C3

◎ **Sights**

2 Cimetière du Montparnasse B2
3 Tour Montparnasse A1

✕ **Eating**

4 Jeu de Quilles B4
5 La Closerie des Lilas D1
   Le Ciel de Paris .... (see 3)
6 Le Dôme C1

7 Marché Edgar Quinet B1

◎ **Drinking & Nightlife**

8 Félicie B4
9 Le Select C1

◎ **Entertainment**

10 Dancing La Coupole C1

🛍 **Shopping**

11 Adam Montparnasse B1

Le Dôme   Brasserie €€€

Map p244 (☎ 01 43 35 25 81; 108 bd du Montparnasse, 14e; mains €43-66.50, seafood platters €66; ⏰ noon-3pm & 7-11pm; Ⓜ Vavin) A 1930s art deco extravaganza of the formal white-tablecloth and bow-tied waiter variety, monumental Le Dôme is one of

the swishest places around for shellfish platters piled high with fresh oysters, king prawns, crab claws and much more, followed by traditional creamy homemade *millefeuille* for dessert, wheeled in on a trolley and cut in front of you.

ST-GERMAIN, LES INVALIDES & MONTPARNASSE EATING

Le Ciel de Paris
Traditional French €€€

Map p244 (☎01 40 64 77 64; www.cieldeparis.com; level 56, Tour Montparnasse, 33 av du Maine, 14e; lunch/dinner menus from €30/45; ⏰7.30am-11pm; Ⓜ Montparnasse Bienvenüe) Views don't get much better than 'the sky of Paris', the Tour Montparnasse's 56th-floor restaurant, accessed by private lift/elevator. Starters include Burgundy snails and pigs' trotters; seafood is a speciality. The gastronomic Grand Écran menu (€128), available at dinner daily and Sunday lunch, includes a guaranteed window table and bottle of Champagne per person. The bar stays open until 1am.

🍷 Drinking & Nightlife

St-Germain's Carrefour de l'Odéon has a cluster of lively bars and cafes. Rue de Buci, rue St-André des Arts and rue de l'Odéon enjoy a fair slice of night action with their arty cafes and busy pubs, while place St-Germain des Prés buzzes with the pavement terraces of fabled literary cafes.

Rue Cler

Pick up fresh bread, sandwich fillings, pastries and wine for a picnic along the typically Parisian market street **rue Cler** Map p238 (rue Cler, 7e; ⏰most shops 8am-7pm Tue-Sat, to noon Sun; Ⓜ École Militaire), which buzzes with local shoppers, especially on weekends.

Interspersed between the *boulangeries*, *fromageries*, grocers, butchers, delis and other food shops, including a wonderful *glacier* (Martine Lambert, at number 39) – many with pavement stalls – lively cafe terraces overflow with locals, too.

St-Germain

Les Deux Magots
Cafe

Map p230 (www.lesdeuxmagots.fr; 170 bd St-Germain, 6e; ⏰7.30am-1am; Ⓜ St-Germain des Prés) If ever there were a cafe that summed up St-Germain des Prés' early-20th-century literary scene, it's this

Wine and cheese for sale along rue Cler

former hangout of anyone who was anyone. You will spend *beaucoup* to sip a coffee in a wicker chair on the terrace shaded by dark-green awnings and geraniums spilling from window boxes, but it's an undeniable piece of Parisian history.

Au Sauvignon — Wine Bar

Map p230 (80 rue des St-Pères, 7e; ☺8.30am-10pm Mon-Sat, to 9pm Sun; Ⓜ Sèvres-Babylone) Grab a table in the evening sun at this wonderfully authentic *bar à vin* or head to the quintessential bistro interior, with an original zinc bar, tightly packed tables and hand-painted ceiling celebrating French viticultural tradition. A plate of *casse-croûtes au pain Poilâne* – toast with ham, pâté, terrine, smoked salmon, foie gras... – is the perfect accompaniment.

Brasserie O'Neil — Microbrewery

Map p230 (www.oneilbar.fr; 20 rue des Canettes, 6e; ☺noon-2am; Ⓜ St-Sulpice or Mabillon) Paris' first microbrewery was opened by a French restaurateur and French brewer over two decades ago, and still brews four fabulous beers (blond, amber, bitter brown and citrusy white) on the premises.

Soak them up with thin-crusted *flammekueches* (Alsatian pizzas).

Café de Flore — Cafe

Map p230 (www.cafedeflore.fr; 172 bd St-Germain, 6e; ☺7am-2am; Ⓜ St-Germain des Prés) The red upholstered benches, mirrors and marble walls at this art-deco landmark haven't changed much since the days when Jean-Paul Sartre and Simone de Beauvoir essentially set up office here, writing in its warmth during the Nazi occupation. It also hosts a monthly English-language *philocafé* session.

Prescription Cocktail Club — Cocktail Bar

Map p230 (www.prescriptioncocktailclub.com; 23 rue Mazarine, 6e; ☺7pm-2am Mon-Thu, 7pm-4am Fri & Sat, 8pm-2am Sun; Ⓜ Odéon) With bowler and flat-top hats as lampshades and a 1930s speakeasy New York air to the place, this cocktail club – run by the same mega-successful team as at Curio Parlor and Experimental – is very Parisian-cool. Getting past the doorman can be tough, but, once in, it's friendliness and old-fashioned cocktails all round.

Garden outside Cinéma La Pagode

Les Invalides

Coutume
Cafe

Map p238 (http://coutumecafe.com; 47 rue Babylone, 7e; ⏰8am-7pm Mon-Fri, from 10am Sat & Sun; 🛜; Ⓜ︎St-François Xavier or Vaneau) 🗒 If you've noticed the coffee in Paris getting better lately, it's thanks in no small part to Coutume, artisan roaster of premium beans for scores of establishments around town. Its flagship cafe – a bright, light-filled, post-industrial space – is ground zero for innovative preparation methods including cold extraction and siphon brews. Fabulous organic fare and pastries, too.

Alain Milliat
Juice Bar

Map p238 (📞01 45 55 63 86; www.alain-milliat.com; 159 rue de Grenelle, 7e; ⏰11am-3pm & 6pm-midnight Tue-Fri, 9am-midnight Sat, 10am-6pm Sun; Ⓜ︎La Tour Maubourg) Alain Milliat's fruit juices, bottled in the south of France, were once reserved for ultra-exclusive hotels and restaurants. But you can pop into his Parisian juice bar–bistro to buy one of the 33 varieties of juice and nectar, or sip them in house. Stunning flavours include rosé-grape or green-tomato juice and white-peach nectar.

Montparnasse

Le Batofar
Club

(www.batofar.org; opp 11 quai François Mauriac, 13e; ⏰bar 12.30pm-midnight Tue, to 6am Wed-Fri, 6pm-6am Sat; Ⓜ︎Quai de la Gare or Bibliothèque) This much-loved, red-metal tugboat has a rooftop bar that's terrific in summer, and a respected restaurant, while the club underneath provides memorable underwater acoustics between its metal walls and portholes. Le Batofar is known for its edgy, experimental music policy and live performances, mostly electro-oriented but also incorporating hip-hop, new wave, rock, punk or jazz.

Félicie
Cafe, Bar

Map p244 (www.felicie.info; 174 ave du Maine, 14e; ⏰7am-2am; 🛜; Ⓜ︎Lourmel) Chances are your first visit won't be your last at this unpretentious neighbourhood cafe with a big heated pavement terrace, fun-loving staff and a laid-back vibe. It's a quintes-

sentially Parisian spot to hang out any time of day, but especially during Sunday brunch, lunches built around bistro classics like steak tartare, and late at night.

Le Select
Cafe

Map p244 (99 bd du Montparnasse, 6e; ⏰7am-3am; Ⓜ︎Vavin) Dating from 1923, this Montparnasse institution was the first of the area's grand cafes to stay open late into the night, and it still draws everyone from beer-swigging students to whisky-swilling politicians. *Tartines* made with Poilâne bread are a speciality.

⭐ Entertainment

Cinéma La Pagode
Cinema

Map p238 (📞01 45 55 48 48; www.etoile-cinema.com; 57bis rue de Babylone, 7e; Ⓜ︎St-François Xavier) This 19th-century Japanese pagoda was converted into a cinema in the 1930s and remains the most atmospheric spot in Paris to catch arthouse and classic films. Don't miss a moment or two in its bamboo-enshrined garden.

Le Lucernaire
Cultural Centre

Map p230 (📞reservations 01 45 44 57 34; www.lucernaire.fr; 53 rue Notre Dame des Champs, 6e; ⏰bar 11am-10pm Mon, 11am-12.30am Fri, 4pm-12.30am Sat, 4-10pm Sun; Ⓜ︎Notre Dame des Champs) Sunday-evening concerts are a fixture on the impressive repertoire of this dynamic Centre National d'Art et d'Essai (National Arts Centre). Be it classical guitar, baroque, French *chansons* or oriental music, these weekly concerts starting at 7.30pm are a real treat. Art and photography exhibitions, cinema, theatre, lectures, debates and guided walks round off the packed cultural agenda.

Dancing La Coupole
Dancing

Map p244 (📞01 43 27 56 00; www.lacoupole-paris.com; 102 bd du Montparnasse, 14e; ⏰2.30-7pm Sun; Ⓜ︎Vavin) Swing, rumba, cha-cha, foxtrot, tango and more at roaring 1920s-style tea dances held in the ballroom of the historic brasserie of the same name. Check the website's *actualités* (current events) section for dates.

Antique Shopping

Art and antique dealers congregate within the **Carré Rive Gauche** Map p238 (www.carrerivegauche.com; **M** Rue du Bac or Solférino). Bounded by quai Voltaire and rues de l'Université, des St-Pères and du Bac, this 'Left Bank square' is home to more than 120 specialised merchants. Antiques fairs are usually held in spring, while exhibitions take place during the year.

 Shopping

Adam Montparnasse   Art Supplies
Map p244 (www.adamparis.com; 11 bd Edgar Quinet, 14e; ⏰9.30am-7pm Mon-Sat; **M** Edgar Quinet) If Paris' art galleries have inspired you, pick up paint brushes, charcoals, pastels, sketchpads, watercolours, oils, acrylics, canvases and more at this historic shop. Picasso, Brancusi and Giacometti were among Édouard Adam's clients. Another seminal client was Yves Klein, with whom Adam developed the ultramarine 'Klein blue' – the VLB25 'Klein Blue' varnish is sold exclusively here.

Gab & Jo   Concept Store
Map p230 (www.gabjo.fr; 28 rue Jacob, 6e; ⏰11am-7pm Mon-Sat; **M** St-Germain des Prés) Forget mass-produced, imported souvenirs: for quality local gifts to take home, browse the shelves of Gab & Jo, the country's first-ever concept store stocking only made-in-France items. Designers include Marie-Jeanne de Grasse (scented candles), Marius Fabre (Marseille soaps), Germaine-des-Prés (lingerie), MILF (sunglasses) and Monsieur Marcel (T-shirts).

Cire Trudon   Candles
Map p230 (www.ciretrudon.com; 78 rue de Seine, 6e; ⏰10am-7pm Tue-Sat; **M** Odéon) Claude Trudon began selling candles here in 1643, and the company – which officially supplied Versailles and Napoléon with light – is now the world's oldest candlemaker (look for the plaque to the left of the shop's awning). A rainbow of candles and candlesticks fill the shelves inside.

Le Bon Marché   Department Store
Map p238 (www.bonmarche.fr; 24 rue de Sèvres, 7e; ⏰10am-8pm Mon-Wed & Sat, to 9pm Thu & Fri; **M** Sèvres Babylone) Built by Gustave Eiffel as Paris' first department store in 1852, Le Bon Marché is the epitome of style, with a superb concentration of men's and women's fashions, beautiful homewares, stationery, books and toys as well as chic dining options. The icing on the cake is its glorious food hall, **La Grande Épicerie de Paris**.

Le Bon Marché
FRED MACK/ALAMY ©

La Grande Épicerie de Paris
Food, Drink

Map p238 (www.lagrandeepicerie.fr; 36 rue de Sèvres, 7e; ⏰8.30am-9pm Mon-Sat; Ⓜ Sèvres Babylone) Among other edibles, the magnificent food hall of **Le Bon Marché** department store sells vodka-flavoured lollipops with detoxified ants inside and fist-sized Himalayan salt crystals to grate over food. Its fantastical displays of chocolates, pastries, biscuits, cheeses, fresh fruit and vegetables and deli goods are a sight in themselves.

Au Plat d'Étain
Games

Map p230 (www.auplatdetain.sitew.com; 16 rue Guisarde, 6e; ⏰10.30am-6.30pm Tue-Sat; Ⓜ Odéon or Mabillon) Tiny tin (*étain*) and lead soldiers, snipers, cavaliers, military drummers and musicians (great for chessboard pieces) cram this fascinating boutique. In business since 1775, the shop itself is practically a collectable.

Hermès
Concept Store

Map p230 (www.hermes.com; 17 rue de Sèvres, 6e; ⏰10.30am-7pm Mon-Sat; Ⓜ Sèvres-Babylone) A stunning art-deco swimming pool now houses luxury label Hermès' inaugural concept store. Retaining its original mosaic tiles and iron balustrades and adding enormous timber pod-like 'huts', the vast, tiered space showcases new directions in home furnishings including fabrics and wallpaper, as well as classic lines including its signature scarves. There's also an appropriately chic cafe, Le Plongeoir.

Le Bain Rose
Homewares

Map p230 (www.le-bain-rose.fr; 11 rue d'Assas, 6e; ⏰11.30am-7pm Mon-Sat, closed Aug; Ⓜ Rennes) The antique and retro mirrors, perfume spritzers, soap dishes, mirrors (hand-held and on stands) and even basins and tapware at this long-established shop can transform your bathroom into a belle époque sanctum.

Alexandra Sojfer
Accessories

Map p230 (www.alexandrasojfer.com; 218 bd St-Germain, 7e; ⏰10am-7pm Mon-Sat; Ⓜ Rue du Bac) Become Parisian chic with a frivolous, frilly, fantastical or frightfully fashionable *parapluie* (umbrella), parasol or walking cane handcrafted by Alexandra Sojfer at this St-Germain boutique, in the trade since 1834.

Quatrehomme
Food, Drink

Map p238 (www.quatrehomme.fr; 62 rue de Sèvres, 6e; ⏰9am-7.45pm Tue-Sat; Ⓜ Vanneau) Buy the best of French cheeses, many with an original take (eg Epoisses boxed in chestnut leaves, Mont d'Or flavoured with black truffles, spiced honey and Roquefort bread etc), at this king of *fromageries*. The smell alone as you enter is heavenly.

Discount Designer Outlets & Secondhand Chic

For previous seasons' collections, surpluses, prototypes and seconds by name-brand designers, save up to 70% off men's, women's and kids' fashions at outlet stores along **rue d'Alésia**, 14e, particularly between av de Maine to rue Raymond-Losserand.

Pick up current designer and vintage cast-offs at *dépôt-vente* (secondhand) boutiques.

Chercheminippes Map p238 (www.chercheminippes.com; 102, 109-111, 114 & 124 rue du Cherche Midi, 6e; ⏰11am-7pm Mon-Sat; Ⓜ Vaneau) Six beautifully presented boutiques on one street selling secondhand pieces by current designers, each specialising in a different genre (*haute couture*, kids, menswear etc) and perfectly ordered by size and designer. There are changing rooms.

Patricia Wells' Culinary Shopping Secrets

Cookery teacher and author of *The Food Lover's Guide to Paris*, American Patricia Wells (www.patriciawells.com) has lived, cooked and shopped in Paris since 1980, and is considered to have truly captured the soul of French cuisine.

What is it that makes Paris so wonderful for culinary shopping?
The tradition, the quality, the quantity, the atmosphere and physical beauty!

Where do you buy your weekly groceries?
All over: the Sunday organic market at Rennes (**Marché Raspail** (p240) – I love the dried fruits and nuts; **Poilâne** (p234) for bread; **Quatrehomme** (p249) for cheese; and **Poissonnerie du Bac** (p240) for fish.

What about for an extraspecial gourmet meal?
I shop regularly at Le Bon Marché's **La Grande Épicerie de Paris** (p249) because it is right down the street from me. But for special meals I always order things in advance and go from shop to shop – **La Maison du Chocolat** and **Pierre Hermé** for chocolate and cakes, and **La Dernière Goutte** for wine. That is the fun of Paris, and of France.

Your top food shopping tip?
If you live in Paris, become a *client fidèle* (loyal customer) so they reach in the back and give you the best stuff. If you only go once in a while, just smile and be friendly.

A perfect culinary souvenir from Paris?
Fragonard, the perfume maker, has a great shop on bd St-Germain. They have a changing litany of *great* things for the home, such as fabulous vases with an Eiffel Tower theme, lovely embroidered napkins with a fish or vegetable theme, great little spoons with a cake or pastry theme. Nothing is very expensive and the offerings change every few months, so you have to pounce when you find something you love. The gift wrapping in gorgeous Fragonard bags is worth it alone!

A La Recherche De Jane
Accessories

Map p230 (http://alarecherchedejane.wordpress.com; 41 rue Dauphine, 6e; ⏲11.30am-7pm Wed-Sat, 1-7pm Sun; MOdéon) This welcoming *chapelier* (milliner) has literally thousands of handcrafted hats on hand for both men and women, and can also make them to order.

JB Guanti
Accessories

Map p230 (www.jbguanti.fr; 59 rue de Rennes, 6e; ⏲10am-7pm Mon-Sat; MSt-Sulpice or Mabillon) For the ultimate finishing touch, the men's and women's gloves at this boutique, which specialises solely in gloves, are the epitome of both style and comfort, whether unlined, silk lined, cashmere lined, lambskin lined or trimmed with rabbit fur.

La Dernière Goutte
Wine

Map p230 (www.ladernieregoutte.net; 6 rue du Bourbon le Château, 6e; ⏲3-8pm Mon, 10.30am-1.30pm & 3-8pm Tue-Fri, 11am-7pm Sat; MMabillon) 'The Last Drop' is the brainchild of Cuban-American sommelier Juan Sánchez, whose tiny wine shop is packed with exciting French *vins de propriétaires* (estate-bottled wines) made by small independent producers.

Pierre Hermé
Food

Map p230 (www.pierreherme.com; 72 rue Bonaparte, 6e; ⊙10am-7pm Sun-Wed, to 7.30pm Thu & Fri, to 8pm Sat; Ⓜ Odéon or RER Luxembourg) It's the size of a chocolate box, but once you're in, your taste buds will go wild. Pierre Hermé is one of Paris' top chocolatiers and this boutique is a veritable feast of perfectly presented *petits fours*, cakes, chocolates, nougats, macarons and jam.

Sonia Rykiel
Fashion

Map p230 (www.soniarykiel.com; 175 bd St-Germain, 6e; ⊙10.30am-7pm Mon-Sat; Ⓜ St-Germain des Prés) In the heady days of May 1968 amid Paris' student uprisings, Sonia Rykiel opened her inaugural Left Bank boutique here, and went on to revolutionise garments with inverted seams, 'no hems' and 'no lining'. Her diffusion labels (including children's wear) are housed in separate boutiques nearby, with other outlets around Paris.

La Maison du Chocolat
Chocolate

Map p230 (www.lamaisonduchocolat.fr; 19 rue de Sèvres, 6e; ⊙10am-7.30pm Mon-Sat, to 1pm Sun; Ⓜ Sèvres-Babylone) Pralines, ganaches and fruit chocolates are the hallmark of this exquisite chocolatier. Other treats include macarons inspired by its signature chocolates, such as Rigoletto (chocolate and salted caramel) and Salvador (chocolate and raspberry), as well as decadent éclairs.

Fragonard Boutique
Perfume

Map p230 (✆01 42 84 12 12; www.fragonard.com; 196 bd St-Germain, 6e; ⊙10am-7pm Mon-Sat; Ⓜ Rue du Bac or St-Germain des Prés) The bd St-Germain boutique of perfume-maker Fragonard (which runs Paris' **perfume museum** (p76)) stocks a heady range of souvenirs – from scarves to cookbooks – evoking the sights, scents and flavours of France.

🏃 Sports & Activities

École Le Cordon Bleu
Cooking

(www.cordonbleu.edu) One of the world's foremost culinary arts schools.

Patricia Wells
Cooking

(www.patriciawells.com) Five-day moveable feast from the former *International Herald Tribune* food critic.

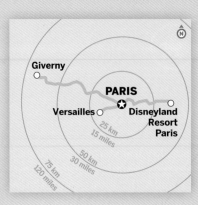

Giverny

PARIS

Versailles   Disneyland
              Resort
              Paris

25 km
15 miles

50 km
30 miles

75 km
120 miles

Day Trips

Versailles (p254)

When it comes to over-the-top opulence, the colossal Château de Versailles (shut Mondays) is in a class of its own, even for France.

Disneyland Resort Paris (p259)

The 'party never stops' at Europe's Disneyland theme park, Disney Village's hotels, shops, restaurants and clubs, and Walt Disney Studios Park, bringing film, animation and TV production to life.

Giverny (p260)

Art and/or garden lovers shouldn't miss Giverny's Maison et Jardins de Claude Monet (closed Mondays and from November to March), the former home and flower-filled garden of the impressionist master.

Versailles (p254)

SYLVAIN SONNET/CORBIS ©

Don't Miss
Versailles

Louis XIV transformed his father's hunting lodge into the monumental Château de Versailles in the mid-17th century, and it remains France's most famous and grand palace. Situated in the leafy, bourgeois suburb of Versailles, about 22km southwest of central Paris, the baroque château was the kingdom's political capital and the seat of the royal court from 1682 up until the fateful events of 1789 when revolutionaries massacred the palace guard. Louis XVI and Marie Antoinette were ultimately dragged back to Paris, where they were ingloriously guillotined.

Map p258

☎ 01 30 83 78 00

www.chateauversailles.fr

passport ticket incl estate-wide access adult/child €18/free, with musical events €25/free, palace €15/free

🕑 9am-6.30pm Tue-Sat, to 6pm Sun Apr-Oct, to 5.30pm Tue-Sun Nov-Mar

Ⓜ RER Versailles-Château–Rive Gauche

Château de Versailles

Few alterations have been made to the château since its construction, apart from most of the interior furnishings disappearing during the Revolution and some rooms being rebuilt by Louis-Philippe (r 1830–48).

To access areas that are otherwise off limits and to learn more about Versailles' history, take a 90-minute **guided tour** (📞01 30 83 77 88; www.chateauversailles.fr; tours €7 plus palace admission; 🕐English-language tours Tue-Sun, tour times vary). Tour tickets include access to the most famous parts of the palace, such as the Hall of Mirrors and the King's and Queen's State Apartments.

The Gardens

Don't miss a stroll through the château's magnificent **gardens (except during musical events admission free; 🕐gardens 9am-8.30pm Apr-Oct, 8am-6pm Nov-Mar, park 7am-8.30pm Apr-Oct, 8am-6pm Nov-Mar)**. The large fountains include the 17th-century *Bassin de Neptune* (Neptune's Fountain), a dazzling mirage of 99 spouting fountains 300m north of the palace, and the *Bassin d'Apollon* (Apollo's Fountain), built in 1668 at the eastern end of the Grand Canal.

Planning for Versailles

By noon ticket queues spiral out of control: arrive in the early morning and avoid Tuesday and Sunday, the busiest days. Save time by pre-purchasing tickets on the château's website or at **Fnac** branches (www.fnac.com).

The estate is so vast that the only way to see it all is to hire a four-person electric car (01 39 66 97 66; per hr €32) or hop aboard the shuttle train (adult/child €7.50/5.80); you can also rent a bike (01 39 66 97 66; per hr €6.50) or boat (01 39 66 97 66; per hr €15).

Getting There & Away

○ **Bus** RATP bus 171 (€1.70, 35 minutes) links Paris' Pont de Sèvres metro station (15e) with the place d'Armes at least every 15 minutes from between 5am and 1am.

○ **Train** RER C5 (€3.25, 45 minutes, frequent) departs Paris' Left Bank RER stations to Versailles-Château–Rive Gauche station.

Local Knowledge

Don't Miss List

BY SYLVAIN POSTOLLE, OFFICIAL GUIDE, CHÂTEAU DE VERSAILLES

1 KING'S PRIVATE APARTMENT
This is the most fascinating part of the palace as it shows the king as a man and very much reflects his daily life in the 18th century. Of the 10 or so rooms, the most famous is his bedroom – where he not only slept, but also held ceremonies. He had lunch here each day at 1pm and also supper, which up to 150 courtiers and people invited from outside the court would watch! By the 1780s, the king's life had become more private – he had an official supper just once a week, on Sunday.

2 HERCULES SALON
I love one particular perspective inside the palace: from the Hercules Salon you can see all the rooms comprising the King's State Apartment, and to the right, through the gallery leading to the opera house. The salon served as a passageway for the king to go from his state apartment to the chapel to celebrate daily Mass.

3 THE ROYAL CHAPEL
This is an exquisite example of the work of a very important architect of the time, Jules Hardouin-Mansart (1646–1708). The paintings, very representative of art fashions at the end of the reign of Louis XIV, are also stunning: they evoke the idea that the French king was chosen by God and as such was his lieutenant on earth. This is the chapel where, in 1770, the future king Louis XVI wed Marie Antoinette – the beginning of the French Revolution.

4 ENCELADE GROVE
Versailles' gardens are extraordinary; my favourite spot has to be this grove, typical of the gardens created for Louis XIV by André Le Nôtre. A gallery of trellises surrounds a pool with a statue of Enceladus, chief of the Titans, who was punished for his pride by the gods from Mount Olympus. When the fountains are on, it's impressive.

Versailles

A DAY IN COURT

Visiting Versailles – even just the State Apartments – may seem overwhelming at first, but think of it as a house where people ate, drank, worked, slept and conspired and you'll be on the right path.

Some two decades into his long reign, Louis XIV began turning his father's hunting lodge into a palace large enough to house his entire court (to keep closer tabs on the 6000-strong army of courtiers). Sparing no expense, the Sun King employed the greatest artists and craftspeople of the day and by 1682 he'd created the most extravagant dormitory in history.

The royal schedule was as accurate and predictable as a Swiss watch. By following this itinerary of rooms you can recreate the king's day, starting with the **King's Bedchamber** ❶ and the **Queen's Bedchamber** ❷, where the royal couple was roused at about the same time. The royal procession then leads through the **Hall of Mirrors** ❸ to the **Royal Chapel** ❹ for morning Mass and returns to the **Council Chamber** ❺ for late-morning meetings with ministers. After lunch the king might ride or hunt or visit the **King's Library** ❻. Later he could join courtesans for an 'apartment evening' starting from the **Hercules Drawing Room** ❼ or play billiards in the **Diana Drawing Room** ❽ before supping at 10pm.

VERSAILLES BY NUMBERS

➡ **Rooms** 700 (11 hectares of roof)
➡ **Windows** 2153
➡ **Staircases** 67
➡ **Gardens and parks** 800 hectares
➡ **Trees** 200,000
➡ **Fountains** 50 (with 620 nozzles)
➡ **Paintings** 6300 (measuring 11km laid end to end)
➡ **Statues and sculptures** 2100
➡ **Objets d'art and furnishings** 5000
➡ **Visitors** 5.3 million per year

Queen's Bedchamber
Chambre de la Reine
The queen's life was on constant public display and even the births of her children were watched by crowds of spectators in her own bedchamber. **DETOUR »** The Guardroom, with a dozen armed men at the ready.

LUNCH BREAK

Diner-style food at Sister's Café, crêpes at Le Phare St-Louis or picnic in the park.

Guardroom

South Wing

King's Library
Bibliothèque du Roi
The last resident, bibliophile Louis XVI, loved geography and his copy of *The Travels of James Cook* (in English, which he read fluently) is still on the shelf here.

SAVVY SIGHTSEEING

Avoid Versailles on Monday (closed), Tuesday (Paris' museums close, so visitors flock here) and Sunday, the busiest day. Also, book tickets online so you don't have to queue.

Hall of Mirrors
Galerie des Glaces
The solid-silver candelabra and furnishings in this extravagant hall, devoted to Louis XIV's successes in war, were melted down in 1689 to pay for yet another conflict. DETOUR» The antithetical Peace Drawing Room, adjacent.

King's Bedchamber
Chambre du Roi
The king's daily life was anything but private and even his *lever* (rising) at 8am and *coucher* (retiring) at 11.30pm would be witnessed by up to 150 sycophantic courtiers.

Council Chamber
Cabinet du Conseil
This chamber, with carved medallions evoking the king's work, is where the monarch met his various ministers (state, finance, religion etc) depending on the days of the week.

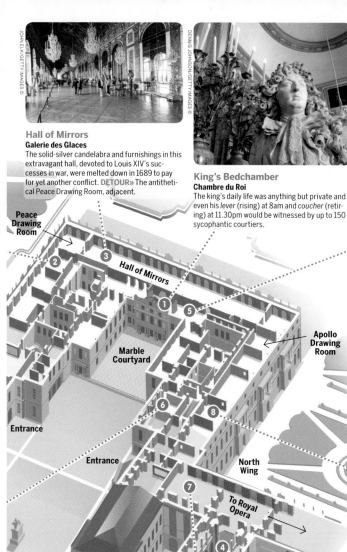

Peace Drawing Room

Hall of Mirrors

Apollo Drawing Room

Marble Courtyard

Entrance

Entrance

North Wing

To Royal Opera

Diana Drawing Room
Salon de Diane
With walls and ceiling covered in frescos devoted to the mythical huntress, this room contained a large billiard table reserved for Louis XIV, a keen player.

Royal Chapel
Chapelle Royale
This two-storey chapel (with gallery for the royals and important courtiers, and the ground floor for the B-list) was dedicated to St Louis, patron of French monarchs. DETOUR» The sumptuous Royal Opera.

Hercules Drawing Room
Salon d'Hercule
This salon, with its stunning ceiling fresco of the strong man, gave way to the State Apartments, which were open to courtiers three nights a week. DETOUR» Apollo Drawing Room, used for formal audiences and as a throne room.

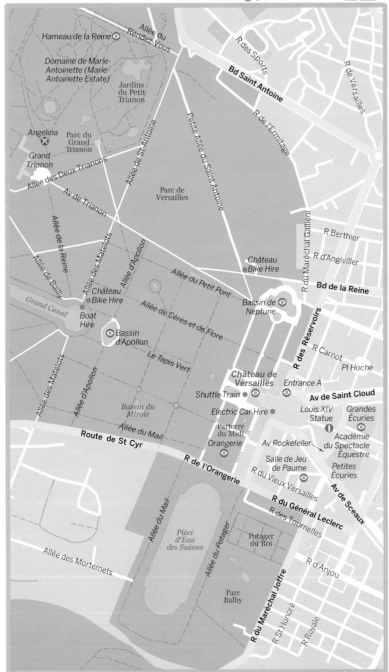

DISNEYLAND PARIS ©

⭐ Don't Miss
Disneyland Resort Paris

Disneyland Park (🕐10am-11pm May-Aug, to 10pm Sep, to 6pm Oct-Apr, hours can vary) has five themed *pays* (lands): the 1900s-styled **Main Street USA**; **Frontierland**, home to the legendary Big Thunder Mountain ride; **Adventureland**, which evokes exotic lands in rides like the Pirates of the Caribbean and Indiana Jones and the Temple of Peril; **Fantasyland**, crowned by Sleeping Beauty's castle; and the high-tech **Discoveryland**, with massive-queue rides such as Space Mountain: Mission 2, Star Wars and Buzz Lightyear Laser Blast.

The sound stage, production back lot and animation studios of **Walt Disney Studios** (🕐10am-7pm May-Sep, to 6pm Oct-Apr, hours can vary) provide an up-close illustration of how films, TV programs and cartoons are produced, with behind-the-scenes tours, larger-than-life characters and spine-tingling rides like the Twighlight Zone Tower of Terror. Its latest addition is the outsized Ratatouille ride, based on the winsome 2007 film about a rat who dreams of becoming a top Parisian chef, and offering a multisensory rat's perspective of Paris' rooftops and restaurant kitchens aboard a trackless 'ratmobile'.

NEED TO KNOW

📞hotel bookings 01 60 30 60 30, restaurant reservations 01 60 30 40 50; www.disneylandparis.com; one day adult/child €64/58; 🕐hours vary; Ⓜ RER Marne-la-Vallée/Chessy

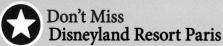

Giverny

Giverny's two main draws, the impressionist museum the Musée des Impressionismes Giverny and, especially, Monet's former home, the Maison de Claude Monet are only open from April to October (as are most places to eat, drink and sleep). If you're here during these months however, the Maison de Claude Monet's gardens are magnificent, so factor in plenty of time to enjoy them.

Getting There & Away

Travel time 50 minutes by train to Vernon, then 20 minutes by bus (or by taxi or bike).

Train From Paris' Gare St-Lazare there are up to 15 daily trains to Vernon (€14.30, 50 minutes), 7km to the west of Giverny.

Bus Shuttle buses (€8 return, 20 minutes, four daily April to October) meet most trains to and from Paris.

Taxi A taxi from Vernon's station to Giverny costs about €15 one way. Call 06 07 01 83 50.

Bike Rent bikes at the Café L'Arrivée de Giverny (02 32 21 16 01, per day €14), opposite the train station in Vernon, from where Giverny is a signposted 5km along a direct cycle/walking track.

Need to Know

○ **Location** 74km northwest of Paris

○ **Tourist Office** (☑02 32 64 45 01; www.cape-tourisme.fr; 80 rue Claude Monet; ⏲10am-6pm Apr-Oct) New office by the Maison et Jardins de Claude Monet.

 Sights

Musée des Impressionnismes Giverny
Museum

(☑02 32 51 94 65; www.mdig.fr; 99 rue Claude Monet; adult/child €7/4.50, incl Maison et Jardins de Claude Monet €16.50/8; ⏲10am-6pm Apr-Oct) About 100m northwest of the Maison de Claude Monet is the Giverny Museum of Impressionisms. Set up in partnership with the Musée d'Orsay, among others, the pluralised name reinforces its coverage of all aspects of impressionism and related movements in its permanent collection and temporary exhibitions. Reserve ahead for two-hour **art workshops** (€12.50 including materials) offering an introduction to watercolour, drawing, sketching or pastels. Lectures, readings, concerts and documentaries also take place regularly.

 Eating & Drinking

Le Jardin des Plumes
Modern French €€

(☑02 32 54 26 35; www.lejardindesplumes. fr; 1 rue du Milieu; 2-course lunch menu €29, 3-/5-/7-course dinner menus €39/62/82; ⏲12.15-1.45pm & 7.15-9pm Wed-Sun; ♿) Opened in 2012, this gorgeous sky-blue-trimmed property's airy white dining room sets the stage for chef Eric Guerin's exquisite, inventive cuisine, which justifies the trip from Paris alone. Its four rooms (€160 to €200) and four suites (€250 to €290) combine vintage and contemporary furnishings. It's less than 10 minutes' walk to the Maison et Jardins de Claude Monet.

La Musardière
Hotel €€

(☑02 32 21 03 18; www.lamusardiere.fr; 123 rue Claude Monet; d €84-99, tr €123-136, f €146, 3-course menus €26-36; ⏲hotel Feb–mid-Dec, restaurant noon-10pm Apr-Oct; ☎) This two-star 10-room hotel dating back to 1880 and evocatively called the 'Idler' is set amid a lovely garden less than 100m northeast of the Maison et Jardins de Claude Monet. Savouring a crêpe in its restaurant is a pleasure.

GRANT FAINT/GETTY IMAGES ©

 Don't Miss
Maison et Jardins de Claude Monet

Monet's home for the last 43 years of his life is now a delightful house-museum. His pastel-pink house and Water Lily studio stand on the periphery of the **Clos Normand**, with its symmetrically laid-out gardens bursting with flowers. Monet bought the **Jardin d'Eau** (Water Garden) in 1895 and set about creating his trademark lily pond, as well as the famous **Japanese bridge** (since rebuilt).

The charmingly preserved house and beautiful bloom-filled gardens (rather than Monet's works) are the draws here.

Draped with purple wisteria, the Japanese bridge blends into the asymmetrical foreground and background, creating the intimate atmosphere for which the 'painter of light' was renowned.

Seasons have an enormous effect on Giverny. From early to late spring, daffodils, tulips, rhododendrons, wisteria and irises appear, followed by poppies and lilies. By June, nasturtiums, roses and sweet peas are in flower. Around September, there are dahlias, sunflowers and hollyhocks.

Combined tickets with Paris' Musée Marmottan Monet per adult/child cost €18.50/9, and combined adult tickets with Paris' Musée de l'Orangerie cost €18.50.

NEED TO KNOW

📞02 32 51 28 21; www.fondation-monet.com; 84 rue Claude Monet; adult/child €9.50/5, incl Musée des Impressionnismes Giverny €16.50/8; ⏱9.30am-6pm Apr-Oct

Paris
In Focus

La Défense business district (p58)
BRUNO DE HOGUES/GETTY IMAGES ©

Paris Today

Eiffel Tower (p52) and Parc du Champ de Mars (p54)

> ❝
> *Europe's mythical 'City of Light' is on the brink of redefinition*
> ❞

living in Paris
(% of population by area)

80	20
Outer Arrondissements	Central Paris

if Paris were 100 people

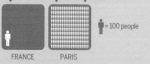

86 would be French
14 would be foreign

population per sq km

👤 ≈ 100 people

FRANCE   PARIS

While the elegance, depth and extraordinary spirit of the Paris of Haussmann, Hugo and Toulouse-Lautrec will never disappear, Europe's mythical 'City of Light' is on the brink of redefinition, with a long-awaited expansion into the suburbs beginning to take shape. Parisians themselves, moreover, are in the mood for change: the 2014 municipal elections ushered in the city's first-ever female mayor.

Madame la Maire

Paris has a history of political subversiveness, and while it's no longer the radical hotbed it once was, it continues to reveal an independent streak that runs counter to nationwide sentiment. This was most recently on display during the April 2014 municipal elections. While the vast majority of the country swung decisively to the right – political payback for President François Hollande's seemingly ineffectual policies – the capital remained resolutely left. But the big story was not that Parisians stuck with the eco-

FABIO CANHIM/GETTY IMAGES ©

the real estate boom of the past decade has pushed most middle-class residents and large companies outside the Périphérique – has created a real need to redefine Paris, on both an administrative and infrastructural scale.

Enter the Grand Paris (Greater Paris) redevelopment project, a Sarkozy-era initiative. The crux of Grand Paris is a massive decentralised metro expansion, with 72 new stations and six suburban lines, with a target completion date of 2025. The principal goal is to connect the suburbs with one another, instead of relying on a central inner-city hub from which all lines radiate outwards (the current model).

In terms of administration, it is expected that the surrounding suburbs – Vincennes, Neuilly, Issy, St-Denis etc – will eventually lose their autonomy and become part of a much larger Grand Paris, all governed by the Hôtel de Ville. It is no done deal, however, as uniting the wildly diverse municipalities will be no easy feat.

leaning Socialists for a third straight term, but rather that the election's two leading candidates were women: the Spanish-born deputy mayor Anne Hidalgo, and the former minister of ecology, Nathalie Kosciusko-Morizet. Hidalgo won with a substantial 55% of the vote, becoming the first-ever female mayor of Paris.

Greater Paris

Most visitors to Paris – and, in fact, many French – continue to think of the city as a self-contained whole, with limits that are both physically and conceptually defined by the traffic-snarled boulevard Périphérique – the ring road that stands on the site of the former city walls. This vision, however, is a far cry from reality: the vast majority of Parisians (8.2 million) now live in the adjacent suburbs, compared with only 2.2 million residents who live in the city proper. The steadily growing suburban population – indeed,

Green Transportation

Fundamentally interconnected with Grand Paris is the issue of transportation. Former mayor Bertrand Delanoë introduced several controversial but ultimately popular green initiatives during his tenure to help improve – or hinder, for those driving cars – transportation in Paris. These included the now famous Vélib' bike share programme, the Autolib' electric-car share programme, and the creation of hundreds of kilometres of new bus and bike lanes. Delanoë's outgoing project was to close the riverside roads along the Left Bank and reinvent a new pedestrian-friendly public area, known as the Berges de Seine. Other recent developments include several new tram lines that serve the city outskirts, with more on the way.

FABIO CANHIM/GETTY IMAGES ©

History

Cimetière du Père Lachaise (p150)

BRUNO DE HOGUES/GETTY IMAGES ©

As the national capital, Paris is the administrative, business and cultural centre of France. Since before the French Revolution, it has been what urban planners call a 'hypertropic city' – the enlarged head of a nation-state's body – and virtually everything of importance in the republic starts, finishes or is currently taking place here. Throughout the city's (and the country's) illustrious history, political rebellion has remained a constant theme.

The Beginnings to the Renaissance

Paris was born in the 3rd century BC, when a tribe of Celtic Gauls known as the Parisii settled on what is now the Île de la Cité. Centuries of conflict between the Gauls and Romans ended in 52 BC, when Julius Caesar's legions crushed a Celtic revolt. Christianity was introduced in the 2nd century AD, and Roman rule ended in the 5th century with the arrival of the

3rd century BC

Celtic Gauls called Parisii arrive in the Paris area and set up huts on what is now the Île de la Cité and engage in fishing and trading.

Germanic Franks. In 508 Frankish king Clovis I united Gaul and made Paris his seat.

France's west coast was beset in the 9th century by Scandinavian Vikings (also known as Norsemen and, later, as Normans). Three centuries later, the Normans started pushing towards Paris, which had risen rapidly in importance: construction had begun on the cathedral of Notre Dame in the 12th century, the Louvre began life as a riverside fortress around 1200, the beautiful Ste-Chapelle was consecrated in 1248 and the Sorbonne opened in 1253.

The Vikings' incursions heralded the Hundred Years' War between Norman England and Paris' Capetian dynasty, bringing French defeat in 1415 and English control of the capital in 1420. In 1429 the 17-year-old Jeanne d'Arc (Joan of Arc) rallied the French troops to defeat the English at Orléans. With the exception of Calais, the English were eventually expelled from France in 1453.

The Renaissance helped Paris get back on its feet in the late 15th century. Less than a century later, however, turmoil ensued as clashes between Huguenot (Protestant) and Catholic groups culminated in the St Bartholomew's Day massacre in 1572.

The Best...
Historical Sights

1 **Musée d'Art et d'Histoire du Judaïsme** (p156)

2 **Cimetière du Père Lachaise** (p150)

3 **Les Catacombes** (p243)

4 **Château de Versailles** (p254)

IN FOCUS HISTORY

The Revolution to a New Republic

A five-year-old Louis XIV (later known as the Sun King) ascended the throne in 1643 and ruled until 1715, virtually emptying the national coffers with his ambitious battling and building, including the construction of his extravagant palace at Versailles. The excesses of this grandiose king and his heirs, including Louis XVI and his Vienna-born queen Marie Antoinette, eventually led to an uprising of Parisians on 14 July 1789, kick-starting the French Revolution. Within four years, the Reign of Terror was in full swing.

The unstable postrevolutionary government was consolidated in 1799 under Napoleon Bonaparte, who declared himself First Consul. In 1804 he had the Pope crown him emperor of the French, and went on to conquer most of Europe before his eventual defeat at Waterloo in present-day Belgium in 1815. He was exiled to St Helena, and died in 1821.

France struggled under a string of mostly inept rulers until a coup d'état in 1851 brought Emperor Napoleon III to power. At his behest, Baron Haussmann razed

AD 845–86

Paris is repeatedly raided by Vikings for more than four decades.

1682

Louis XIV, the 'Sun King', moves his court from the Palais des Tuileries in Paris to Versailles.

14 July 1789

The French Revolution begins when a mob storms the prison at Bastille.

The Best...
Historic Nightlife

1 Comédie Française
(p118)

2 Moulin Rouge
(p142)

3 Palais Garnier
(p83)

4 Au Lapin Agile
(p142)

whole tracts of the city, replacing them with sculptured parks, a hygienic sewer system and – strategically – boulevards too broad for rebels to barricade. Napoleon III embroiled France in a costly war with Prussia in 1870, which ended within months with the French army's defeat and the capture of the emperor. When the masses in Paris heard the news, they took to the streets, demanding a republic.

20th Century History

Out of WWI's conflict came increased industrialisation, confirming Paris' place as a major commercial, as well as artistic, centre and establishing its reputation among freethinking intellectuals.

This was halted by WWII and the Nazi occupation of 1940. During Paris' occupation, almost half the population evacuated, including General Charles de Gaulle, France's undersecretary of war, who fled to London and set up a government-in-exile. In a radio broadcast he appealed to French patriots to continue resisting the Germans, and established the Forces Françaises Libres (Free French Forces) to fight the Germans alongside the Allies. Following Paris' liberation, de Gaulle set up a provisional government, but resigned in 1946; he formed his own party (Rassemblement du Peuple Français) and remained in opposition until 1958, when he was brought back to power. He was succeeded as president in 1969 by Gaullist leader Georges Pompidou.

After the war, Paris regained its position as a creative nucleus and nurtured a revitalised liberalism that peaked with the student-led uprisings of May 1968 – the Sorbonne was occupied, the Latin Quarter blockaded and a general strike paralysed the country.

Under centre-right President Jacques Chirac's watch, the late 1990s saw Paris seize the international spotlight with the rumour-plagued death of Princess Diana in 1997, and France's first-ever World Cup victory in July 1998.

The New Millenium

In May 2001 Socialist Bertrand Delanoë was elected mayor, becoming widely popular for making Paris more liveable through improved infrastructure and green spaces. Chirac's second term in office, starting in 2002, was marred in 2005 by the deaths of two teenagers who were electrocuted while allegedly hiding from police in an electricity substation, which sparked riots that quickly spread across Paris, and then across France.

1889
The Eiffel Tower is completed in time for the opening of the Exposition Universelle (World Fair).

25 August 1944
Spearheaded by Free French units, Allied forces liberate Paris and the city escapes destruction.

1968
Paris is rocked by student-led riots that bring the nation and the city to the brink of civil war.

The French Resistance

Despite the infamy of 'la France Résistante' (the French Resistance), the underground movement never actually included more than 5% of the population. Resistance members engaged in railway sabotage, collected intelligence for the Allies, helped Allied airmen who had been shot down and published anti-German leaflets, among other activities. The impact of their pursuits might have been modest but the Resistance served as an enormous boost to French morale – not to mention fresh fodder for numerous literary and cinematic endeavours.

Chirac retired in 2007. His centre-right successor, Nicolas 'Sarko' Sarkozy, defeated Socialist Ségolène 'Ségo' Royal in the 2007 presidential elections. Sarkozy's win was widely attributed to his platform of economic reform, with many French claiming it was time for 'modernisation'. Following his election, however, many voters were unimpressed at the media hype surrounding the presidency, notably Sarkozy's divorce, whirlwind romance and marriage to actress/model/singer Carla Bruni. Many people believe this contributed to the subsequent defeat of the right at France's March 2008 municipal elections, including left-wing Delanoë's comfortable re-election as mayor.

Recent History

Presidential elections in May 2012 pitted incumbent right-wing president Nicolas Sarkozy against left-wing candidate François Hollande, resulting in France's first Socialist president since 1988. Hollande had campaigned to reduce unemployment (which was at a 12-year high), clear the country's debts by 2017, raise income tax on top-end salaries and steer France though Europe's biggest economic crisis in decades. Some voters, fed up with austerity and desperate for change, welcomed this approach. Legislative elections held a month later sealed the left's grip on power: the Socialists won a comfortable majority (273 seats) in France's 577-seat lower-house National Assembly, paving the way for the new president to enact many of his promised reforms. Rising anger at Hollande's failure to deliver on campaign promises, however, saw his popularity plunge even faster and farther than Sarkozy's and resulted in a near total wipeout for French Socialists in the 2014 municipal elections. The election of Anne Hidalgo as Paris' first female mayor meant the capital was one of the few cities to remain on the political left.

1994
Eurostar trains link Waterloo in London with the Gare du Nord in Paris in just over three hours. Gare du Nord

2004–05
The French electorate rejects the EU Constitution; Arab and African youths riot in Parisian suburbs.

KEVIN CLOGSTOUN/GETTY IMAGES ©

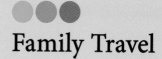

Family Travel

Jardin du Luxembourg (p226)

BRUNO DE HOGUES/GETTY IMAGES ©

Parisians adore les enfants (children) and welcome them with open arms just about everywhere. The French are great believers in doing things en famille (as a family), and children are active participants in many aspects of social life, including visiting museums and dining out. And central Paris' residential make-up means you'll find playground equipment in parks all over the city.

Sights & Activities

In addition to playgrounds, Paris' parks also have a host of children's activities. Among the best are the toy boats, *marionettes* (puppets), pony rides and carousel of the Jardin du Luxembourg (p226); the new millennium playgrounds of Parc de la Villette (p135) adjacent to the fabulous interactive science museum Cité des Sciences (p135); lions, cougars, white rhinos and a gaggle of other creatures at the Bois de Vincennes' state-of-the-art zoo Parc Zoologique de Paris; the kid-friendly Musée National d'Histoire Naturelle (p202) (Museum of Natural History); and the Bois de Boulogne's adorable Jardin d'Acclimatation amusement park (p61).

The shark tank inside the Cinéaqua (p55) aquarium is another winner with animal-mad kids, while a trip to the Louvre (p92) can be a treat, particularly following thematic trails such as hunting for lions or galloping horses.

Further afield, you might consider a day trip to Disneyland Resort Paris (p259).

Eating Out

Many restaurants accept little diners (confirm ahead), but they're expected to behave (bring crayons/books). Children's menus are common, but most restaurants don't have highchairs. Department-store cafeterias and chain restaurants, such as **Flunch** (www. flunch.fr), offer kid-friendly fare, as do a new wave of gourmet pizza, pasta and burger restaurants throughout the city. In fine weather, good options include picking up sandwiches and crêpes from a street stall or packing a market-fresh picnic and heading to parks and gardens where kids can play to their hearts' content.

Need to Know

o **Cots/cribs** Available upon request in many midrange and top-end hotels

o **Highchairs** Rare; bring your own screw-on seat

o **Children's menus** Available in many restaurants

o **Nappies (diapers)** Widely available in supermarkets and pharmacies

o **Changing facilities** Rare; bring a towel and improvise (no one minds)

o **Strollers (pushchairs)** A strict no-no inside Château de Versailles; bring a baby sling

Way to Go

Paris' narrow streets and metro stairways are a trial if you have a stroller (pram or pushchair) in tow; buses offer an easier, scenic alternative. Car-rental firms have children's safety seats for hire at a nominal cost; book in advance. Children under four years of age travel free on public transport and generally receive free admission to sights. For older kids, discounts vary from place to place – anything from a euro off for over fours to free entry up to the age of 18.

The choice of baby food, infant formula, soy and cow's milk, nappies (diapers) and the like in French supermarkets is similar to that in any developed country, but remember that opening hours may be more limited. Pharmacies – of which a handful are open 24/7, and others open for at least a few hours on a Sunday – also sell baby paraphernalia.

Bedtime

When booking accommodation, check availability and costs for a *lit bébé* (cot/crib). Weekly magazine *L'Officiel des Spectacles* advertises *gardes d'enfants* (babysitting) services.

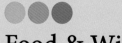

Food & Wine

Macarons at Pierre Hermé (p251)

MING TANG-EVANS/GETTY IMAGES ©

Some cities rally around local sports teams, but Parisians rally around la table – and everything on it. Food is not fuel here; it's the reason you get up in the morning. The freshness of ingredients and reliance on natural flavours combined with refined, often very complex cooking methods – and, of course, wine – means you are in a gourmet's paradise.

Capital Cuisine

Paris doesn't have its own 'local' cuisine but is the crossroads for the regional flavours of France. Dishes from the hot south favour olive oil, garlic and tomatoes; the cooler, pastoral northern regions turn to cream and butter; and coastal areas concentrate on seafood.

Regional French specialities you'll encounter in the capital include the following:

○ **Burgundy** A culinary trinity of beef, red wine and Dijon mustard. Savour *bœuf bourguignon* (beef marinated and cooked in young red wine with mushrooms, onions, carrots and bacon) or snails.

○ **The Dordogne** Black truffles and poultry, especially ducks and geese, whose fattened livers are turned into *pâté de foie gras* (duck- or goose-liver pâté).

- **Lyon** An age-old repertoire of distinctive dishes like breaded fried tripe, *andouillettes* (pig-intestine sausage) and lighter *quenelles* (poached dumplings).

- **Loire Valley** The cuisine refined in the kitchens of the Loire Valley's châteaux in the 16th century became what's often now considered 'quintessentially French': *coq au vin* (chicken in red wine), *cuisses de grenouilles* (frogs legs) and *tarte tatin* (upside-down apple tart).

  - **Alsace** The brasserie, which means 'brewery' in French, originated in Alsace, and brasserie menus often include classic Alsatian dishes like *choucroute alsacienne* – sauerkraut flavoured with juniper berries and served hot with sausages, bacon, pork and/or ham knuckle.

  - **Provence** Sun-ripened fruit and vegetables abound; *à la Provençal* means anything dosed with garlic-seasoned tomatoes. Bouillabaisse, Marseille's mighty fish stew, is Provence's most famous dish.

- **Brittany** Best known for seafood, and sweet, wheat flour *crêpes* and savoury buckwheat *galettes* paired with *une bolée* (a small bowl) of apple-rich Breton cider.

- **Auvergne** Traditional dishes include *aligot* (puréed potato with garlic and Tomme cheese) and *truffade* (sliced potatoes with Cantal cheese). Another speciality is the *lentille verte de Puy* (green Puy lentil).

- **Languedoc** Famed for *cassoulet*, an earthy cockle-warming stew of white beans and meat.

- **Basque Country** Essential ingredients of Basque cooking include deep-red Espelette chillies and Bayonne ham.

IN FOCUS FOOD & WINE

Prix-Fixe Menus

In addition to the *carte* (menu), most Parisian restaurants offer daily *formules* or *menus* (fixed-price menus), which typically include two- to four-course meals. In some cases, particularly at market-driven neobistros, there is no *carte* – only a selection of *menus*.

Lunch *menus* are often a fantastic deal and allow you to enjoy *haute cuisine* at very affordable prices. In this guide, the price for a lunch *menu* generally corresponds to a two-course meal served Monday to Friday. The price for a dinner *menu* generally corresponds to a three-course meal, available every day.

Cheese

France counts upwards of 500 varieties of *fromage* (cheese) made from raw or pasteurised milk, or from *petit-lait* (the whey left over after the milk fats and solids have been curdled with rennet).

Cheeses at the Paris' enticing *fromageries* (cheese shops) are split into five main categories: *fromage de chèvre* (goat's cheese), *fromage à pâte persillée* (veined or blue cheese), *fromage à pâte molle* (soft cheese), *fromage à pâte demi-dure* (semihard cheese) and *fromage à pâte dure* (hard cheese). The selection here or at a Parisian market can be overwhelming – ask to sample before buying.

You can also taste cheese with wine at wine bars, or enjoy it instead of (or as well as) dessert at simple through to celebrated restaurants across the capital.

Charcuterie

Traditionally charcuterie was made only from pork, though other meats – from beef and veal to chicken and goose – are now used in making sausages, blood puddings, hams, and other cured- and salted-meat products.

Every region in France produces standard charcuterie favourites as well as its own specialities. Pâtés, terrines and *rillettes* – potted meat (or fish) that is shredded, seasoned, mixed with fat and spread cold, like pâté, over bread or toast – are essentially charcuterie. They're all often nibbled on with wine, some of the most popular are *jambon* (ham, either smoked or salt-cured), *saucisse* (usually a small fresh sausage, boiled or grilled), *saucisson* (usually a large salami eaten cold) and *saucisson sec* (air-dried salami).

Bread & Bakery Treats

Few things are as tantalising – or prevalent – as the smell of freshly-baked buttery croissants wafting from a bakery door. There are roughly 1200 *boulangeries* (bakeries) in Paris – or 11.5 per sq km. As you'll notice in the extravagant display windows, bakeries not only bake baguettes and croissants but also éclairs, quiches and an astounding array of pastries and cakes.

If it's *pain* (bread) you're after, try to familiarise yourself with the varieties on sale while you're standing in the queue. Most Parisians today will ask for a *baguette tradition* (traditional-style baguette, with a coarse, handcrafted surface and pointy tips). Other breads you'll commonly see include *boules* (round loaves), *pavés* (flattened rectangular loaves) and *ficelles* (skinny loaves that are half the weight of a baguette).

Need to Know

o **Price Ranges** The following symbols indicate the cost for a two-course meal:

€	under €20
€€	€20-40
€€€	more than €40

o **Reservations** Advisable for midrange restaurants (especially dinner) and essential for top-end restaurants (sometimes up to two months in advance).

o **Vegetarians and vegans** Options are emerging but still rare; see www.happycow.net for a decent guide.

o **The Bill** The French consider it rude to bring *l'addition* (the bill) immediately – you have to be persistent.

o **Tipping** A *pourboire* (tip) is not necessary as service is included, but it's not uncommon to round up the bill for good service.

Pastries & Chocolates

Patisseries (pastry shops) are similar to but generally more sophisticated than *boulangeries*. Although they sell different varieties, they're often known for a particular speciality – Ladurée (p76) and Pierre Hermé (p251) do *macarons*, Gérard Mulot (p235) does cakes and *tartes*, and so on. *Chocolatiers* (chocolate specialists) typically sell chocolates measured in 100g increments in mouthwatering flavours like pistachio, lavender, and ginger.

Wine

In Paris you'll find wine from dozens of wine-producing regions throughout France, including the seven principal ones: Burgundy, Bordeaux, the Rhône and

Loire valleys, Champagne, Languedoc, Provence and Alsace. Wines are generally named after the location of the vineyard rather than the grape varietal. Organic and biodynamic wines are increasingly popular.

The best French wines are Appellation d'Origine Contrôlée (AOC), meaning they meet stringent regulations governing where, how and under what conditions they are grown, fermented and bottled. Some regions, such as Alsace, only have a single AOC; others, like Burgundy, have scores. About a third of all French wine carries that AOC hallmark of guarantee.

Specialist wine shops and wine bars are the best places to sample the varieties, or consider a wine-tasting course.

The Best...
Market-Stall Streets

1 Rue Montorgueil, 2e

2 Rue Mouffetard, 5e

3 Rue Cler, 7e

4 Rue de Seine & Rue de Buci, 6e

IN FOCUS FOOD & WINE

Architecture

Palais Garnier (p83)

RUSM/GETTY IMAGES ©

Several key eras are woven into Paris' contemporary architectural fabric. Magnificent cathedrals and palaces took hold from the 11th century. Baron Haussmann created broad boulevards lined by neoclassical buildings. Later additions centred on French presidents' bold grands projets. *Modern and historic complement each other, even if additions take a while to fully appreciate – the now-iconic Eiffel Tower was originally derided as the 'metal asparagus'.*

Romanesque

A religious revival in the 11th century led to the construction of a large number of *roman* (Romanesque) churches, so-called because their architects adopted many architectural elements (eg vaulting) from Gallo-Roman buildings still standing at the time. Romanesque buildings typically have round arches, heavy walls, few (and small) windows that let in very little light, and a lack of ornamentation that borders on the austere. The Église St-Germain des Prés, built in the 11th century on the site of the Merovingian ruler Childeric's 6th-century abbey, has been altered many times over the centuries, but the Romanesque bell tower over the west entrance has changed little since AD 1000.

Gothic – Radiant to Flamboyant

In the 14th century, the Rayonnant – or Radiant – Gothic style developed, named after the radiating tracery of the rose windows. Light was welcomed into interiors by broad windows and translucent stained glass. One of the most influential Rayonnant buildings was Ste-Chapelle, whose stained glass forms a curtain of glazing on the 1st floor. The two transept façades of the Cathédrale de Notre Dame de Paris are another fine example.

By the 15th century, decorative extravagance led to what is now called Flamboyant Gothic, so named because the wavy stone carving made the towers appear to be blazing or flaming (*flamboyant*).

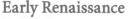

Early Renaissance

The Early Renaissance style of the 15th and early 16th centuries, in which a variety of classical components and decorative motifs (columns, tunnel vaults, round arches, domes etc) were blended with the rich decoration of Flamboyant Gothic, is best exemplified in Paris by the Église St-Eustache. The Marais remains the best area for spotting reminders of the Renaissance in Paris proper, with some fine *hôtels particuliers* (private mansions) from this era, such as Hôtel Carnavalet, which houses part of the Musée Carnavalet.

The Best...
Architectural Icons

1 **Arc de Triomphe** (p70)

2 **Opéra Bastille** (p158)

3 **Musée du Quai Branly** (p59)

4 **Centre Pompidou** (p98)

Baroque

During the baroque period – which lasted from the end of the 16th to the late 18th centuries – painting, sculpture and classical architecture were integrated to create structures and interiors of great subtlety, refinement and elegance. With the advent of the baroque, architecture became more pictorial, with the painted ceilings in churches illustrating the Passion of Christ to the faithful, and palaces invoking the power and order of the state.

Salomon de Brosse, who designed Paris' Palais du Luxembourg in the Jardin du Luxembourg in 1615, set the stage for prominent early baroque architect François Mansart, designer of the Église Notre Dame du Val-de-Grâce.

Neoclassicism

Neoclassical architecture, which emerged in about 1740 and remained popular in Paris until well into the 19th century, had its roots in the renewed interest in classical forms. Neoclassicism was more profoundly a search for order, reason and serenity through the adoption of the forms and conventions of Graeco-Roman antiquity: columns, simple geometric forms and traditional ornamentation. Neoclassicism really came into its own under Napoleon, who used it extensively for monumental architecture intended to embody the grandeur of imperial France and its capital.

The Best...
Neoclassical Sights

1 **Église St-Sulpice** (p228)

2 **Arc de Triomphe** (p70)

3 **Panthéon** (p208)

4 **Palais Garnier** (p83)

Haussman

Baron Haussman's late 19th-century renovation of the medieval city's disease-ridden streets demolished more than 20,000 homes, making way for wide boulevards lined by 40,000 new apartments in neoclassical creamy stone, grey-roofed buildings. And the turn-of-the-century art nouveau movement, which emerged in Europe and the USA in the second half of the 19th century under various names (Jugendstil, Sezessionstil, Stile Liberty), caught on quickly in Paris. It was characterised by sinuous curves and flowing, asymmetrical forms reminiscent of creeping vines, water lilies, the patterns on insect wings and the flowering boughs of trees. Influenced by the arrival of exotic objets d'art from Japan, its French name came from a Paris gallery that featured works in the 'new art' style. In Paris, it ushered in signature sights including the Musée d'Orsay, Grand Palais and Paris' ornate brasseries and wrought-iron metro entrances – and, of course, the Eiffel Tower.

Contemporary

Additions to the cityscape in the late 20th century centred on French presidents' *grand projets* (huge public edifices through which French leaders sought to immortalise themselves). President Georges Pompidou's Centre Pompidou, unveiled in 1977, prompted a furore, as did President François Mitterand's Louvre's glass pyramid in 1989. However, both are now widely admired and considered iconic Paris landmarks. Mitterand oversaw a slew of other costly *projets,* including the Opéra Bastille. In 1995 the presidential baton shifted to Jacques Chirac – his pet *projet,* the Musée du Quai Branly, opened in a Jean Nouvel–designed structure in 2006. Watch this space for future presidental projects.

Monet's *Regattas at Argenteuil* at the Musée d'Orsay (p224)

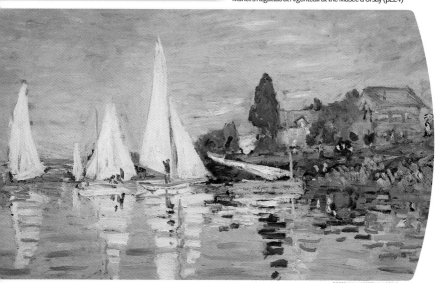

If there's one thing that rivals a Parisian's obsession with food, it's art. Well over 100 museums pepper the city, and whether you prefer the classicism of the Louvre, the impressionists of the d'Orsay or detailed exhibits of French military history, you can always be sure to find something new just around the corner. Viewing art is an integral part of Parisians' leisure time, which accounts for their keen aesthetic sensibility.

Painting

While art in Paris today means anything and everything – metro installations, monumental frescoes, mechanical sculpture, suburban tags and bicycles strung on walls – the city's art heritage is rooted in the traditional genres of painting and sculpture.

Baroque to Neoclassicism

According to philosopher Voltaire, French painting proper began with baroque painter Nicolas Poussin (1594–1665), the greatest representative of 17th-century classicism who frequently set scenes from classical mythology and the Bible in ordered landscapes bathed in golden light. It's not a bad starting point; many of Poussin's finest works now hang in the Louvre.

Modern still life pops up on the canvases of Jean-Baptiste Chardin (1699–1779), who brought the domesticity of the Dutch

The Best...
Art & Sculpture Museums

1 **Musée du Louvre**
(p92)

2 **Musée Rodin**
(p234)

3 **Musée d'Orsay**
(p224)

4 **Musée Marmottan Monet** (p60)

masters to French art. A century later, in 1785, neoclassical artist Jacques Louis David (1748–1825) became one of the leaders of the French Revolution and was made official state painter by Napoleon Bonaparte. Many of his works, including the famous *Oath of the Horatii*, can be viewed in the Louvre.

David's pupil Jean-Auguste-Dominique Ingres (1780–1867) continued in the neoclassical tradition, devoting most of his life to historical pictures such as *Oedipus and the Sphinx*, the 1808 version of which is in the Louvre. Ingres played the violin for enjoyment; the phrase *violon d'Ingres* now means 'hobby' in French.

Romanticism to Realism

One of the Musée du Louvre's most gripping paintings, the *Raft of the Medusa* by Théodore Géricault (1791–1824), hovers on the threshold of romanticism. If Géricault had not died early he likely would have become a leader of the movement, along with his friend Eugène Delacroix (1798–1863), who has his own museum in Paris as well as works at the Louvre and frescoes in St-Sulpice.

Édouard Manet (1832–1883) used realism to depict the life of the Parisian middle classes, incorporating numerous references to the Old Masters. He was pivotal in the transition from realism to impressionism.

Impressionism

Paris' Musée d'Orsay is the crown jewel of impressionist (and postimpressionist) art. Claude Monet (1840–1926) is generally considered the founder of the genre; other impressionists showcased at the Musée d'Orsay include Alfred Sisley (1839–99), Camille Pissarro (1830–1903) and Pierre-Auguste Renoir (1841–1919). The impressionists' main aim was to capture the effects of fleeting light; unusually for the time, they almost always painted in the open air. The term comes from the title of Monet's 1874 experimental painting, *Impression: Soleil Levant* (Impression: Sunrise), displayed at the Musée Marmottan Monet.

Other artists you'll see at the Musée d'Orsay include Edgar Degas (1834–1917) a fellow traveller of the impressionists who preferred painting cafe life and ballet studios; Henri de Toulouse-Lautrec (1864–1901), best known for his posters and lithographs, who chose 'lower' subject including people in the bistros, brothels and music halls of Montmartre; and Paul Cézanne (1839–1906) and Paul Gauguin (1848–1903), who are usually referred to as postimpressionists, encompassing the diverse styles that flowed from impressionism.

20th Century & Beyond

Twentieth-century French painting was characterised by a bewildering diversity of styles, including fauvism, named after the slur of a critic who compared the exhibitors at the 1905 Salon d'Automne (Autumn Salon) in Paris with fauves (wild animals) because of their wild brushstrokes and radical use of intensely bright colours. Among these 'beastly' painters was Henri Matisse (1869–1954); the Centre Pompidou's Musée National d'Art Moderne houses a fabulous collection of his works.

The Literary Arts

Flicking through a street directory reveals just how much Paris honours its literary history, with listings including places Colette and Victor Hugo, avs Marcel Proust and Émile Zola, and rue Balzac. The city has nurtured countless French authors over the centuries, who, together with expat writers from Dickens onwards – including the Lost Generation's Hemingway, Fitzgerald and Joyce – have sealed Paris' literary reputation.

You can leaf through Paris' literary heritage in atmospheric bookshops, hang out in cafes and swish literary bars, visit writers' former-homes-turned-museums, sleep in hotels where they holed up and pay your respects at cemeteries.

Cubism, which deconstructs the subject into a system of intersecting planes and presents various aspects simultaneously, was effectively launched in 1907 with *Les Demoiselles d'Avignon* by Spanish prodigy Pablo Picasso; the Musée Picasso has an astonishing collection of his works.

In the 1920s and '30s the so-called École de Paris (School of Paris) was formed by a group of expressionists including Italian Amedeo Modigliani and Russian Marc Chagall, whose works combined fantasy and folklore.

Dada, a literary and artistic movement of revolt, started in Zürich in 1915. The most influential proponent was Spanish-born Salvador Dalí, who arrived in Paris in 1929 and painted some of his most seminal works here; you can view some at the Espace Dalí in Montmartre.

Artists in the late 20th century turned to the minutiae of everyday urban life to express social and political angst, using media other than paint to let rip – the Musée National d'Art Moderne offers a great insight (as does the building itself). The museum also points to Paris' artistic present – and future.

Sculpture

By the 14th century, sculpture was increasingly commissioned by the nobility for their extravagant, monumental tombs, while in the 15th century Jean Goujon created the stunning *Fontaine des Innocents*. The later baroque style is exemplified by Guillaume Coustou's *Horses of Marly* at the entrance to the Champs-Élysées.

In the mid-19th century, memorial statues in public places came to replace sculpted tombs – the Jardin du Luxembourg is today studded with over 100 sculptures. Jean-Baptiste Carpeaux began as a romantic, but his works – such as *The Dance* on the Palais Garnier and his fountain in the Jardin du Luxembourg – look back to the flamboyance of the baroque era. At the end of the 19th century Auguste Rodin's work overcame the conflict between neoclassicism and romanticism. One of Rodin's most gifted pupils was his lover Camille Claudel, whose work can be seen along with Rodin's in the Musée Rodin.

Among the most influential sculptors to emerge in Paris before WWII was the Romanian-born Constantin Brancusi, whose work can be seen at the Centre Pompidou. Ossip Zadkine was another sculptor who lived and worked in Paris and has a museum.

The Best...
Museums For 20th & 21st Century Art

1 **Musée National d'Art Moderne** (p99)

2 **Palais de Tokyo** (p54)

3 **Dalí Espace Montmartre** (p130)

4 **La Défense** (p58)

In 1936 France put forward a bill providing for 'the creation of monumental decorations in public buildings' by allotting 1% of all building costs to public art. It didn't really get off the ground for another half-century, until Daniel Buren's *Les Deux Plateaux* sculpture was commissioned at Palais Royal. The concept mushroomed, and artwork started to appear everywhere in Paris, including in the Jardin des Tuileries (*The Welcoming Hands*) and even the metro.

The Art of Travel

Metro stations increasingly incorporate artistic themes, including the following:

○ **Abbesses** Hector Guimard's finest glass-canopied, twin wrought-iron lampposts illuminating the dark-green-on-lemon-yellow *Metropolitain* sign.

○ **Arts et Métiers** (line 11 platform) Jules Verne-inspired copper panelling.

○ **Bastille** (line 5 platform) Revolution-era newspaper-engraving frescoes.

○ **Cluny-La Sorbonne** (line 10 platform) A mosaic replicates the signatures of Latin Quarter intellectuals including Molière, Rabelais and Robespierre.

○ **Concorde** (line 12 platform) Lettered tiles spell out the Déclaration des Droits de l'Homme et du Citoyen (Declaration of the Rights of Man and of the Citizen).

○ **Louvre-Rivoli** (line 1 platform & corridor) Statues and bas-reliefs.

○ **Palais Royal-Musée du Louvre** Contemporary twist on Guimard's entrances incorporating 800 colourful glass balls.

Drinking & Nightlife

Experimental Cocktail Club (p116)

OWEN FRANKEN/CORBIS ©

For Parisians, drinking and eating go together like wine and cheese, and the line between a café, salon de thé (tearoom), bistro, bar and even a bar à vins (wine bar) is blurred, while the line between drinking and clubbing is often nonexistent – a cafe that's quiet midafternoon might have DJ sets in the evening and dancing later on. And with legendary venues to choose from, live performances in Paris are a treat.

Drinking

Drinking in Paris as Parisians do could mean anything, from downing a coffee at a zinc counter with locals, getting a fruit juice vitamin fix, sipping Japanese *gyokuro* (green tea) in a sleek *salon de thé* (tearoom) or meeting friends after work for *un verre* (a glass), to savouring a cheese platter with a glass of sauvignon on a pavement terrace, debating existentialism over an early-evening *apéritif* in the same literary cafes that Sartre and de Beauvoir did, dancing on tables to bossa nova beats, swilling martinis on a dark leather couch while listening to jazz, or partying aboard floating clubs on the Seine...and much, much more.

The Best...
Drinking Spots

1 **Le Baron Rouge** (p165)

2 **Experimental Cocktail Club** (p116)

3 **Le Batofar** (p247)

4 **Kong** (p117)

5 **Harry's New York Bar** (p116)

6 **Chez Prune** (p141)

Nightlife

From sipping cocktails in swanky bars to grooving at hip clubs, rocking to live bands, being awed by spectacular operas, ballets and classical concerts, entertained by films, dazzled by high-kicking cabarets, intrigued by avant-garde theatre productions or listening to smooth jazz or stirring *chansons*, a night out in Paris promises a night to remember.

Nightclubs

Paris' residential make-up means nightclubs aren't ubiquitous. Lacking a mainstream scene, clubbing here tends to be underground and extremely mobile, making blogs, forums and websites the savviest means of keeping apace with what's happening. The best DJs and their followings have short stints before moving on, and the scene's hippest *soirées clubbing* (clubbing events) float between venues – including the city's many dance-driven bars.

But the beat is strong. Electronic music is of particularly high quality in Paris' clubs, with some excellent local house and techno, laced with funk and groove. The Latin scene is huge; salsa dancing and Latino music nights pack out plenty of clubs. R & B and hip-hop pickings are decent, if less represented than in many other European capitals.

Entertainment

Paris became Europe's most important jazz centre after WWII and the city has some fantastic jazz clubs as well as *chansons* (heartfelt, lyric-driven music typified by Édith Piaf) venues.

Whirling lines of high-kicking dancers at cabarets like the Moulin Rouge are a quintessential fixture on Paris' entertainment scene – for everyone but Parisians. Still, the dazzling sets, costumes and dancing guarantee an entertaining evening (or matinée).

France's national opera and ballet companies perform at the Palais Garnier and Opéra Bastille opera houses. Virtually all theatre productions are in French but increasingly project English-language subtitles.

The city hosts dozens of orchestral, organ and chamber-music concerts each week. In addition to theatres and concert halls, Paris' beautiful, centuries-old stone churches have magnificent acoustics and provide a meditative backdrop for classical music concerts.

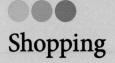

Shopping

Galeries Lafayette (p84)

SENG CHYE TEO/GETTY IMAGES ©

Paris has it all: broad boulevards lined with international chains, luxury avenues studded with designer fashion houses, famous department stores and fabulous markets. But the real charm of Parisian shopping lies in strolling through the backstreets, where tiny speciality shops and quirky boutiques selling everything from strawberry-scented Wellington boots to heaven-scented candles are wedged between cafes, galleries and churches.

Fashion

Fashion shopping is Paris' forte. Yet although its well-groomed residents make the city at times look and feel like a giant catwalk, fashion here is about style and quality first and foremost, rather than status or brand names. A good place to get an overview of Paris fashion is at department stores like Le Bon Marché, Galeries Lafayette and Le Printemps.

Parisian fashion doesn't have to break the bank. Paris' twice-yearly *soldes* (sales) usually last around five weeks, starting in mid-January and again in mid-June, and can yield discounts of up to 80%. Year-round, there are fantastic bargains at vintage and secondhand boutiques (generally, the more upmarket the area, the better quality the cast-offs), along with outlet shops selling previous seasons' collections, surpluses and seconds by name-brand designers.

The Best...
Parisian Shops

1 **Didier Ludot** (p118)

2 **E Dehillerin** (p119)

3 **Village St-Paul** (p174)

4 **La Grande Épicerie de Paris** (p249)

5 **Adam Montparnasse** (p248)

6 **Shakespeare & Company** (p216)

Markets

Many street markets also sell clothes, accessories, homewares and more.

Bric-a-brac, antiques, retro clothing, jewellery, cheap brand-name clothing, footwear, African carvings, DVDs, electronic items and much more are laid out at the city's flea markets. Watch out for pickpockets!

The website www.paris.fr (in French) lists every market by *arrondissement*, including speciality markets such as flower markets.

Art, Antiques & Homewares

From venerable antique dealers to edgy art galleries, there is a wealth of places in this artistic city to browse and buy one-off conversation pieces and collectibles. Paris also has some unique home and garden shops selling colourful, quirky innovations to brighten your living and/or working environment.

Books

Paris' literary heritage has inspired atmospheric bookshops, including English-language bookshops that are a magnet for writers and that host readings, workshops and other literary events. *Bandes dessinées* (comics), known as *le neuvième art* (the ninth art), are big business in France, with dozens of specialist shops.

Top Shopping Tips

○ Dating from the 19th century, Paris' glass-roofed covered passages, such as the Passage des Panoramas (p121), are treasure chests of small, exquisite boutiques.

○ The most exclusive designer boutiques require customers to buzz to get in – don't be shy about ringing the bell.

○ Particularly in smaller shops, shopkeepers may not like you touching the merchandise until invited to do so.

○ Clothing sizes aren't standardised among European countries – head to a *cabine d'essayage* (fitting room) or www.onlineconversion.com/clothing.

○ If you're happy browsing, tell sales staff *'Je regarde'* – 'I'm just looking'.

○ Practically all shops offer free (and beautiful) gift wrapping – ask for *un paquet cadeau*.

○ Greet/farewell shopkeepers and sales staff, with '*Bonjour* (*bonsoir* at night)/*Au revoir*'.

○ Bargaining is only acceptable at flea markets.

○ Food, wine and tea shops make for mouthwatering shopping.

Survival
Guide

Avenue des Champs-Élysées (p72)
PAWEL LIBERA/GETTY IMAGES ©

Sleeping

Paris has a wealth of accommodation, but it's often *complet* (full) well in advance. Reservations are recommended any time of year, and are essential during the warmer months (April to October) and during all public and school holidays.

Accommodation Types

Hotels

Hotels in Paris are inspected by government authorities and classified into six categories, from no star to five stars. The vast majority are two- and three-star hotels, which are generally well equipped. All hotels must display their rates, including TVA (*taxe sur la valeur ajoutée;* valued-added tax), though you'll often get much cheaper prices online, even on the hotels' own websites.

Parisian hotel rooms tend to be small by international standards. Families will probably need connecting rooms but if children are too young to stay in their own room, it's possible to make do with triples, quads or suites in some places.

Cheaper hotels may not have lifts/elevators and/or air-conditioning. Some don't accept credit cards.

Breakfast is rarely included in hotel rates; heading to a cafe often works out to be better value.

Hostels

Paris is awash with hostels, and standards are consistently improving. A wave of state-of-the-art hostels have recently opened their doors, with more in the works, including a 950-bed 'megahostel' by leading hostel chain Generator (www.generatorhostels.com) near Canal St-Martin, 10e.

Only the official *auberges de jeunesse* (youth hostels) require guests to present Hostelling International (HI) cards or their equivalent.

Hostel rates often include basic breakfast.

B&Bs & Homestays

Bed-and-breakfast (B&B) accommodation (*chambres d'hôte* in French) is increasingly popular.

The city of Paris' scheme called Paris Quality Hosts (Hôtes Qualité Paris; www.hotesqualiteparis.fr) fosters B&Bs, in part to ease the isolation of Parisians, half of whom live alone. There's often a minimum stay of three nights.

You can also rent private rooms through Airbnb (www.airbnb.com).

Apartments

Families – and anyone wanting to self-cater – should consider renting a short-stay apartment. Paris has a number of excellent apartment hotels, such as the international chain **Apart'hotels Citadines** (www.citadines.com).

For an even more authentic Parisian experience, sites

such as Airbnb offer entire private apartments, some in unique locations like houseboats. Rental agencies also list furnished residential apartments for stays of a few days to several months. Apartments often include facilities such as wi-fi and washing machines, and can be superb value. Beware of direct-rental scams.

Useful Websites

Lonely Planet (www.lonelyplanet.com/hotels) Accommodation reviews; book directly online.

Paris Hotel Service (www.parishotelservice.com) Specialises in boutique hotels.

Paris Hotel (www.hotels-paris.fr) Hotel booking site with lots of user reviews.

Paris Attitude (www.parisattitude.com) Thousands of apartment rentals, professional service, reasonable fees.

Where to Stay

NEIGHBOURHOOD	FOR	AGAINST
EIFFEL TOWER & WESTERN PARIS	Close to Paris' iconic tower and museums. Upmarket area with quiet residential streets.	Short on budget and midrange accommodation options. Limited nightlife.
CHAMPS-ÉLYSÉES & GRANDS BOULEVARDS	Luxury hotels, famous boutiques and department stores, gastronomic restaurants, great nightlife.	Some areas extremely pricey. Nightlife hotspots can be noisy.
LOUVRE & LES HALLES	Epicentral location, excellent transport links, major museums, shopping galore.	Not many bargains. Ongoing Forum des Halles construction work may be noisy/inconvenient.
MONTMARTRE & NORTHERN PARIS	Village atmosphere and some lively multicultural areas. Many places have views across Paris.	Hilly streets, further out than some areas. Red light district around Pigalle, although well-lit and safe, won't appeal to some travellers.
LE MARAIS & BASTILLE	Buzzing nightlife, hip shopping, great range of eating options in all price ranges. Excellent museums. Lively gay and lesbian scene. Busier on Sundays than most areas. Very central.	Can be seriously noisy in areas where bars and clubs are especially concentrated. Some Bastille areas slightly out-of-the-way.
THE ISLANDS	As geographically central as it gets. Almost all accommodation is situated on the peaceful, romantic Île St-Louis.	No metro station on the Île St-Louis. Limited self-catering options, zero nightlife.
LATIN QUARTER	Energetic student area, stacks of eating and drinking options, late-opening bookshops.	Popularity with students and visiting academics makes rooms hardest to find during conferences and seminars from March to June and in October.
ST-GERMAIN, LES INVALIDES & MONTPARNASSE	Stylish, central location, good shopping, sophisticated dining, close to the Jardin du Luxembourg. Montparnasse area has few tourists and excellent links to both airports.	Budget accommodation is seriously short changed. Some Montparnasse areas slightly out-of-the-way.

Best Places to Stay

OK

NAME		REVIEW
HÔTEL MOLITOR €€€	Eiffel Tower & Western Paris	This art deco complex, built in 1929 (with Paris' swishest swimming pool in the 1930s), and abandoned from 1989, has been restored to stunning effect.
HÔTEL FÉLICIEN €€	Eiffel Tower & Western Paris	Exquisitely designed rooms, with 'White' and 'Silver' suites on the hotel's top 'Sky floor'. Romantics, eat your heart out.
HÔTEL DU BOIS €€	Eiffel Tower & Western Paris	The 39 rooms mix soft hues with Pierre Frey fabrics and well-thought-out touches.
HIDDEN HOTEL €€€	Champs-Élysées & Grands Boulevards	One of the Champs-Élysées' best secrets. It's serene, stylish, reasonably spacious, and it even sports green credentials. The queen-size Emotion rooms are among the most popular.
HÔTEL FRANCE ALBION €	Champs-Élysées & Grands Boulevards	Rooms all have en suite bathrooms and, for Paris, are decently sized (doubles from 14 sq metre), and staff are eager to please.
HÔTEL LANGLOIS €€	Champs-Élysées & Grands Boulevards	Built in 1870, this 27-room hotel has kept its charm, from the tiny caged elevator to sandstone fireplaces (sadly decommissioned) in many rooms as well as original bathroom fixtures and tiles.
EDGAR €€	Louvre & Les Halles	Former convent/seamstress workshop where each room is decorated by a different team of artists.
HÔTEL CRAYON €€€	Louvre & Les Halles	The pencil (le crayon) is the theme, with rooms sporting a different shade of each floor's chosen colour.
HÔTEL TIQUETONNE €	Louvre & Les Halles	This hotel has been around since the 1900s and has a loyal clientele. Rooms sport a mix of vintage decor.
HÔTEL DE LA PLACE DU LOUVRE €€	Louvre & Les Halles	Fairly recent addition to the Parisian hotel scene, with just 20 rooms split across five floors – some rooms have Louvre views.
LOFT €€	Montmartre & Northern Paris	Around the corner from the Moulin Rouge, apartments range from a two-person studio to a loft that can fit a large family or group. Book months in advance.
LE CITIZEN HOTEL €€	Montmartre & Northern Paris	Twelve alluring rooms with iPads, filtered water and warm minimalist design. Artwork is from Oakland's Creative Growth Art Center for disabled artists.
HÔTEL DU NORD – LE PARI VÉLO €	Montmartre & Northern Paris	Prized location near place République. Rooms are decorated charmingly with flea-market antiques. Bikes are on loan for guests.
HÔTEL AMOUR €€	Montmartre & Northern Paris	This former love hotel by the hour features original artwork in each of the rooms. No television – but who needs TV when you're in love?
ST CHRISTOPHER'S GARE DU NORD €	Montmartre & Northern Paris	Just steps from the Gare du Nord, this newer St Christopher's, opened in 2013, has brought more modern hostel accommodation to the city, with six floors of light-filled rooms (600 total). Unless you reserve months in advance, they won't come cheap.
HÔTEL ELDORADO €	Montmartre & Northern Paris	A welcoming hotel with 23 colourfully decorated and (often) ethnically themed rooms, with a private garden at the back. Unfortunately, rooms facing the garden will probably be quite noisy as they look onto the restaurant – earplugs may be a good idea. Cheaper-category singles have washbasin only.

PRACTICALITIES	BEST FOR
☏ 01 56 07 08 50; www.mltr.fr; 2 av de la porte Molitor, 16e; d from €270; ❄ @ 🛜 ⚓ 🚹; Ⓜ Michel Ange Molitor	Splashing out
☏ 01 83 76 02 45; www.hotelfelicienparis.com; 21 rue Félicien David, 16e; d €120-280; ❄ @ 🛜 ⚓; Ⓜ Mirabeau	Indulgent cocooning
☏ 01 45 00 31 96; www.hoteldubois.com; 11 rue du Dôme, 16e; d €230-270, tr €370; ❄ 🛜; Ⓜ Champs-Élysées	Midrange luxury
☏ 01 40 55 03 57; www.hidden-hotel.com; 28 rue de l'Arc de Triomphe, 17e; d €389-454; ❄ @ 🛜; Ⓜ Charles de Gaulle–Étoile	Ecofriendly credentials
☏ 01 45 26 00 81; www.albion-paris-hotel.com; 11 rue Notre Dame de Lorette, 9e; s €77-103, d €97-123, f €163; ❄ 🛜 🚹; Ⓜ St-Georges	Budget Opéra location
☏ 01 48 74 78 24; www.hotel-langlois.com; 63 rue St-Lazare, 9e; s €150-160, d €180-190; ❄ @ 🛜; Ⓜ Trinité	Belle époque ambience
☏ 01 40 41 05 19; www.edgarparis.com; 31 rue d'Alexandrie, 2e; d €235-295; ❄ 🛜; Ⓜ Strasbourg St-Denis	Individuality
☏ 01 42 36 54 19; www.hotelcrayon.com; 25 rue du Bouloi, 1er; s/d €311/347; ❄ 🛜; Ⓜ Les Halles or Sentier	Creative, retro design
☏ 01 42 36 94 58; www.hoteltiquetonne.fr; 6 rue Tiquetonne, 2e; d €65, with shared shower €50; 🛜; Ⓜ Étienne Marcel	Vintage charm
☏ 01 42 33 78 68; www.paris-hotel-place-du-louvre.com; 21 rue des Prêtres St-Germain l'Auxerrois, 1er; d €135-205; ❄ 🛜; Ⓜ Pont Neuf	Louvre lovers
☏ 06 14 48 47 48; www.loft-paris.fr; 7 cité Véron, 18e; apt €100-270; 🛜; Ⓜ Blanche	Self-contained stays
☏ 01 83 62 55 50; www.lecitizenhotel.com; 96 quai de Jemmapes, 10e; d €199 & €269; 🛜; Ⓜ Gare de l'Est or Jacques Bonsergent	Canal St-Martin creative spirit
☏ 01 42 01 66 00; www.hoteldunord-leparivelo.com; 47 rue Albert Thomas, 10e; d €73-86, tr €96, q €125; 🛜; Ⓜ République	Cyclists
☏ 01 48 78 31 80; www.hotelamourparis.fr; 8 rue Navarin, 9e; s €145, d €170-225; 🛜; Ⓜ St-Georges or Pigalle	Adventurous romantics
☏ 01 70 08 52 22; www.st-christophers.co.uk/paris-hostels; 5 rue de Dunkerque, 10e; dm €20-44, d €90-170; @ 🛜; Ⓜ Gare du Nord	Modern hostel accommodation
☏ 01 45 22 35 21; www.eldoradohotel.fr; 18 rue des Dames, 17e; s €43-71, d €65-94, tr €82-102; 🛜; Ⓜ Place de Clichy	Bohemian budget travellers

NAME		REVIEW
MAMA SHELTER €	Le Marais & Bastille	Coaxed into its zany new incarnation by uber-designer Philippe Starck, this former car park offers what is surely the best-value accommodation in the city. Its rooms feature iMacs, trademark Starck details like a chocolate-and-fuchsia colour scheme and even microwave ovens.
HÔTEL JEANNE D'ARC €€	Le Marais & Bastille	Games to play, a painted rocking chair for tots in the bijou lounge and the most extraordinary mirror in the breakfast room create a real 'family home' air in this 35-room house. Book well in advance.
COSMOS HÔTEL €	Le Marais & Bastille	Cheap, brilliant value and just footsteps from the nightlife of rue JPT, Cosmos is a shiny star with retro style on the budget-hotel scene.
HÔTEL FABRIC €€€	Le Marais & Bastille	A stylish ode to its industrial heritage as a 19th-century textile factory. Bright rooms have beautiful textiles and uber-cool cupboards (upcycled packing crates!).
HÔTEL SAINT-LOUIS EN L'ISLE €€	The Islands	This abode brandishes a pristine façade and polished interior. The breakfast room is a 17th-century gem.
FIVE HOTEL €€€	Latin Quarter	Choose from one of five perfumes to fragrance your room at this contemporary romantic sanctum. Rates are often discounted by up to 50% online.
HÔTEL LES DEGRÉS DE NOTRE DAME €€	Latin Quarter	Wonderfully old-school, with a winding timber staircase (no lift) and charming staff, the value is good at this hotel a block from the Seine. Rooms have not been renovated for some time, however.
SELECT HÔTEL €€€	Latin Quarter	An art deco minipalace, with an atrium and cactus-strewn winter garden, an 18th-century vaulted breakfast room and 67 bedrooms with ingenious design solutions to maximise their limited space.
HÔTEL RÉSIDENCE HENRI IV €€€	Latin Quarter	This exquisite late-19th-century cul-de-sac hotel has eight generously sized rooms and five two-room apartments, done up with medieval-style touches. All are equipped with kitchenettes.
HÔTEL VIC EIFFEL €	St-Germain, Les Invalides & Montparnasse	Outstanding value for money, this pristine hotel with chic orange and oyster-grey rooms (two are wheelchair accessible) is a short walk from the Eiffel Tower, with the metro on the doorstep.
HÔTEL SAINT CHARLES €€	St-Germain, Les Invalides & Montparnasse	Located on a quiet, village-like street yet close to the area's lively bars and restaurants. Communal outdoor areas include a timber-decked terrace and fern- and conifer-filled garden.
SUBLIM EIFFEL €€	St-Germain, Les Invalides & Montparnasse	There's no forgetting what city you're in with the Eiffel Tower motifs in reception and rooms (along with Parisian street-map carpets and metro-tunnel-shaped bedheads) plus tower views from upper-floor windows. The small wellness centre/hammam offers massages.
L'HÔTEL €€€	St-Germain, Les Invalides & Montparnasse	This award-winning hostelry is the stuff of urban legends. Rock- and film-star patrons fight to sleep in room 16, where Oscar Wilde died in 1900, or in the art deco room 36 (which entertainer Mistinguett once stayed in), with its huge mirrored bed.
LE BELLECHASSE €€	St-Germain, Les Invalides & Montparnasse	Designer Christian Lacroix's entrancing room themes give the impression you've stepped into a larger-than-life oil painting. Rates include a glass of Champagne.

PRACTICALITIES	BEST FOR
☏ 01 43 48 48 48; www.mamashelter.com; 109 rue de Bagnolet, 20e; s/d from €79/89; ❄@🛜; 🚌76, Ⓜ Alexandre Dumas or Gambetta	Haven-seeking hipsters
☏ 01 48 87 62 11; www.hoteljeannedarc.com; 3 rue de Jarente, 4e; s €72, d €98-120, q €250; 🛜; Ⓜ St-Paul	Value for money
☏ 01 43 57 25 88; www.cosmos-hotel-paris.com; 35 rue Jean-Pierre Timbaud, 11e; s €62-75, d €68-75, tr/q €85/94; 🛜; Ⓜ République	Nightlife
☏ 01 43 57 27 00; www.hotelfabric.com; 31 rue de la Folie Méricourt, 11e; d €240-360; ❄🛜; Ⓜ Oberkampf	Industrial chic
☏ 01 46 34 04 80; www.saintlouisenlisle.com; 75 rue St-Louis en l'Île, 4e; d €159-249, tr €289; ❄@🛜; Ⓜ Pont Marie	Island tranquility
☏ 01 43 31 74 21; www.thefivehotel.com; 3 rue Flatters, 5e; s €255, d €285-305; ❄🛜; Ⓜ Les Gobelins	Romance
☏ 01 55 42 88 88; www.lesdegreshotel.com; 10 rue des Grands Degrés, 5e; d incl breakfast €120-170; 🛜; Ⓜ Maubert-Mutualité	Old-school charm
☏ 01 46 34 14 80; www.selecthotel.fr; 1 place de la Sorbonne, 5e; d €195-332, tr €275-340; ❄@🛜; Ⓜ Cluny–La Sorbonne	Art deco ambience
☏ 01 44 41 31 81; www.residencehenri4.com; 50 rue des Bernardins, 5e; d €285, ste €365-395; ❄🛜👪; Ⓜ Maubert-Mutualité	Families
www.hotelviceiffel.com; 92 bd Garibaldi, 15e; s/d from €99/109; 🛜; Ⓜ Sèvres-Lecourbe	Eiffel Tower accessibility
☏ 01 45 89 56 54; www.hotel-saint-charles.com; 6 rue de l'Espérance, 13e; d/tr/q €170/210/280; ❄🛜👪; Ⓜ Corvisart	Contemporary village living
☏ 01 40 65 95 95; www.sublimeiffel.com; 94 bd Garibaldi, 15e; d from €140; ❄🛜; Ⓜ Sèvres-Lecourbe	Cutting-edge Parisian decor
☏ 01 44 41 99 00; www.l-hotel.com; 13 rue des Beaux Arts, 6e; d €275-495; ❄@🛜🏊; Ⓜ St-Germain des Prés	Literary history
☏ 01 45 50 22 31; www.lebellechasse.com; 8 rue de Bellechasse, 7e; s/d from €183/192; ❄🛜; Ⓜ Solférino	Lavish surrounds

Transport

●●●
Arriving in Paris

Few roads *don't* lead to Paris, one of the most visited destinations on earth. Practically every major airline flies though one of its three airports, and most European train and bus routes cross it.

Paris is the central point in the French rail network, Société Nationale des Chemins de Fer Français (SNCF), with six train stations that handle passenger traffic to different parts of France and Europe. Each is well connected to the Paris public transportation system, the Régie Autonome des Transports Parisiens

(RATP). To buy onward tickets from Paris, visit a station or go to **Voyages SNCF** (www.voyages-sncf.com). Most trains – and all Trains à Grande Vitesse (TGV) – require advance reservations. As with most tickets, the earlier you book, the better your chances of securing a discounted fare. Mainline stations in Paris have left-luggage offices and/or *consignes* (lockers).

On public transport, children under four years travel free and those aged four to nine years (inclusive) pay half price; exceptions are noted.

Flights, tours and rail tickets can be booked online at www.lonelyplanet.com.

✈ Charles de Gaulle Airport

Most international airlines fly to **Aéroport de Charles de Gaulle** (CDG; www.aeroports-deparis.fr), 28km northeast of central Paris. In French the airport is commonly called 'Roissy' after the suburb in which it is located.

Metro & RER Networks

CDG is served by the RER B line (€9.50, approx 50 min-utes, every 10 to 15 minutes), which connects with the Gare du Nord, Châtelet–Les Halles and St-Michel–Notre Dame stations in the city centre. Trains run from 5am to 11pm; there are fewer trains on weekends.

Taxi

A taxi to the city centre takes 40 minutes. During the day, pay around €50; the fare increases 15% between 5pm and 10am and on Sundays. Only take taxis at a clearly marked rank. Never follow anyone who approaches you at the airport and claims to be a driver.

Bus

There are six main bus lines:

Les Cars Air France line 2 (€17, 1¼ hours, every 20 minutes, 6am to 11pm) Links the airport with the Arc de Triomphe. Children aged two to 11 pay half price.

Les Cars Air France line 4 (€17.50, every 30 minutes, 6am to 10pm from CDG, 6am to 9.30pm from Paris) Links the airport with Gare de Lyon (50 minutes) in eastern Paris and Gare Montparnasse (55 minutes) in southern Paris. Children aged two to 11 pay half price.

Roissybus (€10.50, 45 to 60 minutes, every 15 minutes, 5.30am to 11pm) Links the airport with the Opéra.

RATP bus 350 (€5.70, 50 minutes, every 30 minutes, 5.30am to 11pm) Links the airport with Gare de l'Est in northern Paris.

Speed- or Cent-Saver?

Increasingly popular as a means of getting to/from all three Paris airports is the excellent taxi-sharing scheme **WeCab** (www.wecab.com), whereby you book a taxi in advance and split the ride with other passengers going to the same place as you.

For those seeking speed, not a cent-saver, the hot choice is a *taxi moto* (motorbike taxi), whereby you leap on the back of a bike, driver and helmet provided, and zip past the traffic into town at lightning speed. Companies include **Paris Motos** (☏ 06 75 67 56 75; www.parismotos.fr) and **Taxi Moto Paris** (☏ 06 64 65 61 86; http://taxi-motos-paris.com).

RATP bus 351 (€5.70, 60 minutes, every 30 minutes, 5.30am to 11pm) Links the airport with place de la Nation in eastern Paris.

Noctilien bus 140 & 143 (€7.60 or four metro tickets, hourly, 12.30am to 5.30pm) Part of the RATP night service, Noctilien has two buses that go to CDG: bus 140 from Gare de l'Est, and 143 from Gare de l'Est and Gare du Nord.

Gare du Nord

Eurostar (www.eurostar.com) The London–Paris line runs from St-Pancras International to Gare du Nord. Voyages take 2¼ hours.

Thalys (www.thalys.com) Thalys trains pull into Paris' Gare du Nord from Brussels, Amsterdam and Cologne.

Orly Airport

Aéroport d'Orly (ORY; ☏ 01 70 36 39 50; www.aeroports-deparis.fr) is 19km south of central Paris but, despite being closer than CDG, it is not as frequently used by international airlines, and public transportation options aren't quite as straightforward.

Taxi

A taxi to the city centre takes roughly 30 minutes. During the day, pay between €40 and €55; the fare increases 15% between 5pm and 10am and on Sundays.

Metro & RER Networks

There is no direct train to/from Orly; you'll need to change halfway. Note that while it is possible to take a

shuttle to the RER C line, this service is quite long and not recommended.

RER B (€10.90; 35 minutes, every four to 12 minutes) This line connects Orly with the St-Michel–Notre Dame, Châtelet–Les Halles and Gare du Nord stations in the city centre. In order to get from Orly to the RER station (Antony), you must first take the Orlyval automatic train. The service runs from 6am to 11pm (fewer on weekends). You only need one ticket to take the two trains.

Bus & Tram

There are several bus lines and a state-of-the-art tram line that serve Orly:

Air France bus 1 (€12.50, one hour, every 20 minutes 5am to 10.20pm from Orly, 6am to 11.20pm from Invalides) This bus runs to/from the Gare Montparnasse (35 minutes) in southern Paris, Invalides in the 7e, and the Arc de Triomphe. Children aged two to 11 pay half price.

Orlybus (€7.50, 30 minutes, every 15 minutes, 6am to 11.20pm from Orly, 5.35am to 11.05pm from Paris) This bus runs to/from the metro station Denfert-Rochereau in southern Paris, making several stops en route.

Tramway T7 (€1.70, every six minutes, 40 minutes, 5.30am to 12.30am Monday to Saturday, 6.30am to 12.30am Sunday) In service since the end of 2013, this tramway links Orly with

Climate Change & Travel

Every form of transport that relies on carbon-based fuel generates CO_2, the main cause of human-induced climate change. Modern travel is dependent on aeroplanes, which might use less fuel per kilometre per person than most cars but travel much greater distances. The altitude at which aircraft emit gases (including CO_2) and particles also contributes to their climate change impact. Many websites offer 'carbon calculators' that allow people to estimate the carbon emissions generated by their journey and, for those who wish to do so, to offset the impact of the greenhouse gases emitted with contributions to portfolios of climate-friendly initiatives throughout the world. Lonely Planet offsets the carbon footprint of all staff and author travel.

Villejuif-Louis Aragon metro station in southern Paris; buy tickets from the machine at the tram stop as no tickets are sold onboard. Pick up traffic updates on Twitter @T7_RATP

Beauvais Airport

Aéroport de Beauvais (BVA; ☏ 08 92 68 20 66; www.aeroportbeauvais.com) is 75km north of Paris and is served by a few low-cost flights. Before you snap up that bargain, consider if the post-arrival journey is worth it.

Bus

Shuttle (€17, 1¼ hours) The Beauvais shuttle bus links the airport with metro station Porte Maillot. See the airport website for details and tickets.

🚌 Gare Routiére Internationale de Paris-Galliéni

Eurolines (www.eurolines.fr) connects all major European capitals to Paris' international bus terminal, **Gare Routiére Internationale de Paris-Gallieni** (☎ 08 92 89 90 91; 28 av du Général de Gaulle; Ⓜ Gallieni). The terminal is in the eastern suburb of Bagnolet; it's about a 15-minute metro ride to the more central République station.

Getting Around Paris

Getting around Paris is comparatively easy for a big city. Most visitors combine the efficient metro with walking. Buses offer a good view of the city, but can be hard to figure out and slowed by traffic. More tempting is the city's communal bike-share scheme, Vélib'.

🚈 Train

Paris' underground network is run by RATP and consists of two separate but linked systems: the metro and the Réseau Express Régional (RER) suburban train line. The metro has 14 numbered lines; the RER has five main lines (but you'll probably only need to use A, B and C). When buying tickets consider how many zones your journey will cover; there are five concentric transportation zones rippling out from Paris (5 being the furthest); if you travel from Charles de Gaulle airport to Paris, for instance, you will have to buy a zone 1–5 ticket.

Metro

Metro lines are identified by both their number (eg ligne 1; line 1) and their colour, listed on official metro signs and maps.

Signs in metro and RER stations indicate the way to the correct platform for your line. The *direction* signs on each platform indicate the terminus. On lines that split into several branches (such as lines 7 and 13), the terminus of each train is indicated on the cars and on signs on each platform giving the number of minutes until the next and subsequent train.

Signs marked *correspondance* (transfer) show how to reach connecting trains. At stations with many intersecting lines, like Châtelet and Montparnasse Bienvenüe, walking from one platform to the next can take a very long time.

Different station exits are indicated by white-on-blue *sortie* (exit) signs. You can get your bearings by checking the *plan du quartier* (neighbourhood maps) posted at exits.

Each line has its own schedule but trains usually start at around 5.30am, with the last train beginning its run between 12.35am and 1.15am (2.15am on Friday and Saturday).

RER

The RER is faster than the metro but the stops are much further apart. If you're going out to the suburbs (eg Versailles, Disneyland), ask for help on the platform – finding the right train can be confusing. Also make sure your ticket is for the correct zone.

Tickets & Fares

The same RATP tickets are valid on the metro, the RER (for travel within the city limits), buses, trams and the Montmartre funicular.

A ticket – white in colour and called *Le Ticket t+* – costs €1.70 (half price for children aged four to nine years) if bought individually and €13.70 for adults for a *carnet* (book) of 10.

Tickets are sold at all metro stations: ticket windows accept most credit cards; however, automated machines *do not* accept North American credit cards.

One ticket lets you travel between any two metro stations (no return journeys) for a period of 1½ hours, no matter how many transfers are required. You can also use it on the RER for travel within zone 1, which encompasses all of central Paris.

A single ticket can be used to transfer between buses, but not to transfer from the metro to bus or vice-versa. Transfers are not allowed on Noctilien buses.

Navigo Pass

If you're staying in Paris longer than a few days, the cheapest and easiest way to use public transport is to get a combined travel pass that allows unlimited travel on the metro, RER and buses for a week, a month or even a year. You can get passes for travel in two to five zones but, unless you'll be using the suburban commuter lines extensively, the basic ticket valid for zones 1 and 2 should be sufficient.

Navigo (www.navigo.fr), like London's Oyster or Hong Kong's Octopus cards, is a system that provides you with a refillable weekly, monthly or yearly unlimited pass that you can recharge at machines in most metro stations. Standard Navigo passes, available to anyone with an address in Île de France, are free but take up to three weeks to be issued; ask at the ticket counter for a form or order online via the Navigo website. Otherwise pay €5 for a Navigo Découverte (Navigo Discovery) card, which is issued on the spot but (unlike the standard Navigo pass) is not replaceable if lost or stolen. Both passes require a passport photo and can be recharged online for periods of one week or more.

Always keep your ticket until you exit from your station; if you are stopped by a ticket inspector, you will have to pay a fine if you don't have a valid ticket.

Tourist Passes

The Mobilis and Paris Visite passes are valid on the metro, RER, SNCF's suburban lines, buses, night buses, trams and Montmartre funicular railway. No photo is needed, but write your card number on the ticket. Passes are sold at larger metro and RER stations, SNCF offices in Paris, and the airports.

The **Mobilis** card allows unlimited travel for one day and costs €6.80 (two zones) to €16.10 (five zones). Buy it at any metro, RER or SNCF station in the Paris region. Depending on how many times you plan to hop on/off the metro in a day, a *carnet* might work out cheaper.

Paris Visite allows unlimited travel as well as discounted entry to certain museums and other discounts and bonuses. The 'Paris+Suburbs+Airports'

pass includes transport to/ from the airports and costs €22.85/34.70/48.65/59.50 for one/two/three/ five days. The cheaper 'Paris Centre' pass, valid for zones 1 to 3, costs €10.85/17.65/24.10/34.70 for one/two/three/five days. Children aged four to 11 years pay half price.

🚲 Bicycle

Vélib'

The **Vélib'** (http://en.velib. paris.fr; day/week subscription €1.70/8, bike hire up to 30min/60min/90min/2hr free/€1/2/4) bike share scheme puts 20,000-odd bikes at the disposal of Parisians and visitors to get around the city. There are some 1800 stations throughout the city, each with anywhere from 20 to 70 bike stands. The bikes are accessible around the clock.

To get a bike, you first need to purchase a one-/seven-day subscription (€1.70/8). There are two ways to do this: either

at the terminals found at docking stations or online.

The terminals require a credit card with an embedded smartchip – this means the majority of North Americans cannot subscribe here. But fret not because you can purchase a subscription online. Just be sure to do this before you leave your hotel.

After you authorise a deposit (€150) to pay for the bike should it go missing, you'll receive an ID number and PIN code and you're ready to go.

Bikes are rented in 30-minute intervals: the first half-hour is free, the second is €2, the third and each additional half-hour are €4. If you return a bike before a half-hour is up and then take a new one, you will not be charged.

If the station you want to return your bike to is full, log in to the terminal to get 15 minutes for free to find another station.

Bikes are geared to cyclists aged 14 and over, and are

fitted with gears, an antitheft lock with key, reflective strips and front/rear lights. Bring your own helmet (they are not required by law).

In June 2014 the city of Paris launched P'tits Vélib', a bike-sharing scheme for children aged two to 10 years, with bike stations in five sites, including Bois de Bologne, Bois de Vincennes and Les Berges de Seine.

Rentals

Most rental places will require a deposit. Take ID and bank card/credit card.

Au Point Vélo Hollandais (01 43 45 85 36; www.pointvelo.com; 83 bd St-Michel, 5e; per day €15; 🕙 10.30am-7.30pm Mon-Sat; M Cluny–La Sorbonne or RER Luxembourg)

Freescoot (📞 01 44 07 06 72; www.freescoot.com; 63 quai de la Tournelle, 5e; bike/tandem from €15/30; 🕙 9am-1pm & 2-7pm Mon-Sat year-round, plus Sun mid-Apr–mid-Sep; M Maubert-Mutualité)

🚌 Bus

Paris' bus system, operated by RATP, runs from 5.30am to 8.30pm Monday to Saturday; after that, certain evening-service lines continue until between midnight and 12.30am. Services are drastically reduced on Sunday and public holidays, when buses run from 7am to 8.30pm.

The RATP runs 47 night bus lines known as **Noctilien** (www.noctilien.fr), which depart hourly from 12.30am to 5.30am. The services pass through the main *gares* (train stations) and cross the major

axes of the city before leading out to the suburbs. If you have a Mobilis or Paris Visite pass, flash it at the driver when you board.

Boat

Batobus (www.batobus.com; Port de Solférino, 7e; 1-/2-day pass €16/18; 🕙 10am-9.30pm Apr-Aug, to 7pm rest of year) runs glassed-in trimarans that dock every 20 to 25 minutes at eight small piers along the Seine: Eiffel Tower, Musée d'Orsay, St-Germain des Prés, Notre Dame, Jardin des Plantes, Hôtel de Ville, Musée du Louvre and Champs-Élysées.

Buy tickets online, at ferry stops or tourist offices. You can also buy a two-/three-day ticket that also covers L'Open Tour buses for €45/49.

Taxi

The *prise en charge* (flagfall) is €2.50. Within the city limits, it costs €1 per kilometre for travel between 10am and 5pm Monday to Saturday (*Tarif A;* white light on taxi roof and meter).

At night (5pm to 10am), on Sunday from 7am to midnight, and in the inner suburbs the rate is €1.24 per kilometre (*Tarif B;* orange light).

Travel in the outer suburbs is at *Tarif C,* €1.50 per kilometre (blue light).

There's a €3 surcharge for taking a fourth passenger, but drivers sometimes refuse for insurance reasons. The first piece of baggage is free; additional pieces over 5kg cost €1 extra.

Flagging down a taxi in Paris can be difficult; it's best to find an official taxi stand.

To order a taxi, call or reserve online with **Taxis G7** (📞 3607; www.taxisg7.fr), **Taxis Bleus** (📞 01 49 36 10 10; www.taxis-bleus.com) or **Alpha Taxis** (📞 01 45 85 85 85; www.alphataxis.com).

Increasingly big in Paris is **Uber** (www.uber.com/cities/paris) taxi, whereby you order a taxi and pay via your smartphone.

Car & Motorcycle

Driving in Paris is defined by the triple hassle of navigation, heavy traffic and parking. It doesn't make sense to use a car to get around, but if you're heading out of the city on an excursion, then your own set of wheels can certainly be useful. If you plan on hiring a car, it's best to do it online and in advance.

Autolib'

Paris' electric-car-share program, **Autolib'** (www.autolib.eu), is similar to bike-share scheme Vélib': pay €9 per half hour to rent a GPS-equipped car in 30-minute intervals, or subscribe for a week/month (€10/25) to benefit from cheaper rates (€7/6.50 per half hour). Cars can be picked up/dropped off at 1000 available stations around the city and are designed only for short hops; the car battery is good for 250km. Carry your driver's license and photo ID.

Parking

Parking meters in Paris do not accept coins but require either a chip-enabled credit card or a Paris Carte, available at any *tabac* (tobacconist) for €10 to €30. The machine will issue you a ticket for the allotted time, which should be placed on the dashboard behind the windscreen. Municipal public car parks, of which there are more than 200 in Paris, charge between €2 and €3.50 an hour or €20 to €25 per 24 hours. Most are open 24 hours.

Scooters

Freescoot (☎ 01 44 07 06 72; www.freescoot.com; 63 quai de la Tournelle, 5e; ⏰ 9am-1pm & 2-5pm, closed Sun Oct-May) Rents 50/125cc scooters in various intervals (per 24 hours €55/65). Prices include third-party insurance as well as helmets, locks, raingear and gloves. To rent a 50/125cc scooter you must be at least 21/23 years old, respectively, and leave a credit card deposit of €1300/1600. No license required for smaller scooters.

Left Bank Scooters (☎ 06 82 70 13 82; www.leftbankscooters.com) Run by a young Australian-British couple, this outfit rents pastel-coloured Vespa XLV 50/125cc scooters for 24 hours at €70/80, including insurance, helmet and wet-weather gear. To rent a 50/125cc scooter, you must be at least 18/20 years old and have a car or motorcycle licence. Credit-card deposit is €1000. This place runs tours as well.

Tours

Bicycle

Bike About Tours (☎ 06 18 80 84 92; www.bikeabouttours.com; 4 rue de Lobau, 4e; Ⓜ Hôtel de Ville) This expat-run tour group offers daytime city tours (€30; 3½ hours), trips to Versailles (€80), e-bike tours to Champagne (€135) and private family tours.

Fat Tire Bike Tours (☎ 01 56 58 10 54; www.fattirebiketours.com) Day and night bike tours of the city, both in central Paris and further afield to Versailles and Monet's garden in Giverny.

Paris à Vélo, C'est Sympa! (☎ 01 48 87 60 01; www.parisvelosympa.com) Four guided bike tours (adult/child €35/20; three hours), including an evening cycle and a sunrise tour.

🚢 Boat

A boat cruise down the Seine is a relaxing way to watch the city glide by – and is a wonderful way for Paris first-timers to get a quick introduction to the city's main monuments.

Bateaux Parisiens (www.bateauxparisiens.com; Port de la Bourdonnais, 7e; adult/child €14/6; Ⓜ Bir Hakeim or RER Pont de l'Alma) This vast operation runs 1½-hour river circuits with recorded commentary in 13 languages (every 30 minutes 10am to 10.30pm April to September, hourly 10am to 10pm October to March), and a host of themed lunch/dinner cruises.

It has two locations: one by the Eiffel Tower, the other south of Notre Dame.

Bateaux-Mouches (☎ 01 42 25 96 10; www.bateauxmouches.com; Port de la Conférence, 8e; adult/child €13.50/5.50; ⏰ Apr-Dec; Ⓜ Alma Marceau) The largest river cruise company in Paris and a favourite with tour groups. Cruises (70 minutes) run regularly from 10.15am to 11pm April to September and 13 times a day between 11am and 9pm the rest of the year. Commentary is in French and English. It's located on the Right Bank, just east of the Pont de l'Alma.

Vedettes de Paris (☎ 01 44 18 19 50; www.vedettesdeparis.fr; Port de Suffren, 7e; adult/child €14/6; Ⓜ Bir Hakeim or Pont de l'Alma) This company's one-hour sightseeing cruises on smaller boats are second to none. It runs themed cruises too, including 'Paris mystery' tours for kids and boats along the river to Cathédrale de Notre Dame (adult single/return ticket €8/14).

Vedettes du Pont Neuf (☎ 01 46 33 98 38; www.vedettesdupontneuf.fr; Square du Vert Galant, 1er; adult/child €14/7, internet ticket €10/5; Ⓜ Pont Neuf) This company runs one-hour cruises year-round from its centrally located dock at the western tip of Île de la Cité; tickets are cheaper if you buy in advance online. Check its website for details of the wonderful 'Concerts en Seine' the boat company organises – classical music afloat after dusk (tickets €30 to €40).

Bus

Big Bus Paris (http://fra.
bigbustours.com; 1-day pass
adult/child €29/16) Paris' Les
Cars Rouges merged with
London's Big Bus Company to
create Big Bus Paris. City bus
tours are hop-on-off style, with
10 stops around the city. App
for iPhone or Android available.

L'Open Tour (www.
parisopentour.com; one-day
pass adult/child €31/16) Hop-
on, hop-off bus tours aboard
open-deck buses with four
different circuits and 50 stops
to jump on/off at – top for a
whirlwind city tour.

Walking

Ça Se Visite (www.ca-se-
visite.fr; adult/child on foot
€12/10, scooter €15/13)
Meet local artists and
craftspeople on resident-led
'urban discovery tours' of
the northeast (Belleville,
Ménilmontant, Canal St-
Martin, Canal de l'Ourcq,
Oberkampf, La Villette) – on
foot or *trottinette* (scooter).

Eye Prefer Paris (www.
eyepreferparistours.com; €210
for 3 people) New Yorker-turned-
Parisian Richard Nahem leads
offbeat tours of the city.

Localers (www.localers.com;
cost varies) Classic walking
tours and behind-the-scenes
urban discoveries with local
Paris experts: *pétanque*, photo
shoots, market tours, cooking
classes, foie gras-tasting et al.

**Parisien d'un jour – Paris
Greeters** (www.parisgreeters.
fr; by donation) See Paris
through local eyes with these
two- to three-hour city tours.
Volunteers – knowledgeable
Parisians passionate about their
city in the main – lead groups
(maximum six people) to their
favourite spots. Minimum two
weeks' notice needed.

Paris Walks (☎ 01 48
09 21 40; www.paris-walks.
com; adult/child €12/8) Long
established and highly rated
by our readers, Paris Walks
offers two-hour thematic
walking tours (art, fashion,
chocolate, the French
Revolution etc).

● ● ● ●
Discount Cards

Almost all museums and
monuments in Paris have discounted tickets (*tarif réduit*)
for students and seniors (generally over 60 years), provided
you have a valid ID. Children
often get in for free; the cut-off
age for 'child' is anywhere
between six and 18 years.

EU citizens under 26 years
get in for free at national
monuments and museums.

Paris Museum Pass
(http://en.parismuseumpass.
com; 2/4/6 days €42/56/69)
Gets you into 60-odd
venues in and around Paris;
a huge advantage is that
pass holders usually enter
larger sights at a different
entrance meaning you bypass
(or substantially reduce)
ridiculously long ticket
queues.

Paris City Passport (www.
parisinfo.com; 2/3/5 days
€71/103/130) Sold at the Paris
Convention & Visitors Bureau
(p304) and on its website,
this handy city pass covers
unlimited public transport,
admission to some 60
museums in the Paris region
(aka a Paris Museum Pass),

Treasure Hunts

'Treasure hunts' organised by **THATLou** (☎ 06 86 13
32 12; www.thatlou.com; per person excluding admission fees
Louvre/d'Orsay €25/35) inject fun into the potentially
tricky affair of navigating some of the city's most
vast and overwhelming sights, including the
Louvre, Musée d'Orsay and the Latin Quarter.
Hunts are in English or French, can be for two
people or more, and typically last two hours.
Participants form teams (to play alone or against
another team) and have to photograph themselves
in front of 20 to 30 works of arts ('treasure'). Daisy
de Plume, the talented bilingual hunt creator, also
puts together customised hunts.

and a 1hr boat cruise along the Seine. Three- and five-day passes include a hop-on-off open-top bus sightseeing service around central Paris' key sights with Big Bus Paris (p300).

Electricity

230V/50Hz

Emergency

Ambulance (SAMU) ☎15

Fire ☎18

Police ☎17

EU-wide emergency ☎112

Internet Access

Wi-fi (pronounced 'wee-fee' in France) is available in most Paris hotels, usually at no extra cost, and in some museums.

Free wi-fi is available in 260 public places, including parks, libraries and municipal buildings, between 7am and 11pm daily. In parks look for a purple 'Zone Wi-Fi' sign near the entrance. To connect, select the 'PARIS_WI-FI_' network and connect; sessions are limited to two hours. For complete details and a map of hotspots see www.paris.fr/wifi.

Expect to pay between €4 and €5 per hour for online access in internet cafes; **Milk** (www.milklub.com; 31 bd Sebastopol, 1er; 1/2/3 hr €3.90/6.90/8.90; ⊙24hr; Ⓜ Les Halles) has several branches in central Paris.

Medical Services

Hospitals

Paris has some 50 hospitals including the following:

American Hospital of Paris (☎01 46 41 25 25; www.american-hospital.org; 63 bd Victor Hugo, Neuilly-sur-Seine; Ⓜ Pont de Levallois) Private hospital; emergency 24-hour medical and dental care.

Hertford British Hospital (☎01 47 59 59 59; www.ihfb.org; 3 rue Barbès, Levallois; Ⓜ Anatole France) Less expensive, private English-speaking option.

Hôpital Hôtel Dieu (☎01 42 34 82 34; www.aphp.fr; 1 place du Parvis Notre Dame, 4e; Ⓜ Cité) One of the city's main government-run public hospitals; after 8pm use the emergency entrance on rue de la Cité.

Pharmacies

At least one *pharmacie* (chemist) in each neighbourhood is open with extended hours; find a complete night-owl listing on the Paris Convention & Visitors Bureau website (www.parisinfo.com).

Pharmacie Bader (☎01 43 26 92 66; www.pharmaciebader.com; 10-12 bd St-Michel, 6e; ⊙9am-9pm; Ⓜ St-Michel)

Pharmacie de la Mairie (☎01 42 78 53 58; http://pharmacie-mairie-paris.com; 9 rue des Archives, 4e; ⊙9am-8pm; Ⓜ Hôtel de Ville)

Pharmacie Les Champs (☎01 45 62 02 41; Galerie des Champs-Élysées, 84 av des Champs-Élysées, 8e; ⊙24hr; Ⓜ George V)

Money

France uses the euro (€), which is divided into 100 centimes. Check the latest exchange rates on websites such as www.xe.com.

ATMs

ATMs (*distributeur automatique de billets* in French) are widespread. Unless you have particularly high transaction fees, ATMs are usually the best and easiest way to deal with currency exchange; French banks don't generally charge fees to use their ATMs but check with your own bank before you travel to know if/how much they charge for international cash withdrawals.

Changing Money

Cash is not a good way to carry money; it can be stolen

and in France you often won't get the best exchange rates.

In Paris, *bureaux de change* are usually more efficient, open longer hours and give better rates than banks – many banks don't even offer exchange services.

Credit Cards

Visa/Carte Bleue is the most widely accepted credit card in Paris, followed by MasterCard (Eurocard). Amex cards can be useful at more upmarket establishments. In general, all three cards can be used to pay for train travel and restaurant meals and for cash advances. Note that France uses a smartcard with an embedded microchip and PIN. North Americans will thus not be able to use their credit cards at automated machines (such as at a metro station or museum) – they'll have to buy from the ticket window.

Tipping

French law requires that restaurant, cafe and hotel bills include a service charge (usually between 12% and 15%). Taxi drivers expect small tips of between 5% and 10% of the fare, though the usual procedure is to round up to the nearest €1 regardless of the fare.

Travellers Cheques

The most flexible travellers cheques are issued by Amex (in US dollars or euros) and Visa, as they can be changed at many post offices.

Opening Hours

The following list shows *approximate* standard opening hours for businesses. Hours can vary by season; our listings depict peak-season operating hours. Many businesses close for the entire month of August for summer holidays.

Banks 9am-1pm & 2-5pm Mon-Fri, some Sat morning

Bars and cafes 7am-2am

Museums 10am-6pm, closed Mon or Tue

Post offices 8am-7pm Mon-Fri & till noon Sat

Restaurants noon-2pm & 7.30-10.30pm

Shops (clothing) 10am-7pm Mon-Sat, occasionally close in the early afternoon for lunch

Shops (food) 8am-1pm & 4-7.30pm, closed Sun afternoon & sometimes Mon

Public Holidays

There is close to one public holiday a month in France and, in some years, up to four in May alone. Be aware, though, that unlike in the USA or UK, where public holidays usually fall on (or are shifted to) a Monday, in France a *jour férié* (public holiday) is celebrated strictly on the day on which it falls. Thus if May Day falls on a Saturday or Sunday, no provision is made for an extra day off.

The following holidays are observed in Paris:

New Year's Day (Jour de l'An) 1 January

Easter Sunday & Monday (Pâques & Lundi de Pâques) Late March/April

May Day (Fête du Travail) 1 May

Victory in Europe Day (Victoire 1945) 8 May

Ascension Thursday (L'Ascension) May (celebrated on the 40th day after Easter)

Whit Monday (Lundi de Pentecôte) Mid-May to mid-June (seventh Monday after Easter)

Bastille Day/National Day (Fête Nationale) 14 July

Assumption Day (L'Assomption) 15 August

All Saints' Day (La Toussaint) 1 November

Armistice Day/Remembrance Day (Le Onze Novembre) 11 November

Christmas (Noël) 25 December

Safe Travel

In general, Paris is a safe city and random street assaults are rare. The city is generally well lit and there's no reason not to use the metro until it stops running, at some time between 12.30am and just past 1am. As you'll notice, women *do* travel alone on the metro late at night in most areas, though not all who do so report feeling 100% comfortable.

Metro stations that are best avoided late at night include Châtelet–Les Halles and its seemingly endless corridors, Château Rouge in Montmartre, Gare du Nord, Strasbourg St-Denis, Réaumur Sébastopol and Montparnasse Bienvenüe. *Bornes d'alarme* (alarm boxes) are located in the centre of each metro/RER platform and in some station corridors.

Nonviolent crime such as pickpocketing and thefts from handbags and packs is a problem wherever there are crowds, especially packs of tourists.

Take the usual precautions: don't carry more money than you need, and keep your credit cards, passport and other documents in a concealed pouch, a hotel safe or a safe-deposit box.

●●●
Taxes & Refunds

France's value-added tax (VAT) is known as TVA *(taxe sur la valeur ajoutée)* and is 20% on most goods with a few exceptions: for food products and books it's 5.5%, and for medicines it is 2.1%. Prices that include TVA are often marked TTC *(toutes taxes comprises;* literally 'all taxes included').

If you're not an EU resident, you can get a TVA refund provided that: you're aged over 15; you'll be spending less than six months in France; you purchase goods worth at least €175 at a single shop on the same day (not

Practicalities

o **Classifieds** Pick up the free FUSAC (France USA Contacts; wwww.fusac.fr) in Anglophone haunts in Paris for classified ads about housing, babysitting, French lessons, part-time jobs and so forth.

o **Newspapers and magazines** Parisians read their news in centre-left *Le Monde* (www.lemonde. fr), right-leaning *Le Figaro* (www.lefigaro.fr) and left-leaning *Libération* (www.liberation.fr). *Metro* (http://readmetro.metrofrance.com) is the freebie to pick up outside metro stations, and *Le Parisien* (www. leparisien.fr) is the city-news read.

o **Smoking** Smoking is illegal in indoor public spaces, including restaurants and bars (hence the crowds of smokers in doorways and pavement terraces outside).

o **TV and DVDs** TV is Secam; DVDs use the PAL system.

o **Weights and measures** Paris uses the metric system.

more than 10 of the same item); the goods fit into your luggage; you are taking the goods out of France within three months of purchase; and the shop offers *vente en détaxe* (duty-free sales).

For more information contact the **customs information centre** (☏ 08 11 20 44 44; www.douane.minefi.gouv.fr; ⏰ 8.30am-6pm Mon-Fri).

●●●
Telephone

There are no area codes in France – you always dial the 10-digit number.

Telephone numbers in Paris always start with 01, unless the number is provided by an internet service provider (ISP), in which case it begins with 09.

Mobile phones throughout France commence with either 06 or 07.

France's country code is 33.

To call abroad from Paris, dial France's international access code (00), the country code, the area code (usually without the initial '0', if there is one) and the local number.

Mobile Phones

You can use your mobile/cell phone *(portable)* in France provided it is GSM (the standard in Europe, which is becoming increasingly common elsewhere) and tri-band or quad-band. If you meet the requirements, you can check with your service provider about using it in France, but beware of roaming costs, especially for data.

Rather than staying on your home network, it is usually more convenient to buy a local SIM card from a French provider such as **Orange** (www.orange.fr), **SFR** (www.

Charging Devices

There is talk of public transport company RATP jazzing up bus stops of the future with phone-charging stations, but until then charging phones and other devices on the move remains challenging. Carrying your own charger and cable ups the odds dramatically of getting more juice – don't be shy to ask in cafes and restaurants if you can plug in and charge. Ditto for taxi drivers, an increasing number of whom carry a selection of smartphone-compatible cables and chargers. It's easy to recharge at Bibliothèque Nationale de France (p229). Or do it yourself at Gare de Nord, Gare de Montparnasse or Gare de St-Lazare at a pedal-powered charging station.

sfr.fr), **Bouygues** (www.bouyguestelecom.fr) and **Free Mobile** (http://mobile.free.fr) which will give you a local phone number. In order for this to work, you'll need to ensure your phone is 'unlocked', which means you can use another service provider.

Phonecards

Although mobile phones and Skype may have killed off the need for public phones, they do still exist. In France they are all phonecard-operated, but in an emergency you can use your credit card to call.

A *télécarte* (phonecard; €7.50/15 for 50/120 calling units) can be purchased at post offices, *tabacs*, supermarkets, SNCF ticket windows, metro stations and anywhere you see a blue sticker reading '*télécarte en vente ici*' (phonecard for sale here).

You can buy prepaid phonecards such as Allomundo (www.allomundo.com) that are up to 60% cheaper for calling abroad than the standard *télécarte*.

Time

France uses the 24-hour clock in most cases, with the hours usually separated from the minutes by a lower-case 'h'. Thus, 15h30 is 3.30pm, 00h30 is 12.30am and so on.

France is on Central European Time (like Berlin and Rome), which is one hour ahead of GMT. When it's noon in Paris it's 11am in London, 3am in San Francisco, 6am in New York and 9pm in Sydney.

Daylight-saving time runs from the last Sunday in March to the last Sunday in October.

Tourist Information

The main branch of the **Paris Convention & Visitors Bureau** (Office du Tourisme et des Congrès de Paris; www.parisinfo.com; 27 rue des Pyramides, 1er; 9am-7pm May-Oct, 10am-7pm Nov-Apr; M Pyramides) is about 500m northwest of the Louvre.

The bureau maintains a handful of centres elsewhere in Paris, most of which are listed here (websites are the same as for the main office). In addition, find information desks at Charles de Gaulle Airport. For tourist information around Paris, see **Paris Region** (www.visitparisregion.com).

Montmartre Welcome Desk (opp 72 bd Rochechouart, 18e; 10am-6pm; M Anvers) At the foot of Montmartre.

Gare de l'Est Welcome Desk (place du 11 Novembre 1918, 10e; 8am-7pm Mon-Sat; M Gare de l'Est) Inside Gare de l'Est train station, facing platforms 1–2.

Gare de Lyon Welcome Desk (20 blvd Diderot, 12e; 8am-6pm Mon-Sat; M Gare de Lyon) Inside Gare de Lyon, facing platforms L–M.

Gare du Nord Welcome Desk (18 rue de Dunkerque, 10e; 8am-6pm; M Gare du Nord) Inside Gare du Nord, under the glass roof of the Île de France departure and arrival area (eastern end of station).

Syndicate d'Initiative de Montmartre (01 42 62 21 21; www.montmartre-guide.com; 21 place du Tertre, 18e; 10am-6pm; M Abbesses) Locally run tourist office on Montmartre's most picturesque square. It sells maps of Montmartre and runs tours daily at 2.30pm.

Travellers with Disabilities

Paris is an ancient city and therefore not particularly well equipped for *visiteurs* handicapés (disabled visitors): kerb ramps are few and far between, older public facilities and budget hotels usually lack lifts, and the metro, dating back more than a century, is mostly inaccessible for those in a wheelchair (fauteuil roulant).

But efforts are being made. The tourist office continues its excellent 'Tourisme & Handicap' initiative, in which museums, cultural attractions, hotels and restaurants that provide access or special assistance or facilities for those with physical, mental, visual and/or hearing disabilities display a special logo at their entrances. For a list of the ever-increasing places that qualify, visit the website of the Paris Convention & Visitors Bureau (www.parisinfo.com) and click on 'Practical Paris'.

Resources

For information about what cultural venues in Paris are accessible to people with disabilities, surf **Accès Culture** (www.accesculture.org).

Access in Paris, a useful if dated 245-page guide to the French capital for the disabled, can be downloaded in PDF form at **Access Project** (www.accessinparis.org).

Mobile en Ville (📞 09 52 29 60 51; www.mobile-en-ville. asso.fr; 8 rue des Mariniers, 14e, Paris) works hard to make independent travel within the city easier for people in wheelchairs.

For information on accessibility on all forms of public transport in the Paris region, get a copy of the *Guide Practique à l'Usage des Personnes à Mobilité Réduite* (Practical Usage Guide for

People with Reduced Mobility) from the **Syndicate des Transports d'Île de France** (📞 08 10 64 64 64; www. stif-idf.fr). Its info service for travellers with disabilities, **Info Mobi** (www.infomobi. com), is especially useful.

Taxi company **Horizon** (📞 01 47 39 00 91; www. taxisG7.fr), part of Taxis G7 (p298), has cars especially adapted to carry wheelchairs and drivers trained in helping passengers with disabilities.

●●●
Visas

There are no entry requirements for nationals of EU countries. Citizens of Australia, the USA, Canada and New Zealand do not need visas to visit France for up to 90 days. Except for people from a handful of other European countries (including Switzerland), everyone, including citizens of South Africa, needs a so-called Schengen Visa, named after the Schengen Agreement that has abolished passport controls among 26 EU countries and has also been ratified by the non-EU governments of Iceland, Norway and Switzerland. A visa for any of these countries should be valid throughout the Schengen area, but it pays to double-check with the embassy or consulate of each country you intend to visit. Note that the UK and Ireland are not Schengen countries.

Check www.france. diplomatie.fr for the latest visa regulations and the closest French embassy to your current residence.

●●●
Women Travellers

Women attract more unwanted attention than men, but female travellers need not walk around Paris in fear: people are rarely assaulted on the street. However, the French seem to have given relatively little thought to sexual harassment (harcèlement sexuel), and many men still think that to stare suavely at a passing woman is to pay her a compliment.

France's national rape crisis hotline (Viols Femmes Informations; 08 00 05 95 95; 🕙10am-7pm Mon-Fri) can be reached toll-free from any telephone, without using a phonecard. It's run by a group called **Collectif Féministe contre le Viol** (CFCV | Feminist Collective Against Rape; 📞 08 00 05 95 95; www.cfcv. asso.fr).

In an emergency, call the **police** (📞 17). Medical, psychological and legal services are available to people referred by the police at the **Urgences Médico-Judiciaires** (📞 01 42 34 82 85; 1 place du Parvis Notre Dame, 4e; 🕙24hr; Ⓜ St-Michel) inside the Hôtel Dieu.

La Maison des Femmes de Paris (📞 01 43 43 41 13; http://maisondesfemmes.free. fr; 163 rue de Charenton, 12e; 🕙11am-7pm Mon-Fri; Ⓜ Reuilly Diderot) is a meeting place for women of all ages and nationalities, with events, workshops and exhibitions scheduled throughout the week.

Language

The sounds used in spoken French can almost all be found in English. There are a couple of exceptions: nasal vowels (represented in our pronunciation guides by 'o' or 'u' followed by an almost inaudible nasal consonant sound 'm', 'n' or 'ng'), the 'funny' *u* sound ('ew' in our guides) and the deep-in-the-throat *r*. Bearing these few points in mind and reading our pronunciation guides below as if they were English, you'll be understood just fine.

To enhance your trip with a phrasebook, visit **lonelyplanet.com**. Lonely Planet iPhone phrasebooks are available through the Apple App store.

BASICS

Hello./Goodbye.
Bonjour./Au revoir.   bon·zhoor/o·rer·vwa
How are you?
Comment allez-vous?   ko·mon ta·lay·voo
I'm fine, thanks.
Bien, merci.   byun mair·see
Excuse me./Sorry.
Excusez-moi./Pardon.   ek·skew·zay·mwa/par·don
Yes./No.
Oui./Non.   wee/non
Please.
S'il vous plaît.   seel voo play
Thank you.
Merci.   mair·see
That's fine./You're welcome.
De rien.   der ree·en
Do you speak English?
Parlez-vous anglais?   par·lay·voo ong·glay
I don't understand.
Je ne comprends pas.   zher ner kom·pron pa
How much is this?
C'est combien?   say kom·byun

ACCOMMODATION

I'd like to book a room.
Je voudrais réserver   zher voo·dray ray·zair·vay
une chambre.   ewn shom·brer
How much is it per night?
Quel est le prix par nuit?   kel ay ler pree par nwee

EATING & DRINKING

I'd like ..., please.
Je voudrais ...,   zher voo·dray ...
s'il vous plaît.   seel voo play
That was delicious!
C'était délicieux!   say·tay day·lee·syer
Bring the bill/check, please.
Apportez-moi l'addition,   a·por·tay·mwa la·dee·syon
s'il vous plaît.   seel voo play

I'm allergic (to peanuts).
Je suis allergique   zher swee a·lair·zheek
(aux cacahuètes).   (o ka·ka·wet)
I don't eat ...
Je ne mange pas de ...   zher ner monzh pa de ...
   fish   *poisson*   pwa·son
   (red) meat   *viande (rouge)*   vyond (roozh)
   poultry   *volaille*   vo·lai

EMERGENCIES

I'm ill.
Je suis malade.   zher swee ma·lad
Help!
Au secours!   o skoor
Call a doctor!
Appelez un médecin!   a·play un mayd·sun
Call the police!
Appelez la police!   a·play la po·lees

DIRECTIONS

I'm looking for (a/the) ...
Je cherche ...   zher shairsh ...
   bank
   une banque   ewn bongk
   ... embassy
   l'ambassade de ...   lam·ba·sahd der ...
   market
   le marché   ler mar·shay
   museum
   le musée   ler mew·zay
   restaurant
   un restaurant   un res·to·ron
   toilet
   les toilettes   lay twa·let
   tourist office
   l'office de tourisme   lo·fees der too·rees·mer

Behind the Scenes

Author Thanks

CATHERINE LE NEVEZ

Un grand merci to my fellow award-winning Paris authors Chris and Nicola. *Merci mille fois* to Julian, and all of the innumerable Parisians who offered insights and inspiration. *Merci* too to Pierre-Emmanuel, and to everyone at Versailles. Thanks too to Kate Morgan, James Smart, Jo Cooke and all at Lonely Planet. As ever, *merci encore* to my parents, brother, *belle-sœur* and *neveu* for sustaining my lifelong love of Paris.

Acknowledgments

Cover photographs:
Front: Notre Dame on the Seine, Brian Jannsen/Alamy
Back: Gargoyle on Notre Dame overlooking Paris, Sylvain Sonnet/Corbis
Illustrations pp96-7, pp184-5 and pp256-7 by Javier Zarracina.

This Book

This 3rd edition of Lonely Planet's *Discover Paris* was researched and written by Catherine Le Nevez, Christopher Pitts and Nicola Williams, who all also wrote and researched the previous edition. This guidebook was commissioned in Lonely Planet's London office and produced by the following:

Destination Editor Kate Morgan
Product Editor Alison Ridgway
Regional Senior Cartographer Valentina Kremenchutskaya
Book Designer Mazzy Prinsep
Assisting Editor Jenna Myers
Assisting Book Designer Katherine Marsh
Cover Researcher Naomi Parker
Thanks to Cynthia Hoffmann, Kate James, Kam Lam, Anne Mason, Kate Mathews, Virginia Moreno, Wibowo Rusli, Saralinda Turner

SEND US YOUR FEEDBACK

Index

Sights 000
Map pages 000

⊗ Eating

Drinking & Nightlife

⭐ Entertainment

Sights 000
Map pages 000

How to Use This Book

These symbols give you the vital information for each listing:

☑	Telephone Numbers	☎	Wi-Fi Access	▣	Bus
☺	Opening Hours	☒	Swimming Pool	⛴	Ferry
P	Parking	✎	Vegetarian Selection	M	Metro
⊖	Nonsmoking	▤	English-Language Menu	S	Subway
✳	Air-Conditioning	★	Family-Friendly	⊖	London Tube
@	Internet Access	★	Pet-Friendly	▦	Tram

Look out for these icons:

FREE	No payment required
🌿	A green or sustainable option

Our authors have nominated these places as demonstrating a strong commitment to sustainability – for example by supporting local communities and producers, operating in an environmentally friendly way, or supporting conservation projects.

All reviews are ordered in our authors' preference, starting with their most preferred option. Additionally:

Sights are arranged in the geographic order that we suggest you visit them, and within this order, by author preference.

Eating and Sleeping reviews are ordered by price range (budget, mid-range, top end) and within these ranges, by author preference.

Map Legend

Sights
- 🏖 Beach
- 🔵 Buddhist
- 🔴 Castle
- 🟢 Christian
- 🟡 Hindu
- ⚫ Islamic
- ✡ Jewish
- 🔵 Monument
- ⬛ Museum/Gallery
- 🔵 Ruin
- 🟢 Winery/Vineyard
- 🔵 Zoo
- ⚫ Other Sight

Sports & Activities
- 🟢 Diving/Snorkelling
- 🔵 Canoeing/Kayaking
- 🟡 Skiing
- 🟠 Surfing
- 🔵 Swimming/Pool
- 🔴 Walking
- 🔵 Windsurfing
- 🟢 Other Sports & Activities

Eating
- 🔴 Eating

Drinking & Nightlife
- 🔵 Drinking
- 🔵 Cafe

Entertainment
- 🔵 Entertainment

Shopping
- 🔴 Shopping

Sleeping
- 🔵 Sleeping
- 🔵 Camping

Information
- 🔵 Post Office
- 🔵 Tourist Information

Transport
- 🔵 Airport
- ⊗ Border Crossing
- 🔵 Bus
- ⊕ Cable Car/Funicular
- 🔵 Cycling
- 🔵 Ferry
- 🔵 Monorail
- P Parking
- S S-Bahn
- 🔵 Taxi
- 🔵 Train/Railway
- 🔵 Tram
- ⊖ Tube Station
- U U-Bahn
- M Underground Train Station
- • Other Transport

Routes
- Tollway
- Freeway
- Primary
- Secondary
- Tertiary
- Lane
- Unsealed Road
- Plaza/Mall
- Steps
-) Tunnel
- Pedestrian Overpass
- Walking Tour
- Walking Tour Detour
- Path

Boundaries
- International
- State/Province
- Disputed
- Regional/Suburb
- Marine Park
- Cliff
- Wall

Geographic
- 🔵 Hut/Shelter
- 🔵 Lighthouse
- 🔵 Lookout
- ▲ Mountain/Volcano
- 🔵 Oasis
- 🔵 Park
-)(Pass
- 🔵 Picnic Area
- 🔵 Waterfall

Hydrography
- River/Creek
- Intermittent River
- Swamp/Mangrove
- Reef
- Canal
- Water
- Dry/Salt/Intermittent Lake
- Glacier

Areas
- Beach/Desert
- Cemetery (Christian)
- Cemetery (Other)
- Park/Forest
- Sportsground
- Sight (Building)
- Top Sight (Building)

Our Story

A beat-up old car, a few dollars in the pocket and a sense of adventure. In 1972 that's all Tony and Maureen Wheeler needed for the trip of a lifetime – across Europe and Asia overland to Australia. It took several months, and at the end – broke but inspired – they sat at their kitchen table writing and stapling together their first travel guide, *Across Asia on the Cheap*. Within a week they'd sold 1500 copies. Lonely Planet was born.

Today, Lonely Planet has offices in Franklin, London, Melbourne, Oakland, Beijing and Delhi, with more than 600 staff and writers. We share Tony's belief that 'a great guidebook should do three things: inform, educate and amuse'.

Our Writers

CATHERINE LE NEVEZ

Coordinating Author, Le Marais & Bastille, St-Germain, Les Invalides & Montparnasse, Day Trips from Paris Catherine first lived in Paris aged four and she's been returning here at every opportunity since, completing her Doctorate of Creative Arts in Writing, Masters in Professional Writing, and post-grad qualifications in Editing and Publishing along the way. Catherine's writing includes numerous Lonely Planet Paris guides (one of which recently won the British Travel Press Awards travel guide book of the year), as well as newspaper, magazine and online articles. Revisiting her favourite Parisian haunts and uncovering new ones remains a highlight of this and every assignment.

Outside Paris, Catherine has authored, co-authored and contributed to scores of Lonely Planet guidebooks across France, Europe and far beyond. Wanderlust aside, Paris remains her favourite city on earth.

CHRISTOPHER PITTS

Louvre & Les Halles, Montmartre & Northern Paris, Latin Quarter Christopher Pitts first moved to Paris in 2001. He initially began writing about the city as a means to buy baguettes – and to impress a certain Parisian (it worked, they're now married with two kids). Over the past decade, he has written for various publications, in addition to working as a translator and editor.

NICOLA WILLIAMS

Eiffel Tower & Western Paris, Champs-Élysées & Grands Boulevards, Le Marais & Bastille, The Islands British writer and editorial consultant Nicola Williams has lived in France and written about it for more than a decade. From her hillside house on the southern shore of Lake Geneva, it's an easy hop to Paris where she has spent endless years revelling in its extraordinary art, architecture and cuisine. Resisting the urge to splurge in every boutique she passed while walking the length of every street in Le Marais was this trip's challenge.

Published by Lonely Planet Publications Pty Ltd
ABN 36 005 607 983
3rd edition – March 2015
ISBN 978 1 74321 461 9
© Lonely Planet 2015   Photographs © as indicated 2015
10 9 8 7 6 5 4 3 2 1
Printed in China